ETHICS IN AMERICA
STUDY GUIDE

Lisa H. Newton, Ph.D.

Fairfield University

A College Television Course and Prime Time Television Series

Produced by Columbia University Seminars on Media and Society

 Educational Print Materials Produced
by WNET/New York

 An Annenberg/CPB Project

Major funding provided by the Annenberg/CPB Project
with additional support by EQUICOR-Equitable/HCA Corporation

 Prentice Hall, Englewood Cliffs, New Jersey 07632

Editorial/production supervision and
  interior design: Barbara DeVries
Cover design: Lundgren Graphics, Ltd.
Manufacturing buyer: Peter Havens

First Edition

Printed in the United States of America
10 9 8 7 6 5 4 3

ISBN   0-13-290206-0

Prentice-Hall International (UK) Limited, *London*
Prentice-Hall of Australia Pty. Limited, *Sydney*
Prentice-Hall Canada Inc., *Toronto*
Prentice-Hall Hispanoamericana, S.A., *Mexico*
Prentice-Hall of India Private Limited, *New Delhi*
Prentice-Hall of Japan, Inc., *Tokyo*
Simon & Schuster Asia Pte. Ltd., *Singapore*
Editora Prentice-Hall do Brasil, Ltda., *Rio de Janeiro*

To the continuing dialogue

CONTENTS

STAFF FOR ETHICS IN AMERICA TELEVISION COURSE

Editorial Team for Printed Materials: WNET/New York

TIM GUNN, Project Coordinator
ROBERT MILLER, Project Director
JOYCE BERMEL, Project Manager and Editor
NATASHA MOSTERT, Production Assistant
LAURA STEINBERGER, Research Assistant

Television and Audiocassette Production Team: Columbia University Seminars on Media and Society

CYNTHIA MCFADDEN, Executive Producer
MARTHA ELLIOT, Producer
BETSY MILLER, Producer
JAY WARD BROWN, Associate Producer
JEFFREY CRAWFORD BROWN, Associate Producer

Educational Advisory Panel

TOM L. BEAUCHAMP, PH.D.
Senior Research Scholar
Joseph and Rose Kennedy Institute
of Ethics
Georgetown University

SUE COMMANDAY, PH.D.
Coordinator of Special Programs
Rockland Community College

KENNETH E. GOODPASTER, PH.D.
Associate Professor
Graduate School of Business
Administration
Harvard University

LOUIS HODGES, PH.D.
Director
Society and the Professions
Washington and Lee University

PHYLLIS WALDEN, PH.D.
Philosophy Instructor and Director
Credit for Prior Learning Program
Sangamon State University

MARGARET WHERRY, PH.D.
Assistant Director
of Academic Outreach
Kansas State University

FOREWORD

Fred W. Friendly

Man's dignity rises from his ability to reason
and thus to choose freely the good in preference to evil.

Walter Lippmann
September 11, 1945

In my office at Columbia University is a sculpture made of walnut and steel given to me by a very special group of students when I retired from full-time teaching. The inscription on it quotes Socrates: "The unexamined life is not worth living." That is, perhaps, the only indispensable advice anyone has ever given. It is the goal to which we hope this telecourse will lead you.

Our purpose is not to make up anyone's mind but to open minds, and to make the agony of decision making so intense that you can escape only by thinking. Our part in that process, the production of the television programs and the writing of these texts, is now finished. It remains for you to bring the process to fruition by allowing yourself to participate in "the agony" of thinking.

In one of our earlier television programs on the Constitution, Supreme Court Justice Potter Stewart was talking about the legal right of the press under the First Amendment to publish whatever it pleases, including top secret government papers. Justice Stewart wondered whether because something was legal, it was necessarily ethical. He gently scolded me, saying, "The trouble with your profession, journalism, is that you are all confused about what you have a right to do under the Constitution and the right thing to do."

Justice Stewart's admonition is an insightful illustration of what we mean by ethics. Sometimes it is very difficult to discern the right thing to do, and that is what this telecourse is all about: understanding the ancient skill of moral reasoning. The compass which we have used as a logograph for this telecourse is the classic symbol of the ethicists' search for moral direction. While there is no simple formula, no algorithm, by which to identify the right thing to do, the ability to perceive clearly ethical dilemmas and to exercise skilled decision making is critical.

Lisa Newton has been a good teacher for me. This book will be a good guide—a road map, if you will—for you as students as you explore the geography of ethics in America. Together with the **Source Reader**, Professor Newton's text will help you accustom yourself to the workings of your own ethical compass.

Of the ten television programs which make up the core of this telecourse, nine explore the decision making of professionals. These programs are not intended as a primer in professional ethics. Indeed, most of the case studies begin precisely where the professional codes leave off, forcing the participants—and you—to think through these ethical dilemmas from the beginning.

So, for example, the television program concerned with Retributive Justice focuses on the conflicting pressures a criminal defense attorney faces when representing a man accused of murder. Does our system of justice demand of the attorney absolute devotion to his client's cause, even if that means an innocent man will die? Must we accept the "justice" of that system, even if a guilty man goes free? Veteran attorneys and judges who face these ethical decisions daily grapple with them anew here in this course— and you have the opportunity to participate.

Autonomy is the subject of the sixth unit of the course. Conventional wisdom holds that doctor knows best. But when a patient thinks his or her doctor is wrong and insists on a different, perhaps unwise, course of treatment, what should a physician do? That conflict—between the doctor's paternalism on the one hand, and the patient's autonomy on the other—can reach fever pitch in the fast-moving world of modern medicine.

In theory, loyalty makes life simple. But, as the generals, admirals, and soldiers who participate in the program on ethics in the military point out, the choices demanded by loyalty sometimes conflict with the demands of one's own sense of right and wrong. If you were a soldier, trying to rescue five of your comrades held captive by the enemy, and you thought you could get valuable information by torturing one of your prisoners, what would you do? Real soldiers will answer that question in the television program; your job is to understand why they give the answers they do and then to decide whether your answer would be the same.

The first program in the series, which you will view for Chapter 3, is concerned with much more personal, yet no less important, ethical dilemmas. We believe it is important to begin at the beginning, with the very genesis of all our ethics: the personal relationships that bind us together— parent to child, husband to wife, friend to friend, and friend to stranger.

It is from these concentric relationships that we derive our sense of community, however faded and torn it may be in this late 20th-century society. From the community comes our need for ethics and, perhaps, the source of ethics too. What is this community? Walter Lippmann in "The Public Philosophy" defined "We the People" so:

> The people, then, is not only, as Bentham assumed, the aggregate of living persons. The people is also the stream of individuals, the connected generations of changing persons, that Burke was talking about when he invoked the partnership "not only between those who are living" but also with "those who are dead, and those who are to be born." *The People* are a corporation, an entity, that is to say, which lives on while individuals come into it and go out of it.
> ...That is why young men die in battle for their country's sake and why old men plant trees they will never sit under.

Ethics is, after all, a conversation that has gone on for more than 2500 years, stretching from Plato and Aristotle through Aquinas, Hobbes, Kant, Mill, Rawls, and now to you—students of Ethics in America. It is a conversation about nothing less than the essence of humanity; but it is carried on in ordinary settings, day to day, in plain language, by everyone who stops at all to reflect upon personal actions and wonder if he—or she—is doing what is right.

Philosophers contemplating this conversation have created a technical vocabulary that characterizes ethical reasoning. We want to bring to the vernacular enough of that vocabulary so that everyone who participates in this telecourse can join the centuries-old conversation, understand it clearly, and contribute to it. Those who can do so will immediately add to the commonweal of this technologically complex society, by aiding in the resolution of some of the most perplexing dilemmas that confront us. Those who can contribute to this ethical dialogue will join a noble band of thinkers and teachers in this endeavor.

Once, many years ago, I offered praise to a venerable teacher of mine. He dismissed my compliment without hesitation, saying, "There are no great teachers. I was just privileged to be present when the learning process took place."

We who worked on these texts and these videotapes are not privileged to be present with you—distant learners that you are—during the telecourse. But you can be assured that we shall relish our role as this learning process takes place.

Fred W. Friendly
Edward R. Murrow Professor Emeritus
Columbia University
Graduate School of Journalism
New York City, 1988

PREFACE

When Media & Society first suggested that I do the books for this course about ten months ago, my first, and probably most rational, reaction was, that's impossible. A telecourse is not like ordinary college courses, you see. Its leading concepts, and the manner of their presentation, must be determined by the logic of the drama through which the television programs do their teaching. In this case, we aim to dramatize the anguish of choice and the need to think through the painful choices of the moral life. That aim determines the choice of situations to present to the panelists and the order of the programs to present to the students—who are often distant from the classroom, and far from the sort of required course that professors are used to teaching.

From the point of view of the author of the textbooks, the task shaped by these demands is enormously challenging. Between October and May, a whole Reader in the history of ethics had to be collected; an introduction to Ethics had to be incorporated into two chapters of the Study Guide; and ten chapters illustrating the links between ethical imperatives and professional obligations had to be written. And those chapters could not be written until the series had been taped (half in October, half in February), and the order of the chapters was not to be revealed until after the last was written! Such is the nature of the telecourse, and such is the challenge I am increasingly glad I accepted. It has been a tremendous education, lots of fun, and, considering the collected materials of the complete project, enormously satisfying.

But it could not have been done at all without a good deal of help. First, thanks go to my colleagues of the Program in Applied Ethics at Fairfield University: Joseph Coelho, Robert Webber, and Maureen Ford, who helped work on these chapters and took over course and class work displaced by the preparation of these volumes. Thanks also to the advisors of that Program, especially Robert Levine of the Human Investigation Committee of Yale Medical Center, Geoffrey Hazard of Yale Law School, and Margaret Farley of the Yale Divinity School, for help on some of the chapters.

Further thanks to the tireless scholars of WNET/New York, whose responsibility it was to make sure I did the work properly: Joyce Bermel, Robert Miller, Tim Gunn, and the crew of reviewers, Phyllis Walden, Peg Wherry, Sue Commanday, especially Lou Hodges, who saved me from some bad mistakes (I am responsible for the ones that remain), and my long-time friends and colleagues Tom Beauchamp and Ken Goodpaster.

The good people at Prentice Hall, known for their excellence at the trade, outdid themselves in efficiency and cooperation. Special recognition among them goes to Joe Heider, acquisitions editor, his assistant Linda Albelli, June Sanns, who did the page makeup, and especially the production editor Barbara DeVries. And the producers at Media & Society, Jay Brown, Jeff Brown, Cynthia McFadden and Martha Elliott have been a joy to work with.

But a special appreciation is due to my friend and mentor Fred Friendly. He has unlimited enthusiasm in the pursuit of enlightenment and unlimited ability (witness these seminars) to inspire others to undertake the same pursuit. Like Socrates, whom he likes to quote, Fred teaches constantly, just by his eagerness to learn from anyone he talks to. Together with his wonderful wife Ruth, he provides spirit and soul for every project in which he engages his boundless energy. I have tried to make my part of this project worthy of that inspiration.

And finally, I would like to thank my infinitely patient husband Victor and marvelously helpful children (Tracey, my personal secretary, and Kit, chief collator), who helped whenever possible and supported to the end of the project. The help that I have received from them, and from all of those mentioned so far, has enabled me to do my best to meet this challenge, with no excuse for the lapses that remain, responsibility for which is mine alone. I've enjoyed putting these books together; I hope you find your journey through them as educational and enjoyable as I found mine.

Lisa H. Newton
Fairfield University

INTRODUCTION

WELCOME TO ETHICS

One of Moliere's characters, Le Bourgeois Gentilhomme, was delighted to discover, upon taking up learning at an advanced age, that he had been speaking "prose" all his life. "Prose," as you probably know, is any kind of writing that has no rhyme or meter so isn't "poetry." "Ethics," as you may not know, is systematic thinking about right and wrong, good and evil. Ethical presuppositions are built into any decision you may ever have made about the right thing to do, or the right judgment on anyone else's action. I hope that you will be as delighted to find out that you have been doing rudimentary "ethics" all your life, as was Le Bourgeois Gentilhomme to find out that he was speaking prose. Up to now you have probably been doing ethics without benefit of any kind of academic recognition. Now's your chance to get credit for what all people do naturally.

If we all do it naturally, why bother to have college-level courses in ethics? Because we don't all do it very well. Ethical presuppositions are built into all our moral judgments, but they are not all defensible. When the Ku Klux Klansman dons his white robe and in company with his fellows undertakes to burn the houses purchased by black families, he is making a judgment about the respect due to persons whose skin is darker than his own, and it is a very bad judgment. He would probably not try to defend the judgment that "only white persons," or "only persons of whom I personally approve," are worthy of respect. On the contrary, if you asked him, he would probably endorse the Declaration of Independence, which tells us that "all men are created equal," and he would surely support the Constitution, which says that they are entitled to the "equal protection of the laws." But he has never thought through the connection between what he does on those dark Friday nights and what he affirms with his lips when he salutes the American flag, and pledges his allegiance to "liberty and justice for all."

When conscientious public officials violate the law in search of some higher policy good, when irate citizens march to protest the use of property near their own for a group home for the mentally retarded, when astute businessmen close half the company's plants to realize marginally better yields on the remainder of the operations, do they see any link between their actions and the ethical principles that they gladly affirm when asked to teach the morning's lessons at their children's Sunday schools?

These are not easy judgments. We will probably agree—you would not be taking this course if you were not disposed to agree—that the Klansman is doing wrong. I am not sure (you may be) that the officials, the citizens, and the businessmen are wrong; these are matters where good and thoughtful people should not be ashamed to disagree. The agreement is not important, but the thoughtfulness is. There are reasons why we will not always ultimately agree, for ethical principles may ultimately conflict; but we should be clear on *why* we disagree, and learn enough of the terminology, modes of reasoning, and traditional principles of ethics to carry on an intelligent discussion about the ethical disputes of the day.

In this Introduction, we will consider the structure of the course as a whole, the order and goals of the course, the objectives for the student, the relation between the television programs and the printed material, and the orientation of this course in relation to the vast fields of ethics.

THE NATURE OF THIS BOOK

The best way to explain this book is through a simple lesson in logic. To teach my children how to locate things when they were very young, I bought them a book entitled *The Cat in the Box* (no relation to *The Cat in the Hat*). It started with a gray Cat, who was in a Box, that was on a Chair, in a Room, in a House (each of these locations on a separate page with its own picture), in a Street, Town, State, Country, World, Universe. That was half the book, and the second half brought us down the same hierarchy; "Where is my little gray Cat? Look! in the Universe there is a World; in the World there is a Country" and so forth down to "and there in the Box is my little gray Cat!" Aristotle could not have created a stricter logic of inclusion.

The Universe is Thought, or Truth; the Mind of God, if you like. In that Universe we find a World of Philosophy, all human reflection on the ultimate questions of life and experience. Philosophy is traditionally divided into four Fields (which correspond to the Cat's Countries): *Metaphysics*, concerned with questions of Reality; *Epistemology*, concerned with the nature of human Knowledge; *Logic*, concerned with the validity of Argument; and *Ethics*, concerned with judgments on human Conduct.

Ethics in turn is divided into many States; *Metaethics*, or Theoretical Ethics, which considers the meanings of ethical terms and the forms of ethical argument; *Descriptive Ethics*, now largely left to the social scientists, which discusses the moral and ethical beliefs and customs of the peoples of the world; and *Normative Ethics*, which attempts to elucidate established ethical principles; to illuminate actual controversies of the practical world; and sometimes to reach conclusions about what is right and what is not. We will be doing Normative Ethics, with occasional assists from Metaethics (where the concepts we are studying have several meanings and sets of implications) and Descriptive Ethics (where the concepts have emerged into Western consciousness too recently to have built up a normative tradition of their own).

Normative Ethics is the State through which this *Study Guide* will travel, covering the Towns of General Ethics (how, in general, to discuss and apply the terms of ethical discussion); Applied and Professional Ethics (ethics at work in business, the professions, and public service); and, more briefly, Personal Life. Within Applied Ethics, we will explore the Streets of Business Ethics, Medical and Research Ethics, Legal Ethics, Military Ethics, Governmental Ethics, and Journalism Ethics.

There are many ways to treat this subject matter: we can make a scholarly exploration of the professional journals of these fields (medicine, law, business); we can examine the philosophical journals devoted to the problems of ethics in the professions, journals which are increasing daily in number and popularity; or we can simply attempt to identify and elucidate the concepts themselves, the approach we have chosen here. In our Classroom (this *Study Guide*) we will see how these concepts relate to the key philosophical traditions and analyze each concept through a relevant case study. From the professorial Chair in which I sit, I engage in the very traditional form of teaching, a philosophical Essay in conceptual analysis. In the Essay for each chapter, I work from the principle itself, in the light of the traditions that inform our understanding of it (see Chapter Two of this *Study Guide* and the accompanying **Source Reader** for the traditions). I ask here, why is this principle worth fighting about? (Wars have been fought over some of these.) What is its nature? What are its implications for current practice?

The Cat in the Box—the object sought from the beginning—is your understanding of that exercise, and your willingness to join us in the journey just through these thirteen weeks. After that, the Chair is yours, and the Room if you want it. And if the exercise has appealed to you, go on from there: to further explorations of the concepts, to the literature of the various avenues of Applied Ethics, to the whole tradition of Normative Ethics (the **Source Reader** that accompanies this course is a brief introduction to that State of thinking), to the awesome Country of reflection on Ethics since the Saints and Sages of the Ancient World, and on to the World of Philosophy.

THE ORDER OF BUSINESS, IN THIRTEEN PARTS

Chapter 1 will introduce the forms of moral (and other) discourse, the fundamental principles of ethics, and the forms of moral reasoning. This chapter will serve as a reference for the limited technical terminology that will be used in the balance of the book. You are not expected to remember it all on one reading. Refer back to it as you continue with the course, to remind yourself of the terminology.

Chapter 2 summarizes the ethical traditions of the Western World, showing them as, in effect, a continuous conversation within the overwhelming social changes that constitute Western History. The ethical thought of each era can be understood equally as a response to and commentary upon its own age, and as a reply to the philosophers of the last age. This brief chapter merely hints at the traditions; a much fuller account is to be found in your **Source Reader**.

Audiocassettes accompany Chapters 1 and 2, and the concluding chapter, 13.

Chapters 3 through 12 correspond to the televised presentations that constitute the basis for this course. Each chapter follows the same basic outline:

1. Introductory questions. You already work with the concepts we use in this course, in your daily life. They are important to you. One of the best ways to understand the philosophical essay in each chapter is to put down the book for a moment before you begin to read and ask yourself, what does the key concept of the chapter (justice, privacy, loyalty, etc.) mean to *you*, now, before you begin to take it apart and understand its history? Then, when you've completed all the assignments on any concept, ask yourself again: What does this mean to me *now*?

       2. *Essay*. The concept of....this section is an introductory lecture on the core concept for the chapter—what philosophers would call an "explication" of the concept. The concept for the chapter will be considered in itself—why we value it, what areas of the Western tradition may throw light upon it, and what might be entailed in an effort to respect it. In the essay on autonomy, for instance, or privacy, we shall ask why these principles are important to us, where in our traditions that importance is crystallized, and what role they play in the good human life. We will also consider what constitutes violation of the principles and how violation may be avoided. In short, we shall ask of each principle what it demands of us.

       To the extent possible, the essay will draw on the traditions of normative ethics alone, starting with Plato and ending with the present day. This will not always be possible. No civilization, ancient or modern, will set its philosophers to consider problems that do not exist in its experience. Some of our problems are ancient; the legitimacy of political authority and the patterns of distributive justice have been debated at least since the Golden Age of Athens. But some are relatively modern; one of our sessions, for example, will debate the value of community, which involves the obligations that people have to care for others in their society; another will debate the value of privacy, which entails the ability of the individual to keep large portions of life away from others. These problems are new. Until the last century (out of fifty centuries of recorded human experience) the only way for a human being to live was in a community of persons whose lives overlapped in numberless ways: in work, in recreation, in religion, in every expression of the common culture. The creation and preservation of community was no problem because it was everywhere; the protection and limitation of privacy was no problem because it was nowhere. (Delimiting the obligations an individual might have to the omnipresent community *was* a problem, but a different one.) Arguments about discussion of these concepts does not appear in the literature in any recognizable form in ages preceding our own. To a very large degree, then, the treatment of these concepts will rely on the work of astute social scientists, the legal tradition, and analysis of the social institutions within which these concepts acquire meaning.

       But most of the questions are *not* new. Philosophers whose writings are found in your **Source Reader** have provided a continuous commentary on ethical problems for thousands of years. Where I cite a philosopher from the **Source Reader**, the citation appears as "(Aristotle, **Source Reader** p. xxx)"; if you'll turn to page xxx of the **Source Reader**, you'll find Aristotle discussing that subject or one closely related.

       3. *Outline of the television presentation*. Here we include the participants, the questions considered, and the course of the argument. This portion is not meant to be word-for-word accurate, but is just a summary of the themes and issues raised in the seminar.

4. *A review of selections from the* Source Reader. In this section certain selections from the **Source Reader** are recommended for review, and their relevance to the issues raised by the chapter is summarized.

5. *Synthesis, discussion, avenues for further reflection.* The ethical conflicts emerge as we examine all the principles that stand against and limit the principle in question, especially as these issues arose in the television presentation. For example, your autonomy must be respected, but your freedom to do as you please ends when your actions affect my interests or the interests of society as a whole; at that point we must start balancing interests against interests, right against right. For another example, respect for your privacy ends if you use your right to the sanctity of your own home to pack the rooms to the ceilings with illegal drugs or stolen goods. Nor is the good of others, or the public good, the only justification for violating your privacy; if you are seriously suicidal, we may sometimes violate your privacy for your own good, whether you like it or not. Any practical system of ethics must include primary principles (e.g., privacy), secondary principles of limitation (e.g., until the interests of others are affected), and procedural principles for determining when a violation may occur and limiting its damage (e.g., requiring a search warrant when the privacy of a home must be violated, and specifying the times when it is appropriate to obtain one). Where the television discussion has suggested or implied solutions, these will be pointed out, along with all of the unanswered questions.

6. *Questions for your reflection.* These questions take some of the important points from the unit and focus them on individual decisionmaking. Some questions will be taken directly from the **Source Reader,** to help you review that material. Your professor, or the syllabus for this course, will suggest other uses for these questions; as foundation for short papers, or as essay questions for examinations, for instance.

7. *Suggestions for further reading.* This list suggests some further sources on the topic, and will help you follow up topics that interested you. It is not meant to be comprehensive.

Chapter 13 reviews the themes of the book and summarizes the most important requirements of normative ethics. These will turn out to include a tolerance for uncertainty, and a willingness to preserve personal integrity and steadfastness in following a personal moral compass in the face of that uncertainty.

A NOTE ON ETHICS AND LAW

Law is an authoritative system for governing human conduct by rules. Its principles are enacted by the decision of human beings on certain dates at certain places; its terms are precise; its sanctions essentially involve authoritative coercion. In all these respects, law differs from morality, whose principles are everlasting, whose terms are general, and whose sanctions involve primarily the recognition by the actor of the moral nature of the act, that it is right or wrong.

Law is shot through with morality. State governments early in American history routinely incorporated the Ten Commandments into their constitutions, and any strong moral persuasion on the part of the people (unless it runs afoul of a Constitutional protection) will find its way into coercive law. Nor is morality independent of law, which expresses a consensus on what is necessary for the safety and welfare of the people, on the one hand, and on the other, constitutes a contractual agreement with the citizenry, that they will obey it. Thus two moral principles—consideration for the welfare of others and adherence to contract—bind a citizen to obey the law for moral reasons. Law and morality, then, interpenetrate at their foundations.

Given the limitations of space and time—our space and your time—we will not be able to engage in any substantial discussion of the law in this course. We will mention common legal (especially Constitutional) protections as they become relevant; we will examine the law as in itself an ethically problematic field of practice. We will not, however, cite specific cases or statutes, and legal procedures will not figure in the discussions. We gain from this limitation a tighter and more digestible course.

But the loss of this discussion should be mourned, and you should be aware of the loss, for there is a rich legal tradition on many of these values, painfully establishing a public, and publicly enforceable, understanding of their functions in our national life. Autonomy, for instance, in the medical context (in its medico-legal garb of "informed consent") has a history dating back to the beginning of this century, comprising by now dozens of interesting cases. In general, legal histories are well worth exploring for a richer comprehension of the dimensions of a value when it moves from the domain of the private conscience to the judge's bench and the thick, permanent record of case law and precedent.

A NOTE ON LANGUAGE

There are efforts in progress in many academic fields to "de-sex" or "neutralize" the language of human description. Wherever possible, authors are expected to refer to "humankind" rather than "mankind," to discuss human characteristics in the plural (to use the neutral "they" rather than "he" as the appropriate pronoun), and in all treatments of citizens or professions to vary the assumption of gender equally between male and female. We have followed these guidelines in this work, to the extent that the subject matter permits. But it should be noted that the effort fits very awkwardly into the history of philosophy. Virtually all philosophers until the latter half of the twentieth century have written in the gender-specific language now under attack. Some of them (Aristotle, for instance, and St. Paul), wrote that way because they simply assumed that women were unfit for citizenship or professional life. Others, like John Stuart Mill, a passionate campaigner for equal rights for women, wrote that way because that was the way people wrote. While the practice in this book is to use gender neutral language where possible, we are not likely to accomplish significant reforms by tying language in knots. Problems of equality exist in the schools, the workplace, and the nation at large; they will not be solved by campaigns against pronouns.

A fruitful approach, for our purposes, is to assume that when Mill says "he," he means "he or she"; and that when Aristotle says "he," he *should* have meant "he or she." Knowing what we know now about the equality of human potential, we shall take everything that Aristotle said about men as applying equally to women. That assumption made, we can appreciate their arguments without being distracted by their choice of gender attributions.

PHILOSOPHY FOR THE FIRST TIME

If you have not taken any philosophy before this ethics course, you are in for a treat, though the going may be hard at first. Keep the following suggestions in mind as you go through the course:

1. Consult your professor, and read the syllabus through, from start to finish, to get very clear what is expected of you in this course, where you should start, and where the big chunks of work are going to show up. If there's a term paper due at the end of the course, start thinking about it soon.

2. Skim the **Source Reader**, just to find out what's in it. You will be referred to it continually through the chapters of the *Study Guide*, and you will have a much easier time finding and using the material you are referred to if you are already familiar with the **Source Reader's** structure and contents.

3. Then skim the *Study Guide*, to get an idea of what's in store. Each of the topical chapters, 3 through 12, is self-contained; you can read them in any order you like or your professor suggests. Before the course begins, you might want to pick your favorite topic and read that chapter, just to get used to the style and structure.

4. Now read the opening chapters, listen to the audiocassettes that accompany them, and start writing your very first papers in philosophy. Philosophy is one of the oldest recreational activities on record. Enjoy yourself.

chapter 1 _____

ETHICAL REASONING

In this first chapter, we will

1. Introduce the terminology of philosophical reasoning and informal logic (Talking about Talking);
2. Introduce the basic moral concepts and the presuppositions of this book;
3. Derive the basic moral principles from the nature of the human being, and derive from those principles those values or imperatives that can be applied to ethical problems in practice;
4. Set out the forms of moral reasoning;
5. Look ahead to the following chapters;
6. Listen to the first audiocassette.

Of that agenda, the first few items may seem very abstract. If you have not had much in the way of background in academic ethics or philosophy, the terms may seem complex to the point of bewilderment, and you may wonder why such unfamiliar language must be used to introduce such familiar subject matter. Bear with us. In the discussions of the televised sessions, we will use many of the distinctions we introduce here, and it is more helpful to have them all in one place than to introduce them as we go along. Familiarize yourself with the terms here introduced, and refer to this chapter as the course proceeds.

TALKING ABOUT TALKING: THE KINDS OF SENTENCES
THERE ARE

Philosophy is primarily the study of discourse—a particularly thorough examination of the ways that we talk about things, the judgments we make, and the categories and conceptual orders we put upon our experience. It enables us to interpret that experience for ourselves and to find the handles that will let us operate effectively in the world as we experience it. For this reason we call philosophy a "second-order" discipline. The "first-order" disciplines study, record, order, and control either the physical world (through the disciplines of scientific research, medicine, engineering, and other forms of technology) or the world of human conduct (through the disciplines of psychology, law, journalism, politics, and morality). But philosophy in its various branches studies those disciplines for their own sake, in order to understand their terms and their reasoning, and to discover the conditions under which they can be logically coherent and effective.

We are doing ethics, a philosophical study of morality that attempts to extract from our moral codes and moral traditions our most basic beliefs, the concepts on which all morality ultimately rests. We must therefore talk about how we talk about conduct, or how we make moral judgments. Therefore we must first learn to talk about how we talk about anything. How do we use our language? What kinds of sentences are there?

Very early in philosophy, Plato wrote a little Dialogue called the "Euthyphro," in which he apparently discusses the nature of piety and the gods. Actually, he's talking about *knowledge, certainty, ways of arguing,* and *ways of disagreeing.* As Plato sets the scene, Euthyphro (a well-educated scion of the aristocracy) and Socrates are talking about the gods. The gods sometimes disagree about things, Euthyphro believes. Sometimes they fight, he insists, and even wage wars against each other. Now, Socrates wonders, what might they disagree about so violently? And then goes on to distinguish between the kinds of assertions we make that people or gods might disagree about. Not about *mathematical statements,* of course. If you and I add up a sum and come up with different answers, no matter how important the result of the calculation, we won't fight about it—we'll just go back and check our work. (You were probably the one with the right answer.) And not about *factual statements,* either. If you and I disagree about the size of the table, or the number of apples in the basket, or the location of Indianapolis, we'll just agree on a good procedure to get the right answer (measure it, count them, go look at a map) and set about doing it. Where we, and the gods, disagree to the point of getting into fights is in the area of rights, of justice, of the common good—in short, over *moral judgments.* We fight over these issues precisely because there is no agreed-upon procedure to come to a right answer. Nor can there be, as we shall see—but that's getting ahead of the story.

Socrates' distinction, and his conclusion, are as valid now as they were in 400 B.C. Accordingly, we divide assertive discourse into three kinds:

1. *Logical,* or *formal, statements* are definitions or statements derivable from definitions, including the entirety of mathematical discourse (e.g., "2+2=4"). Such statements can be verified by a formal procedure derived from the same definitions that control the rest of the terms of the field in question (i.e., the same axioms define "2," "4," and the procedure of "addition"). True formal statements are *analytic*: they are true logically, "necessarily," or by the definitions of the terms. False statements in this category are *self-contradictory*. (If you say, "2+2=5," you contradict yourself, for you assert "5" and a quantity not equal to 5, or "not-5," simultaneously, and that is a contradiction.) A true statement can never be false, or disproved by any discovery of facts; it will never be the case that some particular pairs of 2 do not add up to 4—and if you think you've found such a case, you're wrong! "2+2=4" is true, as philosophers like to say, in all possible worlds. For this reason we say (following Immanuel Kant) that these statements are true *a priori*: we can know them to be true prior to any examination of the facts of the world, without having to count up lots of pairs of pairs just to make sure that 2+2 *really* equals 4.

2. *Factual,* or *empirical, statements* are assertions about the world out there, the physical environment of our existence, including the entirety of scientific discourse, from theoretical physics to sociology. Such statements are verifiable by controlled observation of that world, by experiment or just by careful looking, listening, touching, smelling, or tasting. This is the world of our senses. Kant called these empirical statements "synthetic," for they "put together" in a new combination two ideas that do not initially include or entail each other. As a result they cannot be known *a priori*, but can be determined only *a posteriori*, that is, after investigation of the world. When they are true, they are true only "contingently," or dependently, as opposed to necessarily; their truth is contingent upon, or depends on, the situation in which they are uttered. (As I write this, the statement "it is raining out" is true, and has been all day. The weatherman tells me that tomorrow that statement will be false. The statement "2+2=4" does not flick in and out of truth like that.)

3. *Normative statements* are assertions about what is right, what is good, or what should be done. We know these statements as *"value judgments,"* prescriptions and proscriptions, commands and exhortations to do or forbear. There is no easy way of assigning "truth value" to these statements. The criteria of "truth" that apply to formal and factual statements do not apply to normative statements. We can certainly say of such judgments that they conform or fail to conform with other moral judgments or with more general and widely accepted moral principles; or that they receive or fail to receive our assent as a society, as compatible or

incompatible with our basic intuitions of what is just or right. We may also say that a judgment succeeds or fails as a policy recommendation on some accepted pattern of moral reasoning, like adducing consequences of that judgment and estimating how human wants will be affected should it become law (see The Forms of Moral Reasoning, below). But the certainties of math and science are forever beyond the grasp of any normative system, which is, possibly, as it should be.

As you have probably guessed, we'll be spending most of the book in that third area, looking at normative statements. In the absence of the certainties of axioms and microscopes, we shall have to proceed as best we can, from the most general principles to their application in particulars. Those general concepts, or principles, follow. The television programs will provide the particulars.

MORAL CONCEPTS AND PRESUPPOSITIONS

From the point of view of theoretical ethics (or philosophy), many approaches to the discipline of ethics are possible; we will start this particular enterprise by laying out the presuppositions of our work. The assumptions that define this book are three in number and very simple: that ethics is intelligible, that ethics is serious, and that ethics is about human beings. We shall take these in turn.

Ethics Is Intelligible

"Intelligible" simply means "understandable," or "meaningful"—something that is intelligible is not self-contradictory and not gibberish. It may seem odd that ethics, the discipline that Socrates insisted ought to occupy first place in philosophy, should have to be defended on this plane. Nevertheless, several twentieth-century schools of philosophy did indeed insist that moral judgments were "meaningless" as assertions—they were only to be understood as expressions of emotion, like "Hurrah!" or "Yuck!," telling us only that the speaker, the one uttering the judgment, felt inclined *for* or *against* whatever the object of judgment might be—at least for the moment. We will spare you the vagaries of "emotivism," "prescriptivism," "logical positivism," and the other varieties of "non-cognitivism": there is time enough for them if you can be tempted to go beyond this course into a more technical "Ethical Theories" course. One temptation along those lines, however, should be noted at this point. It is called "relativism," and deserves a word of explanation. Take note of the following:

1. *We live in a democracy*. "Freedom of Speech" is the name of one of our fundamental beliefs. Each person has the right, indeed the obliga-

tion, to think out ethical and political issues and to come to reasoned conclusions on ethical and political matters. Further, each person has the right (within certain obvious limits) to express that opinion without anyone else having the right to object.

2. *We live in a pluralistic democracy.* We are a collection of very different cultures, but we are agreed on one basic principle: the innate dignity of each individual. That means that we have a duty to treat all citizens with respect; we have the duty to promote tolerance, or, a better word, acceptance, of all our citizens, for what they are and for the culture from which they come.

3. *We consider it very bad manners to go around telling people that we think they're wrong, especially morally wrong.*

4. There are good reasons, as we shall see below, why people, especially if they come from different backgrounds, will disagree on matters of ethics.

All these points add up to "respectful disagreement": In America, it is one of our proudest boasts that *citizens can very seriously disagree with each other on matters of policy and moral right, and yet each will treat the other with respect, and no organ of the state will attempt to suppress either of them*. So far, so good.

But it is psychologically a very short step from respectful disagreement to "indifferentism" or "relativism." *Relativism* can be characterized as the view: "Think what you like, it makes no difference whatsoever. No point of view is more correct than any other; in matters of policy and ethics, there's only *subjective* (personal) opinion, and no *objective* (interpersonal) truth." But it is a very *wrong* step.

We make a large mistake when we confuse a Constitutionally guaranteed right (a *liberty*) with the moral category of "rightness" (*validity*). There is no *logical* connection between *what you have a right to do*, and *the right thing to do*; but there is a *psychological* temptation to move from one to the other. And in logic, there is no connection between "You have the right to think what you like," and "Anything you happen to like to think is right." You have the right, after all, to contradict yourself; you have all the right in the world to think that "2+2=5." That doesn't make it true.

In mathematics, of course, there is one right answer. In ethics there may not be, since the basic ethical concepts are logically independent, and the question of what weight to assign to them must often be decided on the configurations of a particular case. That is why there can be honest, and possibly irreconcilable, disagreement on matters of ethics. But there are always better and worse answers, answers more or less in conformity with those concepts. If it were not so, it would not be worth the effort to reflect on matters of ethics and policy, and to attempt to reach valid conclusions on one's own. There are real moral principles. Two of them, incidentally, are the value of the search for the best answer in moral dilemmas, and respect for honest disagreement on the results.

Ethics Is Serious

Human beings have to live together (see below); but without moral restraints on what they do to each other, they will not live at all. Most people don't have to be *told* that. Ethics, the study of the criteria for right and wrong, is one of the few subjects we have taken seriously as long as we can remember taking anything seriously at all; one of the criteria for a moral judgment (as opposed to other types of judgment) is that it concerns a serious matter. Yet we need this presupposition out front to rule out ethical theories that avoid the serious problems. "Ethical relativism," discussed above, does that, by avoiding the problem of disagreement.

Ethical egoism is another theory that renders all moral problems toothless and relatively easy to solve, by avoiding the problems caused by the necessity of respecting others. According to "egoism," the only principle you should use to guide your life is the principle of advantage to yourself (in the long run). But then you never have any moral tension at all: since there's only one of you, and you know what you want, you can proceed along life's path with nary a qualm, scruple, or twinge of conscience! (Interestingly, egoism does have its dilemmas—fatal dilemmas, in fact. For instance, if someone should ask you for advice on what to do, should you advise what would be in *the questioner's* interest, thereby enabling that person to be a good ethical egoist too, or should you advise the course that is in *your* interests, since the giving of advice is, after all, your act?) But these logical dilemmas are not the kind of moral choice that we are considering in this course. While eliminating the whole moral universe *does* have a simplifying way with moral problems, it is a solution that really has no validity once past our second birthday.

Egoism is not the only trivializer of the moral experience, but we will spare you the others. *Any* theory that attempts to reduce the scope of ethical principles, or eliminate the tension between competing values, is a non-serious theory. Any teaching that seems to produce easy solutions to ethical problems is suspect. There are real values out there; the conflicts that arise in the areas where they overlap are real; and any formula or dogma that makes those conflicts disappear does so by refusing to pay attention to part of moral reality. By limiting the range of human reflection, such "solutions" constrict the mind and hamper our most important function. No such formulae, dogmas, or other "easy outs" will be found in this course. If we can promise nothing else, we can at least promise to leave you with the full complement of moral complexity in your universe.

Ethics Is About Human Beings

If we are to do ethics at all, we have to start from certain basic premises—some fundamental values or principles to which we can refer for the remainder of the course. If ethics is about human beings, we should not have to posit these values arbitrarily, but should be able to discover them in the life of the human being, and derive them from fundamental aspects of human nature. The human being is infinitely complex, of course, and human nature varies enormously from individual to individual and especially from culture to culture. Yet the human being is universally recognizable to others of the species, and it seems that humans everywhere, if they have to, can work together. So avoiding the complexities of the outer limits of human potentiality, it should be possible to say enough about the fundamentals of human morality just from the easily discoverable truths about the human being. This is what we will do in this section. In the course of the discussion, we will make some initial attempts to foreshadow the major ethical orientations which philosophers have, through our history, adopted, as reflective of these most basic moral principles.

Then what are human beings about? Three basic, simple, readily observable facts about human beings determine the structure of our moral obligations:

1. People are animals

People have bodies. They are matter; they exist in time and space and are subject to physical laws. These bodies are organic processes, requiring regular sustenance internally, and suffering all manner of slings and arrows of violent change externally. They experience pain, deprivation, and danger. They are prone to periodic failure unpredictably and to ultimate failure inevitably; they are mortal.

People, therefore, have needs that must be satisfied if they are to survive. They need at least food, water, and protection from the elements and natural enemies. That means that they must control the physical environment to make of it the means to those ends. Failure to do so will lead quickly to pain and suffering. These are inevitable in any case; in this way we are reminded of our mortality.

The immediate implication for ethics is that, if we have any reason to care about human beings, then the relief of that suffering and the satisfaction of those needs should be our first concern. In philosophical terms, human need and vulnerability to harm give rise to duties of *compassion* (for suffering), *non-maleficence* (avoiding harm), and more generally, *beneficence* (working to satisfy human need, maximize human happiness, optimize human interests in all respects).

2. People are social

People are the sort of animals that regularly live in large groups of their own kind (i.e., in groups containing several to many active adult males); individuals raised apart from such groups exhibit behavior that is, as they are themselves, abnormal for the species.

Whatever problems, therefore, that people have with their physical environment (see 1, above), they will have to solve in groups. They will soon discover that this necessity produces a new set of problems; they must cope with a social environment as well as the physical one. That social environment produces two further needs: for a social structure to coordinate social efforts, and for a means of communication adequate to the complex task of such coordination. The need for communication is fulfilled by the evolution of language.

The immediate implication for ethics is that, given that there are so many of us, we must take account of each other in all our actions. We come saddled by nature with obligations, to the group in general and to other members of the group in particular, that we cannot escape or evade. By nature human beings try, most of the time, to do good and avoid evil, in advance of knowing just what counts as good or evil. Again, this condition, all by itself, yields moral principles. *Fairness*, or *justice*, demands that we subject our actions to rule, and that the rule be the same for all. What will make an act "right," ultimately, is not just that it serves individual happiness but that is serves the whole community; people are equal, and since *equality* is itself a value (derived from "equal dignity") the society must deal with them equally unless good reason is given for differential treatment.

3. People are rational

People are able to consider abstract concepts, use language, and think in terms of categories, classes and rules. Since Immanuel Kant, we have recognized three categories of thought ("forms of intuition") that characterize the way human beings deal with the objects and events of the world. These are *time* (*when* did something happen? in the past, the present, the future; and *how long* did it take? duration); *space* (*where* is some object? or *how far* away is it? location, bulk, distance); and *causation* (*how* did something happen? what brought it about? antecedents, agencies, powers, consequences). "Rationality," of course, in our ordinary discourse, means a good deal more than the basic ability to think in terms of when, where, and how. Ordinarily we use the word to distinguish calm and dispassionate decision making from "emotional" or disorganized decision making; we use it to distinguish people capable of making good decisions from people who are not. But for our purposes here, we need go no further with the word. The creature that is "rational" will think, on occasion, in *general* terms, about classes and laws, extending over time, space, and possibility, while the creature that is "not rational" will think, if at all, only about *particular* (individual) objects or events.

Because people are rational, they can make rational choices. When people think about action they think in terms of classes of acts as well as individual acts, future acts as well as past and present acts, of action therefore undetermined, for which real alternatives exist. Since people can conceive of alternatives, they can make choices—having thought over the circumstances, and deliberated on the outcomes, they can decide what to do. People are *free*, as we say, or *autonomous moral agents*. But then they can also realize that they could have done differently, and can feel guilt and remorse and assume *responsibility* for having chosen as they did.

Since people can conceive of classes of acts for which alternatives exist, they can make *laws* to govern acts in the future, specifying that the citizens (or whoever may be bound by the law) *ought* to act one way rather than another. Thus general obligations can be formulated and articulated for a whole society, including, for example, the kinds of obligations we are discussing in this book. Collectively (acting in their groups), people make collective choices, especially choices of rules, rather than relying on instinct; and they are then collectively responsible for those choices and individually responsible for abiding by them.

The immediate implication for ethics is that, as freedom of choice is the characteristic that sets humans apart from the other animals, if we have any duty to respect human beings at all, it is this *choice* that we must respect. Persons are categorically different from the things of the physical world: they have *dignity*, *inherent worth*, rather than mere price or dollar value; they are bearers of *rights* and subjects of *duties* rather than mere means to our ends or obstacles to our purposes. Our duty of *respect for persons*, or respect for persons as autonomous beings, requires that we allow others to be free, to make their own choices and live their own lives; especially, we are required not to do anything to them without their consent. In acknowledging, as social animals, the claims that human society has upon us, we acknowledge our obligation to obey its laws, and law generally.

4. The result of the above:
The human condition

Humans have minds, or as the philosophers call it, a rational nature; and humans have an apparently limitless capacity for suffering. Rationality and suffering are not found together anywhere else; possibly the angels have the first, and surely all beasts possess the second, but only human beings can reflect upon their own suffering and contemplate the suffering of others of their kind, and that sets them apart from all creation. By virtue of rationality, human persons possess *dignity* and command respect. Ultimately, that respect entails the willingness to let other people make their own choices, develop their own moral nature, and live their lives in freedom. By virtue of that abysmal capacity for suffering, the human condition cries out for compassion and compels attention to human *well-being* and the relief of pain. And this condition is shared; we are enjoined not only to serve human need and respect human rights, but to establish *justice* by constructing a political and legal structure which will distribute fairly the burdens and benefits of life on this earth in the society of humans. These most general concepts: *human welfare, human justice*, and *human dignity*—are the source and criteria for evaluation of every moral system authored by human beings.

The same concepts are the source of every moral dilemma. Attention to human welfare requires us to use the maximization of human happiness (for the greatest number of individuals) as our criterion of right action; attention to the needs of groups, and of social living, requires us to set fairness for all above benefit for some as our criterion; yet duty can require that we set aside both the feelings of the groups and the happiness of the individual in the name of respect for human dignity. On the small scale as well as the large, to respect the liberty of persons is not always to further their best interests, when they choose against those interests. To maintain a rough equality among persons, it is often necessary to limit the liberty of some of them. To preserve the community, it is sometimes necessary to sacrifice the interests of the few—but that course seems to discount the worth of the few, and so to violate justice.

Such conflict is fundamental to ethics, and is the major reason why ethics is famous as the discipline that has no clear answers. The human being is a complex creature, and when we extract human values from that complexity, we find them logically independent at the least, and often in opposition. The opposition has two traditional formulations:

1. Conflict of *values*: A value is a desired state, which we try, in our dealings, to advance or enhance or promote. The concepts so far discussed can be treated as values that are difficult to pursue simultaneously—the happiest society, the fairest or most equal society, the freest society or the lifestyle incorporating the most freedom.

2. Conflict of *imperatives*: An imperative prescribes a duty to do or to forbear. It is occasionally more useful to see ethical conflict as a conflict of injunctions or prescriptions telling us what to do in any given situation. We are *told*—by the Law and the Prophets, by our religion, by our parents, by our employers, by the civil law—that we must respect the rights of others,

be fair to everyone, and serve each other's needs. Sometimes it is not possible to do everything at once.

Against every clear value, there is another value, which sometimes conflicts. Against every clear imperative, there is a contrary imperative, equally clear, which sometimes applies. Ethics is the discipline that derives these values and imperatives, works out the consequences of our efforts to protect them, and musters what light it can to show us the possible reconciliations and the necessary compromises that attend their application in practice.

The terms "principle," "imperative," and "value" are sometimes used interchangeably. We will attempt, in the course of this book, to use "concept" to mean the principle in the form of a definition, as above; "value" as a desired end-state, to be achieved or enhanced; "imperative" as a prescription of duty. Morality is sometimes best understood as a system of imperatives, and generally imperatives are cited as the basis for the conclusions of applied ethics. The three concepts elucidated above—welfare, justice, and dignity—correspond to three imperatives for human conduct.

1. *Do Good, or at Least Do No Harm*: Because we must live, and because we can suffer, we must value life and happiness: safety, protection from harm, absence of pain, hunger, or suffering of any kind; enjoyment, pleasure. That is, we have an obligation to help and protect each other, to relieve suffering, to choose each action, or rule of action, according to the amount of pain it will relieve or happiness it will provide. This general duty we may call the duty of *concern for welfare*.

2. *Observe the Requirements of Justice*: Because we must live together, we must value equality: justice, fairness, clear rules and strict enforcement of those rules; trust and trustworthiness, honesty in word and deed. Then we have an obligation to acknowledge our membership in, and dependence on, the human community and the community in which we live—to contribute to its life, obey its laws, customs and policies, to be honest in all our dealings with our fellows and above all to hold ourselves accountable to them for our actions, especially as they affect others. This duty we may call the duty of *justice*.

3. *Respect Persons (as autonomous beings)*: Because we aspire to the full potential of humanity, we must value freedom. We take liberty, autonomy, rationality to be ideals, and value them in others as much as we prize our own. The human enterprise is an endless quest to become better, wiser, more loving people, and we must cultivate people and institutions that will protect that quest. We have an obligation to respect the choices of others, to allow them the space to live their lives, to the end, the way they see fit. For ourselves, we have the obligation to realize our own potential, not only to discern for ourselves the moral course of action, and to take responsibility for the moral choices we make, but to extend our knowledge and the scope of our reason to become as fully as possible the autonomous persons we are capable of being. This duty we may call the duty of *respect for persons*.

Clearly none of these imperatives is optional. We cannot choose not to have bodies. We cannot choose not to need each other, and although we may sometimes wish we could, we cannot choose not to choose, not to be free. And these imperatives are logically independent one from another. They can conflict.

THE FORMS OF MORAL REASONING

From the distinction between imperatives and values, above, two forms of moral reasoning, or reasoning to conclusions on the problems of ethics, may be derived. We call these *consequentialist* reasoning, in which ends are identified as good and means are selected that will lead to those ends, and *nonconsequentialist* reasoning, in which rules are accepted as good and acts are judged right or otherwise according to their conformity to those rules. In consequentialism, the rightness of an act is linked with the goodness of the state of affairs that it brings about; in nonconsequentialism, there is no such link.

We suggested above that moral principles usually take the form of an imperative, setting a duty sufficient in itself to justify action. An imperative serves as the major premise for a line of *deontological*, or *nonconsequentialist*, reasoning. Deontological reasoning states a duty, observes that the present instance, real or hypothetical, falls under that duty, and proceeds to derive the obligation to carry out that duty in this instance. (This form of moral reasoning is particularly well exemplified in the writing of Immanuel Kant, a German philosopher of the late eighteenth century. See Kant, **Source Reader** p. 131). For example, presented with a particularly nice necklace left unguarded on a jewelry counter at the department store, I might be very tempted to snatch it and disappear. But my duty not to do that is very clear:

(major premise)   Thou shalt not steal.
(minor premise)   To take this necklace would be stealing.
(conclusion)   Thou (in this case, I) may not take the necklace.

Or if I take it anyway, and am confronted at the door by the store owner asking if I paid for that necklace, and I want very much to say "Yes sir, I certainly did pay for the necklace, but I seem to have dropped the receipt," again my duty is clear:

(major premise)   Lying is wrong.
(minor premise)   To say I paid for it would be lying.
(conclusion)   I may not say that I paid for it.

Connoisseurs of logical form will note a certain falling short of the strict subject-predicate form demanded by Aristotelian logic, but the point should be clear enough. In deontological reasoning (literally, reasoning from duty), we assume that we are obligated to do what is *right,* that there are *moral laws* which correctly demarcate what is right and what is wrong, and that we can deduce the moral status of a contemplated action by finding what moral laws apply to it. By those laws, an act may have one of three moral statuses: it may be *prescribed* (obligatory), *proscribed* (forbidden), or *permitted* (neither prescribed nor proscribed).

There are problems with this approach, as you may have noted. What, for instance, is the *grounding* of the major premises? Deontological reasoning starts with the assertion of duties, but those duties must be justified externally. In this case, we can go back to our basic principles and derive the prohibitions of stealing and lying without too much difficulty. Occasionally, however, in order to justify a premise, we are forced to fall back on consequentialist reasoning—the reason why we mustn't trade shares of stock on the basis of inside information cannot be traced directly from the original principles, but involves quite some understanding of the stock market and, ultimately, the assertion that insider trading is harmful to the market and thus to the free enterprise system. (Insider trading is usually represented as a violation of "justice." But of course it would not be "unjust" to deal as an insider if the rules permitted it. It would just be conducive to bad consequences—tending to produce a weaker market.)

Note, however, that we could often just as easily couch the same moral argument in goal-oriented or *consequentialist* terms. In such an argument we treat the principles as values rather than as imperatives, and as *ends* to be achieved in society, rather than laws governing action directly. Moral argument then becomes an exercise in evaluating the *means* to the end of the best possible society. The *good,* as opposed to the *right* of right action, becomes the benchmark of moral prescription; that good is generally understood as the greatest happiness of the greatest number of persons in the society in the long run. (This form of moral reasoning is best exemplified in the writing of John Stuart Mill, a nineteenth-century English philosopher, see Mill, **Source Reader** p. 166). Action is right insofar as it brings about *good* results. The most familiar form of consequentialist reasoning is the "cost-benefit" analysis familiar from the business world: To find the right thing to do, you add up the benefits of each of the options, divide the benefits of each course of action by its costs, and select that option with the highest ratio of benefits to costs. (Jeremy Bentham invented the system, using straight add-and-subtract formulas instead of the more sophisticated "ratio.")

Can we deduce the same conclusions as above using consequentialist reasoning? Yes, somewhat more elaborately:

(major premise)   If everyone took objects from stores without paying for them, the economy would collapse; therefore the practice of taking objects without paying for them is contrary to the greatest good of the society.

(minor premise)   Taking this necklace without paying for it would therefore be contrary to the greatest good of the society.

(conclusion)   This act is not right and I should not do it.

We don't have to go through this procedure every time we find a necklace lying around within reach, of course. The experience of the whole human race is that respect for property, however property may be defined in different cultures, is essential for the stability of society, and therefore, on those grounds, such taking of property without payment is appropriately forbidden everywhere (as is lying on matters of commercial interest). Once the act is prohibited, the reasoning proceeds exactly as it did in the nonconsequentialist framework. Most of us find *rule utilitarianism* (consequentialism that establishes rules and then reasons from them) easier to work with on a day-to-day basis than *act utilitarianism* (consequentialism that evaluates every individual act on the basis of its consequences). But any consequentialist will insist on the point that *every legitimate major premise* for such a moral syllogism *is based on consequentialist reasoning*; we need no divine commands, unverifiable intuitions, or arbitrary pronouncements to give us the principles from which we derive the moral status of the act in question.

In any more extensive Ethical Theories course, you will have an opportunity to consider the theoretical problems and refinements of consequentialism, especially in the most familiar form of Utilitarianism. For the moment, we will simply present some very general strictures for these theories. In order to work, consequentialism must satisfy the following conditions:

1. It must be *careful*. The easiest mistake is to forget the bit about the "long run," and conclude that consequentialism just goes after short-term advantage, or "expediency"—what's good for me right now. Working carefully, the consequentialist must make sure that *all* parties involved have been taken into account, and that the long run effects have been calculated.

2. It must be *rule-governed*. A consequentialism (like "situation ethics" or other forms of act utilitarianism) that requires the moral agent to evaluate each situation completely *de novo* to determine the effects of his action, will produce much panic and confusion among those who must decide

and even more panic and confusion among those who will be affected by this seat-of-the-pants decision. And it will be totally incapable of producing justice, which asks only that there be *some* rule, even an imperfect one, known to all and possible for all alike to obey.

3. It must be *sensitive to individuals*. Where the happiness of all people is your concern, there may be a tendency to compress all human experience into the pleasure and pain that we all have in common, and overlook the significant differences between individuals.

4. It must be *sensitive to the differing qualities of pain and pleasure*. In some contexts all we want to know, in order to act or form policy correctly, is the *quantity* of the pain or the pleasure for everyone involved. For instance, in a hospital emergency room, everyone's pain will receive the same attention. But there are pleasures for which refined tastes are necessary, and there must be protection for those tastes, and active efforts to educate people to the point where they can enjoy, for instance, grand opera as much as video games.

Neither form of reasoning, deontological or consequential, is inherently superior to the other. We may use them both, and usually, in the course of a discussion involving ethics, we do. But *it is important to note the difference*, for if we do not, we condemn ourselves to talk past each other and frustrate our dialogue. For example, at a dinner party some years ago, I came across a heated debate on the problem of educating inner-city black teenagers. One side of the debate was arguing that the blacks had been treated so badly in the past, and had been denied such basic amenities and encouragements, that it was *unjust* to expect them to measure up to middle-class educational expectations. The other side, made up of schoolteachers, was arguing that education provided the only *decent prospects for the future*, and indeed, the only way out of the ghetto, for these youngsters, and unless they got their act together and got motivated somehow to finish school, the next generation would be just as disadvantaged and ill-treated as the present one.

Were these two groups really arguing against each other? No. Each could easily have conceded the other's point (and sometimes did) while maintaining its own. Rather, they were arguing *past* each other, one arguing consequentially (toward the future, bleak or somewhat brighter, depending on the means, especially educational means, adopted now), and the other deontologically (from justice). Both, by the way, were making excellent points. You might want to warm up your minds at this point in the course by joining that debate, in imagination, and trying to find a reconciliation. But please, do a better job than they did at keeping straight what kind of argument you are using.

PREVIEW OF THE BOOK AND THE REST OF THE COURSE

Traditions

The next chapter, Chapter 2, will introduce you to the traditions of ethics, keyed to your **Source Reader**. In this chapter we will trace the discipline of ethics through the writings of its greatest exponents.

Concepts

Chapters 3 through 12 will explore the major dilemmas of ethics in contemporary settings, keyed to the television/video series.

Summary

A final chapter will complete the discussion initiated here, of human freedom and the human condition. It will draw together the threads of the Essays in Chapters 3 through 12, to show once more the philosophical unity of apparently disparate principles, and synthesize those conclusions with the discussion of human nature and moral decision making.

AUDIOCASSETTE 1

The audiotape that accompanies this chapter features a dialogue by Professor Fred W. Friendly that elaborates on some of the questions raised here. The participants in the dialogue are:

- Lisa H. Newton, Ph.D., Director of the Program in Applied Ethics at Fairfield University, author of this text
- Willard Gaylin, M.D., a psychiatrist and president of The Hastings Center, an ethics research institute
- Kenneth E. Goodpaster, a philosopher and professor at the Harvard University Graduate School of Business Administration
- The Reverend J. Bryan Hehir, Senior Research Scholar at Georgetown University's Kennedy Institute of Ethics
- Michael Sovern, the president of Columbia University

The dialogue ranges over a number of issues but the fundamental question Professor Friendly explores is what we mean when we say "ethics." Have ethics become synonymous with the law in recent years? Is all that is legal necessarily ethical? You will recognize some of the case studies explored in this first audiotape. Ask yourself if the definition of ethics these scholars give is close to your own definition as you begin this course.

chapter 2 _____

THE TRADITIONS
OF ETHICS

_____

The discussion of ethics began some 4000 years ago. Philosophers since then have joined the discussion, made their contributions, and passed the questions on down to us. In this historical chapter we will briefly survey the major traditions of ethics, examine their tensions and their continuities, and link them with our present concerns. In the audiocassette that accompanies the chapter you will listen to four philosophers who represent the traditions discussed here. You may find this chapter to be a useful roadmap to the **Source Reader** that accompanies this *Study Guide*.

TWO WAYS OF DIVIDING THE TRADITIONS OF ETHICS

The traditions of ethics can be divided according to historical epoch, reflecting the civilizations in which they arose, or according to the type of reasoning they bring to bear on the world of human conduct. In the **Source Reader** attached to this course and in this brief chapter, I have chosen to use the latter division. But the historical division is much more familiar and widely accepted, and deserves a word of explanation.

History, the series of human events throughout the life of the human species, may be seen as a restless sea, constantly in motion, without real breaks or boundaries. But history as an academic discipline needs places to start the semester and places to set the final exam; it also needs coherent themes and patterns to make the events memorable to someone learning them for the first time. (This requirement is not an artifact of the contemporary university; the need to cut history into short and memorable, indeed memorizable, chunks was far greater before we started writing down the historians' accounts.)

For the student, therefore, we have divided the history of the Western world into three (and a half) major eras and many more minor eras identified by century, place, and theme. The three major epochs of Western history are the Ancient Period (the account of Mesopotamia, Egypt, Greece, Rome, and the Mediterranean world in general from about 5000 B.C. to about 500 A.D.); the Medieval Period (the account of Europe and the Mediterranean world from about 500 A.D. to about 1500 A.D.); and the Modern Period (the account of Europe, America, and all the lands they affected from about 1500 A.D. to about 1914). The "half" epoch is usually called "Contemporary," and embraces the twentieth century. The minor eras include such subdivisions of modern history (for example) as Elizabethan England, Colonial America, or The French Revolution.

Before proceeding to the philosophical correlates of these eras, it is worthwhile to enter a protest that has no universally satisfactory response. The assumptions that underlie that division have been aptly summarized as "White is Right and West is Best." In the Modern Period, the only history of most of the nonwhite nations is written, as it were, from the deck of a gunboat of one of the colonial powers. For earlier periods, there often is no written history extant for these nations. We may legitimately ask if the historical division, product of the ignorance of our forefathers, is not out of date and justly to be consigned to the ashheap of history. But there are provisionally persuasive reasons for retaining that schema of history, at least until a great deal more research has been done on the neglected areas.

First, there is a solid written tradition to back up our inquiries into the history of the West. We are bound to rely on the written sources, at least on those that are not known to be unreliable, simply because they are the only sources that survive. When we have so little in writing, relying on written sources may seem like looking for the car keys under the street light, not because that's where they fell but because that's where the light is best. But what alternatives are there? We will always know more about the puny wars of the ancient Greeks than we will about the mighty empire of the Celts, and only because a few Greeks had a penchant for writing things down. (And the Mediterranean air has a penchant for preserving writing in readable condition. The Celts had writing, and did keep commercial records, but apparently consigned rather little else to the page.) Further, we want to know not only what happened, but what people thought about what happened, and for that there is no substitute for an account written at the time of the events we study, by an eyewitness. The first selection in the **Source Reader**, for instance, is taken from an account of the Peloponnesian Wars by an author who participated in the events he recounts, and lived under the governments he describes. Early civilizations in Africa, Asia, and South America have left us with no such sources. For this reason alone, their histories will always be harder to write and much harder to understand.

But there is another and ultimately decisive reason for retaining this division. From before the time that history was taught as an academic subject, we have wanted to know, not history in general, but *our* history, the story of our own people (however we define them), the path over which we ourselves, the people with whom we identify ourselves, have traveled. Before I have become sophisticated enough to know not to ask, I consult the historian primarily to learn, not how time may have passed here and there, but much more crucially, who I am, and why I am the way I am. I expect historians to be able to tell me how my ancestors lived, and thus what stock I come from and what material I am made of. I expect them to be able to chart the directions for my people from their earliest origins, so that, projecting that line into the future, I may discern the path that I will follow and my children after me. Ultimately, I expect historians to show me the personal models that I may emulate, the pervasive strengths of our civilization that I am expected to protect and preserve, and the recurrent problems of the civilization that I will be expected to address as part of my generation's agenda.

In short, I ask historians to give me not an empirical chronology of neutral events, but a normative essay on my rights and my duties in the light of my history, including the background for my ethical orientation and the justification for the ethical choices I make, which brings us full circle to our subject. Even "pure" historians, the recorders of battles and chroniclers of kings, have an ethical agenda to fulfill, one that will not be relevant to me unless they tell me *my* history, *my* story, or the story of the civilization with which I must deal. (Even as a "minority," unwilling to claim that civilization as "mine," I must learn its ways and its directions if I am to chart my course within it.)

Like history, so the history of ideas, specifically of philosophy, can be divided into chronological slices. We recognize an "Ancient Period" in philosophy as well as history: a prelude of pre-Socratic speculation on the nature of things, Plato, Aristotle, and a few schools of post-Aristotelian philosophy to round out the period. By the "Medieval Period" in philosophy we understand the slow intellectual response to religious faith in a religious civilization, suddenly flowering with the rediscovery of Aristotle in the Islamic, Jewish, and Christian traditions (typified by

Averroes, Maimonides, and St. Thomas Aquinas). The "Modern Period" is philosophy's response to modern science and the ideal of Progress, where the dominant perception of the age's thinkers is one of irreversible and substantial change for the better. In each of these epochs the change in focus of the philosophical thought corresponds to a change of political and economic center for the society at large.

Modern philosophy also teaches, more precisely than in the past, the analytic function of the discipline, discovering ways to break problems down, to bring critical thinking to bear on the "solutions" of previous eras, and to establish the logical foundations of the fundamental principles of the subject. It is to modern philosophy, for instance, that we owe the analysis of basic ethical principles employed in Chapter 1 of this volume. Aristotle told us (Aristotle, **Source Reader** p. 45) that ethics was an imprecise discipline, and that we should not expect certainty of our conclusions; conceptual analysis, developed as a philosophical technique in the last two centuries, shows us the logical independence of the fundamental principles, and therefore *why* we may not expect certainty in our conclusions.

Philosophy can be seen as a conversation through the ages on the nature of **reality**, of **man as knower** of that reality, of the **good**, and of the **discourse** in which we carry on that conversation. Ethics is the branch of philosophy that focuses on the good. In the Ancient Period, the focus shifted between the peculiar ideal of personal excellence developed by the Greeks and the stern ethic of obedience to God developed by the Israelites, with every variety of spiritual discipline found between those benchmarks. When the Greek *polis* broke down, new individualistic ethics, notably Stoicism and Epicureanism, arose to fill the gap left by the collapse of the only moral community that the philosophical tradition had recognized. Medieval ethics conceives of the good in a context of religious faith; in the West, the Catholic Church was often the only protector of philosophy after the barbarians destroyed the Roman Empire. Modern ethics, ushered in by the new boldness and individualism of the Renaissance, breaks away from the previous era's reliance on divine revelation and attempts to ground itself in the material world of science and the formal world of logic. It is the failure of that attempt that plagues the contemporary philosophers, wrestling with the dilemmas of nuclear war, environmental catastrophe, and the slow decay of the human institutions (family, church, and community) that helped us weather the last crises.

So dividing the history of ideas into chronological slices makes sense. This historical division is the one most in use in the field. The Suggestions for Further Reading at the end of the **Source Reader** will refer you to a few classical historical approaches to philosophy and ethics. The fact that we have chosen a different manner of exposition should make it all the more worth your while to seek out one of these sources and acquaint yourself with a traditional historical exposition.

DIVISION BY OBJECT OF THE SEARCH

We are employing an alternative structure that divides the conversation on philosophical ethics into four "quests"—for excellence, for holiness, for law, and for happiness. Each tradition includes writings on the nature of moral behavior from ancient times, occasionally extending into the modern era. The structure makes more sense than the chronological division, and also illustrates the persistence of certain fundamental ideas about goodness and right conduct through the length of the conversation. This structure will be followed in this chapter and in the **Source Reader**, as follows:

1. The Greek quest for excellence, with its emphasis on the cultivation of virtue and character;
2. The Biblical commitment to God, to obey God's Laws, and to love God and neighbor;
3. The Moral Law Tradition, in search of the reasonable order of the universe, beginning with Epictetus, continuing through the whole natural law tradition, incorporating Immanuel Kant, John Rawls, and Martin Luther King, Jr.;
4. The Utilitarian Tradition, the pursuit of the greatest happiness of the greatest number in the long run, beginning with Epicurus and continuing through Jeremy Bentham to its culmination in John Stuart Mill.

The **Source Reader** that accompanies this course will give you an opportunity to trace the history and survey the characteristic thinkers of these traditions. In this chapter we will note their peculiar strengths, characteristic tensions, and methods of approaching ethical concerns. This task is analytic and critical in nature, and will give us a chance to apply the distinctions from Chapter 1.

The Greeks

It is fitting to begin any survey of ethics with the Greeks, not just because they left us some of the oldest writings on the subject, but because they took on the questions of ethics from the beginning. Before the philosophers wrote, Greek historians were raising fundamental ethical questions. Herodotus, in the history of the Persian Wars, noted that Greeks and Persians have totally different cultural norms on every important subject of conduct—yet fire burns, here and in Persia. Why can we not discover the same constancy in human law that we discover in nature? Is there anything that is naturally right, *right by nature*? Thucydides, historian of the Peloponnesian Wars, stated the problem so baldly and clearly that excerpts from his history are included in the **Source Reader** (Thucydides, **Source Reader** p. 8): is there anything right *at all*, he asks, or are there simply force, might, and the ability to get your own way and call it justice?

This is the question that every ethical tradition has to answer. It sets the agenda for the rest of the **Source Reader** and the rest of the course. The Greeks of the classical period answered that the only thing that is good without qualification is a good human being, by which they meant a virtuous human being, excellent in character or disposition. The only way to find peace in a world beset with troubles, they argued, is to live an ordered and balanced life, self-sufficient, satisfied with little, and seeking no ultimate justification outside the self. This pursuit of personal excellence is the theme pursued in the selections from Plato, especially in the excerpts from the *Republic* (Plato, **Source Reader** p. 17). In that greatest of all works of philosophy, Plato offers an elegant proof of the proposition: that whether or not the world recognizes and rewards virtue, the just person is the happiest of human beings.

Aristotle approaches the same conclusion systematically, working out a method for exploring questions on ethics and philosophy. He carefully surveys the accepted meanings of the terms he expounds, sorts out their functions, rules out some definitions, adopts others with qualifications, until he reaches an accepted consistent understanding of the concept in question. Thus, to answer the question posed in the first book of the *Nicomachean Ethics*, "what is the highest goal to which a human should aspire?", Aristotle undertakes a step-by-step procedure. First, he identifies the highest goal for human life as "the end for which all means are chosen," since that for the sake of which something is done is superior to that which is done for its sake (or, the end is superior to the means). Then, by a careful analysis of ordinary justification and motive, that highest goal is identified with "happiness." Next, by sorting out human functioning into higher and lower levels, he determines that happiness must be identified with the highest function of humanity. Further, since that which is lasting is superior to that which passes away, it cannot be any transitory or passive state, but must be an ongoing activity of the reason, or rational activity. This "excellence" or virtue of the human being he identifies as activity within a "mean," or actions appropriately chosen between two extremes (Aristotle, **Source Reader** p. 50). Again, in the last book of the *Nicomachean Ethics*, Aristotle takes on the same question from a totally different angle, this time considering various other candidates for "happiness" (Physical pleasure? Money? War? Work?) until only philosophical life and study are left among the candidates for the end-state of human existence (Aristotle, **Source Reader** p. 59).

Does it follow, then, that anyone who understands the conditions of human life will automatically live a life of wisdom, justice, and temperance? It appears so. The philosophers knew that not many people lived that way, but wrote that failure off to (1) misdirected self interest, a form of ignorance; (2) failure of the state and the family to provide a proper education; (3) rare cases of perversity. They had no vision of progress, as did the later Utilitarians—no hope that universal education would make humankind not only universally wise but also universally good. But they did recognize that malleable human institutions could influence how the child grew and the adult behaved.

Having decided what the goal of the moral life was, Aristotle went on to describe how virtue was acquired and how lawmakers should bring it about. Children must be taught good habits, by being told the right things to do and made to do them consistently until right action becomes habitual. Only then should they be told the reasons for the rules they have been taught to follow. Eventually they should be taught to reason right conduct out for themselves. All such teaching presupposes a stable family and an established government that concerns itself with the character of its citizenry. These presuppositions form the core of Aristotle's understanding of the *polis,* the Greek city-state, which devoted itself to the nurture of the citizens' souls just as the citizens devoted their duty to protecting the *polis* and the excellence of its laws.

The Greek solution to the problem that they themselves were the first to pose—why should I be moral?—was simple and elegant: I ought to be moral because the disciplined soul produces the happy human being. To acquire the discipline, I need a strong and disciplined society, and therefore my first responsibility is to participate in creating and preserving such a society, which in turn will train its citizens in virtue and reward those who attain it. Note the dynamics of this approach. There is no reason outside of the individual human life to practice morality; indeed, as Plato has two of his characters point out, the world seems to admire successful injustice much more than quiet justice, and the gods are indifferent to human behavior as long as they get their sacrifices on time (Plato, **Source Reader** pp. 26, 30). But the moral life is very difficult to achieve, requiring socially enforced discipline that runs counter to natural self-indulgent inclinations. If achieved, the moral life is very satisfying, so it is worth our while to create the society that will create it in us. Once we have achieved that life, we should be willing and able to maintain such a society.

But how is this cycle to start? Given either chicken or egg, the cycle can continue; but we cannot create either out of nothingness. Faced with this problem, Plato brings in his "Philosopher King" to set up the institutions that will train the citizens to become the sort of people who will maintain the institutions. But even supposing the King successful, and the state perfectly virtuous, Plato shows that the corrosive influences of human weakness will nevertheless destroy it, gradually, after a period of time. Goodness, after all, no matter how strong in appearance, is only fragile and fleeting.

The real-world equivalent of the decline of the Platonic Republic arrived in Athens in the fourth century before Christ, in the form of Empire—first the Macedonian, then the Roman, which deprived the city-state of its independence and removed forever its ability to create a moral life for the citizenry. The post-Aristotelian philosophers had to project new bases for morality; we will return to them in this chapter's sections on "Moral Law" and "Utilitarianism."

The Bible

Probably the most popular and successful teacher of morality in the Western world, the Bible presents an approach to ethics totally at odds with that of the Greeks. The Israelites never doubted for a moment that moral imperatives were binding on them, nor did they question that the source of morality lay outside themselves, in a righteous God whose clear teachings formed their law. Very little time was spent on intellectual inquiry into the origins and justification of the imperatives they accepted—God had spoken them, they were bound to God as people to sovereign, as children to father, as sheep to shepherd, and that was all the justification they needed.

Two moral commitments set the Biblical tradition apart from the other moral traditions considered in this course. The first was the commitment to justice: the absolute prohibition, enshrined in the earliest formulations of law, against taking advantage of the weakness of the poor, the widow, and the orphan, for personal gain. In the Law, this prohibition shows as a simple insistence on fair dealing in trade ("Thou shalt not keep the labourer's wage over night") and fair punishment for crime ("Thou shalt give life for life, eye for eye, tooth for tooth..." *Bible*, **Source Reader** p. 73). In the Prophets, it emerges as the much more sweeping command to share wealth, no matter how fairly got, with the needy (*Bible*, **Source Reader** p. 78). In later elaborations, we will distinguish between the retributive justice commanded in the Law and the distributive justice commanded in the Prophets; for the Israelites, one Lord commanded justice and justice was all of a piece.

The second commitment was to love, specifically to love God and neighbor. Appearing first in Moses, this commitment becomes the signature of the Prophets and the focal point of Christian teaching. Such a command would have bewildered the Greeks. They tended to understand "love" primarily as the sexual attraction between lovers, and secondarily as the deep affection between friends (that love, exalted in Plato's *Symposium*, that we call "Platonic"); and they understood moral principles essentially as limits to natural, especially sexual, impulses. Whether good or bad, and they certainly did not think it was always good, love could not be commanded. The commitment to love makes no sense without the personal system, and the personal model, of a patriarchal universe ruled by a loving God. We still feel easy telling children that they have a "duty" to love their parents, and it is the same sort of love that is demanded of the Israelites by their God.

While the moral strength, beauty, and effectiveness of the Biblical moral teaching is unquestionable, the intellectual fragility of this system is painfully evident. We may summarize the logical breakpoints as the paradoxes of Fatherhood, Omnipotence, and Idealism.

The paradox of Fatherhood is found in the continual shifts in Divine direction, especially in the earlier books of the Bible. Fatherhood is paradoxical by its very nature. It is of the essence of fatherhood to demand perfect behavior of the child; any conduct less than perfect will elicit violent rage from the father. It is also of that essence to love the child, so that the child in and of itself, without reference to behavior, will elicit instant and unlimited love from the father. But the child is also the image of the father, carrier of his name, bearer of his fortunes—so any endeavor of the child's that seems geared to adult success will meet with instant and tireless support from the father. Just so is the Lord God of Israel: now furious at his people's inevitable derelictions, now taking pity on them and giving them food and favors just because they are His, now helping them win battle after battle, slaughtering all their enemies before them, only to have them turn, in a few generations, to other gods, and the Father's rage starts all over again. Every prophet's message is the same: Israel, you have sinned! and you will be slain, burned out, sacked, looted, pillaged, destroyed, marched into exile, and utterly abolished from the earth. But the Lord will have mercy on you and will then restore you and give you military victories and prosperity and empire forever, because He loves you. And you shall be great among nations. Popular television programs of recent years have made fortunes from the humor inherent in that set of mixed messages; Divine Fatherhood is no different from human fatherhood in its essential ambivalence.

The second paradox results from positing a God who is at once all-good and all-powerful. When the Israelites came out of Egypt, they acknowledged one and only one God for *themselves*, to whom they would give their loyalty; they never claimed that there *were* no other gods. When the Israelites reverted to worshipping Baal under Ahab, God sent Elijah to prove that He could deliver the goods—fire on the altar, in this case—and that Baal could not, and therefore was not worth worshipping. He was not out to prove that Baal did not exist. With the coming of monotheism proper, the belief that there just *is* only one God and that that God is all-powerful, new paradoxes make it very hard to make intellectual sense of the results.

There are paradoxes already present in the notion of an omnipotent Being capable of action: can God make a stone bigger than He can throw? The paradox that presents itself most poignantly to ethicists arises from the combination of omnipotence and goodness. If God is all-powerful, and perfectly good, how can He let evil happen in the world? In his modern retelling of the Job story (*J.B.*; Boston, Houghton Mifflin, 1986), Archibald MacLeish puts the problem in song: "I heard upon his dry dung-heap, That man cry out who cannot sleep: If God is God, he is not good; if God is good, he is not God; Take the even, take the odd; I would not sleep here if I could. Except," and we keep returning to this one, "for the little green leaves in the wood, And the wind on the water." A theological industry has grown up around attempts to reconcile this single, omnipotent, eternal God, and the supposed benevolence of this God, with the agonizing death by starvation of innocent children. No reconciliation is universally accepted or acceptable.

That central paradox is joined by a third one in the Christian elaboration of the Jewish tradition, the paradox of the incomprehensible command. What sense can we make of commands to resist not evil, to love enemies, to turn other cheeks? It is not enough to point out that such commands are very difficult for saints to obey, and impossible for ordinary people. More important, these commands contradict the command to do justice by punishing evildoers, in force since the earliest understandings of the Law. Nor are they good policy, or productive in any political context that we know. On the contrary, such responses to hostile situations tend to be counter-productive in this hate-filled world, emboldening persecutors to persecute further, since impunity is assured. The only ethical sense that can be made, ultimately, of the Christian teaching in its original form is that the ethic as preached was intended not as a guide for actual practice in this world, but as a guide for spiritual preparation for the Kingdom of Christ, also not of this world.

The Biblical tradition yields a final and pervasive irony: despite the paradoxes, from the puzzling tests of Abraham's faith and Job's patience to the crucifixion of Christ and the stoning of Stephen, the Bible has provided more practical guidance in the daily affairs of the inheritors of Western civilization than any of the more philosophical traditions. We will come back to this point in the final chapter of this book.

The Moral Law

There is an intuitive plausibility to these claims: that there is a logical system of moral imperatives inherent in the universe; that our minds are capable of understanding it; and that we are capable of obeying it. Adherence in some sense to each of these claims is the common thread of the Moral Law tradition.

Human beings seek order in the universe, and usually find it, whether the order be a family hierarchy of deities, a metaphysical hierarchy of essences, or a mathematical hierarchy of laws of motion (joined by an evolutionary hierarchy of living beings in species, genus, phylum, and kingdom). But the orderliness of nature may not be a matter of fact, empirically discovered. It may simply be the presupposition of our search for order; the kind of investigation we conduct into the nature of the universe is such that it can find only evidence of order. Disorder, chance occurrences, and random events, like the stray pencil marks on the computer-graded exam, are routinely ignored unless they are so frequent and serious as to invalidate the whole observation. We did not find order in the universe. We knew it was there, decided to find out what kind it was, and automatically excluded from our findings any random events in our field of investigation.

The universe can be explained in several ways, each capable of handling all the observable facts but not capable of subsuming each other. One way of defining the four traditions we discuss in this chapter is by the ordering principles they adopt. The Greeks see a hierarchy of ideas or essences, from the most general (the idea of being itself) to the most particular (the individual snail that crawled across this leaf five minutes ago). The Judaeo-Christian tradition posits an all-powerful God whose Law, willed by Himself as He sees fit, created all things and orders all things. The Utilitarian tradition, to be considered below, is a child of the age of science and mechanism, and sees physical causation in everything. The Moral Law tradition, considered in this section, finds an all-pervading reason, or reasonable order that both explains all that is in the universe and sets the norm and standard for all things. Then deviation from that standard is wrong—is sin, evil, disorder, and injury. The existence of deviation from the natural order, then, is enough reason for the moral being to act, to end that deviation and restore the order to its normal, and normative, state.

Note that in this tradition the universe itself is morally normative. This feature is unique: for the Greeks, the universe might be animated by deities, but it maintained moral neutrality between the good gods and the bad ones. For the authors of the Bible, God alone is moral; His Creation has no moral content independent of His will. And for all of the modern consequentialists, nature is just a matter of physical forces and biological urges; all the moral quality that it has, we impose upon that universe by positing moral premises from which our moral conclusions can be derived. But for the Moral Law tradition, Law is absolute and inherent in nature.

Do you have to believe in God to believe in the existence of a Moral Law in the universe? The question has nothing to do with personal belief in God, let alone personal churchgoing habits. The question is, rather, does any Moral Law or Natural Law theory require a *deus ex machina,* a God to lay down the law in the beginning, in order to make any sense? Apparently it does not. While Thomas Aquinas certainly assumes that the law we discover is identical with the Mind of God, at least with that part of God's Mind that is necessary to our salvation, and Epictetus sometimes talks as if he believes the same, the belief is not universal in the tradition. The Social Contract Theorists, or Contractarians, Thomas Hobbes and John Locke, find their principles in human nature as it is given, while Immanuel Kant and John Rawls deduce theirs from the concepts of duty, law and justice already in the language. To be part of this tradition, you must believe in the orderliness of the subject matter—the physical world, including the human body; the human mind; and human conduct—and you must believe that that order is good; from this all else follows.

The major strength of the Moral Law tradition—its psychological attraction, and the reason for its recurrence—is its power to give meaning to human life and action. Recall the discussion in Chapter 1 of the human being: The human being is at bottom an animal, striving ceaselessly to stay alive and free from pain until its inevitable death. Relationships with others provide some satisfactions, but they are no less transitory, fragile, and painful than life itself. But through the mind, through reason, we can be eternal, and dwell in a realm of certainties above all pain, loss, and change, simply because that realm transcends time. We can overcome the limits imposed on us by distance in a realm apart from all space; our understanding of all of the laws of nature gives us power, not only beyond what we might accomplish through physical effort on our own, but beyond what the entire human race might accomplish by united effort—if it could ever get together in any united effort.

As Plato saw it, that world of ideas was more real than the physical world that points us to it. Mathematics and the ideal certainties of logical relationships lift us out of our human limitations and reveal possibilities of immortality. The ancients also recognized the uniformities of physical nature (on the level of "fire burns"), although, until Newton in the seventeenth century, only the Pythagoreans thought to tie those uniformities to the certainty of mathematics. But a realm of math and science, beautiful as it may be, tells us little about how we ought to live. Mathematics is a purely formal discipline, true in all possible worlds, with no implications for reality as we may find it. Science articulates the uniformities that exist in the natural world but, as a purely empirical discipline, also has no implications for normative discourse and the way we conduct our lives. But if the universe is shot through with law—mathematical law and law of science—why may we not suppose that it contains normative law too, and prescribes for us a proper way of life?

If we may not, the reason *why* we may not was noted by Herodotus. Fire burns, he pointed out, here and in Persia. But our perceptions of what is right vary from time to time, place to place, and cult to cult. We all believe, we say, that there is one unchangeable law, knowable to everyone, open to human reason, written (perhaps) on the human heart. But when it comes down to the chapter and verse of that law, we simply do not agree on what it tells us to do. With all our centuries of trying, and all the talents of the philosophers covered in the **Source Reader** (and countless others) dedicated to the task, that result is disappointing, to say the least.

Why do we look for moral guidance in the universe, anyway? In asserting the existence of a Natural Law, are we just taking an emotionally easy way out? The universe stretches around us in all directions, infinite, mindless, vast beyond imagining, utterly heedless of the existence or needs of human beings. Are we trying to pretend otherwise? Are we trying to pretend that infinite space and cosmic dust really contain a law that was made *just for us*? Is that very likely? On the other hand, why not? The natural world seems to be made just for us: it feeds us, shelters us, gives us just the right amount of oxygen. It is, in short, hospitable—to the point where we are overpopulating it. The regularities of mathematics and science seem perfectly proportioned to our appreciative minds. What is so surprising in the finding that the universe has provision for our moral nature, just as for our physical and psychological natures?

Someone might object that the parallel suggested is entirely misguided: that our pre-human evolution took place in this natural world, so of course our bodies have adapted to its resources; that our survival depended on our ability to assess opportunities correctly, so of course our minds have adapted to its lawlike patterns. But moral nature is not subject to evolution. On the other hand, why is it not so subject? Surely proper behavior towards others, human and divine, is advantageous to survival. Then is it not possible that our moral natures also have evolved and adapted to the moral patterns already in place in nature?

When we return to the four ethical traditions at the end of the course, we will re-examine the Moral Law to see what guidance it may give us in contemporary ethical problems—despite the disagreements about its content, or perhaps *because* of those disagreements.

Utilitarianism

For the Utilitarians, one does not have to scan the universe for the moral law. The imperatives are close to home, in the vulnerability of human flesh and the needs of the human body. Pleasure is good; pain is evil. What leads to pleasure is good; actions that produce pleasure are right. Pleasure for two hours is twice as good as pleasure for one hour; pleasure for two people is twice as good as pleasure for one person. Pleasure for the whole community for the long run is best of all. The approach has the virtue of simplicity.

An examined Utilitarianism, like an examined life, is the only kind worth living. When actions are considered carefully, and paired with their natural consequences, "hedonism" or pleasure-seeking does not lead to the dissolute and shallow life that the passage above might suggest. Pleasure indulged only leads to greater desire; better to live a very frugal and disciplined life, so that desires will not multiply and become insatiable, leading to the pain of frustrated desire. That was the argument of Epicurus, the first of our Utilitarians, a Greek who modified the Platonic argument for the happiness of the just life to accord with his own materialistic approach.

In Jeremy Bentham's hands, that argument reappears. Bentham goes on to argue that, in common experience, service to the community creates more pleasure than service to self, while service to the long term produces more cumulative pleasure than service to the short term. But then if I want to live a happy, pleasure-filled life, I have to restrain my material desires, serve the community, and worry about the long term. So the use of Bentham's "felicific calculus," calculus of happiness (Bentham, **Source Reader** p. 165), actually yields the same common-sense moral conclusions as an ethical system that insists on the necessity of setting aside pleasure in favor of other values.

In the hands of John Stuart Mill, its most famous exponent, Utilitarianism is refined to include other ends (virtue, character, and the more advanced forms of human culture), and more extended means to attaining those ends. Justice, rights, and the full development of individual potential find a place in the system. Yet the fundamental question remains: is Utilitarianism, at bottom, sufficient as an account of the morality of conduct? I know what it is for a course of action to make people happy, and I know (more or less) what it is for a course of action to be right, but are they really the same? Certainly they coincide much of the time; as shown in Chapter 1, human happiness is certainly *one* value. But is it the only value, or the origin of value? Are all other values in fact subsumed under happiness? Put it this way: granted that promoting human happiness is often, or usually, right. But is it the source of right? Does "good" mean no more than happiness? Is the fact that something is in fact *desired* by human beings, even by all human beings, sufficient for the conclusion that it is *desirable*, or good? Put it another way: once I have proved to you that a certain course of action will maximize human happiness in the long run, might you not still be justified in asking, yes, but is it the right thing to do? And if you ask, and the answer is sometimes that it is not, then "right" means something more than "conducive to happiness," and ethics means something more than Utilitarianism will let it mean. (Try to think of examples of that negative answer.)

The strength of Utilitarianism is its immense practicality. It tells you how to go to work immediately to do some good: find out what people need, and get it for them; find out what's hurting people and make it stop. In a world full of famine, war, political prisons, and welfare hotels, that is enough direction to consume a lifetime very profitably. There is no ethical system that is more useful for the legislator, whose only job is to promote the interests of those who elected her. Yet at the end, it does not encompass the whole of ethics. In Fyodor Dostoevsky's *The Brothers Karamazov*, Ivan asks at one point if we would be justified in bringing about the happiness of the whole world if the only price was the death by torture of one, only one, totally innocent person—a baby, perhaps. I do not know the answer to the question. But the fact that we know we have to ask it means that we hold a notion of goodness or rightness apart from happiness, so Utilitarianism is not complete.

At the end of this work we will want to return and ask why not. Why do we insist that the notion of the good must go further than the promotion of happiness, especially in a world so full of unhappiness? Do we want to save for ourselves some glimmer of a value that transcends humanity, happy or unhappy, altogether? Or by a callous "happiness isn't everything," do we hope to free ourselves from the clear duty to alleviate human pain and supply human need, a duty that we shirk as often as we can?

YOUR SEAT AT THE TABLE

It is time to reconvene the Symposium. Plato's *Symposium,* as you may recall, gathered a group of friends around a table to talk about a problem in philosophy—specifically, the true meaning of *love.* There was a bottle of wine going around that table, and Socrates shared in it, but he insisted that there be no heavy or forced drinking, for he wanted to enjoy the conversation as much as the wine.

We will need a larger table, for we have gathered not only Socrates and his friends Plato and Thucydides, but also Aristotle, born about the time that Socrates died, and his younger contemporaries Epictetus and Epicurus. (Of the four traditions we will be following in the **Source Reader**, three are now represented at the table—and we aren't even through the third century B.C., nor have we left Athens, Greece.) And we are adding the Jewish Prophets, who may be very uncomfortable dinner companions, and Jesus of Nazareth, who by all accounts will probably enjoy himself. When we have found chairs for Thomas Aquinas, Thomas Hobbes, and Thomas Jefferson, John Locke, John Stuart Mill, and John Rawls, Jeremy Bentham, and Immanuel Kant, who must not be seated next to each other, Paul of Tarsus, Josiah Royce, and Martin Luther King, Jr., the table may seem quite full. But it isn't, really; there will always be room for those willing to join the conversation. The horseshoe table in the television presentation is an extension, another leaf, of that table. You will be watching, not a new conversation imitating the old, but a continuation of a conversation that is always young.

Now we need you to be a part of it. You need a willing mind, but no prior knowledge of philosophy. (Certainly the people talking with Socrates in the *Symposium* had none, since the discipline had not yet been invented. And still they talked about philosophy, just as friends.) Sometimes you will be asked to concentrate a bit harder, or go over a point a few times if the terms and the method of reasoning are unfamiliar. But there is no need to feel embarrassed; even professional philosophers started out that way; and after all these centuries, your teachers are very patient. If you don't understand them the first time, try again.

The one thing you may not do is sit and passively listen, or let the course drift past as one more set of questions to be answered on an exam, and nothing else for you to do about it. This course is about life, Socrates' life, Cain's life, Hobbes' Life of Man ("nasty, brutish and short"), Jefferson's life, liberty, and pursuit of happiness, Jeremy Bentham's life of desire for pleasure and aversion to pain, and ultimately Martin Luther King, Jr.'s life, laid down for the principles he sets forth in his **Source Reader** selection for this course. And it's about your life, too. You must join the conversation. The syllabus for this course will tell you how to make your initial responses to the conversation as you understand it, but that is only the beginning. After you have turned in, or mailed off, your final exam for this course, your part of the conversation has just begun. We hope to find you at your seat at this table for a long time to come.

AUDIOCASSETTE 2

Now listen to the audiocassette that accompanies this chapter, in which Professor Fred W. Friendly leads a dialogue among four philosophers representing the four traditions presented here. Acting as advocates for their respective traditions, these four philosophers tussle with two difficult ethical dilemmas. The philosophers explain the approach each tradition considers important in making a decision. The participants are:

- The Utilitarian Tradition — Tom L. Beauchamp, Senior Research Scholar at Georgetown University's Institute of Ethics;
- The Greek Tradition — Martha Nussbaum, professor of philosophy at Brown University;
- The Deontological Tradition — Thomas Pogge, professor of philosophy at Columbia University;
- The Biblical Tradition — The Reverend Donald W. Shriver, Jr., president of Union Theological Seminary.

Both case studies concern the ethics of killing, one in a medical context, the other in the context of war. Listen for the justification each tradition gives for its stance. Do the arguments seem logical to you, whether or not you agree with the conclusion? Is there one tradition that seems closest to your own way of looking at these problems?

chapter 3 _____

COMMUNITY:
Do Unto Others

1. When you go in search of Community, or of a community—a place where you can live with neighbors and there will be time to help each other and enjoy each other—what are you really looking for? Is your ideal of community based on selfish goals, or on a longing to be in a situation where you can help others?
2. What has happened to the family in contemporary American life? Can it no longer teach values to its children? What role does the community play in raising the children?
3. Can you think of a time when you should have intervened in other people's lives to help them—against their will? Can you think of a time when you would now?

THE CONCEPT OF COMMUNITY

What does "community" mean? Our first problem is that it has several meanings. It may help to postulate two poles of meaning for the term, one pole designating, very unspecifically, any going organization that exercises limited political authority over a small region—any town or village; and the other pole designating a pattern of life or sociological orientation where collective demands and interpersonal relations are as important as individual goals and choices. There is a general consensus in the literature that "community" in the latter sense is in trouble; we will attempt to say something about how community got in trouble in this place and time. This attempt provides a sociological as well as philosophical agenda for this essay. There is no remedy for that double agenda, as indicated in the Introduction; the concept we are attempting to elucidate (in the second sense) is new on the scene, and its exploration so far has been generally the domain of the sociologists.

"Community" as local political authority is value-neutral; when we set up the traditional dichotomy between the individual and the community, we do not mean to prejudge either, but to adjust the claims of each so that some level of harmony may be achieved. Thus individuals are free to pursue their own private objectives and serve their own private convenience to a certain point; beyond that point they must respect laws and restrictions laid down for the health, benefit, and convenience of all (for instance, in disposing of trash from their homes). Individuals are free to keep what they earn or otherwise obtain by lawful means, but must render a certain amount of their resources each year to the community to provide for services designed to benefit the whole (for instance, the fire department). Intrinsic to our accounts of individual and community is the recognition that neither set of interests is superior to the other.

Put in philosophical terms, "individual" and "community" in this sense are simply two aspects of the social nature of the human being. Humans must live in community or be less (or more) than human; as Aristotle put it, that man who lives outside the polis is either a beast (or psychopath) or a god. By the same token, the citizenry are the material cause of the polis, without which it would have no existence (Aristotle, **Source Reader**, p. 61). The individual owes what is specifically human about her—language, thought, love, responsibility—to the education and social life of the community; the community owes its existence to its legitimacy, and legitimacy is nothing but the recognition given it by the individuals who are its members. This interdependence of meaning is the material for the tragic dramas of conflict between individual and community, as in the trial and death of Socrates (Plato, **Source Reader**, p. 11). Ultimately, community and individual can withhold from each other the value for which each most depends upon the other: the individual may deny the moral authority of the community, and the community may take the individual's life.

In the second sense, "community" is unmistakably a value. As a normative concept, it is closely linked with "intimacy," "trust," "fidelity," or "loyalty," even, if you must, "togetherness." It is that closeness generated in traditional primary relationships, family and friendship, in which people know each other not in function-specific roles, but as whole people in a whole community, living, working, and worshipping together. It is a precious part of human life, strengthening and preserving the individual, protecting religious and moral traditions.

In the contemporary world, "mass society" is seen as threatening "community" in this sense. Mass society, as a sociological concept, deserves a word of explanation. No two writers can be expected to use it in quite the same way. For purposes of this chapter, we will use it to mean a mechanical or bureaucratic organization of people and resources which carries on, in separate locations and institutions, all the functions of human organization that used to be exercised by the community. Thus one set of organizations occupies the individual's working life, another his playtime, another set educates the children, yet a fourth attends to municipal services, and God is worshipped in a fifth group of institutions, by law separated from all the others.

Mass society gives us specialized bureaucracies that serve fragments of us, need by need. Mass society knows no love or anger; it has only functions. It cannot be an object of loyalty or love, so fails to fulfill the need for "membership," or "belonging," one of the more important of the human needs of community. But because the rational division of labor among its functions makes mass society much more efficient at satisfying material needs and providing services for the individual than any informal community ever was, the move from community to mass society is irreversible. Put another way, mass society, preferred by individuals because its specialized institutions are easier and less trouble to work with, competes successfully with community and displaces it. If your understanding of competition is Adam Smith's model of reward for efficient operation, you will approve of the change. If your preferred analogy is the organic process of carbon monoxide poisoning the system by displacing oxygen in the blood through successful competition, your evaluation will be very different.

When mass society replaces community, it leaves tradition at risk, intimacy and faithfulness with nowhere to root and flourish, and individuals dying of loneliness or "alienation." "Community" in this sense, an object of value that we seek to recover or protect, has been examined by the sociologists since Emile Durkheim and Ferdinand Tonnies. The most recent document, *Habits of the Heart* by Robert Bellah and others, traces the consequences of the loss of community in contemporary America, through the lives of representative Americans in different regions and walks of life. The literature on the loss of community is very recent because the problems have arisen only within the last two centuries. Before that the village in which you were born and the family into which you were born determined your religion, your trade, your political activity, your friends, your spouse, your recreations, the clothes you wore, the thoughts you thought, and the dreams you had at night. While this may sound stifling, very few people got lost. Since that simple time, specialized institutions have arisen, with experts to help us order our lives from the cradle to the grave; primary institutions like family, neighborhood, and parish have withered, and "community" has become problematic.

How is "the community" for any individual determined? Is it always my town? Or, if I am a member of an ethnic minority in my town, is *my* community my ethnic group or the part of town where we all live? Could it be some group larger than my town? Could it be, say, "all right-thinking people in the United States, that is, all white Anglo-Saxon Protestants"? Or is that the sort of community I should *not* acknowledge as my own? Could it be the whole world, the whole human race? But then, how will I ever distinguish my community from yours (or should I try)? In short, is my community *given*, as far as I am concerned? Or is it *chosen* by me?

The question is very important. It really asks, is community a *fact of nature*, necessary for human existence, as unquestioned as the oxygen we breathe? Or is it a *conscious project*, adopted by a group of people in order to rediscover, and reinstitute, the values perceived as lost? If it is the first, it is given as a part of our environment, like bodily life and death, and we do no more than adapt to it. If it is the second, then we are responsible for it, for its quality and value as well as for its maintenance. The move from the first to the second understanding of community has created the anguish, and the sense of fragility, over human associations; on the other hand, it has given currency to the notion of individual as well as collective responsibility for the crimes committed by the collective, and to a much higher moral standard for the acts of our own associations (especially our government).

From the answer to that question—whether community is given or chosen—follow the answers to the traditional questions about my duties to my community: What ethical obligations follow from my membership in it? What do individuals and private organizations owe to the community in which they live or carry on business? What are the rights of the private and the public sectors? What, indeed, is the criterion for distinguishing between them? Are their rights and obligations symmetrical, or is there a presumption for the private (as, the defense but not the prosecution has the right to appeal an adverse verdict)? Can the association, in its own person, assert a right to exist, and to maintain certain customs and identifying characteristics even against the wishes of its present members? (For instance, does a Catholic college have the right to maintain its Catholic character even if the vast majority of its present faculty and students have no interest in maintaining that character?) From the fact that human beings are social animals, does anything follow on the rights of individuals or associations?

One way to survey the ethical aspects of community—the identification of the group and the implications for obligations—is to outline briefly three major problematic dimensions, and see how they intersect in the television case study.

1. American individualism: The human being is a social animal. Americans are famous for forgetting that fact. As commentators on our scene have observed since Alexis de Tocqueville in the nineteenth century, Americans are swift defenders of individual interest, fanatical in protection of individual liberty and rights, prickly about privacy, and unaware of their neighbors and the deep streams of society that flow through their lives. "Individualism," a word that Tocqueville may have coined, describes the dominant American orientation to life and society. The notion of the involuntary community—the unchosen framework of human beings among whom one was born, with whom one continues to interact, and with whom one shares a scarcely perceived complex web of interdependence—is no large part of the American's moral universe.

Especially since the Second World War, when Americans began to become self-conscious about the lifestyles of a nation grown so important, our sociologists have traced the damage done to the American soul as a consequence of uncontrolled individualism. At the personal level, we acquiesce readily in personnel transfers, which uproot families and remove us from social ties to local communities, with no reckoning for the disruptions caused by such practices. On the societal level, we find it very difficult to take control of problems like substance abuse, pollution of air and water, acid rain and other assaults on the natural environment, because their solutions require intense collective action over a long period of time, and we have apparently lost the traditions, religious and civic, that would have prepared us to devote a common effort to a common goal. The "Me Generation" was not news in America; we have been the quintessential Me Nation for the last century and a half.

2. Social technology: Americans are also famous for placing a very high value on technological progress, and until very recently, we have been preeminently good at it. The local farm community was destroyed by the explosion of technology that brought first the railroad, and the domination

of commercial powers far from the ken of any previously self-sufficient community; then the factory and the lure of the city that left the country-side an archipelago of ghost towns; and finally the "factory farm," neutron bomb of rural America, rendering the machinery rich and the people un-necessary. The urban neighborhood was destroyed by the automobile, the high-rise office or apartment building, and, ironically, by the very politi-cal and economic advances that enabled the children of the neighborhood to move to previously inaccessible areas to live out the American Dream of upward mobility.

We love to hate our machines, but we will not give them up. The most popular villain of the day is probably the computer. The computer is replacing the teller in the bank, the billing clerk in the department store, apparently the chef at the restaurant, even the stock dealer on Wall Street; we mourn the passing of all but the last. But we have no intention of return-ing to the pre-computer age. Whatever we valued about the old human con-tact, and the web of dependency on human beings that formed the infrastructure of our community, we will gladly sacrifice for the tremendous-ly exciting possibilities that the machines open up for us.

More subtle in their effects on our lives are the elaborate social ser-vice institutions, especially those that are publicly funded. Schools that were not a branch of the Church used to be founded as occasion demanded by a group of families that wanted schooling for their children. Such schools have been largely replaced by sprawling bureaucracies of public school sys-tems, presided over by superintendents, very largely outside the control of parents. Aged parents, who used to be cared for at home (if they lived that long), are now the charges of bureaucracies, which administer all social ser-vices, and all medical care up to and including the last in a network of con-valescent and nursing homes unknown two generations ago.

The removal of education for the young and care for the old from the primary home settings where they developed has been accompanied by similar displacements on many smaller scales: music has moved to the radio, ritual and dance to the television, and gameplaying to the recreation center. Above all, all care for the troubles and needs of people of all ages has moved to the social service agencies set up by municipal, state, and federal government, and out of the realm of family, church, or neighborhood respon-sibility. That, as we shall see in the hypothetical, will come back to plague us.

3. The family: Whatever happened to the good old days when mar-riage was for life and only movie stars got divorced? The family has lost its role, function, legitimacy, meaning, and thus its ability to sustain itself in mass society.

Its role used to be that of sponsor and mediator for the individual in the community. The individual had no independent status, nor any right to enter into the community without family permission and protection. (The forms, if not the spirit, of the last century are preserved in the custom of the "coming out party," in which a young lady is "introduced" to the society by her family, to become for the first time a full member of society.)

Its function used to be that of full caretaker for all its members, responsible for their education, enculturation, health and health care, even their lives (although the father's right to take a child's life has always been severely circumscribed).

Its legitimacy stemmed from the fact that it was, for all purposes, the final authority on matters pertaining to its members, and none could interfere; that understanding ensured, if nothing else, the respect of its members for the family authorities.

And its meaning was that it provided the whole of social life for all its members except the head of the household, who alone was a full member of the larger community. Social interaction for the members occurred only through the family. It was the body, they were the parts of the body. It was one organism, which embodied the meaning of community for its members.

It is commonplace that all these understandings about the place of the family in the life of Western culture are gone, replaced by the complex interaction of all family members with that array of secondary institutions mentioned in the last section. Since the reasons to stay in a family are gone, the very strict rules that people used to follow, that protected the existence of the family, are no longer applicable. Both of these developments have confusing consequences, some of which emerge in the hypotheticals that follow.

THE TELEVISION PRESENTATION: SELECTED QUESTIONS ON PERSONAL ETHICS

This section considers the television presentation or videotape. The recapitulation of the dialogue that follows is not meant to be a word-for-word transcript of the tape, but a summary of the major themes, issues, and opinions that emerged in the conversation. It is for review, and for use as a resource if you include this topic in your term project.

TITLE: "DO UNTO OTHERS"

Moderator: Professor Charles Ogletree, Jr.

Participants: From left to right on your screen

C. EVERETT KOOP
Surgeon General,
U.S. Public Health Service,
Department of Health and Human
Services

MARILYN SMITH
Assoc. Prof. of Philosophy,
University of Hartford

WILLARD GAYLIN, M.D.
President, The Hastings Center

ELLEN GOODMAN
Columnist, *The Boston Globe*

CHASE PETERSON, M.D.
President, University of Utah

J. BRYAN HEHIR
Sr. Research Scholar,
Kennedy Institute of Ethics,
Georgetown University

LINDA ELLERBEE
Journalist

ANTONIN SCALIA
Justice, Supreme Court of the United
States

FAYE WATTLETON
President, Planned Parenthood
Federation of America

MIDGE DECTER
Executive Director, Committee for the
Free World

CALVIN BUTTS III
Executive Minister, Abyssinian Baptist
Church

ANNA QUINDLEN
Columnist, *The New York Times*

ROBERT LEVY
Staff Attorney, New York Civil
Liberties Union

DONALD SHRIVER, JR.
President, Union Theological Seminary

LESLIE GUTTERMAN
Temple Beth-El, Providence, R. I.

Ask yourself, as you review the dialogue:

1. Would you want to inform on someone to break up a scheme of cheating or fixing grades? What if a friend were involved?
2. Do you have the right to tell a person that you think he's doing something seriously morally wrong? Why might you not?
3. Is your right to intervene very different if a child is involved? Why?
4. Ultimately, are you your brother's keeper? Who is your brother?
5. What kind of society would make it easy to be your brother's keeper?

THE COURSE OF THE DIALOGUE

Stolen Tests

The Fairness Argument

The moderator begins with a question for Faye Wattleton. Ms. Wattleton, my name is Robert. I'm a high school senior, and you're an old friend and confidant of mine. My family is poor, but I'm bright and ambitious and I want to get into Harvard. All the rich kids in the class went to College Examination preparation classes to help their scores in the College Examinations, but they cost $500 so I couldn't afford to go to one. Then some friends of mine bought the answers to this year's College Examinations, and gave a copy to me. I've taken the test, the scores were pretty good, and I was planning to use them to support my application to Harvard. Is there anything wrong with that?

Wattleton is troubled by the story, notes that Robert is obviously conflicted on the subject or he wouldn't have come to her, questions him on the circumstances and advises against using the results of dishonesty for a college application. Dr. Willard Gaylin's reaction is just a bit stronger: "I think you want to go to Harvard too badly. And all your life you're going to find things you want too badly, and if you don't learn that you don't do certain things for things you want badly, you're going to end up doing an awful lot of bad things....As far as your being disadvantaged, it's probably another disadvantaged kid you're cutting out of Harvard because you cheated. You can call it anything you want, but you cheated."

Dr. Everett Koop agrees in condemning this "short cut": "You put...a goal in your life so far ahead of ethics and principles and morals that it's going to plague you the rest of your life."

Now Robert goes to Chase Peterson, as the high school superintendent, with a different question. Is he obligated to turn in the others who participated in the scheme? Peterson's answer is a masterpiece of diplomacy. He begins by praising Robert for coming to him to talk about it ("I'm proud of you....You're one heck of a person"), tells him he need not turn in the others, but he hopes he will go and talk to them, describe the pleasant reception *he* got ("Tell them my door is open") and encourage them to come to him on their own. If they won't do that, then we'll get together and decide what to do next.

The Social Consequences of Cheating

Bryan Hehir comments that in the course of this conversation, both major forms of ethical reasoning, the utilitarian and the deontological, have been used to show Robert the error of his ways. "On the one hand, some arguments have been, you might call it, utilitarian. They say, 'If you don't do what's right, sooner or later you may pay for it.' Another set of arguments is, 'You ought to do what's right.' We've now brought together the two major ways that we think about right and wrong and say in this case, you are bound by both...." He objects, though, that most of the conversation has focused on Robert. "Ethics is never just about individual persons. It is always about society." In that larger society, the social bonds can be injured by cheating.

Linda Ellerbee notes that this sort of act is very bad for the individual. You cannot give something in this society without expecting to get it back; if you cheat, you will be cheated. This type of thing is unacceptable (unless, of course, you're running for public office, in which case it seems to be standard behavior). You must set the situation right. Should I turn the others in? Robert asks. Will Gaylin admits that there is an inconsistency in requiring Robert not to use the scores himself but not requiring that the others be turned in for similar penalty. But he would not put the burden of turning them in on Robert.

What does Justice Scalia think? He is not impressed by the "fairness" argument that Robert started out with—all the other kids had $500 to take the course and I didn't. After all, if that was the major argument, you could have stolen the $500, right? and paid for the course and taken it with the others. As a matter of fact that would have been better: it's easier to pay back a stolen $500 than a cheated exam. "Fairness" doesn't cut any ice anyway. After all, some are born with money but no brains. Is it all right for them to cheat to get into Harvard because it isn't fair that they were born without brains? "We do not all start life on an even playing field. But the rules are that we all play it by the rules of honesty and ethics." And pay back what we have taken. The tough question is, whom would you pay compensation to? Who's the victim in cheating?

Bryan Hehir sees this as a fine example of the workings of the lottery of life. We have to learn to play by the rules in an unfair game.

The moderator twists the hypothetical a little. Robert isn't just a friend, Justice Scalia. He's your son. Now what's your advice? Put off college a semester. Retake the exam and turn in honest scores. Thanks for the advice, Dad, but I think I won't take it. I think I'll go to Harvard this year. They're even giving me a scholarship. Are you going to turn me in? There is a very long pause. Finally Scalia says, "You know, I think I will; but I'm doing it more for your own good." Is there something *immoral* about what I'm doing? "Of course there is. You're lying." Gee, Dad, I thought you'd *understand*. Oh, says Scalia, "I do understand. And as your father, I am confident that I am doing what's best for you by holding over your head the threat that if you don't do what's right, I'll do it for you." You won't allow me this one indiscretion? "I've allowed you the indiscretion," says Scalia. "I'm not going to report you to the police....I am just refusing to allow you to profit from what you did wrong."

Wattleton, the old family friend, concludes with the same advice: sit out a semester and retake the test.

Punishing the Wrongdoer

The Cheating Husband

Robert takes everyone's advice, stays out a semester, retakes the test, gets into Harvard honestly, is now launched in his career and married to Carol, a wonderful woman. They're a model couple, it's a great marriage.

Now, Ms. Goodman, you are Robert's old friend and colleague. You know he's having an affair with another woman. What, if anything, do you say or do? Ellen Goodman would bring it up casually in conversation: you know, Robert, your friendship with Dineen is causing comment. None of your business, says Robert. OK, says Goodman, and backs off. Just like that? Just like that. "There's always another day." Marilyn Smith is not satisfied with that conclusion; she'd at least ask him to think about his values. Robert responds to that: Sure, you're right, I'm bringing this to an end, I just need a little time. Not good enough for Anna Quindlen. Stop now, she would say as a friend. The relationship is obvious. Someone is going to tell Carol.

The Right To Know

Who's going to tell Carol? Faye Wattleton wants to know why anyone would want to. Doesn't she have the right to know? Yes, but "not through my sharing it with her." That would be butting into the personal lives and private affairs of our friends, and we have no right to do that. "It may be wrong," Wattleton concludes, "but I don't see myself as a savior to go around cleaning up the world of all wrong." Linda Ellerbee, who is now convinced that Robert is running for public office, would do no more than withdraw moral support: she would not join Robert at the dinner table until this affair ended.

The Obligation Not To Do Harm

At this rate no one's going to tell Carol. The moderator thickens the plot just a bit: Carol tells you that she and Robert are doing so well they've decided to have a baby. *Now* will you tell her? Will Gaylin thinks that the structure of the obligations just changed. Before, to tell Carol would be doing good unnecessarily; now that a baby is contemplated, keeping silent would be to do harm, or at least to be an accessory to harm. The obligation not to do harm is much stronger than the obligation to do good.

Would Everett Koop tell her? Not unless she asked directly, and then he could not lie. Ah, but what if Carol were your daughter? Would you tell her then? Yes, he would, and would take Robert along for the interview, and the whole thing would be thrashed out right there. Scalia would also tell Carol in that situation, for the same reason that he would have turned in his son for cheating; it will be painful, but the special relationship creates a special obligation. Marilyn Smith would tell her, adding that Robert is a skunk and she should get out of the relationship as fast as possible. Wattleton would not tell her daughter; she would, instead, go to Robert and tell him to get out of the affair *before* she tells her daughter. Goodman is not happy with this new secret relationship with her son-in-law, excluding her daughter. Quindlen would be afraid to go to her daughter; what we might get here is the kill-the-messenger syndrome, where daughter blames the bearer of bad news.

Child in Love

Now the moderator changes roles to become Nancy, a fifteen-year old who wants to tell her friend, Faye Wattleton, a very happy secret if Wattleton will promise not to tell. Wary by this time, Wattleton is interested but will not pledge confidentiality. Nancy decides that Wattleton is not her friend after all and goes on to Ellen Goodman. I want to tell you about this great relationship I have with Robert. He's 30 and he's married but he's getting out of that marriage at some point and I love him so much. I know it's a little unusual but I hope you understand.

Goodman is appalled, and tries to do some fact-finding. She strongly advises Nancy to talk to her parents. Nancy will have to get out of the relationship.

Midge Decter can't understand this deep and meaningful conversation with a manipulative child. "Why don't you say to her, 'Listen, punk, you don't know what the hell you're doing.'...And I now have to get on the phone to my friend, Robert, and tell him that if he doesn't leave you alone, I'm going to call the cops." Can't see this pussyfooting around with a fifteen-year-old.

Goodman doesn't like that course. I am trying to keep the conversation going, she points out. Ellerbee also would talk, and try not to close the door. She would ask the teenager to think about what she's doing. Built on this basis, what future do you think this relationship really has? You're lying to yourself. And you're hurting Carol. Try to imagine Carol's face. That line of thinking goes nowhere. The fifteen-year-old has no interest in "Carol's problems." Fr. Hehir adopts a slightly different approach. "Robert is tied to his wife, so you are engaged with someone who is already tied to someone else....It is futile to let a fifteen-year-old talk about her happiness without talking about the impact she's having on other people. They're old enough to know that much."

The Battered Child

Let's try another story. Rabbi Leslie Gutterman is in the supermarket, where he sees a woman haul off and slap, hard, the child that is with her. What do you do? Nothing. She does it again. What are you thinking?

At this point I'm very concerned, says Rabbi Gutterman. If I'm nearby, I might ask her if there's some problem, just to show her that there are some consequences for this kind of behavior in public. All right, she says there *is* a problem. The kid is disobedient. I told him not to touch the bleach and he did and got the top off and poured bleach all over the floor. That's the problem. Rabbi Gutterman is not prepared to take the matter further. Scalia remarks that the child is probably chewing on his leg by now. Linda Ellerbee recalls the swift and certain justice of her own upbringing, similarly meted out to her two children, and doubts if the description given constitutes child abuse.

Will Gaylin is a bit more concerned for the fate of the child. If that was a real blow, why do you start out by asking the mother if there is some "problem"? This is the topsy-turvy world of social worker/psychiatry mentality, and it's morally bankrupt. "Where the hell are the values here?"

Obligation to Strangers

Ellen Goodman points out that intervention may not be in the best interest of the child, who may be blamed for the embarrassing intervention and beaten very badly as soon as they're home. There's a point beyond which you simply can't protect that child. Gaylin suggests that an intervention in this situation might be at least a start—to build up a history of attempts to help the child. Koop points out that this is not a neighbor but a stranger, to whom we have no ongoing relationship; it is not clear that we can or should do very much to intervene.

Will Gaylin comments that we have a countervailing value here, the integrity of the family. "We do respect family integrity. The family is still a structure of our society. We don't cast...all moral and ethical issues into the legislature and into litigation. So there is a family which can go wrong, but up until now has been one of the social forces that has served us reasonably well in modern times. The other value we have to be concerned about is...family autonomy—we're just chipping away at it constantly now by bringing the courts, the legislatures into things that used to always be family."

Scalia ends with the comment that we have a special duty to help the young, simply because they cannot help themselves.

Alms for the Poor

The situation changes again. Ms. Quindlen, I'm a homeless person near where you live, and right now I'm in your path. I want you to give me a quarter. Will you do it? I'd rather buy you a tunafish sandwich. No, no; I'm allergic to tunafish. I want the quarter. Will you give it to me? Probably. Will you help me across the street? Sure. And for another two blocks? Uh, yes. Why, this is the apartment house where you live! You know, I've been on the streets for some weeks, and I'm awfully grubby. Can I come up and take a shower? *No.* Why not? Quindlen: That's where I draw the line. I'll do anything I can to get you appropriate shelter, but I don't know you well enough. Of all I've done, this is the first request that would put me at risk.

What do you think about, when homeless people ask you for money? That they might spend it on booze. That's why I'd rather buy the sandwich. Yes, but I'd rather have wine; will you get a bottle of wine for me? No, because it's not good for you. You're judging me? I thought you were concerned for me? "When you asked for the white wine the sense of concern is overtaken by my refusal to participate in your slow destruction of yourself."

Robert Levy would give money to a street person, and not judge him. If someone asks you for a dollar to get a drink, you'll give it? No; fifty cents is all right, but a dollar is not. Rev. Donald Shriver would not give the money if he knew it would go for drink. "I see again the tip of that iceberg, of a growing, major problem in this society and I go home and mourn, for the fact that we have the richest country in the world which doesn't have apparently enough resources to put a roof over the heads of growing numbers of people in our midst." Rabbi Gutterman would not give a dollar for a drink. Linda Ellerbee would gladly give the money without judging how it would be spent, and picks up on Shriver's theme: "I would also give money to defeat the policies of the government that wants to use our money for weapons instead of finding homes for these people."

Koop would give the dollar for the drink. He's supervised medical students working with Skid Row alcoholics, and has been struck by the extreme unlikelihood of changing anyone's ways. Will Gaylin would not give one penny, largely because of his "Marxist pre-pubescence," in which he was taught that the giving of private charity is degrading to the recipient and unnecessary in any decent society; it also enables society to ignore the problems. "I don't know what is served except a cheap service to my conscience." Calvin Butts has no patience with this approach. "I have a another code that says that if someone asks, you give. And that's based on a principle I get out of my own faith. And if a man is hungry, a woman is hungry, shivering, cold or needs a drink, I will give. And I will give what I can."

Public Responsibility or Private Charity

Quindlen asks, what if it's a seven-year old child panhandling? Gaylin is unmoved. To give charity to a beggar is to salve your conscience, so you can sleep well at night, when you shouldn't be sleeping well until we have the society structured to take care of all the poor and homeless, visible and invisible. Wattleton points out that the child might have a perfectly good home and just enjoy panhandling. Decter finds no contradiction between public responsibility and private charity.

Calvin Butts points out that charity saves lives, immediately. It prevents homes from being vandalized. In the long run, it may make us recognize that we are challenged to do something ourselves.

Gaylin is unimpressed, backing up his scepticism with a story of a young tough on the subway platform panhandling rich and poor alike.

A cleaning lady gives him what he wants for fear of being thrown off the platform. So should I give money so the boy doesn't push people off the platform?

Chase Peterson points out that such depths of poverty paralyze us into thinking we can't do anything. At least the act of charity expresses commonality between us and the homeless poor. Levy agrees that we should help them somehow. Shriver would rather run a soup kitchen than give charity at random. Quindlen would try to do both.

Justice Scalia, the homeless person who followed you home now hangs around. She's living in the alley behind the apartment house, defecating there, sleeping on cardboard, burning money, generally acting weird. The tenants' association wants to call the cops to take her away. How will you vote?

Scalia won't do that unless he's sure she will be cared for. Gaylin would have us look into the matter more. She might need help. It is ironic that the defense of the "civil liberties" of the homeless has made it impossible for us to call them sick and hospitalize them, so now we have to call them nuisances and put them in jail. Levy isn't sure she's mentally ill. "And if the solution to our housing problem is to call the police, I think we're barking up the wrong tree. If she hasn't committed a crime and she's not dangerous to other people, I don't think that the police have the right to remove her." Maybe's she's schizophrenic. Levy doesn't think that's the issue. We have two questions here. "First, when society can permissibly intervene to take someone off the street. And I would draw the line at when someone neither commits a crime nor is dangerous. And secondly, how can we help that person? And the way to help that person so far has not been to lock people up in mental hospitals...."

The Limits of
Protection

Gaylin points out that by the logic of the child-abuse case, if you can go out of your way to protect an infant, why can't you intervene to protect an infantilized adult?

Bryan Hehir, reviewing the scenarios to this point, comments that in every case played out there was a presumption of a bond among the actors. "So that one thing we've clearly established is that we don't live our lives in moral autonomy...in the sense that we only have those obligations that we choose to make with others....You neither want to institutionalize every moral responsibility we have, nor do we want to leave the whole world an open space where people come to recognize their moral responsibilities on their own, or don't do anything. The middle ground we're trying to find is where you institutionalize those responsibilities that I would generally call public order. But beyond that minimal public order, you...try to shape people's moral responsibilities so they will respond to human needs when they don't have to by law, but when they ought to by moral responsibility....And in that kind of society I think you hit the balance between public and private that you'd like."

A REVIEW OF SELECTIONS FROM THE SOURCE READER

Every reading in the history of ethics is relevant to this unit. Ultimately ethics is all about the painful adjustments that people have to make in order to live as free people with each other without hurting each other. Every reading in the **Source Reader** is all about individuals learning to live in community with other individuals. We have selected for review those that seem to balance the elements most satisfactorily.

Selections for this chapter:

> Plato, *Crito*, **Source Reader** p. 14
> Aristotle, *Nicomachean Ethics*, Book II, **Source Reader** p. 47
> The *Bible, Deuteronomy*, **Source Reader** p. 75
> The *Bible, Luke,* **Source Reader** p. 86

The order of readings is not chronological. The reversal is intentional. Plato poses the question: Is this the only way a good man can live within a good community—to defy its moods and die of its whims in order to bring it to its senses? Aristotle describes a much more settled social life, in which the young person is gradually led to become thoughtful and moral by careful training from the laws. Moses infuses both visions of social life with passion: I am the Lord; keep my Law. And above all love the Lord, and love your neighbor, and in that faithful relationship between people and God that the Israelites called the Covenant, those three duties are the same. The story of the Good Samaritan raises the classic question, who is my neighbor, to whom do I owe this love? And the answer is, your neighbor is the person in your path who needs your help.

SYNTHESIS AND DISCUSSION

One theme runs through all the hypothetical cases posed in the course of the television discussion: As the functions of the family are taken over by other institutions, the family is increasingly unable to control the interactions between those institutions and the members of the family. The possibilities raised by these outside relationships tempt individuals into new means of pursuing interesting objectives, and the family is increasingly unable to enforce the rules that might keep it functioning well. Ultimately the breakdown of the family plays itself out in public, and we are helpless to decide whether or how to intervene. Above all the anonymity of the urban-suburban society strips interactions of all "neighborly" character, lowering both our concern for the victims and our ability to help them.

A useful way to trace the collapse of the family and the retreat of the community is by considering the main characters of those hypotheticals in order of age. The youngest is the child in the supermarket. How did the situation come to the severe blows that concerned Rabbi Gutterman and made Will Gaylin want to open a case record? Suppose I had been in that supermarket, and had seen my close friend's child spilling the bleach while my obviously exhausted friend tried to attend to the marketing, the dripping child, the spill on the floor, and the infant in the child carrier. I would have gone over immediately, helped to sort out the situation, and taken charge of enough of the damage so my friend would not have been in such desperate shape by the time she reached the checkout. There would have been no blows. If we could arrange to have a close friend around every time things got bad, or maybe a live-in nurse or grandmother to help at home, there would be much less of the sort of desperation that leads to child abuse.

We cannot arrange this, but there is an alternative. Suppose instead we made a rule, that if someone's child spills bleach near you in the supermarket, or if something similar happens, you must immediately act as that person's best friend would act, were that best friend there. That rule, which Plato passed for his ideal state in the *Republic*, would go a long way toward solving the problem of child abuse, and most other problems as well. (Do you recognize it? That's Jesus' rule, from the story of the Good Samaritan. "I know I have to help my neighbor, but who is my neighbor?" "Just decide that the person who needs help is your neighbor, and act as a neighbor would.")

It's a very good rule, but we cannot put it into effect as law, and enforce it, for two reasons: (1) It violates the individual liberty of the Samaritan, to require that help be supplied, without contract and without pay, regardless of cost or inconvenience to the helper. (2) If we ask people to react quickly in response to perceived need, there will be a good deal of bumbling and well-intentioned mistakes—some of the "help" will be unwanted. But it violates the individual liberty of the recipients to require them to endure perfect strangers butting into their private affairs against their wishes. So a Good Samaritan requirement can be shot down by the claims of liberty; unless, in the interests of a much better society at all levels, we Americans decide to waive those claims in this case. But we won't; at least, we have not done so yet.

Next we find a fifteen-year-old having an affair with a married man over twice her age. There is little to be said in defense of statutory rape, and the panel does not linger long on the case. But the interesting question is not, is she right to carry on this affair? or even should we try to understand how she feels? The question is, who was asleep at the switch while a fifteen-year-old started hanging around with a married man with whom she had no business at all? Why wasn't the fifteen-year-old told to come straight home from school each day? And when this relationship started, why didn't everyone around them put a stop to it? The answer is that such rules cannot be enforced any more, and that it was, by our present understandings, no one else's business to interfere with their relationship. In a vicious cycle of moral decline, our capacity for outrage, and our courage to speak up and to act when outraged, have undergone the same attenuation as our capacity to sympathize with overburdened mothers in supermarkets and our generosity with time and energy to help them.

Now the son of the family comes home with SAT and College Board scores that are unusually good, only to tell you that he's cheated to get them, by stealing the answers to the tests. Here the remedy is not so plain. It is not, as Justice Scalia points out, just a matter of paying back something you may have stolen. In order not to profit from that cheating, the boy is going to have to sit out a year of school; and at his age, that is quite a penalty. The question, why did he take that year off, especially when his scores were so good, will follow him around for quite a while.

The panel did not hesitate; but would other parents, intent on their sons' success, tell them to use the scores, and just pray they won't get caught? What if there had been the added pressure of a military draft and inevitable combat duty for boys who drop out of school between the ages of seventeen and twenty? Would some of the panelists have become less certain of the moral course of action? Again the major question will have to be, who provided this opportunity? Why are we so hesitant to attempt to restrict the contact our children have with people who will do them harm, primarily by preying on their inexperience and leading them into temptation?

Now the respectable and well-educated husband is having an affair. We know both husband and wife. Do we intervene, tell the husband to stop, tell the wife what's going on? Such is the hesitation of any member of the panel to agree to intervene, that the moderator must change the hypothetical: the abandoned wife, possibly pregnant or thinking of becoming so, is your daughter. *Now* will you tell her? Still they hesitate, and so they should. There is no point in grieving someone with painful information when nothing can be done about a situation, and nothing can be done about adultery. Its status as a crime is laughable. As a prohibited action, it is no more than breaking a promise, which is unenforceable in the courts since it does not involve property. (Whatever Biblical history there may be of treating sexual favors as property in marriage has been quietly set aside in our contemporary understandings of "privacy.") In the libertine logic readily available in our culture, adultery is an expression of freedom of association, which is protected by the Constitution. Adultery is gratifying to individuals, and as a society, we can support very little in the way of countervailing values to individual gratification. The pursuit of self-fulfillment is encouraged by every aspect of our culture, and every adulterer discovers, in the self-serving perspective of the self-absorbed, that the new extramarital relationship is the necessary means to personal growth and self-fulfillment.

Adultery is not new. We have known since Moses that adultery would always be a temptation; why else would the Israelites have dealt so ferociously with it? The contrast of earlier penalties and current practice raises the question, why was adultery taken so very seriously then and not at all seriously now? (except by those directly injured, who are usually portrayed as objects of pity and ridicule rather than as rightfully angry).

The answer is simple enough. In earlier times, the family was the essential economic unit (basis for all industry), educational unit (whose chief function was to socialize the children into the moral tradition, so that they would be able to carry it on), social unit (relations were interfamily, not interpersonal), and therefore legal unit (the family alone had legal standing and legal responsibility for the actions of all the members.) Then, as now, adultery destroyed families. Therefore adultery was terribly wrong and was punished with all the force at the law's command. Now that the agencies of the state have taken over the family's functions, the institution is apparently no longer necessary, so the picket fence of prohibitions that kept it in existence is quietly being dismantled. It should be pointed out that in our history, no attempt has ever been made to run a society without the family as its basic unit. This generation will face the consequences of this experiment, and will have new evidence on the dispensability of the family unit.

One of the consequences of the collapse of the family is evident now. The teenagers and the younger adults in the last two scenarios discussed can, if pressed, fend for themselves. But if the family falls apart, who will take care of the aging parents, the chronically ill, all (besides the children) who cannot care for themselves? The answer to that appears in the last part of the hypothetical—the street, with its wandering, lost, friendless, "familyless" vagabonds, victimized by agencies of crime and agencies of the law alike, protected even from help by their civil liberties. Even in the television presentation, with no threat of embarrassment at stake from real encounters with real people, the panel divided neatly into three views on what to do about the drunk, deranged, or defeated homeless wanderers of our streets. We will juxtapose their answers, and the contradiction that underlies each of them, as a summary of all the dilemmas of this section:

1. The Good Samaritan's answer: Give people in need what they need, and give it to them immediately, to the limit of your ability, either by yourself or through private agencies. This at least makes some people happier, even if only for awhile, which the other answers do not; as Butts points out, it can very well save lives. The disadvantage of this course is that you

cannot ensure that the differences you make will last. The contradiction is that you cannot, in this society, force real help on people if they don't want it, and if you just give them what they want, not what they need, you may do them more harm than good.

2. Plato's answer, in which he is joined by Karl Marx: Assign to the whole society, the State or government, the duty of caring for those who cannot individually care for themselves. Care is a right, not something for which we should have to beg, and resort to private charities is humiliating. The advantage to this course is that if care is integrated into a system of lifelong support, an individual can be followed and helped to become a fully productive citizen. The disadvantage is that the help got this way is much more expensive than the help got through private charities, since a government program must fund its quarters and its staff as well as the help actually distributed to the poor; and that ultimately, this help becomes too expensive, for we cannot supply all the needs of all the needy. The contradiction lies in the nature of our effort to help the poor; we push the beggar aside on the way to the legislature to do our lobbying, yet lobbying is totally unproductive of help if it fails, and, given the nature of the political process, very unpredictable in result even if it succeeds.

3. The Libertarian way: Do nothing. There is no way, privately or publicly, that you can help the poor, for their need is endless. Moreover, you have earned that money, and it is justly yours. Neither beggar (through manipulation of your guilt) nor government (through taxes for welfare programs) has the right to take it away from you to use it himself or give it to someone else who didn't earn it. Some redeeming value could be found if you could prevent further self-destruction, by controlling the lives of those you help—but you cannot. Therefore we should quietly discourage private charity and abolish all government programs designed to help those who cannot help themselves.

One advantage of this course is that the productive people retain their resources. A more important advantage is that the withdrawal of outside resources will force people to rely again on family and neighbors, and such reliance will strengthen the family again. The disadvantage is that doing nothing is totally contrary to everything we've ever known about our duty to those in need, and that we cannot live that way. The contradiction lies in that last: that we find ourselves advocating that help be withheld in order to diminish harm (if only in the form of the further erosion of the family), while what the needy need is help.

Let us end on that paradox. We see need all around us, from the anguish of a neighbor over a wayward teenager, to the mentally defective homeless on the streets of the city. We feel like helping (that's bred in the bone) and we know we should help (our traditions have no stronger message). We have the resources to help, if only to sit and sympathize for awhile. And yet very often we cannot move to give help. This is something we knew how to do, it seems, just a few generations ago. Individuals gave to charity, often grudgingly; neighbors helped neighbors over the rough spots; there was an ordered system for family and parish to care for the poor and the helpless. Now, as in some nightmare where safety is just across the room but we have forgotten how to walk, we are helpless before the simplest forms of suffering—afraid to interfere with someone else's liberty, afraid that the help we give will really harm and we will be held legally liable. Where do we go from here?

QUESTIONS FOR YOUR REFLECTION

1. Is there a contradiction between our demand that our children be honest and moral persons, and our demand that they be successful? Present an argument that there is, and see if you can answer it.

2. What are the scenarios of intervention? At what point do you either intervene yourself or call the police?

- A noisy quarrel next door?
- A brawl on the street?
- A parent dragging a howling child?
- A ragged man with vacant eyes wandering in the traffic?
- A woman lying face down in a doorway?
- A man lying face down in the gutter?
- A child torturing a kitten?
- A woman kicking a dog?

3. What is the role of laws like those forbidding adultery or the abandonment of children in preserving the family? Will normally good families stay together because of love, without any social penalties for breaking up? Should we have such laws? Why?

4. What is the role of sexual exclusivity in marriage and family? Do you think experiments with "open families," where sexual activity is unrestricted, could work? How? If not, why not? Should they work? Can you give an ethical argument for sexual exclusivity?

5. Compare and contrast the views of law and love presented by Plato and by Jesus of Nazareth. Between the two, where does Moses come down? How do the two principles work together in his last sermon?

SUGGESTIONS FOR FURTHER READING

Special Supplementary Text:
ROBERT BELLAH, et al. *Habits of the Heart: Individualism and Commitment in American Life.* New York: Harper and Row, 1985.

BELL, DANIEL. *The Cultural Contradictions of Capitalism.* New York: Basic Books, 1976.

DURKHEIM, EMILE. *Suicide.* (Paris, 1897) trans. Spaulding and Simpson, ed. Simpson. New York: Free Press, 1966.

GOFFMAN, ERVING. *The Presentation of Self in Everyday Life.* New York: Doubleday Anchor Books, 1959.

HOCHSCHILD, ARLIE R. *The Managed Heart: Commercialization of Human Feeling.* Berkeley, CA: University of California Press, 1983.

MACINTYRE, ALASDAIR. *After Virtue.* South Bend, IN: University of Notre Dame Press, 1981.

MERELMAN, RICHARD M. *Making Something of Ourselves: On Culture and Politics in the United States.* Berkeley, CA: University of California Press, 1984.

NISBET, ROBERT A. *The Quest for Community.* New York: Oxford University Press, 1953.

RIEFF, PHILIP. *The Triumph of the Therapeutic.* New York: Harper and Row, 1966.

RIESMAN, DAVID, NATHAN GLAZER, AND REUEL DENNEY. *The Lonely Crowd: A Study of the Changing American Character.* New Haven, CT: Yale University Press, 1950.

SHILS, EDWARD. *Tradition.* Chicago: University of Chicago Press, 1981.

TOCQUEVILLE, ALEXIS DE. *Democracy in America.* trans. George Lawrence, ed. J. P. Mayer. New York: Doubleday Anchor Books, 1969.

TÖNNIES, FERDINAND. *Community and Society (Gemeinschaft und Gesellschaft).* (Berlin, 1887) trans. and ed. Charles P. Loomis. East Lansing, MI: Michigan State University Press, 1957.

WHYTE, WILLIAM H. *The Organization Man.* New York: Simon & Schuster, 1956.

chapter 4

RETRIBUTIVE JUSTICE:

To Defend a Killer

1. "Don't get mad, get even." It's a common rule in a heartless society. But is it right? If you are a victim of some injury, do you always have a right to get even, to punish in return?

2. Have you, or any of your friends, ever been in trouble with the law? If so, what did you think of the workings of the criminal justice system by the time you were free of it? Do you follow the sensational cases in the newspapers? Should their sensational aspects dominate the news?

   Do you find yourself more likely to be angry at the defendant for the terrible crime, or sorry for the defendant because of all the publicity?

3. Since the law of Moses told us to give "an eye for an eye and a tooth for a tooth," we have known that society has a responsibility to punish all offenders. On the other hand, American society has a duty to presume the innocence of all accused of crime. Can you think of incidents where these two rules have seemed to conflict with each other?

THE CONCEPT OF RETRIBUTIVE JUSTICE

In order to understand the workings of the criminal law, we must begin the story with Thomas Hobbes. Early in the *Leviathan* (**Source Reader**,

p. 104), he sets the stage for his Social Contract with a brief and candid description of human nature. Human beings are fearful of and hostile to one another, he tells us. They resent the least detriment to themselves—to their bodies, their property, their liberty or opportunities, their pride and their reputation. Fear of detriment leads to pre-emptive attack as a defensive measure. What begins as a quest for individual safety rapidly becomes a quest for enduring safety and the property, power, and reputation for fierceness that will protect it.

That last—the reputation for fierceness—creates unendurable danger in the society. For let anyone hurt me, intentionally or otherwise, and I am immediately obligated not only to return the hurt, but to punish him terribly, so he becomes an example to others, to teach them that they must never hurt me but must leave me alone. At that point, of course, he must do the same to me; he must show the world that he cannot be hurt by anyone with impunity, so he must do much more damage to me than I did to him. Unless, of course, I kill him, in which case his family takes over the obligation to kill at least me and two members of my family, whereupon my family....But in accounts by Gregory of Tours, of the lawless civilization of early medieval Europe, we find documentation of real feuds that dwarf such State of Nature fantasies.

For Hobbes, and for any strategist of social life before law, retribution—getting even with someone for what has been done to you—is no part of justice in itself, but a simple necessity of life where your safety lies in your reputation for vengeance. But this pattern of escalating vengeance must be stopped. Revenge unrestricted will destroy the people, or, as Hobbes points out, at least make progress and civilization impossible. So the first move that the people should make is to agree to a common government that will protect them from each other (Hobbes, **Source Reader** p. 108). This move launches Social Contract theory, still the basis of our assumptions concerning the legitimacy of government.

The decision to move from State of Nature to Civil Society is in fact unnecessary, since people have always lived in organized groups. But the need to restrain the unfettered course of private vengeance persists, for the simple psychological reason that the injury that has been done to me seems in my eyes much more serious than the same injury done to the person who did it to me. So even without the need for a reputation as a terrible avenger, I will tend to overpunish in the case of any injury. Therefore in any society, the lawgivers' first move is to restrain the taking of vengeance. Look again at your **Source Reader**, this time in the Biblical tradition, for a record of what some of Western civilization's earliest lawgivers did about vengeance. First, the repayment for any hurt shall be strictly limited by what we now call the *lex talionis*, or "law of the claw": no vengeance shall exceed the original hurt, "...you shall give life for life, eye for eye, tooth for tooth, hand for hand, foot for foot, burn for burn, wound for wound, stripe for stripe"

(*Bible*, **Source Reader** p. 73). Second, not even that penalty may be exacted if there appears to be no malice in the original hurt, or if that malice is mitigated in some way by circumstances. A murderer shall be put to death. But if the crime seems to be one of passion, or recklessness, or otherwise not premeditated, exile to a city of refuge is the appointed penalty (*Bible*, **Source Reader** p. 72).

In the earliest of our traditions' writings on law, then, we find the society intervening in the natural course of vengeance to protect itself against the fury of injured individuals. Society cannot afford private wars, so it imposes the *lex talionis*. But beyond that minimum, it can ill afford to lose valuable citizens, punished for being the unwitting causes of accidental maimings or deaths. So recognition of mitigating circumstances, the requirement of *mens rea* ("guilty mind") or intent to injure, and the assignment of lesser penalties for lesser degrees of guilt appear very soon in the history of our law. From these earliest practices we forge our notion of retributive justice: it is just and fitting to repay every injury with a similar injury to the one who inflicted it, unless mitigating circumstances make a lesser punishment appropriate; and in all cases, inflicting a punishment *greater* than that called for by justice is unjust for the same reasons that the original injury was unjust.

It is in theory a short step from the right of society to mitigate punishment in order to save its resources, to the right of society to determine all punishments, including whether or not there shall be punishments, on grounds of what is good for society—that is, on strictly utilitarian grounds. This step was never taken in the early part of our ethical tradition. For religion and philosophy, a higher Order not only permitted but required that revenge be taken in case of crime. Beginning with fragments of the Greek tradition that preceded Thucydides, Justice has always been represented by the scales, and understood in the philosophical tradition (as opposed to the legal tradition) as a matter of balancing interests, rights, and powers. In its earliest representation, that order of the universe that the Greeks knew as *Moira*, justice was seen as conformity to the initial, and therefore correct, distribution of powers and prerogatives. Should a violation of that order occur, in the form of a trespass or usurpation of a portion of moral turf by one who has no right to it, that violation was an injustice, which had to be made right for the sake of the order of the universe itself. Therefore retributive justice—the restoration of that order—was not optional. Throughout the Biblical tradition also, we find that justice is required by the Lord, to the extent that the Lord will occasionally kill, or cause to be killed, the merciful kings or warriors who have spared people whom the Lord wanted punished by death. This requirement of retributive justice informs and gives impetus to all theatrical tragedy, from the Greeks through Shakespeare to O'Neill.

In later parts of the tradition, such requirements have been denounced as superstitious, and reforms of systems of legal punishment have been urged for the greater good of society. Jeremy Bentham, founder of Utilitarianism, was himself dedicated to the reform of the correctional system, to bring it more in line with the good of society as he saw it. For Bentham, "revenge" was a psychological urge that is unworthy of civilized persons, and no state should impose punishment for that reason alone. Rather, punishment should be selected and administered with the objective of doing the maximum good for the maximum number of persons. Utilitarian considerations alone, aside from all anger and thought of revenge, yield several justifications for legal punishment that may figure in determination of the punishment best suited for any crime:

- Disablement. The convicted criminal is, we may suppose, dangerous. Putting the convict in prison will at least "get him off the streets," and ensure that he will not commit a further crime of that sort or any other sort.
- Deterrence. Other potential criminals, seeing how this one has fared, will be deterred by fear of the same fate from committing crimes themselves.
- Rehabilitation. The time spent in prison, under the control of the state, can be put to good use. This may be an excellent opportunity to put the criminal through school and teach her a useful trade so that she will not have to live by crime when she has served her sentence and emerges from jail.

In debates over the justification of socially imposed punishment for crime, the "utilitarians," emphasizing the long-term interests of society, tend to cluster on one side; on the other we have the "retributivists" or "retributionists," emphasizing the requirement under justice to punish crime just because it *is* crime. In many cases, their conclusions converge. For instance, if a crime turns out to have been committed by a feebleminded person, or one who was insane at the time the crime was committed, neither position holds that he ought to be punished. The retributivists will point out that since he did not know what he was doing, he did not intend the crime, does not *deserve* to be punished, and therefore it would be *unjust* to punish him. The utilitarians will point out that since he is permanently disabled, he cannot be rehabilitated, and since he is pitiable rather than fearsome, his punishment would not edify the community or deter potential offenders who do not suffer from the same handicap; so it would be of no *benefit to the community* to punish him. Yet there are powerful differences between the positions in theory.

One major difference is that if the utilitarian position is to be completely consistent internally, it can justify, on all three justifications, "punishing" the innocent. The value of *disablement*, after all, is not limited to those convicted for crimes; there are many dangerous persons roaming the streets who just don't happen to have committed a crime, at least not one that we could establish in court, but we would all sleep easier if they were behind bars. The value of *deterrence* certainly does not depend on whether the person punished has actually committed the crime. If we can't find a person who has committed a crime that we want to deter, we can just arrest someone who might have committed one, or looks like he did, and let that person stand in for the criminal. Believing him guilty, future criminals will be just as deterred by his terrible punishment as they would have been by the similar fate of someone who is actually guilty. And the value of *rehabilitation*, under the stern control of the legal authorities, is certainly not limited to criminals. Sometimes I think I could use some, and I know *you* could. An excellent law would allow the police to pick up anyone who could use some more education or training and keep her in jail until she has been educated to our satisfaction. Or at least, so the utilitarian position would entail. Utilitarians, of course, deny that any such suggestions are consistent with their position. They only meant to talk about the disposition of people who have been convicted of crime in the ordinary way—not about finding new ways to put innocent people into the correctional system.

When Cain killed Abel (*Bible*, **Source Reader** p. 68), God knew right away who had done it. Since the arrival of more humans on the earth, it often is very difficult to tell who committed a crime. For the moment, let us assume that there *is* a clear crime in question: a *corpus delicti* with knife protruding from back, an empty jewelry store with back door forced. Our law is quite clear on how parties and nonparties to that crime should be treated. The guilty person shall be identified, apprehended, charged, held, and (once the evidence is assembled), indicted, tried, convicted, sentenced, and punished. All innocent parties shall be left strictly alone; all their liberties shall be respected; they shall not be coerced into any course of action repugnant to them. If there is any doubt on how any given party shall be treated, the presumption is that this person is one of the innocents. The two provisions create an obvious tension in the treatment of the one suspected of the crime, in the struggle to balance the state's need to gather evidence and the individual's right to be left alone and at liberty. The Constitution holds this balance, leaning always to the side of the individual. The state is strong and rich, and commands the cooperation of all the citizens. The presumption of innocence demands that in all cases we favor the accused individual.

THE TELEVISION PRESENTATION: SELECTED QUESTIONS ON CRIMINAL LAW

This section considers the television presentation or videotape. The recapitulation of the dialogue that follows is not meant to be a word-for-word transcript of the tape, but a summary of the major themes, issues, and opinions that emerged in the conversation. It is for review, to pick up any parts you may have missed, and for use as a resource if you explore this topic further in a term project.

TITLE: "TO DEFEND A KILLER"

Moderator: Professor Charles Ogletree, Jr.

Participants: from left to right on your screen

RODERIC DUNCAN
Judge, Superior Court,
Alameda County

JOHN E. SMITH, PH.D.
Clark Professor of Philosophy,
Yale University

JAMES F. NEAL
Partner, Neal and Harwell

WILLARD GAYLIN, M.D.
President, The Hastings Center

JACK LITMAN
Partner, Litman, Asche, Lupkin and
Gioiella

VERNON MASON
Attorney

ELLEN YAROSHEFSKY
Attorney

FAYE WATTLETON
President, Planned Parenthood
Federation of America

ANTONIN SCALIA
Justice, Supreme Court
of the United States

ANNA QUINDLEN
Columnist, *The New York Times*

LEAH SIMMS
Ass't U. S. Attorney, S. D. Florida

SCOTT HARSHBARGER, D. A.
Middlesex County, Massachusetts

REV. DONALD SHRIVER, JR.
President, Union Theological Seminary

MARILYN HALL PATEL
U. S. District Judge, N. D. California

STEPHEN GILLERS
Professor, N. Y. U. School of Law

As you read through the dialogue, ask yourself:

1.   What do I need to know in order to know that a crime has been committed?
2.   What do I need to know in order to determine how guilty the offender is?
3.   When should society be angry at an offender, when should it forgive him, when should it pity her?
4.   If I were the victim's mother, how would I want the police to treat the offender?
5.   If I were the offender's mother, how would I want the police to treat him?

THE COURSE OF THE DIALOGUE

Crime and the Priest

In this case, the hypothetical begins with Fred Friendly's introductory remarks, from which we learn the basic facts of the situation. Wendy Wright is a stocktrader for an investment banking firm, John Barnes is an advertising executive. They have been engaged to be married; then she broke it off; then, Wendy is found stabbed. The scene opens with the moderator, as John Barnes, seeking solace and advice from his spiritual mentor, the Reverend Shriver. "I killed Wendy," he tells him. "Will you forgive me?" Somewhat taken aback, Shriver is not sure that he is capable, or entitled, to forgive John. He is sure about one thing; John must go to the authorities. He may stay in the church overnight to think it over—"ancient right of sanctuary"—but then he must go to the appropriate authorities.

"But I'm coming to you for forgiveness," John protests.

Justice or Forgiveness   Shriver at the moment is unforgiving. "You have to reckon with a crime that you have committed. And in that reckoning God and some of your neighbors will be with you. But at no point in the midst of all of that is any of us going to forget that you have committed an important crime...." But at the moment, he will not turn Barnes in to the police on his own.

Stephen Gillers, lawyer and law teacher, provides a different perspective: As to "confessing" to the authorities, "In my world, it's not the moral thing to do....In my world [as defense lawyers, we will] get you the best possible deal....I'm not out to save your soul. I'm out to save your time and your life."

Donald Shriver rejoins: "Judgment against your deed is something that has to be talked about and reckoned with as a part of the forgiveness process....[Nowhere is it said that] you can be forgiven for something that you haven't confessed, engaged in a process of repentance to, maybe done restitution for....and endured some punishment...one thing we must avoid in all this forgiveness business is cheap forgiveness...that thinks you can thereby avoid the process of changing your orientation, changing your mind, doing some restitution and enduring some punishment."

What does the prosecutor, Leah Simms, think of the case? Is it important? Yes, "the death of anyone is important." The first thing she will do is gather evidence. "If Reverend Shriver is still in the scenario it's going to be terribly important whether or not I can get his testimony...."

Shriver will resist testifying, since testifying would be a breach of confidentiality. Resist to the death? Not that far. But you'd be willing to go to jail for contempt of court to defend confidentiality? "Yes. But don't ask me for how long!"

Crime and the Prosecutor

The
Public's
Right To
Know

Leah Simms is asked to comment on how the case is to be handled. She will treat it, as far as possible, as a typical homicide. District Attorney Scott Harshbarger agrees, tracing the procedures that the D. A.'s office must follow to maintain the "very tricky balance between the public's right to know" and "the rights of the defendant here to have a fair trial in this process." Since the media are likely to classify this as a "high-society" crime, it will get a lot of attention. "It doesn't sell newspapers if a homeless person is murdered."

Vernon Mason observes that the information that comes to the media has been filtered through the prosecutor's office, and is not necessarily objective. Anna Quindlen defends the amount of media attention given to cases like this one. It's not what people expect; these are professional people, and therefore interesting. And "there's also sort of a broad category of stories that we've come to realize readers like. They come under the heading of lovers' quarrels. And this is the ultimate lovers' quarrel." It's all right to work on what sells newspapers; it's important to know what the readership considers news "and to balance that with what you consider news."

Justice Antonin Scalia points out that it is the identity, or the status, of the murderer that causes the interest here. The Greeks wrote their tragedies about kings, not about common folk, because the fall of a highly placed person is inherently interesting.

Crime and the Psychiatrist

A Higher
Moral Code

If Dr. Willard Gaylin had been approached by John Barnes that morning, how would he have felt about maintaining confidentiality? Gaylin continues the conversation. How did you kill her? I stabbed her. Where did you get the knife? We're getting off the subject that interests Barnes. The question is, are you going to turn me in? The answer from Gaylin is, eventually, yes: "John, I have to tell you. It's painful for me to turn you in. It violates a professional code which I take very seriously. But I have to tell you, I'm a lot of things. And a psychiatrist is not the first person I am. I'm a citizen of the country, I'm a human being with a moral code. And I have a kind of hierarchy of those things." He honors his profession, but recalls that under law, even law that Stephen Gillers would accept, had he cooperated with "professional" practices under the Nazis, he'd have been found guilty at the Nuremberg trials. He admits that he is, as the situation stands, in a "moral dilemma, a situation of anguish, where good and bad are done either thing that I do. And considering the nature of your crime, I am going to, if I cannot convince you....I am going to turn you in....Now you can take comfort in the fact that this is going to cause me a lot of pain and...." Barnes grumbles that it will cause *him* a lot of pain, too. "Yes, yes. And the pain you experience may be the first step in the expiation that your Reverend has told you he wants."

What would Professor Gillers advise? Gillers' response is brief and to the point: *Get yourself a defense lawyer.* "You go to Will Gaylin and he anguishes and he intellectualizes and then he becomes an informant against you. Stay away from the hereafter. Stay away from the people who are going to help your mind. Get yourself a good defense lawyer before you do anything else."

Crime and the Lawyer

Barnes goes off to get himself a lawyer. Jack Litman is a likely candidate for a defense lawyer in this case. Barnes tells him the story of the relationship, the final conversation, the killing that he can't quite remember. Did you talk to anyone else about this? Litman asks. Well, I talked to Rev. Shriver, didn't tell him much. Don't talk to anyone else, advises Litman. Don't do anything. Don't go to the police. Let's talk for awhile, see if this really is a crime, and if it is, what crime, and how we should go about defending it, before you go to the authorities.

Would Ellen Yaroshefsky represent him? Maybe. She's not sure. "What's your hesitation? Because I'm a man?" "Not because you're a man. It's because of the way I might be used in the courtroom. The very fact that I am a woman standing up in the courtroom says something to the jury about what has happened in this case....I'm not certain that I'm the right person for you. You see, the role of the defense lawyer is a very important one and it's important that you can zealously, and very zealously, represent somebody. Once you're in that courtroom, no one is going to presume you innocent anymore....You need somebody in there who's really going to be able to stand by your side and believe every second of the time that they're in there, they're doing absolutely the right thing with their time."

Vernon Mason points out that you need a defense lawyer who will have no hesitation about representing you. Justice Scalia adds that Yaroshefsky has no duty to accept any client at all. She should not be criticized for refusing a client on any grounds; after all, the inability of a potential client to pay the lawyer's customary fee is a perfectly acceptable ground for refusing to represent him. And Faye Wattleton adds that Yaroshefsky is doing Barnes a service by revealing her hesitations at the beginning, rather than waiting for them to surface later in the trial.

Would James Neal be willing to take the case? "John, you've already got my attention," Neal says. "I understand you are a man of some means." Now, for starters: "I don't want you to tell me anything....I am bound by a code of professional responsibility and there are certain things I can and cannot do. For example, if you tell me that you stabbed Wendy, I can't put you on the stand and have you lie about stabbing Wendy. Do you understand?" So maybe we want to talk about what kind of defense we want to prepare before you tell me too much more. Meanwhile don't go talking to any more preachers and psychiatrists. "There are very few deaf and dumb people in the penitentiary. Always remember that."

Loyalty to Clients

Gillers comments on the lawyers' duty in these cases. They can refuse a case, but once they have accepted, "their autonomy is out the window. Then they know only one person in the world, and that person is their client. And regardless of how repulsive the case might be to them as human beings, as lawyers they have to be loyal to an infinite degree....It is an incredible burden and I think...over a lifetime it takes a real psychic toll. You can say, 'I'm doing the right thing. This is the job I was assigned. I'm following the rules laid down. Let them call me names. I don't care.' But over a lifetime,...it takes a psychic toll because they get mixed signals between their responsibility as professionals and their responsibility as human beings. Dr. Gaylin reconciles those mixed signals by putting his human responsibility above what he perceives to be his professional responsibility. And he may be right for his profession, but he's not right for the defense lawyers."

Professor John Smith is appalled. "But the way you're talking about this autonomy and the lawyer-client relationship and the adversary system, I have the impression that all things are permissible. Are there any boundaries?..." He points out that defense lawyers can mislead the jury in many silent ways that will not get into the court transcript. "...is all permitted when one has this absolute obligation to defend the client?...we...tend to think that it's an intrinsic value that doctors should cure disease. Do we have the same sense that winning all the cases is an intrinsic value?"

Litman takes on that question. "I don't know that winning all the cases is an intrinsic value, but it certainly is an intrinsic value to have the awesome power of government constantly checked by defense lawyers so that mere accusations don't inevitably turn into guilt....Everyone is presuming that prosecutors do their job not only zealously, but properly and correctly and that is certainly not a fact. Everyone's presuming that judges are fair and impartial and wonderful to the rights of everyone. That is also not a fact. Everyone presumes that jurors come into court unhampered by what they read in the press, fair-minded and impartial. And that, too, is not a fact. You need a zealous criminal defense lawyer in order, as Brandeis said, in order to promote liberty we need eternal vigilance. And I think that it's the criminal defense lawyer that must stand up to government at every moment."

The hypothetical expands. See, John Barnes tells the lawyer, a few years ago I was involved in another case like this. I killed her, too. No one ever found out. I just wanted to tell you about it. Are you going to reveal that?

Litman will never reveal that story. Wattleton has distinct ethical problems with the notion that there could be a killing and yet no crime, which she finds "very strange…in the ethical framework of our societal values. And I would feel very much driven to persuade this gentleman to go to law enforcement officials, to confront the results and the acts that he has committed."

Lawyers as Amoral Agents

Gillers explains once more the lawyer's role: "Lawyers, especially criminal defense lawyers, are amoral agents who can justify their behavior only by being part of an adversary system that is based largely in the Constitution, and that is [therefore] moral. Now we could change it. It's not that Jack and Ellen are arrogating to themselves a certain prerogative that no one else can. They're told to behave that way. Jack squeals, we disbar him. You and I and society disbar him."

The Limits of Law and of Lawyers

The moderator tightens the screws once more. I killed someone a few years ago and they arrested the wrong person for it. It's been through several appeals, all of which he lost, and now he's about to be executed for the crime. *Now* are you going to tell the police about it?

Confidentiality and the Attorney/ Client Privilege

James Neal is undeterred. "Not only would we be disbarred, but in most states it is a felony for a lawyer to violate the attorney-client privilege. Now I will not tell about that fellow …unless I conclude that this is an ongoing fraud on the court, which would be an exception to the attorney-client privilege, sometimes called the client fraud exception."

Scalia denies that this is protected information. The only information that is protected is that which enables the lawyer to give his client the best possible defense, and this doesn't count as that.

Neal does not agree. Everything about his past is necessary for me to defend him. And "my sole duty at that point in life is to stand beside the man accused of the crime because, believe me, you can be the most popular man in the world, but once you're accused of a crime, there's only one man who will stand up with you and that is your defense counsel. He's the only person in the world who tries to help you. Society does not. Your friends leave you. And that is my only goal while I am defending that man. But I must do it within the Code of Professional Responsibility. And that's where I look. If I'm not violating the code—before I took that case, I had to agree that I would do anything ethical to defend that man."

You will let an innocent man be executed?

"Absolutely…people die every day. It may sound harsh, but we have values to serve."

You know, Litman points out, there are other ways to bring that man's innocence to the attention of the courts. And Neal agrees that he would use one of them, if he could find a way to do it without implicating his client.

The lawyers are now the object of some concern among the others. In their defense, Harshbarger reiterates Gillers' point above: this is the system that we have created in which they must function. Don't blame the lawyers. Duncan comments that those rules were not made by "society" or "us"; they were made for lawyers by lawyers.

Is the System Ethical?

Then, says Will Gaylin, it's time we questioned the system. If the system "somehow or other drives us into an unethical position we are free in a democratic society to alter—by legislation, litigation, discussion of ethics—to alter the system."

Quindlen points out that whether or not we collectively change the system, there must be a point at which the system-bound professional is willing to step outside the system, and this looks like one of them. "I can tell you quite well what I think the media reaction would be if Mr. Neal stepped outside the system and said, 'I cannot let an innocent man be executed.' Because look at the reaction here. The society would say, 'Damn right.'" Neal is not swayed. "Oh, I'd be very popular. But I'd be wrong." Simms disagrees. This rule might be worth testing. Get yourself a lawyer, Mr. Neal, and we'll litigate their right to disbar and indict you for divulging that information. He will do no such thing. "I won't litigate because I believe in it. I believe in it. I think value is served far beyond a life by the attorney-client privilege. I do believe that. I would not litigate it."

The case moves closer to trial with a new witness for the defense. This witness, male, claims he had a relationship with the victim some years ago, a relationship very similar to that of John Barnes, and suffered similarly from her behavior. There's also a photo album showing her posing nude, and evidence that she used drugs on occasion. Shall we use this? Shall we put the ex-boyfriend on the stand? Is his evidence worthwhile? Jack Litman thinks it probably is, as throwing light on probable circumstances surrounding the killing.

Blaming the Victim

Faye Wattleton disagrees about the relevance of this evidence. What it seems to show is that the victim "deserved" to die, and that is always a poor idea to introduce into the court. Quindlen is "not crazy about" this kind of defense; she does not see the relevance of that past relationship, and she thinks it is "morally wrong to blame the victim."

Judge Patel is not sure. The evidence does not seem to be relevant to the case, from what she has heard so far. "We're not concerned about the victim's intent here. We're concerned about the defendant. And her prior conduct is really not relevant, based upon what I've heard so far, to his intent." She might not admit it. This is an ethical dilemma: Should the past of a dead person, no longer around to defend herself, be splashed across the front page? The law determines relevance, and she will have to follow the law.

Justice Scalia would be more inclined to admit it. This is a serious matter. The life of the accused may be at stake. "This evidence is relevant to establishing, if not a defense—at least a matter in mitigation of the seriousness of the crime." He is sorry to sully the reputation of the deceased, but the accused is still alive and needs a defense.

Sentences and Revenge

The hypothetical proceeds. Barnes is convicted of manslaughter. He can get anything from probation to 20 years. Judges, what are you going to give him?

Judge Patel argues that it is not a simple matter to decide these things. She will need reports, memoranda, background. How remorseful is he, for instance? What does he now say about his crime? What other information is there? The moderator asks: Will you listen to the victim's parents? Will you listen to a Victims' Rights Organization? Answer: I will listen to anyone. But with no prior record, "We're probably looking at something like between 10 and 15 years." Judge Duncan agrees. "I think the fact that judges are so all over the map in this sort of decision is why Congress and state legislatures all around the country have now started to say, "We want to make you follow some guidelines...."

Will Gaylin points out that all these considerations aid a utilitarian decision. But the judges "forget that certain crimes demand certain punishments. They demand it. As Kant said, 'The last murderer should be punished.'...I'm not allowed to wreak my vengeance on my daughter's murderer. I'm protected by the fact that society will give a retributive punishment....My daughter is dead. That death demands it."

Justice in Sentencing

Litman argues that this is just one more instance of hard cases making bad law, but denies that anything would be helped by dictating maximum penalties at the legislative level. Sentencing power lies not with the legislature but with the judges. "We expect this kind of discriminating, careful judgment. Certainly there should be uniformity and certainly there should be fairness, but somewhere along that continuum there have to be a variety of different sentences."

Gaylin retorts that we have too much of that sort of thinking. We need a "greater emphasis on the retributive aspects and the recognition that taking a life may demand, with all of the exculpations and everything else, a certain price. And what the price is I'm happy to let the legislature dictate."

The final twist to the hypothetical: John Barnes' manslaughter conviction is reversed on appeal, on technical grounds. He's a free man. But not for long. Driven beyond the bounds of endurance by this latest travesty of justice, Wright's mother kills him. Now she's the defendant in your court. Justice Scalia, how do you feel about her?

Justice Scalia feels mostly sadness. The system let off someone who should have been punished, to involve someone else in a crime that never should have been committed. I would have to give her at least five years, to deter others. Will Gaylin suggests that juries have a residual supply of common sense, and probably would not convict her. But if something in the case caused them to convict her, she should get the maximum sentence. Donald

Retribution and Moderation

Shriver ends the discussion with a reminder that the system owes us two things: "One, retribution for the crime," just as Will Gaylin and John Smith claimed; and second, "the moderation of our popular propensity toward revenge and for disproportionate retribution. What this mother was doing was imposing capital punishment....You owe us retribution. What you also owe us is the moderation of our natural willingness to always take an eye for an eye or a tooth for a tooth, and maybe two eyes and two teeth while we are at it."

A REVIEW OF SELECTIONS FROM THE SOURCE READER

Before going on to synthesize the philosophical background and the television presentation, this would be a good time to review certain of the readings in the history of ethics that pertain especially to this topic.

The criminal law has always had a special fascination for philosophical ethics, possibly because several of its practitioners—Socrates, Thoreau, Gandhi, and Martin Luther King, for example—spent time behind bars themselves. The readings relevant to this topic comprise an unusually rich and varied feast.

Selections for this chapter:

Plato, *Crito*, **Source Reader** p. 14
Aristotle, *Nicomachean Ethics*, Book III, **Source Reader** p. 50
The *Bible*, *Genesis*, **Source Reader** p. 68
The *Bible*, *Exodus*, **Source Reader** p. 72
Thomas Aquinas, *Summa Theologica* II, 1, q. XCV Art. 2, **Source Reader** p. 102
Thomas Hobbes, *Leviathan*, **Source Reader** p. 104
Thomas Jefferson, *The Declaration of Independence*, **Source Reader** p. 124
Martin Luther King, Jr. "A Letter from a Birmingham Jail," **Source Reader** p. 152

You might begin the review with a re-reading of Hobbes: there is no clearer exposition of the reason why we need a criminal law and a government strong enough to enforce it. Without law, we are at each other's throats. In Plato's *Crito*, there is an acknowledgment of our dependence on law for the life we live and value. Why do you think Socrates was willing to go to his death apparently for the sake of obedience to law? Is the person *within* the law a different sort of person from the person *without* the law, out-lawed, in Hobbes' state of nature? Read the two together and form your own judgment.

The Biblical story of Cain and Abel opens the book on crime for the civilization with which we are familiar. Here is murder pure and simple, and God's hatred of the crime, and anger, followed by punishment. Even here, in the passages following the ones quoted, God modifies the punishment by affixing the "seal of Cain" to the murderer's brow; while it will not save him from terrible punishment, it will keep him from the *inhuman* state of nature, or outlawry, where anyone who finds him may slay him like some wild beast of the wood.

In the Ten Commandments we find the prohibition against murder. In the passages that follow in the book of Exodus, we find the law forbidding murder made specific. The laws seem harsh in their punishments, but then it would be impractical for a nomadic tribe to hand down prison sentences for serious offenses. Yet in their assignment of degrees of guilt, the laws seem fair. Translate some of those provisions into modern events and laws: would those circumstances influence you, as a member of the jury? The philosophical background of those distinctions is given in the passages from Aristotle's *Nicomachean Ethics*, Book III, on the nature of the voluntary. This is the background that gives rise to our notion of the domain and the limits of free will.

But is human law absolute? Not in our tradition. Augustine claimed, and Aquinas agreed, that "That which is not just appears to be no law at all." But then revolutions against unjust law are justified, as Jefferson boldly asserts, and civil disobedience that changes that law in the direction of justice is morally praiseworthy. Yet Martin Luther King, Jr., and Socrates are not in disagreement. Can you explain why?

SYNTHESIS AND DISCUSSION

Our endless fascination with crimes of violence has predisposed us to pay attention to details in accounts of crime and punishment. We know that the unnoticed shoe or the crumpled note may be the crucial clue to the identity of the murderer or the degree of her guilt. The detective stories and courtroom dramas that dominate prime-time television have taught us to look for complete accounts of these crimes and careful analyses of prosecution and defense. On this program, however, directed as it is to discussion of the ethical dimensions of the behavior of lawyers and other professionals, such a detailed presentation would be impossible. In deference to our expectations of the matter, I will begin with the *unasked* questions that must still be in the viewer's mind at the end of the presentation, and then proceed to the central ethical questions that came up in the course of the dialogue.

The unasked questions would have to start with the very basic. We know only that John Barnes and Wendy were publicly engaged to be married, and that Wendy has been found stabbed, presumably dead. But the crucial facts that we would need to know in order to assess John's culpability, and to prepare his defense, are not known. For instance, if the police have found the body and are now looking for a murderer, how close are they to John? He'd be a natural suspect, and I wonder why he's still at large. Who else saw him go to Wendy's apartment, or leave? What did he do with his bloodsoaked clothes? (people do not die neatly when you stab them.) How many people saw him stained with blood? Barnes' cheerful assessment of his situation—that he is the only evidence—is very unlikely, as any lawyer would know.

Where did he get the knife? That question, asked by Will Gaylin and never answered, is crucial, as we have known for 3000 years: "Whoever strikes a man so that he dies shall be put to death. But if he did not lie in wait for him, but God let him fall into his hand, then I will appoint for you a place to which he may flee...." If John brought the knife with him, intending to kill Wendy if she did not do what he wanted, then he is guilty of murder in the first degree. If in the middle of a fight, he ran to her kitchen and took her bread knife and came back into the room intending only to brandish it, that might be murder in the second degree. If the verbal fight had just turned violent, and in an unspeakable rage John had groped on the sideboard for something to hit Wendy with, and his hand had found the knife left there by Wendy the day before, that sounds like manslaughter. The penalties for these crimes are very different.

And so forth. The point here is not to discuss a different tape, but to point out that the answers to the asked questions depend in large measure on the answers to the unasked questions; and that those questions, having been with us since Moses, are part of our understanding of the moral dimensions of crime.

Much of the dialogue turns on the duty of the lawyer to keep his client's secrets. Confidentiality is a value for all the professions, not just the law. We will discuss this value more completely elsewhere in this volume. Here we are interested only in the lawyer's confidentiality as it relates to— or frustrates—justice.

The position of the lawyer in this regard is well described by Stephen Gillers, backed up by prosecutor Harshbarger. The lawyer *may not* reveal his client's confidences: if he does, he is guilty of violation of the rules that define moral conduct for his profession (the *Code of Professional Responsibility* and the *Model Rules of Professional Conduct*); since those rules have, in this profession alone, the force of law, he might be guilty of a crime, a felony; and he has acted unprofessionally and might be disbarred. The system could not be clearer about its expectations of the defense lawyer in a criminal case. Such, at least, is Neal's claim, although we might be hard put to find a lawyer convicted of crime for giving evidence against his client to save the life of an innocent man. The exceptions, the circumstances in which breaches of confidence are allowable, are very carefully circumscribed: the lawyer may intervene to prevent *future* crimes from being committed; the lawyer must report any *ongoing* fraud upon a tribunal (whenever the deception began, it continues now and will require fraudulent acts in future); and the lawyer must not knowingly permit his client to lie to the court. You'll notice how the conscientious lawyer, in the person of James Neal, handles *that* one: *don't tell me* the truth about anything you might want to lie about later! Further, absent these excepting circumstances, no combination of evil consequences can induce the lawyers to break silence—even the likely death of an innocent man for their client's crime does not stir them. If the man's life can be saved, the execution stayed, without involving their client, well and good; otherwise, too bad for him.

Why these queer rules and practices, all apparently aimed at the suppression of truth and the frustration of justice? The answer seems to be that there are values we treasure more than truth and justice. The protection of the dignity of the individual is one of them. We are terribly dependent upon the complex web of society around us. Accused of a crime, we find all the elements of that web on which we have depended suddenly turning against us (Neal put the case rather well). Employer (and income) are gone, friends don't have the time to help or visit, family is ashamed; every setting to which we used to contribute, we now damage by our presence. So terrible is the force of social disapproval of this sort that it has been known to kill all by itself; this is the power of "hex," curse, or "pointing the bone" in many less developed societies. That, indeed, used to be the way the human group kept order. Undesirables were simply "cut off out of the land of the living," thrust from the group. And with no one to speak to them, or recognize them, it was as if they never existed—as individuals, outside the group, they had no value at all.

That is the outcome our complex, occasionally clumsy, system forbids. No matter what the person has done, he remains a person, of infinite worth. That means that worthy status must be attributed to him, and recognition and credence granted him. This is one of the points, in our accepted social philosophy, where utilitarian considerations are simply set aside. It would be better for the interests of the society at large, no doubt, if criminals could be brought speedily to punishment, and if their lawyers would cooperate in securing justice—against their own clients, and for the innocent people who are suffering (one way or another) for their clients' crimes. But this is not the way we have decided to go. We have decided that the dignity of the individual whose dignity is endangered is more important than other social values, and so we provide for the reinforcement of that dignity at its most threatened point. For the man accused of crime, his defense lawyer is appointed to be what the whole society is to the successful individual at large: a mirror in which the individual can see his own worth as a human being.

QUESTIONS FOR YOUR REFLECTION

1. The following hypothetical, a classroom standard, follows an original by Immanuel Kant: Suppose a crew of ruffians were cast ashore on a desert island with a very small amount of food taken from their sinking ship. Quickly discovering their own tendency to greed and violence, and anticipating no ship in the area for a matter of weeks, they pass a law, effective in their own society only, that all food shall be rationed by a trustworthy second mate, and that any taking of food otherwise shall be a violation punishable by death. The law keeps things orderly for some days, but then two men are caught stealing food. They are sentenced to be hung in the morning. At dawn the first sentence is carried out, but as the ropes are being readied for the second one, miracle of miracles, a ship comes in view, responds to their signal, and starts for them. What should they do about the second thief? Why? What would Kant have answered?

2. Does one who kills another "deserve" to die? Why or why not? Are there circumstances that would change your answer? Make two lists (two columns on a piece of paper, perhaps), one of the circumstances in which a killer would deserve to die and the other of circumstances in which a killer would *not* deserve to die. Now figure out what factors set the two lists apart:

- Some qualities of the person of the killer?
- Some qualities of the victim?
- Some qualities of the intention behind the act?
- Some features of the society in which the killing takes place?
- Some calculation of the likely consequences of assigning that kind of penalty to that kind of act?

What does the exercise tell you about your tendency to rely on deontological or utilitarian reasoning? What does it tell you about your sense of the sacredness of human life?

3. What would an ideal criminal law process look like? An ideal society, of course, would not have any crime. Is there a way of shaping our

criminal law and correctional system to eliminate crime? How? If not, what system would be the most morally defensible?

4. Take a look at your answer to the previous question. What does it tell you about your assumptions about human nature? For example, do you assume that people are entirely the products of their environment and education, or do you assume that there is a certain native goodness (or perversity) that evades environmental modification? Do you assume that people are most likely to change their ways as a consequence of punishment, persuasion, reward, education, or something else? What?

5. Look over the passages from Bentham and Mill again. How does Mill's approach differ from Bentham's? How would you describe the basic perceptions that guide Mill's thinking, as opposed to Bentham's? (Find, if you can, a copy of Mill's "Essay on Bentham," and incorporate its insights into your answer.)

SUGGESTIONS FOR FURTHER READING

Special Supplementary Text:
JAMES S. KUNEN. *"How Can You Defend Those People?" The Making of a Criminal Lawyer*. New York: Random House, 1983.

BAILEY, F. LEE. *The Defense Never Rests*. New York: Stein and Day, 1971.

BENTHAM, JEREMY. *Rationale of Judicial Evidence*, in *Collected Works* volume VII, ed. J. Bowring. Edinburgh: Tait, 1827.

BROWN, M. K. *Working the Street: Police Discretion and the Dilemmas of Reform*. New York: Russell Sage Foundation, 1981.

CAHN, EDMOND. *The Sense of Injustice*. Bloomington: Indiana University Press, 1949.

CARTER, LIEF. *The Limits of Order*. Lexington, MA: D. C. Heath, 1974.

CLEAR, TODD R., AND GEORGE COLE. *American Corrections*. Monterey, CA: Brooks/Cole, 1986.

COLE, GEORGE. *Criminal Justice: Law and Politics*. Pacific Grove, CA: Wadsworth (Brooks/Cole), 5th edition 1988.

CURRIE, ELLIOTT. *Confronting Crime*. New York: Pantheon Books, 1985.

DERSHOWITZ, ALAN M. *The Best Defense*. New York: Random House, 1982.

DWORKIN, RONALD. *Taking Rights Seriously*. Cambridge, MA: Harvard University Press, 1977.

FEELEY, MALCOLM. *The Process is the Punishment*. New York: Russell Sage Foundation, 1979.

FOUCAULT, MICHEL. *Discipline and Punish*. tr. Alan Sheridan. New York: Pantheon Books, 1977.

FRANKEL, MARVIN E. *Criminal Sentences: Law Without Order*. New York: Hill & Wang, 1972.

FREEDMAN, ESTELLE B. *Their Sisters' Keepers*. Ann Arbor: University of Michigan Press, 1981.

FREEDMAN, MONROE. *Lawyers' Ethics in an Adversary System*. Indianapolis: The Bobbs-Merrill Company, 1975.

GAYLIN, WILLARD. *The Killing of Bonnie Garland*. New York: Simon and Schuster, 1972.

GOLDMAN, ALAN. *The Philosophical Foundations of Professional Ethics*. Totowa, NJ: Rowman and Littlefield, 1980.

HALL, JEROME. *General Principles of Criminal Law*. Indianapolis: Bobbs-Merrill, 2nd edition 1947.

HAZARD, GEOFFREY C. *Ethics and the Practice of Law*. New Haven, CT: Yale University Press, 1970.

KADISH, SANFORD H., et al., eds. *Encyclopedia of Crime and Justice*. 4 volumes. New York, NY: Free Press, 1983.

KALVEN, HARRY, JR., AND HANS ZEISEL. *The American Jury*. Boston: Little, Brown, 1966.

KIPNIS, KENNETH. *Legal Ethics*. Englewood Cliffs, NJ: Prentice Hall, 1986.

LEWIS, ANTHONY. *Gideon's Trumpet*. New York: Vintage, 1964.

McGINNISS, JOE. *Fatal Vision*. New York: New American Library, 1983.

MOLEY, RAYMOND. *Politics and Criminal Prosecution.* New York: Minton, Balch & Co., 1929.

ROTHMAN, DAVID J. *The Discovery of the Asylum.* Boston: Little, Brown, 1971.

SILBERMAN, CHARLES E. *Criminal Violence, Criminal Justice.* New York: Random House, 1978.

WALKER, SAMUEL. *Sense and Nonsense About Crime.* Monterey, CA: Brooks/Cole, 1985.

WAMBAUGH, JOSEPH. *The Blue Knight.* Boston: Little, Brown, 1973.

WILSON, JAMES Q., AND RICHARD J. HERRNSTEIN. *Crime and Human Nature.* New York: Simon & Schuster, 1985.

WISHMAN, SEYMOUR. *Confessions of a Criminal Lawyer.* New York: Times Books, 1981.

Code of Professional Responsibility (American Bar Association)

Model Rules of Professional Conduct (American Bar Association)

chapter 5 _____

ACCOUNTABILITY:
Public Trust, Private Interests

QUESTIONS TO KEEP IN MIND AS YOU READ THE CHAPTER

1. What is it to be accountable, or answerable, to someone else—say, your boss at work? Do you sometimes worry what the boss would say if she knew what you were doing? Do you think about what the boss would want before you act?

2. What do you expect of your public servants, the people who govern you? Do you envy or admire their power? Do you think of them as "persons in authority"? Would you like to run for office, or serve on an executive branch or Congressional staff? Why or why not?

3. According to our form of government, government officials are our servants, accountable to us. How do we hold them accountable? How do we make sure they do what we want them to do?

THE CONCEPT OF ACCOUNTABILITY

Certain values arise only with certain social systems, which need them to function. In the traditional Western aristocracy, for instance, the honor of the peerage, the class of noble birth, was the highest and most necessary value in the realm. *Noblesse oblige* is precisely the obligation incumbent upon them who are answerable to God alone, against whom no law can be enforced nor coercion be made effective. They undertake that obligation just because they have the power to do good.

Democracy nullifies the worth of such honor. It is the essence of government of and by the people that those who appear to be in positions of "authority" or "rulership" are really not so, but are the humblest of servants. There is a reason for this paradoxical state of affairs.

This unit is about respect for persons, or what, in a previous century's philosophy, used to be called "the dignity of man." Each individual has a certain worth or dignity, merely by virtue of being human, being a rational moral agent responsible for actions (Kant, **Source Reader** p. 137). Democracy as we know it is that form of government crafted to incorporate that dignity into governance, and it's never been an easy job. The logic is simple enough: if we are and ought to be autonomous agents, no one at all should have the right to tell us what to do, for all acts performed on someone else's orders are *heteronomous*—literally, another's law, as opposed to *autonomous*—my own law. The same goes for obedience to rules or laws passed by others. I must govern myself or be less than human.

But how can I govern myself with all those other people I have to live with—rather, how can each of us live in the complete freedom of individual self-governance in any universe that contains more than one person? Clearly we cannot, so we try the next best scheme: we will live together, leaving each as much individual liberty as is compatible with a like liberty for all (Rawls, **Source Reader** p. 149), and on matters that have to be decided collectively, we will do only what we all can agree on. But that last part turns out to be impossible, since we cannot all agree on *anything*. So we move to the *next* best scheme: we will live together, leaving each as much liberty as we can (so far the same); but collective matters will be concluded by *majority vote* rather than unanimity (Locke, **Source Reader** p. 119), with provisos that certain rights of minorities will be protected from all legislation in derogation of those rights (see, for instance, the first ten amendments to the United States Constitution), and further provisos that each citizen will have a voice in any piece of legislation in which he feels that his interests are affected. The resulting form of government—with its exhausting campaigns, frequent elections, endless hearings, extended negotiations, all of which end in constitutional challenges that can drag on for years—may be, as some have complained, the most inefficient form of government known to the human race, but that is not the point. The point is that this form of government preserves as far as possible the right of individual citizens to make their own decisions about how their lives shall be lived, while permitting them to live in association with other human beings.

So much decided, the practical question arises: in a nation of 250 million people, how shall we ever count the vote to find out which measure has a majority? For that matter, how shall the citizens of a town of 50,000 fit into one town meeting? And so we become, not a "democracy," where everyone votes on everything, but a "republic," where representatives—people chosen to represent us, to be present at the meeting for us, to serve as our voice and our proxy—do the actual voting. As *our* voices, they have none of their own. (Recall that magnificent story of the Speaker of the House in Royce, **Source Reader** p. 139.) We have voted for them, we have chosen them, they are our servants and we are their *constituency*, to which they are responsible, or *accountable*.

The most puzzling, persistent ethical dilemmas of our form of government arise when we try to spell out the duties of the representative vis-a-vis that constituency. As a group, constituents are varied, often anonymous, and often very troublesome. Their interests may conflict, giving them stakes in conflicting pieces of legislation. They usually represent a wide spectrum of wealth and education. They certainly differ in their preference for their current representative and his or her political party.

Along that last line, they differ significantly in the financial and other support they have given their current representative in his efforts to be elected to office, and in the support that they promise to supply in future, should he turn out to be the loyal and intelligent representative they expect him to be—i.e., if he continues to champion the projects and causes that serve their interests. But while the constituents are equal to each other in no respect save that they are that representative's constituency, this is the only equality that the representative is to take into account, by the rules of the system. As citizens, their rights and interests are equally to be respected and protected. It is their representative's responsibility to make sure that that is done.

Given the realities of political life, is the expectation of utterly even-handed treatment of all constituents the least bit realistic? If it is, it treats as of no account the moral duty of "gratitude." This is one of hundreds of places in our moral universe where a clear and familiar duty suddenly loses moral weight because of the special circumstances of the moral agents to whom it should apply.

The elected representative is the complete servant of the electorate. What is involved in this type of servitude to the public? Surely we are not talking about "obedience to commands," as in the comparatively simple situation of private service, for the constituency has no single voice. In certain circumstances, even large majority support for a measure or the clear findings of a poll need not be binding upon a conscientious representative. The people may, for example, be responding to media hysteria, misinformation or partial information, or to an appeal by a popular President or TV personality (it's getting hard to tell them apart), and may not be in a position to say what they really want. The representative needs to take such circumstances into account. If I am a salesclerk, and the customer asks for a purple scarf, I will sell her one, even when I know that purple is *just* not her color—that's not my business, after all. But if I am a faithful servant, I will try to serve the real needs of my master, and to ignore the momentary whims.

The role of the elected representative is then very seriously circumscribed. It may help to define the responsibilities if we rule out the sins:

1. As above, the representative may not be *arrogant:* He may not decide on the basis of personal liking, whim, or conscience, that such a course is good for the constituency, and proceed to follow it without regard for what his constituency might prefer or think to be right.

2. On the other hand, the representative may not be *slavish*: He may not simply accept the results of the poll or the latest flood of mail and proceed on that basis to select what measures shall be supported. Both arrogance and slavishness are called "irresponsibility," in different senses of the word: arrogance is failure of *accountability*, unwillingness to account for one's actions to those who have a right to such an account; slavishness is a failure of *leadership*, which is part of the task attached to the office.

Where, between the two poles of arrogance and slavishness, does the representative's responsibility lie? The representative may not speak for virtue as a whole, or even his constituency's virtue; that would be arrogant. He may not speak for their present desires only; that would be slavish. Between these lie the middle term interests of the constituents: their interest in jobs, income, the material goods of this world, education, recreation, a fair allotment of the goods disposed of publicly, and a fair voice in the management of the public affairs. The representative is best seen, perhaps, as the *agent* of the public, serving their real interests—not their apparent interests, and not his own.

Arrogance and slavishness are misinterpretations of the work of public office and can be seen as public sins. Beyond these are the private sins of the public servant, all too much with us in the news of the day. At least the following should be noted and avoided:

3. Conflict of interest, or self-dealing: If I, as a representative or appointed public servant, make decisions that will benefit me (and mine) rather than the public I serve, that is dishonest. Thus the congresswoman

may not vote for legislation that will serve only those that she knows will contribute to her campaign, and ignore the interests of everyone else in her constituency. Thus the regulator may not regulate misery on all the companies he regulates except the one that has promised him a job as soon as his term is over, on which he regulates nothing but happiness. The aide to the President may not spend her public career carefully feathering a consulting nest in the society of Washington lobbyists. And the retiring general may not order procurement of goods from just those companies that have promised him adjunct executive status upon retirement.

4. Appearance of conflict of interest, or self-dealing: Supposing, as an honest representative, I support the most vital industry of my area, which just happens to have contributed 87 percent of my campaign funds. Suppose, as an appointed member of a regulatory agency, I vote in favor of a petition by a corporation, within a week after the *Wall Street Journal* has announced my appointment to the corporation's board of directors. Suppose, as Postmaster General, I appoint as postmaster to an affluent post the most qualified applicant, who just happens to be my brother-in-law. In all three instances, I may have violated no precept of law or morals, but I must take seriously into account the possibility that I have disedified the people, for I have made it *appear* that my tenure in a position of power is entirely aimed at promoting my own interests and those of my relatives. It is not enough that *I* know that no wrongdoing is involved. As representative, I have a responsibility to educate the public. Justice must not only be done, it must appear to be done, or the people will be demoralized and feel themselves licensed to pursue their own interests, contrary to law and public interest.

Where does all this leave the public servant? To come back to our original question, what do we require of the holders of public office? First, we are talking about the most exacting standard of openness anywhere in the Western tradition, for the people deserve to know everything about the person who is serving them—any bad habits, any health history, any predilections at all that may reduce the service they receive. Second, we are talking about the most exacting standard of altruism in the same tradition, for the public servant must avoid even the hint, or the most superficial appearance, of using public office for personal ends. And third, we are talking about the most complex job in that tradition, for it requires that the official learn the technology involved with space travel, the medicine involved with all matters of public health (AIDS, for instance), and the cultural history of every group here and abroad that he might be involved with, the better to serve a varied group of citizens, a local, state, or national constituency.

THE TELEVISION PRESENTATION

This section considers the television presentation or videotape. The recapitulation of the dialogue that follows is not meant to be a word-for-word transcript of the tape, but a summary of the major themes, issues, and opinions that emerged in the conversation. It is for review, and for use as a resource if you include this topic in your term project.

TITLE: "ETHICS IN GOVERNMENT: PUBLIC TRUST, PRIVATE INTERESTS"

Moderator: Professor Arthur R. Miller

Participants: from left to right on your screen

LLOYD CUTLER
Counsel to President Carter (1979–80)

ARTHUR LIMAN
Partner, Paul, Weiss, Rifkind, Wharton & Garrison

STANLEY BRAND
General Counsel, U. S. House of Representatives (1976–83)

LOUIS STOKES
U. S. Representative, 21st District, Ohio

PETER JENNINGS
Anchor and Senior Editor, ABC News

JOSEPH CALIFANO, JR.
Secretary of HEW (1977–79)

JEANE KIRKPATRICK
U. S. Permanent Representative to the United Nations (1981–85)

JEFF GREENFIELD
Media and Political Analyst, ABC News

ALAN SIMPSON
U. S. Senator, State of Wyoming

ANN LEWIS
Political Consultant and Commentator

R. W. APPLE, JR.
Chief Washington Correspondent, *The New York Times*

ROBERT BECKEL
President, National Strategies

NEWT GINGRICH
U. S. Representative, 6th District, Georgia

RUDOLPH W. GIULIANI
U. S. Attorney, Southern District, N. Y.

BARNEY FRANK
U. S. Representative, 4th District, Massachusetts

LEONARD GARMENT
Partner, Dickstein, Shapiro and Morin

THE COURSE OF THE DIALOGUE

Ask yourself, as you review the dialogue:

1. Who is the real employer of Abel and Upstart? How does public account-ability affect them?
2. What is the role of image and image-making in political campaigns? To whom is the political image-maker responsible?

The Incident

The scene opens at a Washington dinner party, given by the White House chief of staff, Bob Abel. Joseph Califano, now serving as White House counsel, is a guest at that party. He is enjoying the conversation in the kitchen when the host and his wife get into an increasingly noisy argument, culminating in Abel's striking his wife. They recover quickly before the horrified guests, and continue with the party. Would Califano, in his position, want to do anything about the situation? Yes, he would talk to Abel, find out if he's been under a lot of pressure, that sort of thing. And indeed he has. Would Califano tell the President? No, not without more evidence that this is serious and ongoing.

A gossip columnist calls. Seems she heard that at Abel's party, Abel really belted his wife. You were there; is it true? Califano would probably tell her that he doesn't talk about private parties. He would not lie to her. From all his experience in Washington, he learned that you never lie to reporters. Those who do get into terrible trouble. All right, now it's Mrs. Abel's sister on the phone, and she tells you this violence goes on all the time. *Now* what do you do? Talk to Abel about getting help; talk to him about maybe leaving government while he gets help. Not talk to the President yet.

Accountability to the President Jeane Kirkpatrick, the designated President, disagrees. Just *be-cause* I'm overloaded with problems I don't need this sort of thing sneaking up on me. I would want to know immediately, for I think this is fairly serious. It wouldn't surprise me to find out that I am taking this *much* more serious-ly than my counsel is.

Covering the News

The hypothetical expands. Someone calls Peter Jennings and tells him that the President's chief of staff beats his wife, and has been doing so for at least three years. What do you do? Immediate answer: Call Sam Donaldson. Ah, more experienced in these matters? No, but as our Washington correspondent, a lot closer to all parties in the situation. I will suggest that we keep this story very quiet for the present. Why? Because, as you can appreciate, it's very hard to check out, because the most important part of the story concerns how the White House will handle it, and so I don't want it sneaking onto the air, our air or anyone else's, until it's been thoroughly checked.

Johnny (R. W.) Apple is interested in other aspects of the story. Is this White House "the kind of place that drives people to this sort of behavior? Does that tell us anything about the way decisions are made? Is it such a hothouse, such a fervid looney bin, that people behave like this? As some recent White Houses have been." First thing I'd do is call the White House counsel, Califano. And what would Califano do? Put Apple off until late afternoon, by which time I'll have been able to talk to *everyone* about how this situation is to be handled. If the President is a man, we'll have the President's wife prepared to issue a compassionate statement. That sort of thing.

Drugs, Tests, Suspicion, and Trust

Phase three of the hypothetical: the phone call to Peter Jennings, from a White House source, mentions not wifebeating but cocaine. Jennings is very hesitant about this story; it will need a lot of confirmation. This might just be someone out to get Abel's job, and I don't want to play his game. Suppose you get confirmation? I still don't know if it's true. Let's say that two White House aides say that it *is* true. Now what do you do? I call the White House, tell them the story, tell them I'm going with it on the news, would they like to comment? No comment. All right, I go with it.

Madame President, what do you do? Call the White House counsel! Califano would take this very seriously, get a special prosecutor....Wait a minute, says Abel. None of this is true. I don't take drugs. Never touched cocaine. Don't even smoke cigarettes. But then where did the story come from, Abel? Someone's obviously out to get me. Now, Madame President, whom do you trust?

Madame President is very hesitant. Are you sure it's just someone out to get you? Madame, is that a note of doubt I detect in your voice? Not doubt, really. Just caution. Look, Abel says, I'm telling the truth. Tell you what, I'll take a drug test. Are you going to ask me to do that? Absolutely not, says Kirkpatrick. If we're living in a White House where the chief of staff has to take a drug test to prove his innocence to the President—this is impossible. The press secretary would be happy to see Abel take a drug test on his own.

What would Lloyd Cutler advise? The Attorney General should be called in, and Abel should get himself a lawyer. Arthur Liman is promptly appointed Attorney General. He would welcome a drug test. We cannot afford to have Abel destroy the credibility of this Presidency. But Abel still says it is not true. Who believes him? Peter Jennings, do you believe him?

Wait a minute. "I've already gone on the air and broadcast this because you told me it was true." No: someone in the White House told you it was true and you chose to believe him or her and maybe one or two others. Now, of course, Jennings will give Abel equal time to refute the charge.

The Value of Trust

Kirkpatrick is still unwilling to impose a drug test. "It isn't the respect for civil liberties that would cause me not to request a chief of staff to take a drug test. It's a sense of what kind of relationship there has to be between a President and his or her intimate advisors....there's got to be trust." But wouldn't it help to restore credibility if everyone had a drug test? No, that makes it worse. "It's very important to restore the fabric of trust in our society. It's been torn really almost to pieces. And you can't do that by...requiring drug tests from all your principal advisors. It just won't work. Really won't work. Least of all in a democracy would it work."

Cutler still wants Abel to have a lawyer of his own, and recommends Leonard Garment. Garment immediately accepts the job, and tells Abel that really, his first task is to extract the truth from *you*, Abel, since we can't have you damaging this Presidency. I'm going to hit you with some verbal two-by-fours, maybe some real ones, to get the true story; I'm going to get the FBI into it....Cutler changes his recommendation, fires Garment and appoints Liman to be Abel's lawyer. Abel needs someone thinking about *him*. Liman accepts. He'll go to the White House and say that it's an absolute outrage, how this man was defamed. If whoever did this can hurt Abel with false accusations today, he can do it to you tomorrow, Madame President. You're going to have to deal with this problem in the White House: infighting, lying, false accusations, and creation of distrust.

The Fall and Rise of Arthur Upstart

The hypothetical advances. Tests are done, they come back with sure proof that Abel is drug-free. Now what do you do, Madame President? Well, we have to stop this. We seem to have people on my staff who are willing to lie to the press, to sacrifice the Presidency, to do in another staff member, one of their own. I'd ask my counsel to look into who it might be. Mr. Califano? If I'm where you say I am, I already know within two or three who it might be. Good enough: as a matter of fact, all the evidence points to one man—Arthur Upstart, the Wunderkind of the White House. He's terribly bright, a graduate of the best schools, excellent on foreign policy, the best man you have on environment, known to be ambitious, and he's probably the one in the best position to pull this stunt.

You confront him, Madame President, and what do you say? Answer: I probably don't confront him. I probably just move him over to Justice, where he'll be out of the way and can continue on his career without bothering us. Repeated attempts by the moderator to argue Upstart's credibility, and his sense of injury at being shifted, and his right to "due process" before being reassigned, meet with variations on one theme: that an aide in Upstart's position serves where he serves at the pleasure of the President and can be moved at the service of the same pleasure. The fact that his continued presence might, through no fault of his own, prove an embarrassment is quite sufficient to move him to Justice—or Guam, for that matter.

So Upstart moves. But his parting shot—look, Madame President, this mistake leaves that sniper still on your staff, and you're going to have to deal with that sometime—continues to bother. Could we persuade the journalists who got a whiff of the cocaine story early on to tell us who their source *was*? Upstart is still eager to have them say who it was *not*, namely, him. Some of the journalists will not do this. Their basic obligation in this case is to their sources, who are dead meat if it gets out that they leaked any story from the White House, and protection of those sources means not even saying who it was *not*; there are only two or three possibilities, after all, and denying one may well finger the real source. But Jeff Greenfield is unhappy about this solution: after all, according to the hypothesis, the source fed the journalists a *lie*, for the purpose of advancing his career by bringing about the political death of another. To the extent that you protect that source, you protect a useless resource, since we need truth, not lies, and, given his motivation, you cooperate in a base design. What interest is at stake here?

A Conflict of Interest

The hypothetical continues: Upstart wants to leave government and open up shop as a consultant. He figures he can use all his good government connections to help clients and make a good living. Anything wrong with that, Mr. Brand? Yes, quite a bit. There are fairly extensive laws governing how, and how soon, Upstart can come back and work for his clients. For one year, he may not return to the people he worked with or talk about anything he worked on. Mr. Giuliani, if an associate leaves your office, and sets up in practice for himself, can he practice law against you—defend the people you are prosecuting? Answer: Sure, as long as the case was not in the United States' Attorney's Office when he was working here.

Mr. Gingrich, how about a congressman? It's not as strict. There is an ethical restriction against a former congressman using his privilege of visiting the floor of Congress to lobby his former colleagues *on the floor*. But even that is not a legal restriction. And he certainly can lobby anyplace else. And there's no restriction at all on the aides. Stokes agrees that there seems to be a double standard for executive and legislative branch employees, but insists that it is justified by the unique power wielded by the executive branch, which makes misuse of executive power that much more dangerous. Simpson growls that the abuses in the legislative branch are quite bad enough, citing especially the practice of hiring for a lobbyist the most recently retired senator from your state or congressman from your district, and having him catch you in the office, or better, in the swimming pool, to deliver his pitch.

Gingrich agrees that the law can be abused in either branch, and proposes that it be made uniform. "In this cold and ruthless city, I think the center of hypocrisy's Capitol Hill. Either the law is a stupid law and we ought to change it, or the law's a good law, and ought to apply to congressional staffs and to congressmen. Because we have congressional staff directors...who are extraordinarily powerful, extraordinarily influential, far more valuable than the head of the IRS, in terms of getting what you want, and it's just hypocritical to say that we ought to block the executive branch while the pigs on the Hill gorge at the trough. It's just wrong."

Campaigning for Office

By the next phase of the hypothetical, Upstart has made it to the Supreme Court of his state. Now a Senate vacancy opens up, and he decides to run for office. Ann Lewis will help him with his campaign. First we'll go over your background, she tells Upstart; I want to know everything you've ever done. How much money will we need? For a medium-sized state, four to six million dollars. If you pass the initial screening, we'll go to Washington and make the rounds—of the PACs. [A "PAC," or Political Action Committee, collects money from a single constituency, like a corporation or trade group, to contribute to the political campaigns of candidates who favor their constituencies' interests.] They're the ones with the thousands to commit at one time. Fundraising in Washington is wholesale, not retail, and we're going to have you strut your stuff before the big guys.

Accountability to Contributors You're putting me on display! Upstart objects, disgusted. Right, says Lewis. After all, you're asking people to put out a lot of money for you, and they have a right to see you, to hear you, to figure out if you're a viable candidate, and to know where you stand on the issues. Aren't they buying my vote for their purposes? Oh no, says Lewis, no one can do that....

This happens to be one of the sensitive issues of electoral politics. Barney Frank jumps in. Does he use PACs? I *hope* I use them more than they use me, Frank replies. Sure I do. But isn't that *grubby*? Yes, and if there were a better way—publicly funded campaigns, for instance—I'd gladly use it. But I'm not going to put myself at a disadvantage because of scruples that no one else seems to share. You have to cultivate a certain quality: being an ingrate. Nowhere else are you expected to take thousands of dollars that you don't have to pay back and then pretend that you forget who gave it to you. But that's what you do in this game.

Let's advance the campaign. We are now taking polls. The polls, Upstart notices, show that he has a nasty problem with his rural constituency. His problem is that his image is purely urban—pinstripes, watch chain, the works—and worse, that he's against farm subsidies. While all election advisors tell him not to try to look like something he isn't—please, no bib overalls, no climbing on a horse (you'll fall off), no pulling up peanuts— nevertheless we can blunt some of those effects. Take off the watch chain now. To Upstart's grumblings, Lewis replies that this image work is not a matter of "trying to be what you aren't," it's rather a matter of showing respect for what your constituents *are*. And Robert Beckel urges that in talking about farm subsidies, you announce your intention to "review" them, and appoint a board including farmers to do just that.

Simpson objects: all you're trying to do is fuzz every issue you've got. No, you're just trying to find an acceptable way to reconcile your background with your constituents' expectations.

The Deals of Politics

Upstart wins and goes to the Senate. The big issue before the Senate right now is low income housing. Barney Frank, from an urban state, is working hard for it. Upstart's rural state doesn't need it much. It needs jobs. What Upstart needs is a big military base in his state. If he votes for Frank's housing, will Frank vote for his base? Depends on the type of base, Frank says. If it's a big nuclear weapons system, no. If it's just a training camp, and the public interest is indifferent to its location, sure, I'll vote to put it in your state in return for your vote on housing. I'm easy to handle. As long as the public interest is served, I'll deal.

Congressman Stokes, is this right? Sure it's right. This is the way the system works. Nothing wrong with trading. (Stokes likes it better if he knows that his vote for the other guy's project won't influence the outcome, but admits that trades are unlikely in those circumstances.) Simpson objects: vote-trading isn't a given, a completely acceptable process. He doesn't like it. When you trade votes, you end up with two bad bills instead of one (or none). Trading turkeys for the good of the republic? That doesn't make sense.

Accountability to Constituents

"Do you always vote pure conscience?" That depends, says Simpson. "Yeah, I vote conscience, and then sometimes I vote it with unalloyed brilliance, and other times I vote it with *aaagh*. Like that." That's the nature of the legislative process.

That's the American system, Giuliani cuts in. It helps to put this in perspective. There were allegations of sexual misconduct in George Washington's presidency. The first cabinet almost fell apart in the fighting between Alexander Hamilton and Thomas Jefferson. Actually all the people in this situation are acting in accordance with conscience in a democratic government. You raise the tough questions, and you try to answer them in a decent way. Sometimes you agree and sometimes you disagree.

A REVIEW OF SELECTIONS FROM THE SOURCE READER

Before going on to put the philosophical background together with the television presentation, this would be a good time to review certain of the readings in the history of ethics that pertain especially to this topic.

The readings for this chapter are on politics: the Greek ideal of politics, or statecraft, and the Enlightenment ideal that gave rise to our own government.

Selections for this chapter:

> John Locke, *Treatise of Government*, II, **Source Reader** p. 110
> Aristotle, *Politics* Book I: Chapters 1 and 2, **Source Reader** p. 61

The readings are put in reverse chronological order for a reason: it is easier to understand Aristotle's organic view of the state if the full structure of an example is before us. (You would find it easier to construct a chicken from a goose than from the egg of a chicken, even a very good egg. Mature specimens resemble each other more than either resembles its embryonic form.) Without getting too much into the current details of the workings of the government, Locke gives us just such a mature organism to contemplate. And the outlines of Aristotle's explanation are clear in the operations of a modern republic, even when, by virtue of its size and its policies, it fails to meet Aristotle's limits.

Ask yourself, as you review these passages, what Aristotle would have thought of the kind of democracy Locke had in mind, and the kind of democracy that the United States turned out to be.

SYNTHESIS AND DISCUSSION

The purpose of this section is to tie together the theoretical background of the opening essay, the selections from the **Reader** just reviewed, and the practical considerations raised by the experienced lawyers, statesmen, and stateswomen of the seminar. Do you sense an awkward fit between the two? Why?

There is a gap between theory and practice in the government of a very large and powerful nation that tries to maintain the character of a democracy. We said at the start that this unit is really about the dignity of the human person, the inherent right to self-governance, and the accountability of the representative. But the other side of this unit is about the enormous difficulty of keeping in focus the respect due the citizens, and the outlines of the government formed to embody it, when you are actively engaged in governing, at the very power center of the nation.

Our scene opens at an in-group party, travels through the gossip circles to the journalists, involves White House counsel, chief of staff, junior aides, in a wicked round of accusations, career ambitions, sniping, backstabbing, furious efforts to discover the truth, private lawyers.... Except for the President, *not one* of the cast of characters for the first and longest part of the hypothetical was elected by the people to do the people's business. How can we reconcile the two visions of American governance that we are given here—Locke's understanding that governance is nothing but the expression of the (minimal) agreement of autonomous agents to manage some of their affairs in common, and the practical reality that governance is a rich and delightful world of its own, self-contained, turning on the court intrigues of ambitious favorites, barely governable by the public figures at its center?

There is a way to reconcile the two notions of governance, but its path is more tortuous than the simple Lockean logic set forth at the beginning. This is a large and complex country, with a very large array of responsibilities devolving on the President's office. The President of the United States is, for better or worse, the single most important person in the world as far as international politics goes (as legislative leader and Chief of State of the largest power in the world), Commander in Chief of the most dangerous military force in the world, leader of his party and responsible for aiding the political fortunes of every member of it, National Teacher, National Preacher and Priest, National Symbol, and National Teddy Bear. In all the demands placed on the person of the President, a large and multiply talented staff is essential. The President needs all those people, to keep contact with the political constituencies and help the party, to keep the social occasions in order and running properly, to keep the President abreast of developments in rocket technology, Albania, the polar ice cap, and the Catholic Church, and above all to keep the Presidential schedule sane and productive. But the very confluence of all those people instantly creates a problem of its own.

There is a Law of Numbers, developed by the nuclear physicists (in the notion of a "critical mass" of radioactive material), employed by evolutionary biologists (to explain how collections of cells began to differentiate into complex organisms—in sponges, for example), and adapted by students of bureaucracies. The Law claims that when you get enough of any stuff together, quantitative increase becomes qualitative change. In accordance with that law, many people gathered together supposedly to pursue the purposes of one elected official become a world in themselves. They develop their own internal agendas, create hierarchies that appear on no organizational chart, and eventually, in their pursuit of objectives entirely internal to their own pattern of interaction, forget completely about the nation that brought them into existence. The intrigues are infinitely fascinating for those involved in them, but the public is served by none of this. To keep these staffs functioning as resident experts while keeping the internal "politics" under control is an endlessly frustrating task.

What we see on our television screen, then, is one of the vortices of twentieth-century democracy, one of the places where our eighteenth-century notion of justifiable government tangles in the technological realities of the twentieth century. The theory of our democratic form of government is the product of philosophy: a logical derivation of an institution from a primary moral principle. The technological complexity is the product of history: the inexorable rise of science and its applications in the last century. Our task is not to resolve "in favor of" one side or the other. We cannot do away with history, or science, or the proper management of our progress through expertise, or, therefore, all the people we need to help us with that management; nor can we do away with morality, nor logic, nor democratic theory, nor, therefore, the imperative to make these "staffs" responsive to the public voice and the public good. Our task is to discover resolutions that will make it possible for a government that exists primarily to honor the dignity of the human to function in a technologically complex world.

Meanwhile, other issues of democratic roles and democratic accountability are raised in the latter portion of the presentation. The political "image-makers" are functioning like advertising agencies in the private sector, aiming to get you to buy (quite literally: you'll be paying her salary for several years) their product. It has been argued that they are doing no more than helping the candidate put her best foot forward, so the voters will get a true picture of her abilities. On the contrary, it has been argued that these agencies distort the political process; certainly that is what they are *trying* to do. (After all, if the candidate were going to win anyway, they would be useless.) Whether they succeed in changing minds or no, the fact that some candidates use them makes it essential for all candidates to do so, and that at least distorts the campaign—in favor of the candidate with money.

Vote trading collects some votes and loses some, among the panel. Is vote trading simply a common-sense way of getting legislation passed that is vital to your constituents' interests, when your constituents are in the minority nationally? Or is it, as Simpson suggests, just "trading turkeys"? As representative, were you elected to vote only for what your constituents would have voted for? (If you were Barney Frank's constituents, you would vote *for* the housing but probably *against* the new military base in Upstart's state.) Or were you elected to further your constituents' interests, using such means as are necessary to get Upstart's vote for the housing? Democratic theory is simply not clear on the subject. Vote trading is universal, but we have no final verdict on its desirability.

QUESTIONS FOR YOUR REFLECTION

1. As we learned in Civics class, the President is elected by the people primarily to execute the laws of the land. As we know further, the President is expected to embody the people's ideals, protect the national interest, and establish whatever agencies are necessary to implement the complex agenda of the office. For these purposes, the President hires a staff of qualified people. Suppose you are a staff member, hired to keep the President posted on all matters concerning the natural environment.

To whom or to what are you accountable:

- The person of the President (your friend);
- The interests of the White House and its staff;
- The elected representatives of the people;
- The people;
- The natural environment?

2. Are there better ways of handling the complexities of government than by appointing these proliferating staffs? Invent one, and defend it on the following grounds (any and all that apply):

- Effectiveness (ability to get the job done);
- Efficiency (economical use of resources for a given result);
- Happiness of the people involved;
- Service to the republic as a whole;
- Conformity to moral principle, especially those principles that apply particularly to government service.

3. The imperative of accountability—that the representative of the people must serve, and appear to serve, only his constituents—has some odd moral consequences. These include, as Rep. Barney Frank mentioned in the television presentation, the demand that the representative cultivate the vice of ingratitude, so that he can accept large sums of money and forget where it came from. What other odd moral behavior seems to follow from the imperative of accountability?

Can you think of other professions where the duties incumbent upon the professional demand conduct that would violate ordinary moral principles in nonprofessional situations?

4. Do we demand higher moral standards of public servants than of other citizens? Why? Because they are public servants, and the public deserves the best? Or just because they are in the public eye and misbehavior is harder to conceal?

5. Can you show how Jefferson's theory of revolution (found in shortest form in the Declaration of Independence) follows from John Locke's theory of government? Could it follow from Hobbes' theory of government? Under what circumstances?

6. What does it mean for a representative to "vote her conscience"? On democratic theory as we have presented it, is it permissible to "vote your conscience" as a representative? Show how.

7. Would public financing of elections ease the moral dilemmas of the elected representative? How? Or Why not?

SUGGESTIONS FOR FURTHER READING

Special Supplementary Text:
PETER FRENCH. *Ethics in Government*. Englewood Cliffs, NJ: Prentice Hall, 1981.

ARENDT, HANNAH. *On Revolution*. New York: Compass Books, 1965.

BARRY, BRIAN. *Political Argument*. London: Routledge and Kegan Paul, 1965.

BEAUCHAMP, TOM L., WILLIAM T. BLACKSTONE, AND JOEL FEINBERG. *Philosophy and the Human Condition*. Englewood Cliffs, NJ: Prentice Hall, 1980.

BEAUCHAMP, TOM L. AND TERRY P. PINKARD, EDS. *Ethics and Public Policy*. Englewood Cliffs, NJ: Prentice Hall, 1983.

BOWIE, NORMAN E., ED. *Ethical Issues in Government*. Philadelphia: Temple University Press, 1981.

BURKE, EDMUND. "Address to the Electors of Bristol" (November 3, 1774) in *Works of Edmund Burke*, vol. 2. Boston: Little, Brown, 1865.

COHEN, CARL. *Democracy*. Athens, GA: University of Georgia Press, 1971.

The Constitution of the United States of America
Declaration of Rights of Man and of Citizens (1789)

FEINBERG, JOEL. *Rights, Justice and the Bounds of Liberty*. Princeton, NJ: Princeton University Press, 1980.

HART, H. L. A. *The Concept of Law*. Oxford: Clarendon Press, 1961.

HART, H. L. A. *Law, Liberty and Morality*. Stanford, CA: Stanford University Press, 1963.

HOLDEN, BARRY. *The Nature of Democracy*. New York: Barnes and Noble, 1974.

MILL, JAMES. *An Essay on Government* (1820) Cambridge: Cambridge University Press, 1937.

MILL, JOHN STUART. *Considerations on Representative Government*. Oxford: Oxford University Press, 1946.

PATEMAN, CAROLE. *Participation and Democratic Theory*. Cambridge: Cambridge University Press, 1970.

PITKIN, HANNA F. *The Concept of Representation*. Berkeley, CA: University of California Press, 1967.

ROUSSEAU, JEAN-JACQUES. *Political Writings of Jean Jacques Rousseau*, ed. C. E. Vaughan. Cambridge: Cambridge University Press, 1915.

United Nations Universal Declaration of Human Rights (1948)

WERHANE, PATRICIA H., A. R. GINI, AND DAVID T. OZAR, EDS. *Philosophical Issues in Human Rights*. New York: Random House, 1986.

WOLFF, ROBERT PAUL. *In Defense of Anarchism*. New York: Harper and Row, 1970.

chapter 6 _____

AUTONOMY:
Does Doctor Know Best?

QUESTIONS TO KEEP IN MIND AS YOU READ THE CHAPTER

1. How much do you value your freedom—your right to make choices for yourself, at least where your own life and interests are at stake? When someone takes away your autonomy, and overrules your choice "for your own good"—and turns out to be *right* about your own good—are you thankful or angry?

2. When you go to a doctor, what do you expect the doctor to do for you? In deciding what course of treatment will be used (if what's wrong with you is complicated enough to require treatment), how much of the decision do you expect the doctor to make and how much do you expect to make?

3. Do you expect the doctor to *make sure*, somehow, that your mother and younger brother get the right treatment even though they're too ignorant to see what's best for them? Do you expect that the doctor will do the same for you if you're too scared, or hurried, to understand a situation properly? Or do you expect to take the responsibility for your care?

THE CONCEPT OF AUTONOMY

For the purposes of philosophical ethics, "autonomy" is understood as a union of two components. The first is rationality or understanding (variously

103

defined, but always including the ability to evaluate situations accurately and choose appropriate means to cope with them); the second is freedom or "noncontrol" (meaning the right and ability to do what you choose to do, or at least to act without coercion or restraint). The notion of "informed consent" bridges the components perfectly, since information is essential to rationality (we have to understand the situation before we can decide what we ought to do about it), and consent presupposes freedom. An action is "autonomous" if it is intended (otherwise it wouldn't be an action at all), understood in its nature and consequences, and freely chosen. Consent to medical treatment is autonomous if it is deliberately or intentionally given, if the treatment and its alternatives, projected risks and benefits, are understood, and the patient is not coerced into giving it. "Informed consent" is what the doctor has to have from you before any course of treatment can begin.

Autonomy is a central value in any Western ethical system. Different philosophical traditions, as might be expected, have provided a variety of methods for deducing its centrality. In Book I of the *Nicomachean Ethics*, Aristotle derives "activity of the rational element" as the proper function of the human being—thinking, deliberating, and deciding make us human. The derivation presupposes a fixed human nature, in which a clear hierarchy of functions can be observed (Aristotle, **Source Reader** p. 46). Because of the centrality of the rational decision, Aristotle takes very seriously the problem of ascertaining the "voluntariness" or freedom of acts and consents (Aristotle, **Source Reader** p. 50).

Immanuel Kant starts with logic and the meanings of the words rather than with a notion of human nature, but comes to the same conclusion. In brief, he proves that if we place *value* on anything at all, if we take value choices seriously, then we must place the highest value on autonomy—the ability to make moral choices in the first place (Kant, **Source Reader** p. 136). In contrast to Kant, John Stuart Mill attempts to derive the value of liberty from the consequences of policies of freedom alone. If we leave people free to make their own choices, they will be happier in the long run; liberty is thus established on utilitarian grounds (Mill, **Source Reader** p. 182).

From all of the above it follows that respect for autonomy, respect for rationality, freedom, and the activity of rational choice made possible by them, is one of the most important moral principles that we acknowledge, and that protection of autonomy is one of the first duties of law and policy. Very little of practical value follows from that consensus, however, because two essential elements of agreement are missing. First, there is no agreement on the order of priority of the components, which are logically completely independent of each other, and have no natural (conceptually determined) order of priority. Second, both rationality and freedom are subject to degrees. Rationality may vary from complete ignorance or derangement to an ideally complete understanding of all that is entailed in a choice. Freedom may vary from complete coercion (the gun at your head, or better yet, the head of your child) through infinite degrees of pressure and manipulation to some ideal of "reflective equilibrium" inhabited only by reasons in which choice is entirely free. We have no consensus on what makes withholding of information "material," pressure "irresistible," nor the minimum point below which either may sink before we decide that action or consent is not autonomous.

Two different notions of autonomy can result from placing one or the other component first in importance. We may call these the Libertarian and the Rationalist notions.

1. The Libertarian interpretation is associated with Jeremy Bentham, J. S. Mill, and Anglo-American ethical, legal, and economic theory in general. In this view, freedom comes first. What the individual *in fact* chooses is an accurate expression of his autonomy, no matter how unwise the choice may appear to others. He has a right to all available information, and to advice as long as he'll take it, to make his choice as rational as he wants it to be—but his want is final. For example, the competent young adult patient who rejects life-saving surgery (e.g., an appendectomy in acute appendicitis), knowing the consequences, is making an autonomous decision which should be respected. Doubts as to the patient's real understanding of what he is choosing—doubts about the "authenticity" of the decision—tend, in this tradition, to be resolved in favor of respecting the patient's wishes, even when we are not sure that we are respecting the patient's autonomy.

2. The Rationalist interpretation is associated with Jean-Jacques Rousseau, Immanuel Kant, Karl Marx, and Continental ethical, legal, and economic theory in general. In this view, reason comes first. The real rational interests of an individual correctly express his autonomy, and to the extent that the individual happens to choose against these interests, to that extent he is deceived. The young adult who refuses an appendectomy, or amputation of a gangrenous limb, would on this view be held to be deceived; his "freedom" being therefore illusory, need not be taken into account. The source of the deception may lie in the surroundings—the situation may be obscure, or someone may be lying—but it could equally lie within the individual's personal and family history. On the other hand, it may lie primarily in the institutions of society, which are very likely (at least according to Karl Marx) set up to perpetuate deceptions useful to the ruling class. On this view, it would be the height of cynicism to regard the misguided "choice" that emerges

from this web of deception as expressive of the real person, and to pretend to take it seriously as "his" choice.

The result of this type of analysis is to justify "paternalism," literally "acting as a parent." The parent, or the authority acting as parent, justifiably makes decisions for the child or dependent ward in the ward's best interests, regardless of the ward's desires. In a medical context, paternalism means overriding or ignoring the patient's choice or other rights (e.g., privacy) in favor of the patient's interests. Doubts about the authenticity of the decision tend to be resolved in favor of paternalism.

Our duty to respect autonomy, then, can have two different objects, depending on whether we tend to give pride of place to the patient's expressed desire or to the patient's real interests. Put into the practical setting of medicine and hospitals, how shall we make decisions appropriately respectful of human dignity and moral agency? Right now we have no sure criteria for determining the presence or absence of autonomy in any human being on either the libertarian or rationalist interpretation. We have no sure knowledge that autonomy is even a possible condition for humans. After all, if we count any self-deception, or lack of complete or completely understood information, as negating rationality, no one can ever be "rational." And if we count emotional stresses, or felt constraints, or strong desires as coercive, no one can ever be totally "free." So we could argue that "autonomy" expresses an angelic ideal that may help to guide human theory but can never be a reality in human life. But back in the real world, there are times when we have to know whether or not a person is "competent," or autonomous enough to make decisions for himself and protect his own interests; if not, we have to protect those interests for him. And there are times when we have to know if a person has enough of the deck together to stand trial, sign a will, or participate in medical decisions to start, continue, or end treatment. If we set our standards of information and liberty too high, we will succeed only in making our highest value completely useless for evaluating human conduct.

In medical settings, questions about autonomy arise under three different headings, all of which include both problems in determining degree of autonomy (*how* free and informed is the patient?), and problems of deciding whether freedom or rationality is more important.

1. Patient competence: Is the *patient* autonomous? We know that when we are sick we have trouble "thinking straight." When a patient is not only sick, but in pain, under sedation for pain, possibly suffering from some brain damage as well, and suffering from identifiable clinical depression,

both reactive (from unhappiness at being sick and hospitalized) and chronic (due to chemical changes in the brain brought about by sickness and medication), should the patient's refusal of further treatment be honored? Should it even be taken seriously?

2. Fitness of means to ends: Is the *choice* reasonable? When a patient seems competent, relaxed, and lucid, yet repeatedly insists that a clearly gangrenous limb is not to be amputated because it will get better, or that her diseased appendix must not be removed because that would keep her from getting well, what assumptions must we make about the nature of the treatment decision? Should it be honored anyway?

3. Authenticity: Is it the patient's *own* choice? Does the decision express the patient's real wishes? When a friend deep in his cups makes a tactless remark about me, or my car, or my living room sofa, I'll dismiss it by saying that "It wasn't him talking; it was the drink." When a patient has cooperated eagerly with all prenatal care, but after many hours of fruitless labor refuses a necessary Caesarean section, we are tempted to wonder, is that the patient *herself* talking, or is that the fear? When a comatose patient's surrogate decision maker, who has agreed for months that no resuscitation is to be undertaken in case the patient's heart stops, suddenly cries out for the nurses to *do* something when the heart actually stops, we are tempted to wonder, is that the person talking or is that the panic? On the one hand, we want to allow patients (on their own or through surrogates) to change their minds. On the other hand, we want to make sure that those are *their minds* that are changing.

This problem penetrates deeply into medical practice. If a Jehovah's Witness refuses a blood transfusion repeatedly, and all next of kin and friends concur in the decision, should we honor that refusal? The weight of law and tradition says that we must. Now, close to death, the same Witness suddenly cries, "Save me! Save my life!" Has the patient just changed his mind (in which case we should give the transfusion), or is this just a cry of fear, expressing no authentic desire of the patient's in these circumstances? In which case what *should* we do? If a pregnant woman agrees ahead of time that no painkillers should be used during her labor, but starts crying out for drugs during the very last contractions of a normal delivery, that request is routinely ignored. If a patient dying of cancer has agreed ahead of time that no mechanical or artificial aids to breathing or nutrition should be introduced during the ebbing of his life, and then, *in extremis*, cries out for help in breathing, should we ventilate him? or routinely ignore such requests?

The primary debate in all of the above is whether we should accept a person's choices as valid and unchallengeable when the major objection to those choices is that they damage no one except the person herself. That is the situation assumed in most of the debates over "informed consent" in medicine, especially when the decision is to withhold life-sustaining treatment. If the decision materially affects the interests of others, it is generally accepted that those others must have a hearing before the decision is carried out. But what counts as "affected"? Patients' spouses will always be affected by patients' decisions; they should certainly have the right to say something. But should they have a veto? If there are minor children in the family, a mother's choice to forgo treatment that is likely to save her life and restore her to health will almost certainly be overruled. And in the television hypothetical, there is an unborn child in the patient's womb. Isn't that a minor child? Or is it part of the mother's body, not "an other" at all? May the child be considered independently of the mother? May his interests override hers?

Suppose the decision affects only some policy or practice? Contemplating the practice of removing feeding tubes from a dying person, a nurse of my acquaintance remarked, "You know, there are lots of places in this world where a person can starve to death. My hospital should not be one of them." Traditionally, medicine has not "given up" on a patient until everything has been tried to improve her condition. Suppose a patient refuses further treatment before that point has been reached. Is the traditional medical practice standard an appropriate limit on autonomy? Or should autonomy be taken most seriously *precisely* at that point where some set of professional standards, developed by professionals for the greater happiness of professionals, imposes unwanted invasions on the person?

THE TELEVISION PRESENTATION: SELECTED QUESTIONS ON THE PROFESSION OF MEDICINE

This section considers the television presentation or videotape. The recapitulation of the dialogue that follows is not meant to be a word-for-word transcript of the tape, but a summary of the major themes, issues, and opinions that emerged in the conversation. It is for your review, and for use as a resource if you include this topic in your term project.

TITLE: "DOES DOCTOR KNOW BEST?"

Moderator: Professor Arthur R. Miller

Participants: From left to right on your screen

FRANK YOUNG, M. D.
Commissioner, U. S. Food and Drug
Administration

WILLARD GAYLIN, M. D.
President,
The Hastings Center

ELLEN GOODMAN
Columnist, *The Boston Globe*

MILDRED STAHLMAN, M. D.
Professor of Pediatrics/Pathology,
Director of Neonatology, Vanderbilt
University School of Medicine

MORTIMER ROSEN, M. D.
Chairman and Professor, Department of
Ob/Gyn, Columbia Presbyterian
Medical Center

JOSEPH CALIFANO, JR.
Secretary of HEW, 1977–79;
Senior Partner, Dewey, Ballantine,
Bushby, Palmer and Wood

ROBERT MERHIGE, JR.
U. S. District Judge, E. D. Virginia

C. EVERETT KOOP, M. D.
Surgeon General, U. S. Public Health
Service, Department of Health and
Human Services

FAYE WATTLETON
President, Planned Parenthood
Federation of America

DIANE HEGENER, M. D.
Radiation Oncologist, Central Maine
Medical Center

VINCENT T. DEVITA, M. D.
Director, National Cancer Institute

ALEXANDER CAPRON
Professor of Law, Medicine and Public
Policy, University of Southern California

PAUL MARKS, M. D.
President and CEO, Memorial
Sloan-Kettering Cancer Center

MARCIA ANGELL, M. D.
Sr. Deputy Editor, *New England
Journal of Medicine*

As you read through the dialogue, ask yourself:

1. If you were in trouble and were trying to figure out what to do about it, whom would you ask to help you sort out the best course of action?
2. If you were in serious trouble, would you like your friends and family on the phone to each other trying to protect your welfare without your knowledge?
3. How would you fit that unborn child into your plans if you found yourself suffering from cancer that could be easily treated—only at the cost of the child's life?
4. At what point would you want to intervene in a loved one's choices, if the choices did not seem to be in her best interests, or reflective of his settled dispositions?

THE COURSE OF THE DIALOGUE

The Alarming Test Results

The moderator begins by addressing Dr. Everett Koop. Dr. Koop, I'm Betty Bright, your long-time patient and family friend. You have scheduled a special appointment with me this morning to discuss the results of my last Pap smear, which were positive. I come rushing into your office, Hi, Uncle Chick! I'm in a big hurry, film crew downstairs, off to Arkansas, I'm a film producer now, lots of work to do. Betty, says Everett Koop, I'm going to have to ask you to postpone that trip. Remember that Pap smear? Well, there were changes in some of those cells that might mean an early cancer. Cancer! Yes. I'm not going to mince words. Your life could be at stake. We've got to do something about it now. But, Betty protests, I'll be back from Arkansas in two days. Not soon enough, Koop says. We're going down to see Dr. Hegener now. How about tomorrow morning? Look, half a day wouldn't get you to Arkansas and back anyway. We're going down now.

Suppose she convinces you, Dr. Koop, and you let her go. An appointment is made with Diane Hegener for after Betty comes back. A while later, Dr. Hegener calls Koop. Your patient missed the appointment, and I can't find her. Koop is concerned; he calls once more, but she's out of town again. Does Betty have a husband? Yes, says the moderator, name's Dan, an old golfing buddy of yours. (Now why didn't I remember that? wonders Koop.) Are you going to talk to him? Yes, says Koop. I'm their friend as well as their doctor, and I don't think this is an invasion of privacy. He talks: Dan, I'm worried about Betty. I'm delighted that she's so successful, but she had some worrisome test results, and I'm a little scared about her. She might have an early form of cancer. Cancer!

Invasion of Privacy

The moderator turns to Will Gaylin. Has Koop done anything wrong here? No, I don't think so, says Gaylin. He has every right to use the word "cancer," if that's what you're worried about. If the phone call to the husband is at issue, the concept of privacy or confidentiality between doctor and patient is almost sacred. Not absolutely? No, nothing is absolutely sacred; but the doctor is frightened, he cares about Betty. She's acting irrationally—after all, she doesn't want to die—and he's worried that he may have pushed "cancer" a little too fast. He has a right to talk to her husband. Dr. Frank Young agrees that Koop should have talked to her husband; to keep silent would have been to betray the confidence of longstanding friendship. What about the confidence between doctor and patient? That is a trust, an important one. But it is bilateral. Confidentiality is not a one-way street, nor does the right to privacy in the relationship belong to the patient alone. The doctor assumes part of the responsibility, part partnership, for Betty's welfare.

Doctor-Patient Confidentiality

Alexander Capron is in flat disagreement. This is a clear violation of doctor-patient confidentiality. They're just deciding what's right for her, regardless of her right to privacy. But her life is at stake! Yes, "but it's *her* life. That's the point."

Marcia Angell is also disturbed by this paternalism. Betty Bright is a grown-up, after all. There could be many reasons why she hasn't returned those phone calls. She could just be very busy right now. She could know that the two days, or weeks, are not going to make that much difference in the treatment. She could be digesting the information before talking it over with her husband. It could be that, contrary to Dr. Gaylin's speculations, Koop didn't push the C-word hard enough. They should keep phoning, try harder to get through to her, get *her* to talk to her husband. What if it turns out she's been lying to her husband? That's her business and her right.

Who Chooses the Treatment?

Well, Dr. Hegener, the news is good and bad. Betty has come back. Turns out she has cervical cancer in the early stages, stage I-A. What do you do? You are convinced that radiotherapy is clearly indicated. But Betty has a few questions first. As a matter of fact, she wants a reading list; wants to know everything possible about the disease and the options before her. Hegener *likes* that. The patient is taking this seriously, and I'll be able to work with her. But you're convinced that radiotherapy is the correct treatment. Why encourage this? As a matter of fact she comes back, having read everything, convinced that a radical hysterectomy is the best course of treatment. Well, Hegener says, I'd go over it with her, make sure she understood what she read, and if that's what she still wants, I'd refer her to the best oncological surgeon I know. But she's vetoed your professional judgment! Doesn't that bother you? It bothers me, but it's her decision to make: it's her body, it's her choice, and she has to live with the consequences.

Vincent DeVita comments that for those two treatment modalities, the consequences for the disease are exactly the same, so the patient might make the decision based on the side effects. But don't you care at all, that you know the best choice of treatment and your judgment is being questioned? Hegener's answer is as before: the patient is the one who will have to live with the consequences.

Will Gaylin disagrees. The attitude that Hegener and DeVita adopt is not appropriate. As a physician, I serve not your desires but your health and your needs. The moderator encourages: they're denying their own autonomy, right? They're catering to her? Gaylin assumes, for the sake of argument, that the hysterectomy is not indicated. In that case, he is a little disturbed by the physicians' willingness to do what she wants, removing parts of her. I know it's her body, but I cannot mutilate her on a whim. But if you don't do what she wants, she'll walk out of the office, the moderator

Autonomy vs. Health

says, and she'll see nobody else, she'll die! I still cannot ethically do this surgery, says Gaylin. "I still would not violate her body for some imaginary anxiety of hers. That would be, it seems to me, a violation of my commitment to this religion called health."

The Mother or the Child

The hypothesis gets more serious. When she comes back, Dr. Hegener, Betty has Stage II-A cervical cancer. And she's now 14 weeks pregnant. (How does she know? Saw a gynecologist. OK.) Now it's clear that she needs radiotherapy. Will she lose the baby? Yes, radiotherapy will abort the fetus, eventually. But will she survive? She has a very good chance of survival. Even at this advanced stage, there is a 60 percent survival rate.

Betty doesn't like the sound of the odds. I never beat the odds; I'll probably die. And the baby will be dead. I don't think I want to give up the baby. It's a gift from God, and it will be all Dan will have left. Dr. Hegener respects and understands that.

Betty goes back to Uncle Chick. Uncle Chick, I don't want to lose this child. Am I crazy for wanting to keep it?

Koop knows how she feels. He also knows that Dan has always wanted to be a father. But he doesn't know enough about the subject to advise her. He wants to ask physicians he trusts to join the conversation—Dr. Mildred Stahlman, to comment on the baby's chances and Dr. DeVita to assess the cancer and say how much Betty is increasing her own risks by putting off radiotherapy.

We assemble the panel and yes, she's really increasing her risks. It's practically suicidal to put off therapy for the rest of the pregnancy. Now what would Koop advise?

Maybe we'd better reconsider this. Does Dan really want a baby that he's going to have to raise all by himself? Does he want it more than he wants a good chance of keeping Betty? Let's be sure we're not just giving in to a "romantic notion" of sacrificing yourself for your child.

Will Gaylin is less interested in Dan's wishes than in Betty's. "I don't believe in God, particularly, and in that situation I'd want to leave a child behind, as a piece of immortality....I think we're at that point...where we don't have the rules to protect us. We have to agonize with ourselves and our conscience....I would have a high respect for Betty's opinion on this and give her—and I am someone who is very paternalistic, as you know—here is where I would give her an absolute autonomy. I have no real preferences in this until I've talked to her."

Absolute Autonomy

Betty goes to Dr. Mortimer Rosen as her obstetrician and gynecologist. I want to save the baby. Dr. Rosen says that they will work together, and that he will do his best. Remember, Doctor, it's the baby first, and me second. He understands how she feels; he will work with her. Dr.

Stahlman agrees. As of now, our responsibility is for two lives. It is the mother's choice. If she knows what is at stake, and she knows the chances she is taking, there is no objection to proceeding with her chosen course.

The Crisis

Betty's condition worsens, Dr. Rosen. Finally, in her twenty-eighth week of pregnancy, Dan comes to see you. Betty's dying soon. Can we save the baby? The problem is, she won't agree to a Caesarean section to take the baby at this time; she thinks she can live long enough to bring it to term.

Rosen needs a clearer definition of the medical situation. I need to know how long, realistically, we can expect her to live. What are the risks to my two patients? There is probably no "risk" for Betty; no matter what we do, she will die in a very short time. But if she's going to die, we must deliver the child immediately, or the child will die too. If death is imminent, as you say, I will need help from support personnel to talk to her, to tell her she's dying, and that it's important that we give the child every chance.

Marcia Angell has difficulty seeing where the dispute comes from. What is the hesitation? Haven't we already established that the baby's life takes priority over the mother's? The disagreement seems to hinge on facts: Betty thinks that she "can hang on," keep herself alive, for a significant amount of time; the physicians' prognosis is for a very short survival.

So Rosen talks to Betty. Tells her she's dying. He will do the best that he can for the baby; that is his only obligation and only guarantee. He cannot cure her. But he may be able to give her one very precious thing: a chance to see her baby before she dies. The moderator grumbles that he's pulling emotional cords. Yes. He'd bring Dan in to plead for the baby to be delivered. He has a role to play here, one he believes in. "If this patient, in the beginning, had chosen to seek no medical care, I would have supported her...It would have been her right...to refuse all medical care....But it was a different situation; now we have two people to consider."

So you and Dan are going to pull my emotional cords to push me into a decision that I might not want. How does Ms. Wattleton react?

Faye Wattleton is upset. This started out as a *partnership* between you two. Let's try to preserve that. "You can't turn the tables on Betty at this point." This looks like a revival of that paternalism we saw earlier. Ellen Goodman is not at all sure the doctors are right about the prognosis. Betty says she can hang on until 30 weeks, well, maybe she can. I don't think the doctors have a direct line to God. Betty's gone this far because she wants to give her baby the best possible chance; let her go on. I am less than impressed with medical expertise. Give her one day at a time, and we'll see. But that's just temporizing! Temporizing is all we can do now, says

The Ethics
of
Persuasion

Goodman. What Betty has wanted is for the baby to live. "She and her baby are in a partnership for survival, and they seem to see that partnership differently than the doctor does."

Rosen finds the suggestion quite acceptable. We'll take it from day to day, let her make the decision each day as long as she can. The trouble is, if she becomes incompetent, and cannot make the decision any more, he has no clear guidance on what to do next, and he cannot make the decision to operate without the support of someone authorized to decide. What he would like to do is take the patient to the operating room and deliver the baby. Last time this type of case came up, he had to wait until the patient died; the baby was delivered after the mother's death, but it died too. "Who speaks for the fetus when the fetus has a right?"

Suppose Betty continues saying no. Will Rosen just accept that? No, he'll try administrative means to get the operation authorized, maybe a court order. Paul Marks says that at this point, with the patient still lucid and clearly refusing surgery, he'd have to back the patient. Califano, the lawyer, points out that since the mother is lucid, and either choice she makes is supportable, we are not likely to get a court to help out by ordering the Caesarean section.

Who Speaks for the Fetus?

Coma

Just as Dr. Rosen had feared, Betty slips into a coma. Now Dan announces that he's the surrogate decision maker, grabs the consent form for the surgery, signs it, and tells Dr. Rosen to go ahead. Will Rosen now perform the operation? Yes, after explaining the risks and benefits to Dan, who will have to assume the responsibilities of raising the child.

Mildred Stahlman points out that the father's contribution to a pregnancy is not negligible. His rights should be taken more seriously because he will be left with the total nurture of this baby. By the way, we are not reduced to guesswork when it comes to the condition of the fetus: We can monitor fetal condition with a great deal of accuracy and frequency, and simply put off the operation until the baby is noticeably getting into trouble. "If the baby is dying and there is a chance to save the baby's life, I will be the baby's advocate—I must be the baby's advocate."

Califano thinks that Rosen is indeed playing God, but perhaps that is what he has to do. Califano would love to have a court order for that surgery. Would Judge Merhige give such a court order? Califano presents an argument to the judge that it is in the best interests of all parties to have the baby delivered by Caesarean section immediately. Alex Capron, the opposing attorney, suggests that there is no reason for the judge to have to make the decision. Every move this woman has made is to save the baby.

Her wishes should prevail. If you take this to court to try to force surgery, I will oppose that attempt.

Faye Wattleton argues that the court and the physicians should honor Betty's desires. The only reason why she wanted to postpone the surgery was to get to viability.

Judge Merhige keeps hearing about the rights of the mother and father. He wants someone to represent the rights of the fetus. Dr. Stahlman has already said that she would do that. All right, now he has someone he can trust. He agrees with Dr. Rosen that new law is needed in this field. This difficulty is frequently encountered in the courts, and....The moderator interrupts. Would Judge Merhige please render a decision without foot-notes? Sure. The State has an interest in the preservation of the baby's life. Take the baby.

Autonomy or Authenticity

Will Gaylin is a bit upset by the course of part of this conversation. "We do have another principle that we haven't mentioned. We've mentioned autonomy, that she has a right, and I would not have the operation against her will. But Betty is not a case history, she's a human being. And there is a concept of authenticity. There is a lifetime that we have....This is a woman who made a tremendously courageous...statement that she wanted this child to live...." We all know her. "And we've seen a consistency of dedica-tion to that child. I'm willing to supplement without the courts the autonomy expressed by this woman, that after she's passed into the coma...the consent of the husband...is an authentic action consistent with the Betty we all knew and worked with over all these weeks."

The moderator concludes this section with a restatement of the problem: We are all working to do what Betty would have done. But what was that?

Endgame

Let's go back one step. Betty is just about to slip into the coma. This time there is no talk of waiting for viability. She just doesn't want a Caesarean, period. No surgery. She's weak, she's dying, but she's very clear: no surgery. Now you know "what she would have wanted." Are you going to go along with it?

A Conflict of Rights

Rosen is bothered: "I have difficulty that the law says to me one day, when I can hold the child in my hand, the same person, I must do everything that I can as a physician to protect the child's rights, and the next day, because it's in a shell, within a body, I am violating one person's rights to protect another person's rights. I can save the child if we deliver it today. I violate my patient's rights, but who is my patient? I think today I have to speak for the fetus. Yester-day I may have spoken for the mother." Faye Wattleton reacts immediately:

When did you change your mind? You started out willing to work with Betty, whatever she wanted. Now all of a sudden you're speaking for someone else. When the transition?

Rosen points out that the question now is only, who can live? When all this started, the mother could live. Now only the baby can. Wattleton retorts that he is going beyond the bounds of consent. Rosen replies that he is not God, but that he has an obligation to save lives if he can.

Angell points out that there is a sharp change here. We started out with a partnership between Betty and Dr. Rosen. Well, then, when the patient becomes incompetent, the partnership continues with the surrogate decisionmaker substituting for the patient. The natural move is to go to Dan and let him authorize the surgery, which he's wanted all along. Now, suddenly, it seems she changed her mind. Then the surrogate must honor her wishes on that, too. We should be using substituted judgment—the judgment of the surrogate on what the patient would have chosen.

Substituted Judgment

Judge Merhige is still in favor of surgery, if we have a viable fetus.

Dan suddenly changes his mind. Now he thinks that Betty's last decision should prevail. Besides, he doesn't think he's capable of raising the child by himself. Let them both die. The panelists immediately discover a doting grandparent willing to raise the child. Judge Merhige's decision is unchanged: if the child can survive, deliver it. But Betty was clear that she didn't want surgery, protests the moderator.

Rosen's position is also unchanged. If he can get legal support, he will deliver the baby. If not, he will walk away. Sadly, and feeling wrong, but he'll do it.

Wattleton protests that Betty's rights seem to have gone into that coma with her.

The Right to Refuse Treatment

Judge Merhige articulates the assumption underlying his position throughout: The mother does not have all that autonomy to refuse treatment when there's *another party*, an innocent person, the baby, involved.

Koop points out that Rosen has done an extraordinary job of carrying out an extraordinary contract.

Wattleton is distressed by this turn of the argument. What, doesn't the woman have a right to change her mind? For a while she was talking surgery at some point, now she's changed her mind and doesn't want it. What's wrong with that? Gaylin asks if she does not find this a very strange change of mind. She gave up a very good chance of survival in order to carry this fetus to viability and give it the best possible chance of survival. Now, dying, she says she doesn't want surgery, dooming the baby to death and rendering her death useless. Couldn't this be a whim, the terror of the moment? Is that Betty talking?

Well, why not? asks Wattleton. People do strange things all the time. "Is she not still a part of the human race, that has the right to make these decisions? And indeed, imperfect as we are, to change her mind?"

A REVIEW OF SELECTIONS FROM THE SOURCE READER

The sense of self and the value of self-determination are late arrivals on the intellectual scene. We have always known that people could be "self-willed" and "selfish," but such "idiotic," or idiosyncratic, behavior was always condemned as "antisocial" and therefore wrong. A strong current of such social orientation still underlies every going society, as it must if the society is to survive. Yet despite this orientation to community, our greatest thinkers in the modern period have affirmed the value of individuality. This would be a good time to review some of them.

Selections for this chapter:

> Aristotle, *Nicomachean Ethics*, Book III, **Source Reader** p. 50
> John Locke, *Second Treatise of Government*, Ch. V, , **Source Reader** p. 114
> Immanuel Kant, *Foundations of the Metaphysics of Morals*, **Source Reader** p. 137
> John Stuart Mill, *On Liberty*, **Source Reader** p. 182

Locke derives the right to freedom from property rights. I own myself, therefore I have the right to use myself as I see fit, just as I would use any other types of private property. The person, in this derivation, is just one more object of ownership. For Kant, the person is very definitely *not* an object. The worth of an object is in its price, but the worth of a rational being is in dignity, beyond all price. Mill rejects both of those *a priori* derivations of the value of autonomy, insisting that Libertarian policies can be justified entirely *a posteriori*, by observing their consequences in human happiness. Those three derivations are mutually incompatible; that is, if one of them is the "right" derivation, the other two are wrong. (The conclusion is the same in all cases, so there is no difference in application.) Which derivation do you find strongest, or most persuasive? Why?

SYNTHESIS AND DISCUSSION

What are they really arguing about? The concept of "autonomy" is the most complex of ethical concepts; its literature is deep, difficult, and (as pointed out in the preceding paragraph) often contradictory. As the introductory essay for this chapter explains, the conflicting elements in the notion of "autonomy" often lead to irreconcilable disagreements in practice; many of these emerged in the course of the dialogue.

For purposes of this brief discussion, let us isolate three sets of questions on autonomy, not to resolve them, but to get them clear enough so that we can appreciate how terrifying they are. The televised dialogue mercifully begins with relatively inconsequential questions on professional prerogative and client autonomy. It proceeds next to the agonizing questions surrounding the determination of competence, authenticity, or true autonomy of a decision made by a person incapacitated for decision making; and it ends with the very fundamental, and often ugly, set of questions concerning who is to count as morally considerable, and to what extent individual rights should be set aside for the sake of other people or the public at large. We will take these one at a time.

1. Professional Prerogative and Client Choice: should the physician impose medical decisions upon the patient? The first part of the dialogue turns on the efforts of the medical profession to treat Betty Bright appropriately for her cervical cancer. According to the physicians, appropriate treatment is relatively simple to obtain and very effective. There is even a choice of treatments (surgery and radiotherapy), between which the patient may choose. (They have identical outcomes but different side effects.)

But Betty doesn't seem to be interested; off she goes to Arkansas, or anywhere else, and doesn't keep her appointments. The physicians are frustrated; here's a case where they are really certain that they know what's best for the patient, and the darn patient won't do the obvious thing. First of all, why? They bandy around possible answers: you scared her too much and she's blocking; you didn't scare her enough and she didn't take you seriously; she's in the phase of Denial. Marcia Angell introduces an intriguing suggestion: it isn't the *physician's* state of certainty that matters here, but the patient's. Just possibly, Betty is taking into account lay "wisdom" on the subject that the physicians do not know.

If so, the wisdom is wrong. Can the physicians do anything to change Betty's mind? "Doing something" would mean violating the traditional right of confidentiality, or privacy, between doctor and patient, in order to put pressure on people around Betty to get her to treatment. Can they do that? Where does professional right and obligation leave off, and necessary respect for patient choice begin? Do the doctors have the right to let Betty make choices that will kill her—without even trying to stop her? On the other hand, are they *that* certain of their diagnosis and their prescription?

Underlined throughout this part of the dialogue, and again in the debates over the need for an immediate Caesarean, is a constant paradox of medical practice. Looked at from the perspective of lay society, the physicians' art is uncertain, doctors can make mistakes, they are only advisors, there are many sources of healing knowledge outside of medicine, and their insistence on *their* way of knowing and healing is the sheerest arrogance. Looked at from the physicians' perspective, if doctors are ever to help anyone, they must proceed confidently and certainly even if there is always a risk of mistake; and in the case of cervical cancer, there isn't very much risk. Where their diagnoses are well established and their treatments standard and successful, they can even get in legal trouble if they do not insist that the patient heed their advice. Now what should they do?

2. The mood becomes darker when we move from a heedless patient with a curable condition to a terminal patient with a cliff-hanging choice: do we perform the Caesarean today, or do we wait until tomorrow and make the choice all over again? What will be best for the baby? Both mother and obstetrician agree that each day or week in the womb of its living mother gives the baby a better chance of survival; presumably they agree that no matter how soon after death the operation is performed, the baby will be severely endangered by its mother's death while it is still in the womb; and they disagree about how long the mother has to live. The law is clear: the hospital must honor the lucid mother's choice, even if there is disagreement about the quality of the factual knowledge on which she bases her choice. But is she lucid?

All she wanted was to bring the baby to term, or at least close to term, so Dan would have a child. Now the best judgment is that the baby is as close to term as it is going to get, and the time has come to take the baby out of the mother by Caesarean section. So logically she should agree, right? Is she *not* agreeing because she is incompetent—dazed by pain, confused, crazy? If autonomy is based on rationality, may we say that she has lost her autonomy because she is now not thinking well, she is irrational—she is crazy? Given the entire trend of her decisions to this point, may we say that her present "decision" is not hers at all, is inauthentic? Or should we turn the tables on all such thinking? On the contrary, is it possible that we think she is incompetent, unfree, and inauthentic because she is not agreeing with us, the rational medical community? What duties do we have to her now?

3. Until now the decision has belonged to Betty. Betty decided on the course of treatment that would give her baby the best chance. Betty decided to put off the Caesarean to give the baby a better chance. Then Betty decided "no surgery" regardless of the baby's chances. With the coma, the decision still belonged to Betty, as articulated by surrogate decision makers—Dan and the others who were most recently the closest to her. Did she want to save the baby or did she want no surgery? But the final twist of the hypothetical asks a different question. Suppose we know for sure she wanted no surgery. Suppose Dan decides, as surrogate, that there should be no surgery because he doesn't really want a child anyway. But suppose the pregnancy is far enough advanced to give the baby an excellent chance for survival if delivered by Caesarean section before Betty's death. Now should the community intervene, not to preserve the force of the woman's choice, but to save the life of its youngest citizen, the child of her womb?

Two positions immediately crystallize. One, represented by Rosen and Merhige, in which the entire medical and legal tradition join, dictates immediate measures to save the child's life. No question of the woman's right to control her own body, life, and future is involved in this decision; she has none of those any more, and her "right" is history. The only element in the situation that is worthy of moral consideration is the endangered baby.

The other position, represented by Wattleton and Goodman, embodies a relatively new argument. There have been scattered attempts to put it on a philosophical basis, under the heading of "respect for persons," a variant of autonomy. On this reasoning, the woman who, living, had every right to refuse surgery for cervical cancer to save her own life, has the same right, dying, to refuse surgery that would save the life of her child. In both cases, the right of the individual to protect the integrity of her own body takes precedence over every other interest. The attempt does not take us very far. The right of a dead person to "protect the integrity of the body" is implausible on the face of it, and we can easily imagine circumstances in which it would be overridden (for instance, in an epidemic of new and deadly disease, where autopsy of all disease victims was made mandatory for public health reasons). But the assertion of the right to protect the integrity of a dying body when a living person will suffocate as a result is altogether novel. There is a living baby in that dying body, and if an endangered baby can be saved without deadly injury to another (irrelevant in this case), then we are under an obligation to save it—unless babies in this condition have no right to our consideration at all.

That last possibility illustrates why the position defended by Faye Wattleton is characterized in some of the literature as "abortion logic." By the decision in *Roe v. Wade*, so the argument goes, you can perform an abortion until the ninth month of pregnancy if the mother's life or health is at stake, regardless of state law on the subject. (Marcia Angell mentioned this during the televised presentation.) Abortion always entails the death of the abortus, or we wouldn't call it abortion. You're never allowed to kill a human being; such killing would be murder, which is terribly wrong. So logically, if under certain circumstances you can bring about the death of whatever it is in the woman's uterus, up to and including the ninth month of its residency therein, then whatever it is is not a human being up through that month. But if it's not a human being, then it cannot be the object of a physician's care and obligation. So the obstetrician, and the pediatrician, and the law *have no right* to consider delivering the baby for *its* sake. *It* has no right to moral consideration, and they have no right to give it any.

Can we live with this? Suppose we have got to the 36th week before Betty takes a sudden turn for the worse, and a healthy infant kicks and struggles inside her. If we'll give Rosen some support, he'll have that baby out now and it may (depending on actual length of gestation) be guzzling formula within the hour. If we won't, he will have to walk away, and the infant will die as the placenta's oxygen is replaced by poison in the body of its dead mother. On the other hand, our support reintroduces a tradition of medical paternalism that we have successfully challenged in the last decades. What should we do?

QUESTIONS FOR YOUR REFLECTION

1. Whose life is it, anyway? The question is usually rhetorical. In a play by that name, the answer clearly given was, Mine! But is that the right answer? Who else might your life belong to? In what senses?

2. At what point may the medical community intervene for the medical welfare of the individual? Intervention is suggested at several points in the presentation: phoning the husband to get the wife in for an appointment, manipulating the patient to accept an unwanted therapy that the physician knows is the best one, surgical intervention to separate a baby from its dying mother. This question is an instance of the larger issue, at what point may the general community intervene for the welfare of the individual in general? What background circumstances alter your answer? On ethical grounds, which of the following should we take into account?:

- Age of the individual;
- Apparent composure of the individual;
- Apparent intelligence of the individual;
- Apparent wealth of the individual;
- Whether or not individual has sought any kind of medical help before;
- How the individual got into this situation;
- Threats of lawsuit.

3. Betty isn't alone in that hospital. What is the role of her primary nurse in her last illness? What is the role of her mother? What roles can be played by other participants in the health care professions and in the neighborhood? Can the nurse serve as Betty's advocate? How? Who else might?

4. At what point may, or must, the physician begin to consider the embryo, fetus, or unborn child, as a separate patient, whose interests may, or must, be balanced with the mother's?

5. How do J. S. Mill and John Locke work together to produce the standard American notion of the autonomy of the individual with respect to matters of health and the body? Trace the arguments in each that lead to the libertarian position presupposed by supporters of "patient autonomy" such as Goodman and Wattleton?

SUGGESTIONS FOR FURTHER READING

Special Supplementary Text:
JAY KATZ. *The Silent World of Doctor and Patient*. New York: The Free Press, 1984.

BOK, SISSELA, AND JOHN A. BEHNKE, EDS. *The Dilemmas of Euthanasia*. Garden City, NY: Anchor Doubleday, 1975.

CARLTON, WENDY. *"In Our Professional Opinion...": The Primacy of Clinical Judgment over Moral Choice*. Notre Dame, IN: University of Notre Dame Press, 1978.

CASSELL, ERIC J. *The Healer's Art*. New York: Lippincott, 1976.

CHILDRESS, JAMES. *Who Should Decide?* New York: Oxford University Press, 1984.

CULVER, CHARLES M., AND BERNARD GERT. *Philosophy in Medicine: Conceptual and Ethical Issues in Medicine and Psychiatry*. New York: Oxford University Press, 1982.

FADEN, RUTH R., AND TOM L. BEAUCHAMP. *A History and Theory of Informed Consent*. New York: Oxford University Press, 1986.

GRISEZ, GERMAIN, AND JOSEPH M. BOYLE, JR. *Life and Death with Liberty and Justice: A Contribution to the Euthanasia Debate*. Notre Dame, IN: University of Notre Dame Press, 1979.

HIPPOCRATES. *Hippocrates*. trans. W. H. S. Jones, 2 vol. Cambridge, MA: Harvard University Press, 1962.

JAMETON, ANDREW. *Nursing Practice: The Ethical Issues*. Englewood Cliffs, NJ: Prentice Hall, 1984.

KOHL, MARVIN, ED. *Beneficent Euthanasia*. Buffalo, NY: Prometheus Books, 1975.

KUBLER-ROSS, ELISABETH. *On Death and Dying*. New York: Macmillan Co., 1969.

LAIN-ENTRALGO, P. *Doctor and Patient*. New York: McGraw-Hill, 1969.

NOONAN, JOHN T., JR., ED. *The Morality of Abortion: Legal and Historical Perspectives*. Cambridge, MA: Harvard University Press, 1970.

SUMNER, L. W. *Abortion and Moral Theory*. Princeton, NJ: Princeton University Press, 1981.

VEATCH, ROBERT M. *Death, Dying and the Biological Revolution*. New Haven, CT: Yale University Press, 1976. (Second edition forthcoming 1988).

VEATCH, ROBERT M. *A Theory of Medical Ethics*. New York: Basic Books, 1981.

The President's Commission for the Study of Ethical Problems in Medicine and Biomedical and Behavioral Research: all volumes of its Report, especially *Decisions to Forego Life-Sustaining Treatment* and *Making Health Care Decisions*, Washington, D.C: Government Printing Office, 1982-1986. See especially Gerald Dworkin's essay on Autonomy and Informed Consent in the latter volume.

DISTRIBUTIVE JUSTICE:

Anatomy of a Corporate Takeover

QUESTIONS TO KEEP IN MIND AS YOU READ THE CHAPTER

1. Probably the first moral judgment you ever made was, "That's not fair!" (when your sister took all the Halloween candy, perhaps). Children have a natural sense of fairness. So do adults. What's fair in the world at large, now that you're grown up? Does the question still have meaning?

2. Do you think all business is just organized greed? Does that mean all businessmen are greedy? Do you know any? Are they? At this time, do you think you might go into business? Are you greedy? (Or, will you be then?)

3. We will be looking at some very recent practices in the world of business—the "leveraged buyout," "hostile takeover," "payment of greenmail," and the like. From popular press reports, what do you think of these practices? Do you admire the "raiders"? Do you think that someone should put a stop to them? See if your opinion changes in the course of reading the chapter and viewing the video presentation.

THE CONCEPT OF DISTRIBUTIVE JUSTICE

How should the goods of a nation be distributed among its citizens? When the classic formula is read, "From each according to his ability to each according to his_____", how shall we fill in the blank? "Worth" or "merit" (as

Aristotle would probably say, and aristocracies everywhere have practiced)? "Work" or "transformation of resources" (as Locke and capitalist democracies everywhere would have it)? "Need" (Karl Marx's suggestion, and the simplest formula for any socialism)? What distribution is *fair*, in a high-technology, economically developed country? Or is the whole question wrong-headed? Is it like asking, what sort of religion shall we impose on the people? Is it a question that we have no right to ask, for all answers are wrong?

Since the Greeks, we have assumed that distributive justice entailed giving to equals equal shares (of the pie, or whatever was to be shared) and to unequals different shares, the difference in proportion to the inequality. What that formula does not tell us is (1) who *we* are, who are authorized to do the sharing; (2) what this famous pie is—what goods are available for "sharing;" (3) who is an eligible recipient for a piece, of whatever size; (4) since all conceivable recipients are equal in some respects and unequal in others, what aspects of equality are relevant to the distribution; (5) how we judge the proportions for unequal distribution. Our intuitions on all these questions are remarkably unclear, and our justifications are accordingly difficult to prove.

Take a paradigm case of just distribution, to set the stage for discussion. I need help to get my hedges trimmed, and have the money to pay the going rate for casual labor. I repair to a place frequented by available workers, and offer $15.00 to any who will spend six hours trimming my hedges. Two hours later I recruit other workers, and in my rush to finish I hire a few more to work the final two hours. There is no question on any of the five problematic dimensions enumerated above: The money is my own, and I, as owner, am authorized to distribute it; the pie in this case is the cash put aside for hedge trimming; eligible recipients are the workers; the relevant inequality is hours worked; and proportion is determined by prorating dollars per hour. Those who worked the whole six hours get $15.00, those who joined on later get $10.00, and those who checked in for the last two hours go home with $5.00 each.

That distribution is just. It is not, of course, necessary (see the Gospel according to St. Matthew, 20:1–16, not in your **Source Reader**), for the money is mine, and as long as I give what I promised to all, I can certainly give more to some of the workers, or even to people who have not worked at all, if that is what I feel like doing.

The paradigm does not exhaust the matter. In fact, its very simplicity shelters a fatal flaw: precisely because it is *my* money, private money, justice appears as a very distant limit: it would be unjust of me to deprive people of cash that I have promised them for work done, when they have done the work, but beyond that justice does not govern my expenditure of what is my own; spending is at my discretion. In the public domain, the imperative bears with much more force: it is unjust for the city department of welfare to withhold benefits from those who deserve them, but equally unjust to give out benefits to those who do not deserve them, or have lied, stolen, and cheated to get on the welfare rolls.

So it is with the public's money that we are most bound to be just in distribution. But ultimately, what is the public's money? For ordinary purposes, I know what is mine and what is not. My house is my own, the post office belongs to the public. But let a highway be planned, in the way of which stands my home, and I may be in for a rude shock about where the rights of ownership *really* lie. Children are hostages to fortune; property is hostage to the state. In the end, "private ownership" is a matter of law or policy rather than of natural right. And that is as it should be. As Adam Smith pointed out in *The Wealth of Nations* (1776), everyone's property is the product of collective effort, often over many generations, and only legal conventions define what sorts of effort, merit, or desert shall be blessed, in the appropriate circumstances, by bestowal of "property rights."

But then it is surely appropriate to ask about the justice of the distribution of wealth throughout the whole society. All that property is the result of effort beyond that put forth by its present holders—*that* has been true of all private property since the hunter-gatherer society disappeared. Why can't we decide to redistribute private property whenever it is clearly in the public interest to do so? There are good policy reasons to let individual effort be rewarded by secure possession of desirable goods (it keeps people working harder, for instance). That was Adam Smith's contention, certainly. But the assumption that private property is to be protected—that people are *entitled* to the property they hold—is even older.

Probably the first and most persuasive exposition of this point of view is Aristotle's (*Politics*, II, 4), in his attack on Plato's collectivist "Republic." Property, he noted, is usually held privately, although occasionally commandeered for public use. And that is as it should be—for private satisfaction (since people like things to be their own), for the good of the object owned (since people take better care of the things that are theirs), and for the promotion of virtue (since people can only be generous with things that are genuinely theirs to keep or to share). On the whole, the Western tradition has agreed with Aristotle. After Plato, we wait until Karl Marx to find another major thinker willing to abandon the sanctity of private property, even over a very limited part of the economy. Only fragmentary groups of religiously motivated communitarians have advocated property in common as the norm of economic life.

But while the ethical tradition of the West clearly presupposes the existence of private property as an institution, very few writings have acquiesced in a policy of letting wealth lie in the laps of whosoever can get it, no matter how they get it. On the contrary, an underlying duty of redistribution of wealth in the form of support for the poor is found very clearly stated in the Bible. The Biblical prophet Amos was no socialist, nor was socialism possible in his era; but precisely *because* there was no bureaucratic apparatus to enforce it, the duty of the rich to support the poor applied with all the more force. The Lord is uncompromising: the wealthy of the society must provide for the widow, the orphan, and the beggar at the gate, or suffer the wrath of God and eternal damnation.

Note that Amos's anger (*Bible*, **Source Reader** p. 78)—and the anger of Jesus of Nazareth, for that matter (*Bible*, **Source Reader** p. 85)—is directed at the rich simply because they *are* rich and they are not providing for the poor. They are not accused of individual crimes in acquiring their wealth, so the notion of retributive justice does not enter the moral picture. No one is claiming that they don't deserve their money. All that is claimed, and claimed, in the Biblical tradition, at the top of the prophet's voice, is that being rich, they have a duty before God to provide for the needy, and that duty overrides any duties of ritual or sacrifice or prayer. For Amos, and Hosea and Jesus and Karl Marx, the inequality of distribution of goods in a society was a collective crime all by itself, which cried to Heaven for remedy.

Western thought has never strayed very far from the Bible, and when John Locke essayed to ground the all-important right to private property, he limited it strictly: we have a right to own the goods of this world, only if we have taken the resources to make them from a virtually unlimited commons (so as to leave "as good and enough" for the next to come), have mixed our labor with them, and have taken no more than we need (Locke, **Source Reader** p. 116). On that last point he is emphatic; the echoes from the Bible (the legend of the manna, the commands to Christ's disciples) are unmistakable.

Distributive justice, then, is a principle of morality that limits the right to hold and to use private property, and by tradition, strictly limits its arbitrary use and the amount that can be acquired. We are reminded of this tradition in the present spate of wildly disproportionate fortunes: while billions change hands in a typical day on Wall Street, our television documentaries linger over the bloated bodies of dying children in Africa and the cardboard cartons used by the homeless citizens of our major cities for sleeping quarters in the winter. We believe in the "sanctity" of private property, or at least in the wisdom of founding our economic system on its secure possession. But when we come to the very rich, that policy seems to make a lot less sense, since no billionaire can enjoy any more steak, beer, or comfortable clothes than your run-of-the-mill millionaire. As for fortunes made with very little effort or hard work, the policy simply does not seem to apply. Of course we're not averse to rewarding luck, or skill in parlaying less money into more money. But when the effort is minimal and no hard-won skill is in evidence, when luck does not seem (as it does seem when a plumber wins the lottery) to be playing its usual impartial role, and when the fortune is so vast that it boggles any imaginative attempt to see how it might be spent on the goods of this life—a policy of letting the money lie in the lap into which it fell may seem open to question, if not entirely wrongheaded. This is doubly so if other, less fortunate, harder working persons have been injured in the transfer of money to the billionaire. The transaction may have been entirely legal, but something in us cries that it is not fair, and we may be right. Certainly, in our protest against these casually got fortunes, according to our own traditions, we have the Lord on our side.

Justice, in the Western mind, is firmly bound up with equality. Our propensity to use "equality" as a baseline of just distribution, however, may be an accident of modern philosophy. The Bible tells us to take care of the poor, the widow, and the orphan; it does not tell us to equalize incomes or establish a system that will provide for all equally. Aristotle specifically rejects the "Pythagorean" idea that the reciprocity that characterizes justice is to be equal reciprocity (Aristotle, **Source Reader** p. 56). When Jefferson wrote that "All men are created equal," or the framers of the French Declaration of Rights of Man and Citizen stated that "all men are created and remain free and equal in rights," they emphatically did not mean economically equal. The political equality that characterizes citizens, from Plato's Athens to the present time, has nothing to do with economics.

But modern Western history, from the late eighteenth century to the present, has been characterized by stunning advances in material existence, and a corresponding emphasis on material goods, the means to make them (the means of production), and the means to obtain them. If equality is important, and material goods are the means by which all goods are measured, then the only equality that means anything must be material equality, right? And so the modern approach to fairness in distribution, from the nineteenth century Romantics onward, has been to assume that equal distribution of resources is normative and argue from that point to any other fair distribution.

The most serious recent attempt to articulate the Western tradition of distributive justice is that of John Rawls of Harvard University, in his *A Theory of Justice* (1971) (Rawls, **Source Reader** p. 145). Rawls' work perfectly exemplifies this shift from the insistence on political equality as normative to the assumption that economic equality is the only condition that requires no explanation. According to Rawls, as the **Source Reader** passages show, we must find our principles of justice in the rules that any group of rational, self-interested people, assigned to plan their society, could agree to be governed by. If they knew what roles they would fill in the society for which they were planning—whether they personally were to be rich or poor, black or white, slave or free—then they would be able to tailor their rules to favor their own class. (Remember, they're *supposed* to be selfish.) So Rawls won't tell them what roles they will play, and thereby forces them to choose rules that will maximize advantage, or at least minimize disadvantage, for everyone in the society. The rules they would agree on in those circumstances, he argues, would provide for liberty first (the maximum liberty for each compatible with a like liberty for all) and equality second—no inequalities unless the creation of a privileged post works out to everyone's advantage, including the least well off in the society, and the post is open to all on the basis of equal opportunity.

The formulation has its critics. As Robert Nozick (also of Harvard) points out (in *Anarchy, State and Utopia*, New York, 1974), Rawls' preference for equality in distribution is not itself morally derivable from anything. Any pattern of equal distribution is arbitrary with respect to the way things are, to any other pattern, and to any exercise of liberty, since almost any exercise of choice in distributing goods under your control is likely to upset the pattern. Further, Nozick argues, Rawls misses the whole notion of "entitlement," which may be just as basic as equality to our understanding of justice. If I legally own something, whether or not I earned it, or you want me to have it, or a democratic election would award it to me, or it's more or less than anyone else has, it's *mine*, and you have no earthly right to take it away from me just because it doesn't fit some ideal pattern of just distribution you have in mind. I'm entitled to it.

Who's right? Both Rawls and Nozick home in on fundamental intuitions about justice. Both sets of intuitions, contradictory though they may be, are built into the traditional justification of our system of "free enterprise." That convergence of contradictions in the system suggests in advance of observation that free enterprise will develop kinks and tensions now and again. For we argue, following Adam Smith (*Wealth of Nations*), that private property is absolutely sacred, that it is to be left in private hands, and that only the most limited restrictions should be put on its free use. So far, we sound like Nozick. Then, following Adam Smith's argument further, we learn that if such free use is permitted, of course inequalities will result, but that they will redound to the material benefit of even the least advantaged, since the wealth of the whole nation and the goods available to all will be increased without limit. There is no way that the greedy and selfish can expand their own prosperity without building that wealth, Smith argues, so all will (as by an Invisible Hand) be led to serve the common good while thinking all the time that they serve only their own. This part of the argument sounds like Rawls.

But does the business system always operate that way? Smith makes a persuasive argument that while we are dealing with farmers and simple manufactories, it does. But what happens when something like Wall Street enters the picture? This could be the point at which the delicate union of entitlement and redistributive justice parts at the seam.

THE TELEVISION PRESENTATION: SELECTED QUESTIONS
ON THE CONDUCT OF BUSINESS

This section considers the television presentation or videotape. The recapitulation of the dialogue that follows is not meant to be a word-for-word transcript of the tape, but a summary of the major themes, issues, and opinions that emerge in the conversation. It is for review, and for use as a resource if you include this topic in your term project.

TITLE: "ANATOMY OF A CORPORATE TAKEOVER"

Moderator: Professor Lewis B. Kaden

Participants: from left to right on your screen

LESTER C. THUROW
Dean, M.I.T., Sloan School of
Management

RUDOLPH W. GIULIANI
U.S. Attorney, Southern District, New
York

FREDERICK H. JOSEPH
CEO, Vice Chairman, Drexel Burnham
Lambert

T. BOONE PICKENS, JR.
General Partner,
Mesa Limited Partnership;
Chairman of the United Shareholders
Association

ARTHUR LIMAN
Partner, Paul, Weiss, Rifkind, Wharton
& Garrison

SIR JAMES GOLDSMITH

WARREN E. BUFFETT
Chairman, Berkshire Hathaway Inc.

ROBERT E. MERCER
Chairman and CEO, Goodyear Tire and
Rubber Company

JANE BRYANT QUINN
Financial Columnist, *Newsweek*;
Syndicated Columnist, *The Washington
Post*

TIMOTHY E. WIRTH
U.S. Senator, Colorado

JOSEPH FLOM
Partner, Skadden, Arps, Slate, Meagher
& Flom

JAMES F. BERÉ
Chairman and CEO, Borg-Warner
Corporation

JOHN H. GUTFREUND
Chairman and CEO, Salomon Brothers,
Inc.

EDWARD JAY EPSTEIN
EJE Publications

HARRISON GOLDIN
Comptroller, City of New York

THE COURSE OF THE DIALOGUE

Ask yourself, as you review the dialogue:

1. Why are these people, each of them, doing what they're doing? What motivates them? Is it just money? Does anything they say make you doubt that?

2. As a citizen, do *you* have any real interest in these proceedings? Are you a stakeholder in Peachtree Industries? How? Do you deserve to be heard? What would you say, and why?

The Meeting and the Interview

The scene opens at Peachtree Industries, Plum Valley. Peachtree was founded by Harry Oldman many years ago, to make good airplanes. A few years ago Chairman Oldman brought a new president on board, who talked him into picking up a financial services company in New York. That's the big profitmaker right now. But the chairman's heart is in technology, as always, and the meeting he's called is to talk about his new hypersonic airplane which will fly from New York to Tokyo in a few hours and has enormous potential for both military and civilian uses. Suddenly, even as he is describing the hypersonic plane's certain domination of the air and the market in the twenty-first century, he slumps back on the couch, mutters that he can't feel his left side—his speech is slurred. Mr. Mercer, you're the CEO. You immediately bundle him into the company ambulance, which heads for the nearest hospital, and call his doctor. That done, looking at your watch, you realize you are already late for an interview you had scheduled with reporter Sally Quinn, to talk about this new plane.

Under the circumstances, Mr. Mercer, do you go through with the interview?

"We go ahead with the interview, but we avoid what's happened to Harry at this point." Sally Quinn asks about Harry's whereabouts, but her curiosity is not rewarded. Harry may be back later; he's got his own agenda; my time is limited, Ms. Quinn, and if you want to talk about this project....

Mr. Beré, what would you tell her? "I would say that he's ill, he's been taken to the hospital and we do not know the consequences of the event." Even if Harry had asked you to tell no one? Yes. We have an obligation to the shareholders and other stakeholders; this is important news.

Lies, Evasions, and Telling the Truth

Quinn is furious. Mercer lied to me, she protests, and I feel very strongly about that. I did not lie to you, insists Mercer. You did too. Didn't. Did. There was a story, I was right there, and you didn't tell me; you misled me. What about Warren Buffett, the major shareholder?

Would he want to know? Sure, if it's important. How will *you* get the information, Mr Buffett? Oh, Mercer will tell *me*. He will? Mr. Mercer, would you tell Mr. Buffett if he called you? Yes, I'd tell him if he asked me. See, the interview with Ms. Quinn was for a specific purpose, to discuss a certain aspect of the company's future....Quinn is beside herself by now. You'd tell him, but you would not tell me, because you wanted to use me as a promotional device! Mr. Mercer, I am not in your PR Department... Oh, come on, says Mercer. You knew the rules of the game when you came after the interview.

Mr. Flom, what would a lawyer say? That Mercer creates legal liabilities for the company, especially exposure to suit by the stockholders, if he withholds from the public information that might influence decisions to buy, hold, or sell stock in his company. And if he then tells some people, and not others, he creates insider trading liabilities for the ones he's told. Mr. Liman, do you agree? Absolutely. He has a choice of saying that Harry's in the hospital, or canceling the interview. For all the reasons that Joe Flom gave, and for one other—that this sort of evasion destroys the credibility of the company—you may not mislead a reporter. (Hear, hear! says Quinn.)

Insider Trading

New question: Mr. Pickens, are you interested in this sort of news? Well, says Pickens, the odds are if Harry goes, the price goes up, because then it becomes a prospect for a sell-out. Fine. Now you get a telephone call from one Desmond Gruntled, a former employee of Peachtree who was fired several weeks ago. He tells you that Harry's not long for this world—may be gone within the week. Mr. Pickens, can you buy stock on that information? Absolutely not. That counts as inside information; I know something the other shareholders don't know, and it would be unfair to them for me to act on it. Does Mr. Giuliani agree that transactions under these conditions would be suspect? He sure does. If Pickens traded on that information, he would certainly be sued by other stockholders, the SEC would go after him in an enforcement action, and he might also be indicted. As Flom said, in this case law and fairness coincide: the point is to keep all players on an even footing, to keep a level playing field.

Mr. Liman, do you agree? Well, every time a CEO goes to the doctor, he doesn't have to publish his cardiogram. And if Harry looks a little peaked on the golf course, and you draw some conclusions about the future of the company, you don't have to abstain from the market. The major problem with company officers using company secrets is that they don't belong to them. If you take those secrets you can be accused of appropriating them just as if you took any property.

Obligations of Insiders

Flom suggests that we forget the level playing field. What the law can do is say there are certain people, the insiders, "who have a duty to the shareholders, and they should not be able to use the information they have against the interests of those shareholders and for their own benefit." [Such a duty is called a "fiduciary" obligation.] The doctor is not one of those insiders. The company lawyer obviously is.

Senator Wirth, are these the right distinctions? Wirth, with a little smile, says, well, "the Congress has been wrestling with this for the last three or four years. And many of us have wanted to leave this area deliberately ambiguous...we'd rather leave it in a situation where that ambiguity is out there and management of companies and raiders of companies are a little bit afraid of that, afraid that there might be a very ambitious DA out there who might go after them in some way...so therefore, they're gonna behave, they're gonna behave...."

Mr. Epstein, does that make any sense? Not much. There is no level playing field out there; the attempts to preserve one only protect an illusion. There is an alternative. Respect the fiduciary obligations that Mr. Flom was talking about, but after that, let the market fix the price of the stock. No restrictions on the flow of information absent a fiduciary obligation.

Mr. Giuliani? Not so fast. There may very well be violations of principles other than the fiduciary one, which will get you in trouble. If you guess wrong about that you can be sued. If you violate a principle deliberately, you can be indicted. For example, if Ms. Quinn talked to CEO Bere and found out about Harry Oldman, and stopped on the way back to her office to buy stock, would she be in trouble? She sure would be, sued at least, and certainly misusing her position as reporter.

Quinn agrees. I would expect to be investigated under those circumstances. It's just wrong—illegal, immoral, and fattening. My job is to go and do the story and publish it. It would be totally unethical to trade on that information, and would blow my career, among other things. It's my duty to publish that information. If I then want to buy the stock, I buy the stock. Duty to whom? To the readers, to the job, to myself. This comes from the ethics of being a journalist, nothing to do with markets.

You know, Lester Thurow muses, "lots of stock markets elsewhere in the world don't have our insider trading laws or don't enforce them. And I know of no evidence that they have any more fraud than we do. And see, I would square Mr. Epstein's comments: ...you can't make the playing field level. And therefore what you tell people is, that this is very *unlevel*. There are land mines everywhere, and Joe Sixpack doesn't have an equal chance with Warren Buffett. And anybody who tells Joe Sixpack he does, is lying to Joe Sixpack. And I think these insider trading laws are basically high level lying. They're telling the public something that isn't true. It's more than the 'illusion.' It really is fraud of a high order, and I think everybody here who is participating in that process is contributing to fraud." If the playing field were really level, he points out, there'd be no reason to have a stock market, where every advantage comes from having information before someone else does. Giuliani objects that just because a condition can't be made perfect is no reason to ditch the law.

The Takeover Attempt

Moving on in the hypothetical: Mr. Pickens, you've been interested in Peachtree for some time, as we noted before. Now, why are you in this business? To make money, Pickens replies. Primarily, however, he seems to regard himself as a "geologist" heading up a company that invests in energy companies, bound by a fiduciary obligation to his shareholders, and therefore a large investor who sometimes becomes active. (Both he and Sir James admit to being "raiders," sometimes.) Goldsmith sees the first work of investment in start-ups. You see an opportunity, a group of people trying to do something, and you back them, and it works or it doesn't, depending on the accuracy of the judgment.

"But then you have the opposite thing, somebody's mistake of the past," Goldsmith says. "And when there's somebody's mistake of the past, the market must be free to clean up that mistake....During the 1960s, the fashion was to conglomerate....The purpose of conglomeration was to build big groups by financial use of market multiples. They couldn't do it in an integrated way because the law stopped it in antitrust..., so they created these extraordinary contraptions of multi-industry companies...socks to electric engines to aerospace to whatever you like. Anything. These conglomerates didn't work. Now there are two ways in which you can handle that. You can either enshrine them, ossify them, make them into a monument and say, ...Wonderful! They didn't work, but they're there, just like a monument! And then you have inefficient industry forever. Or you can say, set the market free. And let the market cleanse itself. And somebody... has to go and do a *re*start-up, by the action of the free market, cleanse it of a structure which was wrong, liberate the pieces so they can become valid companies and of course make a profit at the same time. And that is just as constructive a thing to do as the start-up."

And, the moderator suggests, you're the cleansing agent, the Ajax? Sometimes, yes. But you only move when a company needs something.

A Free
Market
Ethics

"I do not know of a well-managed company that has been taken over by force. I only know of those that have not been good. And, by the way, well managed companies have got better because of the fear of being taken over."

And what is the motive? "If I'm in business, it is for money. That's the best reason for anybody to be in business....A demagogue will tell you that he's in business for all these constituencies of suppliers, communities, employees, everything else. That's not true, and if it's true, it's a mistake. If you start talking this nonsense about how we're only in business for the sake of our employees, you will featherbed, you will become uncompetitive and you will let them all down. That's pure demagoguery." Ah, but *you* make quite a bit of money on all this cleansing? I certainly do. "That's the purpose I'm in business for. I'm not in religion, I'm not in politics, though I'm not certain you don't make money in politics. I'm in business." And if you just wanted to clean it up...? "I might join the Church."

Let's move along to the acquisition moves on Peachtree. Mr. Pickens, as a general principle, we can say that you'll look after the business interests of your company and the community of Plum Valley will have to look after itself, right? Wrong! I care very much about the communities. When I was going after Phillips, I even offered to move to Bartlesville, Oklahoma, and that is a *real* personal consideration.

Very well. Let's get on with our interest in Peachtree and then we'll be able to see what the consequences might be. Pickens is the raider, Joseph is an investment banker, Liman is the lawyer. Pickens: they pushed me into it. Mr. Joseph, is that conceivable? Yes. That's part of our business. He probably asked us to look for acquisitions, and one service that investment bankers perform for a company is to show them acquisition opportunities in the marketplace. For a fee. What kind? On a $5 billion deal, maybe $5 million. That's our incentive to bring him the idea, and to work with him on strategy, tactics, etc., including disposition of any parts that have to be broken off. If you help him raise the money? That would cost more, depending on how much he needs, and whether it's high-grade (well-secured) debt or low-grade. Might be a couple hundred million dollars, depending on the size of the deal and how much equity he's put into it.

Sir James, you're going after Peachtree. You buy stock? Yes, up to the five percent permitted by law, before I disclose anything. (We establish that it is *not* insider trading to trade on the basis of *your own* intentions.) That acts as insurance if the deal does not go through. Once the five percent is bought, you plan to file a form 13D indicating an intention to buy the rest, so you call the CEO of the company and tell him that you're

Short- or Long-Term Benefits

after the company. Such conversations are set up between Goldsmith and Bere, Pickens and Mercer, duplicating the conditions of earlier actual takeover attempts by those raiders against the companies of those CEOs. The conversations, and subsequent meetings, are civil, informational, very brief, scripted by lawyers. (The last thing Sir James wants is to learn so much about the company that he becomes an insider and *can't* trade in that stock anymore.) When the raider makes an offer for the stock, above what the stock has been selling for, will the CEO accept it, or will he fight to defend his company, in order to make the raider go away? Of course I'll fight, says Mercer. "Because I don't see a plan that's going to be beneficial to the corporation. It's a one-time hit, where we get a spike in the share price and we cash out a corporation instead of operating it as a viable entity a long time into the future."

The Meeting of the Board

After this conversation, the CEO has no choice but to convene his board of directors and talk over the offer. The moderator quickly convenes a board: the retired mayor of Plum Valley, Harrison Goldin; the dean of the university's business school, Lester Thurow; the president of that university, Tim Wirth; the head of corporate legal staff, Joseph Flom; and their investment banker, John Gutfreund. Well, gentlemen, what shall we discuss? The interests of the community? The interests of the nation, or the employees? No, the legally sophisticated members immediately reply: We are chartered for one purpose only, and that is to represent the interests of the shareholders. Bounded only by U.S. or state law and the charter of the company, the good of the shareholders alone is in view.

You know, points out Thurow, there is no evidence, long term, that these mergers and takeovers have any effect at all. Track ten takeover victims with ten companies that were not touched, and you find no difference at all. Meanwhile, just because management is fired doesn't mean we close the local facility. So this dichotomy we're trying to set up here, this opposition between the interests of the community and the interests of the shareholders long term, is not yet clear.

Shareholders or Community   Buffett wants all options taken into account, and then he wants a decision that will be in the best interests of the shareholders. What about the community? The shareholders should vote on that. Regarding his own role, Tim Wirth disagrees. "I'm on the board because I'm president of the university and because the shareholders see some value in my being able to go to Washington and maybe foul up Boone Pickens a bit. There is also a deep relationship between Peachtree and the university and the community, and so I have an obligation and I'm on the board, not only to represent those shareholders, but also to represent the university and the community....I think there are a variety of other values that are at stake in this as well."

Liman says that the board of directors cannot do otherwise than serve shareholders. Wirth rejoins that "we have been arguing...for almost a hundred years in this country about the responsibilities that corporations have to their communities. We have tried for a long time to get corporations more responsible. We've done it at Peachtree. We're reaching out, supporting this university, supporting cultural activities and so on. We are the ultimate of what America believes corporate responsibility is; and yet you lawyers from Wall Street are coming in and telling us what to do with our community and our responsibilities." Mercer chimes in that shareholder value isn't just price; it's price and value. We're only talking very short term here. "We're gonna give you ten bucks and you can sell your stock and then we'll cash out the company. If you're sitting in front of a computer and that spike comes up and you have a fiduciary responsibility to that fund that you're managing, that stock is gone. It has to be."

Nor is appeal to the "long-term interests of our shareholders" going to do the company any good. Once the process of takeover has begun, most of "our shareholders" are short-termers, the arbitragers who mediate between the original price of the stock and what will turn out to be the final price.

The board meeting continues. When John Gutfreund tells the board that the offered price of $30 is too small, they agree to tell the raider "no thanks" and start to plan defenses. The moderator takes Flom through several standard moves—pre-takeover cost-slashing, self-tender, defensive tactics designed to make the company more expensive for the raider, the search for a white knight, and so forth. Sir James objects that these options are not the moves of choice today. "How do you defend today? You don't defend on economic grounds. You don't defend on being able to get a better offer. You defend by being able to go to Washington....get the Senate and the Congress,...who believe in the sort of stuff that Senator Wirth believes in, which he has just talked about, which is a pastoral America with a little company, and the church, and the university, and the whole thing is going to stay there and be there forever. And that they don't have to compete with anybody....This is totally mixed up. They are losing the fundamental difference between doing business and doing good. Doing business is what gives you the fuel to do good. Don't mix them up. The bee doesn't make honey because he's

Who
Shares the
Pie?

doing good....He's confusing it, and that's why this country is losing its vigor."

Mercer points out that in this country it's the state legislatures that would be involved, not Congress, and adds that if it's economic vigor in question, this country's best companies got that way by competitiveness, reinvestment of resources, expenditures on research and development. In his view the money spent on warding off raiders—which we have seen is substantial—is totally wasted as far as competitiveness is concerned.

Thurow thinks the polarization of these disputes into good guys and bad guys is a mistake. "That's what all the analysis indicates, that 10 to 15 years later the companies involved in this kind of behavior look exactly like the companies that weren't involved in this kind of behavior. Their stock doesn't outperform the market any more on average, their productivity doesn't grow any faster on average....It makes a lot of difference who manages these companies to the guys who are actually managing them. But if you ask does it make much difference to the American GNP, the answer is no...." Except that you attract a lot of talent to this high-paying field, talent that might have been at the service of new products and new services. Joseph complains that the "10 to 15 years" comparison isn't fair, since back then we had conglomerations, and we *all* agree that conglomerates are....Wait a minute, Thurow cuts in. Ten to 15 years ago you guys were telling us you were building a better economy through conglomeration, and you weren't; now you tell us you're building a better economy again, through takeovers, but how do we know that is true?

Joseph says it's a judgment call. But Sir James argues that the proposition is proven. Consider the "strategy" adopted at Peachtree's board meeting to make the company more competitive: Cut the overhead, cut excess positions, close obsolete factories. "That was the defense. Now what if there's no one there to trigger the defense? Suppose all managements were enshrined, that you could never get rid of them, that they were totally entrenched. Why would they have to do that? The only reason that the board has considered these things, which they've been paid to do for years, is because they are under attack. Take away, as our politician friends want to do, the capacity to attack, and those fellows will never do it."

And the plant in Plum Valley? If it's working well, of course it stays open, and it will be a better plant, for we will have married management with capitalism. The manager who is a major shareholder will be a much better manager. And if the plant is inefficient, then you have to close it. "What are you running, a charity or a business?"

The Ongoing Dilemma

The
Changing
Ethical
Agenda

Beré sums up the difficulties: "I was trained that a corporation was a guest in this society, to present quality goods at a reasonable cost. We were not trained to react to financial markets as such. We were trying to find a balance between long term and short term, and trying to be sensitive to our community because we genuinely believed that that would optimize our profits." Now the situation is different, and boards discuss different matters. Beré is not sure what he would do: accept Sir James' offer, buy back stock, or restructure the company. "But at this juncture the Street is telling us that the trader or the short-term investor prevails and, therefore, it's my duty to react to that. As difficult as it's going to be, it must be done."

A REVIEW OF SELECTIONS FROM THE SOURCE READER

Before going on to synthesize the philosophical background with the television presentation, this might be a good time to review certain of the readings in the history of ethics that pertain especially to this topic.

Justice is the oldest topic of philosophical dispute, and the literature, much of which is mentioned in the introductory essay to this chapter, is particularly rich.

Selections for this chapter:

> Plato, *The Republic*, Book I, **Source Reader** p. 18
> Aristotle, *Nicomachean Ethics*, Book V, **Source Reader** p. 54
> The *Bible*, prophecies of *Amos* and *Micah,* **Source Reader** p. 77, 79
> The *Bible*, Scribes and Pharisees, *Matthew*, **Source Reader** p. 85
> John Rawls, *A Theory of Justice*, **Source Reader** p. 146

There is a clear progression of method between Plato's treatment of the subject and Aristotle's. Plato shows that popular intuition is insufficient to the task of discovering a clear and usable notion of justice. His demonstration is completed by Aristotle's systematic approach to the concept, which discovers in "reciprocity" the common core of the several meanings of "justice."

The Biblical approaches provide a foundation for reformist or revolutionary understandings of "justice," intent as they are on unmasking the moralistic hypocrisy that makes systematic injustice appear acceptable to the good citizens of the land. Karl Marx built upon this foundation in his most effective and influential writings. In another course, you may have read *The Communist Manifesto* by Karl Marx and Frederick Engels. (If not, you may want to look at it now; it's short.) Can you see the connections between the religious condemnation of injustice found in the Bible and the atheistic condemnation found in Marx?

John Rawls picks up from Aristotle, with a systematic attempt to define and frame the justification for a notion of social justice adequate to an advanced society.

SYNTHESIS AND DISCUSSION

A number of questions are raised in the video presentation. Among the most obvious are the identity and roles of the major characters. First, what is, or who is, the businessman, the capitalist, and the manager? What do they do? Conflicting images compete in the presentation. Second, what is the moral status of the practices involved? Why is insider trading wrong, if it is? Why are hostile takeovers wrong, if they are? On what grounds can it be claimed that these, and indeed many, of the practices of Wall Street are "unjust," or damaging to our ability to create a just society? Are the laws that attempt to limit these practices more unjust than the practices themselves? Let us take these questions in order.

1. Who is the *businessman* (or businessperson)? Conflicting images recur in our social history. Consider the most popular ones:

The businessman as insatiable destroyer. This is the shark of the takeover dramas, the moustache-twirling villainous landlord of the early 1900s melodrama, the factory-owner as Charles Dickens saw him, the banker foreclosing on the family farm. This enemy of the human race will do anything, absolutely anything, to make more money, to get richer. Already wealthy beyond belief, he is not deterred in his predations by any considerations of justice or the welfare of anyone beyond himself. His desires are financial, not political; otherwise, he is indistinguishable from Thucydides' Athenians, who casually assumed that "might makes right," and would allow no argument from moral principle to slow down their attack on a weaker adversary (Thucydides, **Source Reader** p. 8).

The businessman as community fixture. Someone, after all, had to stock in the groceries, peddle the tin, bring in tools and dry goods. The American small town businessman is often portrayed as beneficent, fulfilling a necessary function in the life of the town: making a living but nothing beyond a living, hiring the youngsters, hosting the gathering of the old boys around the cracker barrel, and contributing to all the local charities and parades. We find the closest parallel to this pastoral image in the contented citizens of Plato's communities, cheerfully accepting assignment to those tasks for which they are best suited, grateful for whatever the community gives them for a living, avoiding the accumulation of wealth (Plato, **Source Reader** p. 31)

The businessman as visionary. This is the hero of the bestselling autobiographies, committed to some machine, product, or service and committed to bringing it to the public. (One thinks of Henry Ford in his younger days.) This is the brilliant executive, able beyond her contemporaries to see the role of her industry in the distant future, toward which she guides it. And these are the heroes of the business writers—devoted to value, committed to the company, obsessed with quality—characterized, in a word, by "excellence." As far as I can tell, they mean the same by that word as Aristotle did by *arete*, which he made the keystone of his Ethics, and which we still translate as "excellence" or "virtue" (Aristotle, **Source Reader** p. 47).

We bring up these types (or stereotypes), along with their ancient parallels, for two reasons: First, they were all there on the videotape that you have seen. Epstein, Joseph, Goldsmith, and Flom defended the businessman's unlimited right to go after money and more money (for the shareholders), an approach that Wirth found infuriating. Wirth was defending the businessman as having a function within the community, providing jobs, supporting the university, altogether being a good citizen, an image for which Goldsmith had complete contempt. And Mercer and Beré defended the product-orientation of the visionary businessman as essential to long-term competitiveness. (Harry Oldman, the main character of the hypothetical, seems to have been that type of businessman.)

Second, the point of the Greek parallel is to show that there is nothing new under the sun while human beings are the subject of discussion. Business as we know it did not exist in the Athens familiar to Thucydides, Plato, and Aristotle. The arena in which they strove with each other was politics, and in the three forms of political activity—the unbridled pursuit of conquest or power, the acceptance of a function in the community appropriate to your talents, and the disciplined effort in pursuit of preeminence in virtue—is a rough but perfectly workable model for the types of the American businessman.

2. Who is the *capitalist* and who is the *manager*? These are questions that used to be easier to answer. Once, the only resources for a businessman to invest were his own (on hand or borrowed), and no one else could run the company because no one else knew what he had in mind for

it, so management and capital were one. Now the company is owned by distant investors, "represented" by a board of directors that they "elect" at a distance, the managers are products of the business schools, and the vision is nowhere at all. Here is where the trouble begins.

The *capitalist* is someone with money who does not need all of the money to live and is therefore willing to invest some of it in enterprises that are not guaranteed to succeed. The assumption of risk—the willingness to give your money to someone else to spend, knowing you may never see any of it again—defines the capitalist investor, and the practice of funding business enterprise, especially at the outset of the enterprise, with risk capital, defines "capitalism" as an economic system. Investors come in two types, "free" and "bound" (or "early" and "contemporary").

The *free investor* is the true capitalist: her money is her own, to invest as she sees fit. Why would she want to put her money into new or otherwise risky businesses? One reason might be to make more money, at a higher return than she can get from the bank or government savings bonds. That, at least, is what the system assumes she wants. But she might have quite different reasons to invest: she might believe in the product, or the industry, or the service they are performing for the country, or she might just like and trust the entrepreneur who asked for the money—either because she thinks she's a good business manager or simply because they're friends. The important point is that the money is hers to increase or lose; she is free to choose to take no dividends at all for four years while research and development proceed, or to watch the price of a share of the stock dip, or peak, while doing nothing at all about it.

The *bound investor* enjoys none of those freedoms. He is not investing his own money, but managing someone else's. He is a hired money manager who will lose his job if the investments he picks do not yield profit abundantly, more abundantly than the market as a whole. He wields enormous power—typically the funds that he is managing outweigh those of any combination of individual investors—and he cannot choose to accept anything but the highest possible immediate yield. If the price of a share of stock shows no sign of rising soon, the manager must look for ways to sell it; if it peaks because of takeover rumors, the manager must immediately sell it to the arbitrager, for there is no more efficient way to increase the value of the fund for which he is responsible.

The bound investor becomes a major problem for most publicly owned corporations, especially corporations where major research projects or reinvestment are periodically required if the company is to remain competitive, for any halt in the flow of earnings to shareholders will put the company in play and probably result in breaking it up. There is no villainy here: the largest funds that those money managers manage are the pension funds of the employees of America, and their astuteness in the market results in comfortable retirements for millions of secretaries and teachers. One of the most powerful of these funds, CREF, is quietly accumulating the money that I myself will live on after I retire; I am hardly in a position to condemn their practices. But the resulting pressure on the corporation to abandon long-term ventures, where success is not certain anyway, in favor of the instant distribution of cash, may be damaging to the corporation and bad for American industry in the long run. So at least, think the corporate directors on the television presentation.

The *corporate manager* is a professional, whose skills in management were acquired in business school and are equally applicable in any industry. She may very well choose to go into an industry whose product excites her, or whose good fortunes she thinks are essential to the future of the U.S. But the essence of her management is skill in turning resources into distributable profits and wise reinvestments. She's under a fair amount of pressure to concentrate on the profits as is our "capitalist" above.

The manager bears a *fiduciary* responsibility to the company and its owners, the shareholders. The word comes from the Latin *fides*, or "faith"; the manager must keep faith with the owners, and not betray their trust. Those are unabashedly moral terms: they mean that the obligation that the manager has to serve her company is not just prudential (in her best interest, if she wants to stay employed at that high salary) or legal (accountable at law if her actions should work against the interests of the shareholders), but also moral. She has made them a promise, a promise that they will find very difficult to enforce, given their distance from the firm and its affairs. Therefore it is her responsibility to make sure that she keeps that promise faithfully.

The content of that promise and the side-constraints that limit its execution have been a matter of serious dispute in the last decades. Everyone agrees that the manager must not be "selfish," but must faithfully carry out his responsibilities. But to whom are those responsibilities finally owed, and what behavior counts as selfish? In the end, is the manager doing the responsible thing when he withholds profits from the shareholders to serve the community? Or does responsibility require the reverse? Since the 1960s, we have reversed our assumptions about shareholders' rights and managers' motivations; see the attached chart for a summary of the reversal.

3. What is *insider trading* and why is it *wrong*? *Insider trading* is not defined on the taped presentation, nor can it be defined. As Lester Thurow points out, insider trading does not name a *malum in se* (something wrong in itself), which is universally recognized, like murder or horse

THE DILEMMA OF THE RESPONSIBLE MANAGER: THE NOTION OF FIDUCIARY RESPONSIBILITY

Everyone agrees that in managing a large publicly-held corporation, the managers must not act selfishly, but must act according to their responsibilities to the people they serve. But just what *that* means depends on your theory of management:

	THEORY I (1960s) "LIBERAL"	THEORY II (1980s) "CONSERVATIVE"
Statement of the Theory	The corporation is a guest in society, which by its laws allows it to accumulate money and power. It must use these goods to help the community.	The corporation is created by its owners for the sole purpose of producing a return on their investment. All other purposes are irrelevant.
RESPONSIBILITY: What managers are supposed to do	Take care of the employees, the community, and only then the shareholders. Be "socially responsible," or exercise "corporate responsibility."	Return the maximum amount to the owners, for whom the managers are merely "agents." Cut all costs; boost price of share of stock.
SELFISHNESS: What managers are *not* supposed to do	Hog all the money the company makes for themselves and the shareholders.	Hog all the money the company makes for themselves and their private purposes: luxurious offices and contributions to pet charities.
Dilemma	How to keep the company profitable enough to survive.	How to protect the people who keep the company going.

WHAT IS THE MANAGER REALLY SUPPOSED TO DO?

Note: In the early nineteenth century, the terms "liberal" and "conservative" would have meanings diametrically opposed to those above. The community-centered "conservative" (Edward Burke) would have denied that any private party had a right to make a profit at the expense of the community; the "liberal" (J.S. Mill) was in favor of economic liberty and free enterprise.

143

thievery; most countries don't have any such prohibitions. It is criminal because our regulations and regulators (the Securities Exchange Commission) say it is. And as Representative Wirth points out, the SEC has no intention of giving it a clear definition, because brokers and lawyers will behave themselves much better if they *do not know* what acts may land them in jail.

Can we live with this? The topic of the day, after all, is "justice." As Thomas Aquinas points out, a law is no law at all if it is not just, and one of the defining characteristics of just law is that it be clearly promulgated, to all who are affected by it (to whom it might be applied), in advance of any attempts to enforce it. Yet here is a "law," or attempt at a law, which exists only because an enforcement agency says it exists, and which is defined only by selective enforcement action. Is it just to deprive a citizen of liberty or property for an act that is defined as criminal only after the fact and at the convenience of the enforcement agency?

As to "why is it wrong," it is wrong, apparently, because it is unjust. But three different, and logically distinct, types of injustice are presented in the television discussion as the reason why insider trading is a breach of justice:

a. It tilts the level playing field. Hence it is unfair, as a race is unfair if one runner has to run in the tall grass, or against the wind, or under some other handicap, and the others do not (unless the handicap was introduced *in order to* make things fair among unequally qualified runners). When one player in the game has information that the others do not have, he has an unjustifiable advantage and it isn't fair that he should win.

But does this justification make any sense at all? Is the playing field ever level when Boone Pickens and I are playing against each other? Lester Thurow calls these laws "a species of high-level fraud" because they give the impression that a fair game is being played by all when really, the pros, who are the experienced players, have all the advantages of information they have legally gained and instant access to the selling floor, and you and I have no chance at all.

b. It is a violation of that fiduciary responsibility mentioned above: If an officer of a corporation uses information for his own benefit that he has received because of his position of responsibility in the corporation, he breaks his promise to serve only the corporation, and not himself, in the use of those powers that he has by virtue of his office. He accepted the powers of office under a set of rules governing how they should be used, and now he breaks them to his own advantage, and that is not fair.

c. It is violation of property rights, or theft, in that he is taking secrets that belong not to him but to the company for his own use without the permission of the company.

All three explanations of the wrongness of insider trading are species of justice, and all of them are sensible enough. But they apply in slightly different circumstances. Whatever you did to become an insider trader, under (a) you must have gained an advantage others did not have, under (b) you must be an officer of the company, and under (c) you must have come by the information illicitly, without the company's permission. So if you are charged with insider trading, you may successfully defend against one ground for the charge only to find yourself faced with the same charge on totally different grounds.

With this discussion in front of us, we are led to ask, on two counts, do the insider trading laws aid the cause of justice or hinder it?

a. From the point of view of the small investor, no one satisfactorily answered Lester Thurow when he charged that the field cannot be made level and that keeping laws in place ostensibly in order to keep the field level presents the appearance that the field *is* level; that therefore the laws tempt people into unfair games, in which they are sure to lose.

b. From the point of view of the trader, he may be prosecuted at any moment for violating an undefined law on one of several grounds; he may know no more about the law when he has been fined millions and sent to jail than he did before he was indicted. Nowhere else in our law do we tolerate such kangaroo justice. Should we tolerate it here?

Perhaps not. On the other hand, if we give an understaffed enforcement agency the job of keeping practices fair in a very complex field, a field where the best and the brightest of the nation labor daily to find new ways to make millions for their equally clever clients, we may make a grave error if we define law too clearly or provide precise information about our enforcement practices. All such guidance will do is reassure those who, even now, are devising the newest set of shady deals and shadowy practices, that they are home safe in what they do, since the law did not foresee what they are doing and forbid it by name.

4. Is this where we want to concentrate the *wealth* and *talent* of the nation? Stand back from the situation and consider for a moment:

Wealth. The amount of money that changes hands on Wall Street on any given business day equals the GNP of several smaller countries. The amount that changes hands during a hostile takeover (the scenario on the television presentation) could house all the homeless in New York City. The amount made by any big player in the course of one of these deals equals the life earnings of most of the working people in the country. And nothing gets accomplished. We are told that the company under attack is "cleansed," and that that is somehow good for the competitiveness of America; but there is no evidence of any general economic benefit or growth in exports as a result of this activity. Not one widget is produced, no grain is grown, no lunches are served. Nothing, but a good deal of money changing hands. Is this *their* money, to spend as they like, with as much right to seek $100 million profit as the boy next door has to set up a lemonade stand? Or is this *our* money, the public's money, which we have a right to see is spent toward the general good—toward saving or creating jobs, toward changing the balance of trade in our favor, toward housing the homeless and healing the sick? None of these questions, first raised at the start of the chapter, have been answered by the television presentation.

Talent. In general, the bright young people will go where the rewards are highest; that is why we call them "rewards." A society states its basic values when it assigns its rewards and sets the conditions for getting them. A society is in balance when its rewards are distributed, not evenly, but in a proportion that will secure an appropriate number of practitioners in any trade, business, or profession.

Our assignment system has been, historically, the free market, surrounded by legal conditions (like licensing) for participation in free market rewards. We assume that when the number in a given occupation falls below the society's need the material reward of that occupation will rise until enough talent is lured into it to fill the need and restore the society to equilibrium. The licensing requirements will make sure that the occupants are well qualified to fulfill their function, and the laws surrounding the practice will be sufficiently severe to discourage shady dealings.

But new financial practices came up so fast on the Street that all those balances didn't work. Suddenly the free-market rewards for wheeling and dealing on the stock market were so high that a disproportionate number of bright youngsters were attracted into the trade, which expanded beyond belief, and well beyond its function in the society, if, indeed, it ever had one. Should there be better, more directive, more balanced ways of assigning talent?

The question is not a minor or short-term personnel problem. On a national level: Can we afford to starve medicine, and agriculture, and manufacturing, for the sake of the "freedom" of the least mature of our citizens to choose their own "calling"? Since the Greeks, we have known that most citizens are greedy to the point of total loss of self-control when large amounts of money suddenly seem to be available (recall Plato's Oligarchic State; Plato, **Source Reader** p. 36). Young people will ordinarily choose a career that promises to satisfy that greed, simply because they have not lived long enough to know better. In this case, the trade promises rewards beyond the power of most youngsters to resist.

When we let them follow the dollar sign to Wall Street and the twilight world of the traders, we foresce terrible damage to them spiritually, to the rest of our society economically, and to the nation politically. May we, or must we, permit this to happen in the name of "freedom"? Put it another way: when the immediate and specific material welfare of the individual seems to conflict with the long term and diffuse welfare of the society, which should take precedence? And when the freedom of the individual seems to conflict with justice in the distribution of goods in the society, which should take precedence?

QUESTIONS FOR YOUR REFLECTION

1. You have seen, in the Insider Trading issue, a case where inadequate law desperately tries to keep up with current practice. Consider the following questions:

- What makes *this* regulation so difficult? Why do we not have the same trouble regulating the practice of medicine? What is peculiar about financial practices in this regard?
- Can you think of any other areas where we want to keep the law unclear to deter wrongdoers? If so, what? What are the similarities and differences between that field and this?
- Can a level playing field be maintained? How? Or why not?
- In this ambiguous situation, what do we do? Abandon the Market to the professionals? Work harder to keep it open to all? Abolish the Market altogether? What do you think?

2. What were Adam Smith's presuppositions about the necessary conditions for making money, that made him so sure that freedom to seek money for the individual would lead to wealth for the nation? How does the hostile takeover fit into that system? If it does, show how; if it does not, show why and draw the implications.

3. We seem to agree that the wealth of the nation will be best taken care of, in general, in private hands, saved or spent on private initiative. What exceptions to that rule do we draw now? (The answer could run to hundreds of items; select representative ones.) Why do we make exceptions in those cases? Does the rationale for any one of those cases suggest a basis for public intervention in the exchanges of wealth that take place in the financial markets?

4. Where, in general, does the responsibility of the corporate executive lie? Is she primarily accountable to the shareholders, to the local community, or to the polity at large? Say what the law is, but also say what it should be, say why, and give some examples of implementation.

5. Construct a skit in which the major characters are Plato, the prophet Amos, and Sir James Goldsmith, discussing the desirability of current financial practices on Wall Street. On what matters would they agree? On what would they differ?

6. Suppose a long-lost uncle died and left you $100,000. What would you do with it? On what principles would you base your decisions on how to use it? How important is the concept of distributive justice in your decision-making process? How important is making more money?

SUGGESTIONS FOR FURTHER READING

Special Supplementary Text:
ROBERT HEILBRONER. *The Nature and Logic of Capitalism*. New York: W. W. Norton, 1985.

BARRY, BRIAN. *The Liberal Theory of Justice*: a *Critical Examination of the Principal Doctrines in A Theory of Justice by John Rawls*. Oxford, England: Clarendon Press, 1973.

BEAUCHAMP, TOM L. AND NORMAN E. BOWIE. *Ethical Theory and Business*. Englewood Cliffs, NJ: Prentice Hall, 3rd ed. 1988.

BELLAH, ROBERT N., ET AL. *Habits of the Heart*. New York: Harper & Row, 1985.

BLOCKER, H. GENE AND ELIZABETH SMITH, EDS. *John Rawls' Theory of Social Justice*. Athens, OH: Ohio University Press, 1980.

BOWIE, NORMAN E. *Business Ethics*. Englewood Cliffs, NJ: Prentice Hall, 1982.

BOWIE, NORMAN E. *Towards a New Theory of Distributive Justice*. Amherst, MA: University of Massachusetts Press, 1971.

BUCHANAN, ALLEN. *Ethics, Efficiency, and the Market*. Totowa, NJ: Rowman and Allenheld, 1985.

BUCHHOLZ, ROGENE A. *Essentials of Public Policy for Management*. Englewood Cliffs, NJ: Prentice Hall, 1985.

CAVANAGH, G. F. *American Business Values in Transition*. Englewood Cliffs, NJ: Prentice Hall, 1976.

CHAMBERLAIN, NEIL W. *The Limits of Corporate Responsibility*. New York: Basic Books, 1973.

DANIELS, NORMAN, ED. *Reading Rawls: Critical Studies of A Theory of Justice*. New York: Basic Books, 1975.

DEGEORGE, RICHARD T. *Business Ethics*. New York: Macmillan, 1982.

DONALDSON, THOMAS. *Corporations and Morality*. Englewood Cliffs, NJ: Prentice Hall, 1982.

FREEMAN, R. EDWARD. *Strategic Management: A Stakeholder Approach*. New York: Columbia University Press, 1984.

FRIEDMAN, MILTON. *Capitalism and Freedom*. Chicago: University of Chicago Press, 1948.

HALBERSTAM, DAVID. *The Reckoning*. New York: William Morrow and Company, 1986.

HAYEK, FRIEDRICH. *Individualism and Economic Order*. Chicago: University of Chicago Press, 1948.

HAYEK, FRIEDRICH. *The Mirage of Social Justice*. Chicago: University of Chicago Press, 1976.

KIPNIS, KENNETH AND DIANA T. MEYERS. *Economic Justice*. Totowa, NJ: Rowman and Allenheld, 1985.

LADD, JOHN. "Morality and the Ideal of Rationality in Formal Organizations," *Monist* 54 (October 1970): 488-516.

MACPHERSON, C. B. *The Life and Times of Liberal Democrats*. New York: Oxford University Press, 1977.

MARX, KARL. *Economic and Philosophical Manuscripts*, in *Karl Marx, Early Writings*. ed. T. B. Bottomore. London: C. A. Watts, 1963.

NAISBITT, JOHN AND PATRICIA ABURDENE. *Re-inventing the Corporation*. New York: Warner Books, 1985.

NOZICK, ROBERT. *Anarchy, State and Utopia*. New York: Basic Books, 1974.

O'TOOLE, JAMES. *Vanguard Management*. Garden City, NY: Doubleday, 1985.

PETERS, TOM (THOMAS J.), *A Passion for Excellence*. New York: Random House, 1985.

PETERS, TOM (THOMAS J.), *Thriving on Chaos*. New York: Knopf, 1987.

PETERS, THOMAS J. AND ROBERT H. WATERMAN, JR. *In Search of Excellence*. New York: Warner Books, 1982.

POSNER, RICHARD A. *The Economics of Justice*. Cambridge: Harvard University Press, 2nd ed. 1983.

RAWLS, JOHN. *A Theory of Justice*. Cambridge: Harvard University Press, 1971.

REGAN, TOM, ED. *Just Business*. New York: Random House, 1984.

SETHI, PRAKASH S. *Up Against the Corporate Wall: Modern Corporations and Social Issues of the Eighties*. Englewood Cliffs, NJ: Prentice Hall, 1982.

STERBA, JAMES. *The Demands of Justice*. South Bend, IN: University of Notre Dame Press, 1980.

TRUMP, DONALD J. *Trump: The Art of the Deal*. New York: Random House, 1988.

TULEJA, TAD. *Beyond the Bottom Line: How Business Leaders are Turning Principles into Profits*. New York: Facts on File Publications, 1985.

VELASQUEZ, MANUEL G. *Business Ethics: Concepts and Cases*. Englewood Cliffs, NJ: Prentice Hall, 1982.

WALTON, CLARENCE C. *Corporate Social Responsibilities*. Belmont, CA: Wadsworth, 1967.

WATERMAN, ROBERT H., JR. *The Renewal Factor*. New York: Bantam, 1987.

WOLFE, TOM. *The Bonfire of the Vanities*. New York: Farrar, Straus and Giroux, 1987.

chapter 8 _____

LOYALTY:
Under Orders, Under Fire (Part 1)

1. What does loyalty mean to you? What has it meant to the leading philosophers of the Western tradition? Is loyalty always exclusive—separating those loyal to one cause from those loyal to another?
2. What commitments are demanded of the soldier, simply because he is a soldier? What conflicts does loyalty raise in military life?
3. Can we understand more of what loyalty, and duty, and discipline, demand of us in everyday peacetime life by looking at the dilemmas peculiar to the military in wartime?

THE CONCEPT OF LOYALTY

The moral universe, as suggested in the first chapter, is one, and essentially unified. We can derive from the requirements of human nature three basic concepts—justice, happiness, and autonomy—and show, as we construct societal values and moral imperatives from these concepts, that they are logically independent and can, in practice, conflict. But we can also show that in theory each should entail and encompass the others, such that anyone who would accept only one of them could easily be committed to the other two.

Thus Plato, in his elaboration of the results of justice in the soul, readily concludes that the person in whom justice resides must be also the most generous of people, honest, free, and respectful of the freedom of others (Plato, **Source Reader** p. 34). And John Stuart Mill and other Utilitarians have no difficulty in deriving the essentials of justice and freedom from the basic value of human happiness (J. S. Mill, **Source Reader** p. 166).

Loyalty, too, extends as a value to encompass the whole of morality, at least in the hands of its most famous advocate, the American philosopher Josiah Royce. For Royce, "loyalty" springs from the most basic recognition by a human being that there is real value outside the self. That recognition of value—the greatness of God, the value of society, or the dignity of the individual—is followed by an internal act, an engagement of the self to the service of that value, that the modern mind will call "commitment." It follows that if we are loyal to a value, we are committed to respect the individuals who share that value, to promote the happiness of all who fall under its sway, and to preserve the formal structures that make personal commitments permanent and functional (Royce, **Source Reader** p. 143).

Above all, loyalty can never undermine itself. If we are to be loyal to anything we must be loyal to loyalty itself, just as, if we are bound to obey this or that moral imperative, we must also be bound to obey the imperative that instructs us to obey moral imperatives. "Loyalty to loyalty" (Royce's phrase) entails the duty to respect the commitments, or the loyalties, of others, (i.e. to respect them as moral agents, as we find in Immanuel Kant, **Source Reader** p. 137). It entails further the duty to promote the interests or happiness of persons to whom we are bound by loyalty; it entails the duty to respect justice, constitution, and law in the society to which we are loyal. So loyalty is simply one way of focusing the whole duty of man; it is appropriate to no particular profession, practice, group, or orientation, but is, according to Royce, the most general moral notion there is.

For purposes of this chapter, however, we will consider only a narrower sense of loyalty appropriate to a specific situation—that of the military in combat. When we focus our attention on the particular type of loyalty expected of the military, especially in time of war, we are dealing with a much more specific concept. The soldier has *chosen* to serve his country, in a hierarchical order where he must obey commands, in certain types of situations for a certain length of time. These duties, once he is in uniform, are no longer to be debated. It is the soldier's duty to serve his country by placing his life between that country and its enemies, in the branch of military service to which he is assigned, through obedience to his commanding officer. If doubts assail him on the goodness of any of these objectives, it is his moral duty to extract himself from the situation, at whatever cost to himself, as rapidly as possible.

That "duty," a moral concept that recurs throughout the discussions of this chapter, can also be understood in two senses. In itself, the term "duty," like "justice" or "loyalty," has the broadest designation in ethical discourse. "It is my duty to do this" is all but synonymous with "I should do this," or "It is right to do this," sentences that apply no matter what ethical theory or argument is about to be offered to justify the claim. But in ordinary speaking about matters of morality, "duty" has a tone, or aura, to it that distinguishes such claims from, say, Utilitarian claims that a certain action will bring happiness to many, or a claim that certain courses of action will make us wiser or more virtuous people. Duty is what you *must* do, whether or not it will make anyone happier, whether or not it will make us better people. The notion of duty calls attention to the fundamentally deontological nature of moral perception: do what you must do, though the earth should perish, though the heavens should fall in ruins. Duty is not oriented to consequence or goal, hence we cannot ordinarily avoid our duty simply because undesirable consequences may follow from doing it. When you are told to do something *because it is your duty*, you are not being invited to think out the consequences of obeying, nor to devise creative ways to reach the same goal without doing what you were told to do. You are being told to do what you are told and save the thinking for later.

Now, why would we ever want people to work this way? As we have seen, creative moral thinking is one of the highest functions of the human being, if not the highest. The ability to think through the moral imperatives that we are given by our tradition or our superiors, to understand them, to make them our own—or, alternatively, to rethink and ultimately reject them—is our most characteristically human faculty. To be autonomous—to obey laws that we ourselves have laid down—is as serious an imperative as we have in the moral life. Why would we ever want humans to suspend that ability and become, like trained animals, mindless obeyers of orders?

Three characteristics of imperatives would make it desirable to have human beings obey without thinking: (1) With respect to *content*: if the act commanded is inherently repugnant to those who have to act, it is good for them to learn to obey as automatically as possible, in order to maintain their emotional distance from the act. For example, while things may be different now, medical students traditionally were handed scalpels and pointed at their first cadavers without having any opportunity to discuss the significance of carving up dead bodies. The less they thought about it, and the quicker they got on with it, the thinking went, the sooner they would develop confidence in dealing with the body, the confidence that they need as practitioners. (2) With respect to *context*: if the situation requires very rapid, unforeseeable, deployment of large amounts of highly coordinated human effort, you must have people drilled to obey orders without thinking—for any delay can destroy the effectiveness of the whole effort. (3) With respect to *complexity*: if what these large numbers of people have to do, quickly, is so inherently complex that explanations are impossible—even if time permitted and emotional distance were not a factor in the circumstances— then again, we will need people willing to obey orders without asking questions.

Given these three characteristics of commands that must be carried out without question, the exigencies of military life clearly justify the stress on "duty" and discipline that has characterized the traditions of the armed services. We ask the soldier to leave home, family, and career, and enter a situation where his life will be continually at risk. We ask him to learn how to slaughter his fellow human beings, in situations where tens of thousands of troops must move at once or all will be lost. We ask that he risk his life in support of a strategy that is not only monstrously complex but also Top Secret—even if we had time to explain it to him, we would not be permitted to do so. Moreover, in the particular case of military combat, the soldier is required to carry out his duties in fear, with emotion clouding his reason. The military, then, provides an excellent setting to observe and discuss these narrower senses of loyalty and duty.

Of course, that raises a larger question. Granted, *if* we are going to send men off to slaughter on the battlefield, we must train them to act on orders, out of duty, and not out of independent moral assessment of each situation as it comes up. But what justifies our decision to send them out there? If we must turn men into animals or robots in order to fight a war successfully, what can justify war? We know independently that it is wrong to treat individuals only as means to a larger end; wrong to discourage the use of moral judgment; wrong to allow people to kill each other; and therefore completely wrong deliberately to turn men into killing machines for some abstract purpose we may have in mind. Then how shall we ever justify the practice of war, which demands that we do that?

The question is really two questions merged into one. First, is war ever justifiable? The answer to that is, yes, unfortunately. (That's *my* answer. But see representative opinions on the other side in Supplementary Readings, below.) No one, military or otherwise, is in favor of wars. But we live in an imperfect world, where evil and ignorance are real factors in international as well as personal life; delusions of grandeur, power, or historic mission will ever and again seduce nations into waging war upon their neighbors. And when they do, their neighbors have the right, and the duty, to retaliate: to make war in return, to defend themselves and to punish the enemy for the aggression. No one wants war, but in this world, sometimes, we get it. By extension of that right, we may also fight to prevent aggression, or to help an ally defend itself, or to prevent aggression against an ally. This chain of purposes can lead, as we know, to wars that stretch on for years for obscure political purposes. These wars need moral scrutiny, but the appropriate examining body is political, not military.

Second, if war is inevitable, can we tolerate what happens to the human beings fed into its bloody maw; can we even tolerate what happens to the humans fed into the military machine as it prepares for possible war? Royce is helpful in answering this question: as long as personal choice is involved at the outset of any commitment, then the subjection of individual energies to duty is not only harmless, but brings out the best that is in us.

This was Plato's point, in his definition of courage and description of the ideal soldier (Plato, **Source Reader** p. 32).

The ideal soldier has a strong "spirited element" (that we might call "will") which enables him to set aside his own desires, inclinations, and interests in favor of what he sees to be right—his duty. Ideally, the soldier does everything from a sense of duty, and nothing for any other reason. The soldier's goal is honor, and the only appeal that should move him is appeal to honor, which requires that over the length of his life in the military he adhere to his duty. The virtue that distinguishes the soldier from the person unfit for military service is "courage." In popular literature, "courage" seems to apply only during combat; the same quality operative during the boredom of peacetime duty seems better described as "fortitude." They mean the same, and both describe the person who fights when he is called upon to fight, without fear and without Rambo-style emotional involvement, and forbears from fighting when he is called upon to forbear, without complaint or ambition.

The soldier acquires courage through discipline. Instilling discipline is the fundamental purpose of basic training. It teaches a soldier to forget his own desires and impulses by systematically overriding them in compelling dramas of humiliation and teamwork. In basic training, or "boot camp," every scrap of idiosyncrasy or individual pride is eradicated, by a schedule that leaves no time for personal considerations, and by deliberate suppression. That is the reason for the short haircuts and the uniforms. Meanwhile, every successful team effort is rewarded. (The inculcation of discipline is necessary for any institution that makes similar demands of selflessness; many of the same dramas take place in the training period for the Society of Jesus and similar religious orders.)

So the young soldier learns to transfer his desire for personal preeminence and reward (which is brutally discouraged) to a new desire, for the preeminence and reward of unit, team, and country. These become the objects of his loyalty.

Without that discipline, no one, in his right mind, would run *toward* someone who was shooting at him. Nor would soldiers be likely to conform their conduct to group objectives in crisis situations. Above all, no one would be able to tolerate "preparedness"—the meaningless round of drill, inspection, and spit and polish that fills the days of the peacetime army. In sum, no one could count on any band of men in the field in times of real danger. The disciplined soldier, like the Stoic, does his job regardless of the terrors of this life (Epictetus, **Source Reader** p. 94). Ideally, the soldier will do his job completely free of all passion, desire, fear, or anger; it is discipline, a Stoic discipline, that teaches him to do this. Discipline makes courage possible for the individual and national defense possible for the society; it enables the soldier to do his duty and honor his commitment to his nation's defense. Loyalty is an ideal, the fulfillment of which demands subordination of competing desires by discipline.

**THE TELEVISION PRESENTATION: SELECTED QUESTIONS ON
THE MILITARY EXPERIENCE**

This section considers the television presentation or videotape. The recapitulation of the dialogue that follows is not meant to be a word-for-word transcript of the tape, but a summary of the major themes, issues, and opinions that emerged in the conversation. It is for review, and for use as a resource if you include this topic in your term project.

TITLE: "UNDER ORDERS, UNDER FIRE (PART 1)"

Moderator: Professor Charles Ogletree, Jr.

Participants: from left to right on your screen

NEWT GINGRICH
U. S. Representative from Georgia

EVELYN P. FOOTE
Brigadier General, AUS

LOUIS STOKES
U. S. Representative from Ohio

BRIAN JENKINS
Chair, Political Science,
RAND Corporation;
Captain, U. S. Army Special Forces
(1965–68)

TIMOTHY TATUM
Chaplain (Colonel),
U. S. Army War College

EDWARD C. MEYER
General, AUS (Ret.)
Chief of Staff, (1979–83)

PETER JENNINGS
Anchor, Sr. Editor, ABC News

FREDERICK DOWNS, JR.
Director, Prosthetic/Sensory Aids,
Veteran's Administration;
Lieutenant, U. S. Army (1966–69)

DAVID C. JONES
General, USAF (Ret.)
Chairman, Joint Chiefs of Staff
(1978–82)

WILLIAM C. WESTMORELAND
General, AUS (Ret.)

GEORGE M. CONNELL
Colonel, USMC

MIKE WALLACE
Correspondent, CBS News

BRENT SCOWCROFT
Lt. General, USAF (Ret.)

J. BRYAN HEHIR
Department of Social Development and
World Peace,
U. S. Catholic Conference

ROBERT C. STUART
Major, USMC

JAMES E. SERVICE
Vice Admiral, USN (Ret.)

As you read through the dialogue, ask yourself:

1. What is being asked of the soldier? Do we have a right to ask it? Why?
2. What is the soldier's "duty"? Does the prohibition against obeying illegal orders limit that duty?
3. Is the Platonic and Stoic ideal of freedom from all passions appropriate to military life in combat? Why?
4. Is "loyalty" specifically appealed to in the life of the soldier? If not, how is it manifested in military life?

THE COURSE OF THE DIALOGUE

Training Soldiers to Kill

The scene opens in a recruiting center. Gerard Irving Joe (henceforth just call him "GI") has just seen *Rambo* for the third time and wants to go out and fight and shoot guns. Major Stuart readily agrees that GI should join the Marines. But first he must pass certain examinations.

GI passes, and the scene shifts to Boot Camp. Lieutenant Downs, his drill instructor, tells him what to expect. Boot Camp will be hard; especially hard will be learning to obey orders without any "back lip." He will learn to obey instantly; discipline is the purpose of all this training. He will learn hand-to-hand combat—how to kill not only with guns but with grenades, bayonets, trench shovels, whatever comes to hand. GI gets a little nervous; this begins to sound bloody. "It sounds like you're teaching me to become a killing machine." You got it, says the drill instructor. "The bottom line of what you're to do is to kill men and take ground."

Loyalty to Nation

At this point Joe begins to have qualms about all this killing, and seeks out the Chaplain (Tatum). I was taught "Thou shalt not kill," he says; how can it be right for me to kill a man? Chaplain Tatum suggests that they sit down and talk about it for awhile. The killing that is forbidden is the voluntary, premeditated taking of human life, on your own, for your own purposes, Chaplain Tatum explains. Presumably, if you are sent out with the Marines to kill people, it is because your nation has declared war, and therefore you are justified in killing, and therefore it is right to train you to kill. But I certainly hope you don't take that training out into the street and start killing people at random, Tatum says.

Loyalty to Conscience

Fr. Bryan Hehir joins the discussion: It is given that "the function of the military involves the possibility of using force." But that means force legitimately applied—not against just anyone, anytime, in any circumstances. Remember that at the conclusion of the Second World War, the Nuremberg Principles established law for military situations: some orders are unlawful, and you should retain enough of your individuality to know "that you could say 'no' to an order."

Downs swivels in his seat, and grimly concludes the conversation: "He'd better not say 'no' to *my* order."

Covering the News

Phase two of the discussion: We have learned what we have to learn to be good soldiers, and now we are ready to test our training in combat conditions. The chance arises immediately. It seems that South Kosan, our ally, has just been attacked by North Kosan. We have a battalion or so stationed at the point of the attack; we've taken very heavy casualties and lost some ground. What would General Westmoreland do? Activate the chain of command, fight back, get reinforcements, and wage war.

A new question: how will the media deal with this attack? The question is put to Peter Jennings. You have ten minutes before the six o'clock news. Do you report the attack?

Jennings' reply: Yes, very cautiously. Like the generals, we will need reinforcements, more information, a better grasp of the situation. We will say, on the news, that there is an unconfirmed report of an attack; that military sources in Washington will not comment at this time; that we will seek information and continue reporting; that, again, this is unconfirmed.

Is General Westmoreland bothered by these reports? No, he is not—"I could care less" what the reporters are saying at this point. Would Mike Wallace seek more information from him? Yes, he would, in a simulated telephone call: "General, what is going on out there? How much can you tell us about what is going on out there?" Answer: "I will not give you any information."

How would Admiral Service respond to the press? Admiral Service would talk with Jennings—he has "a cooperative arrangement with Peter Jennings, whom I trust implicitly." How does such a relationship develop? Answer: This kind of trust has to be built up over a long period of time. Essentially, it is trust that the situation will not be *mis*represented by the press, that the military will not end up taking the blame for the inevitable blood and pain of combat. Vietnam showed the military how vulnerable it is on this score.

Newt Gingrich joins the conversation, pointing out the new problems raised by "an instantaneous world at the opposite end of morality." Do we really want the mother of a young soldier to find out that her son is dead by seeing him blown to bits on the evening news, before the special duty officers of the

Loyalty to
Truth

armed services have had time to get to her home, tell her in person, soften the blow? We live now in an electronic neighborhood that includes the whole world, and we are going to have to get used to it. "One last comment as a history teacher. December 1861, *The New York Times* printed the exact structural fortifications around Washington and what unit was in each part of the structure. It is the nature of a free press to do its job....aggressively, without much regard for the problems of the military. And I think it's been that way through all our history except for the largest of wars, World War II, and we just have to learn to live with it."

Combatants and Noncombatants

Phase three of the hypothetical situation: A hill, lost in a North Kosanese attack early in the battle, must be retaken. A platoon, led by Downs, is given the job. What do you tell your men? Answer: I tell them what the mission is; that we are outnumbered; that we're to get to the top of that hill; that the hill is full of enemy soldiers, and we are to kill every one—Every one?—yes, I don't want any prisoners—Wounded?—that depends on the situation. "My squad leaders and my platoon sergeant know how I feel about these matters. They'll pass the orders down to the men."

Would "Lieutenant" Jenkins say the same? Answer: We must maintain the difference between combatants and noncombatants. Someone who surrenders has made himself a noncombatant, and you can't kill him. On the other hand, if you're not sure.... In the end, this is a decision that every man is going to have to make for himself. As an officer, I am certainly not going to give that kind of order.

Downs agrees that we are talking about difficult decisions, but reemphasizes: My concern is to protect my men; I really don't care about the enemy; I have an obligation to complete that mission, and I must balance these things. Each officer has his own moral orientation, which he has to live by and live with, and his men better know what it is.

Major Stuart agrees that snap decisions will have to be made in the heat of combat; but has no doubt that the order to "kill everybody" is an improper order.

Fr. Bryan Hehir rejoins the discussion: We have to distinguish here the rules you have to live by and the individual situation that may undermine the application of the rules in a specific instance. We need to know beforehand what is objectively the right thing to do. Here Mr. Jenkins is absolutely right to distinguish between the combatants and the noncombatants—you cannot kill noncombatants, and killing the wounded is wrong. But in combat an individual may be overwhelmed by fear and commit an act

Loyalty to the Unit

that is objectively wrong without being subjectively "guilty" of committing a crime.

George Connell, a colonel, comments: Presumably, we have gone to war to fight evil. We can't break those basic moral rules, forbidding us to kill noncombatants, because then we would become the evil that we are out there to fight. So we can't say simply, "no prisoners." If an enemy soldier is a threat, we kill him. If he surrenders, we *can't* kill him.

Chaplain Tatum is asked to bless the guns for the mission and to pray for its success. Will he do this? No, answers Tatum; I will not bless this or any other mission. I will pray for you, for the men, for everyone's safe return. General Scowcroft comments that he would put no pressure on a chaplain to bless a mission; the chaplain is there to comfort the men, not to play any military role.

Now the scenario changes, just a bit: the mission turns out to be impossible. The hill is much too well defended for this platoon to take it. Everyone's pinned down; people are dying. Lieutenant Downs, what do you do? Retreat? No; radio back for reinforcements to complete the mission. Ah, but it seems that General Meyer already knew the mission could not be completed: it was only a "decoy" (diversionary tactic). Should General Meyer tell Downs of this? Do the men have a right to know they're being used as decoys? Meyer answers: No, nor is the information significant in context. There are not "real" and "decoy" missions, there is only the whole front and a war to win. Whatever deployment of troops will accomplish the overall objectives is justified. Such operations are often militarily advisable, and have been used throughout history.

Downs comments: Your job in this mission, whatever you think of it, is to obey your orders, fulfill your particular role, and if you die doing it, to die honorably. What role is handed to you is of no concern to you. Meyer concurs: The general's professional duty is to deploy the men as effectively as possible; "it is unethical not to be professional."

The Disobedient Soldier

The plot thickens again: One private, seeing the impossibility of the attack and the orders, refuses to go up that hill. What do you do about it? Downs: I will scare him into following orders if I can, drag him if I can't get him moving any other way, and if that fails, shoot him. "This is not a situation in which I have time for argument....And if I have to kill you in order to save the lives of my men, I will make that decision. I will face up to the consequences of that later in a court martial and explain myself, but I know at that exact moment in time, I've got to make that decision. And I will live with it. But you are dead." Would you do the same to another soldier, who won't go up that hill because he is paralyzed by fear? No, says Downs; I'd get him moving somehow. I have no policy on these matters: every man is a different case.

Now suppose that Jennings is there as newsman. He sees the lieutenant shoot the private. Downs: He is *not* there. Jennings: Yes, I am. I would try to stay out of the officer's way. I would not intervene. I *would* get as much as possible on tape. "To use one of the great cliches of journalism, this is the first rough draft of history." I would make no judgments on what happens.

General Westmoreland joins in, questioning the usefulness of press presence at this point. Meanwhile, we need clarification of that "no prisoners" order. There are rules, after all. "You perhaps may have had a psychological warfare unit there broadcasting to the troops, 'Lay down your arms and you'll be safe.' So you attack the hill, and suddenly you see a lot of the soldiers of Kosan throwing down their weapons and holding their hands up. You're not going to kill them." Downs agrees; of course not. The situation determines the possibilities. If everyone starts surrendering, I take prisoners.

General Jones joins the discussion. It might be worthwhile to point out that as policy, "we don't kill prisoners, we don't kill the wounded, we don't shoot our own troops." It is always a possibility that a lieutenant would have to shoot one of his own men, but in all of World War II it never happened. Under the highly unusual, dire circumstances posited here, there are terrible responsibilities on that young officer. He is going to have to live with the responsibility, and the consequences, of that act.

Now let's make the incident public. Mike Wallace is sent the tape of Lieutenant Downs shooting the private. Question: Would you air it? First, Wallace replies, it would take a very long discussion, much the same kind of discussion as we're having here. We would not put it in a slot on the evening news. My hunch is that after due reflection, yes, we would air it, under the rubric that "war is hell," with enough context to make it understandable. The American people have a right to know what goes on in their wars.

The story continues with the introduction of a new scenario. Guerrilla fighters are hiding in a village of about 200 people, including a guerrilla leader (Scarface) who was responsible for the deaths of a number of American soldiers some days ago. It is Colonel Connell's responsibility to search the village. How would he do it? Very thoroughly. He will search people for weapons—yes, women too—he will unbandage the wounded at the hospital to see if those are gunshot wounds, he will search house to house. He doesn't need a search warrant. All of this is unpleasant, but a greater good justifies it.

Now we find Scarface, in an alley. Do you shoot him? Yes. Even if he surrenders? Of course not. I'd *like* to take him prisoner. But most likely, if he makes any threatening gesture at all, I'll kill him.

Loyalty to History

The Right to Know

The Ethical
Choice

The same question is put to Brian Jenkins. There is the guerrilla. He's trying to get away. You can't stop him. What do you do? And Jenkins concludes the program with the theme that has run through it consistently:

I will have to decide, in that split second, what I will do. I should not be in this situation: there should be others surrounding this place, there should be alternatives to killing him. I have my own fear to deal with, and my own uncertainty. In the end, "I would do what I would have to do, and what that would be would be another of the secrets that I will live with for the rest of my life."

A REVIEW OF SELECTIONS FROM THE SOURCE READER

Before going on to synthesize the philosophical background and the television presentation, this might be a good time to review certain of the readings in the history of ethics that pertain especially to this topic.

The virtue, or quality, under consideration in this chapter is a composite of several virtues, treated in various parts of the philosophical literature. We expect of the soldier unflinching service to the cause for which his nation does battle, through uncomplaining obedience to commands from his superior officer, despite the dangers of war. The virtues that comprise this disposition are variously called "courage," "steadfastness," "faithfulness" (or "fidelity"), or "loyalty," and are often summarized under the very general heading "adherence to duty."

Selections for this chapter:

The *Bible*, the story of the Covenant, **Source Reader** p. 69
Plato, *The Republic*, **Source Reader** p. 32
Epictetus, *The Moral Discourses of Epictetus*, **Source Reader** p. 93
Josiah Royce, *Philosophy of Loyalty*, **Source Reader** p. 138

The Covenant between the Israelites and their God may be the first recorded pledge of loyalty or fidelity: the Israelites will remain faithful to their God by exclusive worship and obedience to His Law, and He will remain faithful to them by protecting them (ultimately) in their endeavors and in their occupation of the land that He has promised them. Such a pledge gives the people identity, and gives meaning to their lives and their tribulations. It fills the being of the individual and the agenda of the nation. Josiah Royce takes the subject from that point, placing loyalty in modern contexts.

Plato and Epictetus are dealing with the same quality, from the point of view of the Greek ideal of manhood. One of the qualities that the Greeks considered essential for a man was the ability to endure hardships without flinching (as in the story of the Spartan boy who carried a young fox in his shirt, on his father's instructions, without complaining even as the panicked animal tore through his chest into his heart). The philosophers generalized that quality into the ability to adhere to duty without being swayed by any pain, desire, fear, or other passion.

SYNTHESIS AND DISCUSSION

What points did you find most noteworthy in the video presentation? As the introductory essay for the chapter tries to unify contemporary practical questions with classic sources in philosophical ethics, the Synthesis attempts to unify that background with the elements of the dialogue on the television presentation or videotape.

Points for consideration:

1. Note the person of the soldier, as described in the program. The term that General Meyer used is "professional": a professional soldier makes the best military decision under the circumstances. That decision is the one best calculated to take and hold ground, eliminate enemy troops, protect his own men, and abide by operant rules and policies, given the information that he has at the moment. He is not influenced by desire (ambition, greed, haste), fear (for self or career), or sentiment (compassion for troops). What he does, he does dispassionately, rationally, without joy if he triumphs (he spends that energy preparing for the next encounter) or self-pity if he fails. He accepts his role, his job, and carries out his duty according to his orders, knowing that his task forms a part of a larger whole which depends for its success on his faithfulness to his duty. This soldier derives from Plato, as above (Plato, **Source Reader** p. 32); his approach to life and death, however, is best captured by the Stoics, exemplified by Epictetus (Epictetus, **Source Reader** p. 93).

2. The loyal soldier, faithful to his mission and to his men, was not born that way. As Aristotle points out (Aristotle, **Source Reader** p. 47), virtues are acquired by practice. The soldier in training first performs acts of the appropriate kind under compulsion, and through imposed discipline becomes habituated to performing only acts of the required type. Military discipline explicitly aims to eliminate individual self-assertion, even individual self-consciousness. This suppression of individuality makes habitual performance of duty easier, but moral reflection and the exercise of conscience become much harder. Given that the soldier is required to slaughter his

fellow humans, an act which he is proscribed from performing on his own, it is probably just as well that individual reflection is discouraged. As the chaplain points out, the killing of battle is justified only because the soldier acts, not as his own man, but only as an instrument of the cause. Discipline teaches him to think and act only as a member of the group, an extension of the officer's mind.

Here, of course, is the first of the ethical conflicts. Let us grant that individuality can survive the battering of military service and does not need protection. But when he stands firing his rifle as a member of the group, does the soldier remember that, by the Rules of Land Warfare drawn up after the War Crimes Trials in Nuremberg, Germany, in the years following World War II, he is fully responsible as an individual for any acts that fall outside the Rules, no matter who gave the orders? As Fr. Hehir points out, he had best not *totally* lose touch with his conscience. But as Frederick Downs points out, a disposition to question orders may endanger the survival of his unit, which is why it is the officer's responsibility to make sure that he does obey the orders. Who's right?

3. In the heat of battle, the orders come down: no prisoners, no mercy—and no questions. With luck, the men "understand" the "values" of their officer by this time, so that the orders do not have to be issued in a way that might later prove embarrassing—or incriminating. The orders are clearly improper, as Major Stuart points out. Can they possibly be justified? And when a dissenting soldier protests and refuses to go up that hill, the lieutenant first brutalizes him, and finally kills him, deliberately shooting him through the head. Can "the heat of battle" justify *that* killing as well—isn't this arrest, trial, and execution for a capital crime with no attempt to set in motion the processes of justice? Isn't that murder? Can any of these acts find justification in ethics? Could loyalty require them?

It could be argued that they are indeed justified, by the same values that govern the Rules of Land Warfare. The point is survival. As Thomas Hobbes reminds us (Hobbes, **Source Reader** p. 106), the primary right of all humans, whose search for protection first brought them together in societies, is the right to life. The individual's right to life can be set aside only in the interests of the group's survival; the group can lay its own survival on the line only for the survival of society. In war, the survival of the nation is at stake. That is what gives the war its moral warrant, or justification for being. (And that is why "police actions," like Vietnam, where only policy is at stake, sit so awkwardly on the conscience of the society.) For the sake of the war, one may sacrifice the group: the mission comes first, the men second. Consistent with the accomplishment of the mission, the survival of the group is paramount. For the sake of its own survival in this very dangerous mission, the unit may not encumber itself with prisoners (unless all of the enemy surrender at once, in which case, as Downs indicated, his orders immediately revert back to the Rules). Nor can the unit risk attacks from behind by enemy soldiers spared out of mercy. Nor can the unit stand idle, helpless targets of enemy fire, while the captain argues patiently with a private whose training is not up to the present set of orders. Nor can it tolerate dividing the unit into those who choose to go up the hill into likely death—the smaller the number, the likelier the death—and those who choose to remain below watching. Killing the individual is entirely justified by the need to protect the group.

On the other hand, the nation will not survive if it does not affirm, in general observe, and as far as feasible enforce, the Rules of Land Warfare or some reasonable equivalent. A nation must not attempt to survive on power alone; without a conviction that it is good, that it is engaged in a good fight against an evil power, it will not fight well. The soldiers must be convinced that their fight is justified because they are fighting for something worthy of their sacrifices.

The second conflict, then, is between the unit on the battlefield and the moral consciousness of the nation as a whole. Can we as a nation maintain our moral warrant if our soldiers shoot prisoners as a matter of (informal) policy? *Do we want to know about it?* What's the matter with us if we don't?

4. That brings us to the final point: the nature of, and conditions for, the "just war." It is very significant for our purposes that North Kosan apparently attacked South Kosan. Refer at this point to the special supplementary book for this teaching unit, Michael Walzer's *Just and Unjust Wars*. To summarize, somewhat more simply than he has it, the paradigm case of a just war, recall that it requires:

- The pre-existence of two identifiable, independent political entities; we may call them Aggressor and Innocent. (The theory does not tell us whether the entities are admirable or otherwise, but it helps in practice if Aggressor is otherwise nasty—fascist, whatever—and Innocent is otherwise lovable.);
- A clear-cut boundary between them;
- An attack across that boundary by Aggressor, unprovoked by Innocent;
- An injury suffered by Innocent, clearly intended by Aggressor.

At this point, Innocent's retaliatory attack, continuing on if possible into Aggressor's territory to punish Aggressor, is just.

Every public relations (propaganda) effort carried on by any nation at war attempts to make that nation look like Innocent in the scenario above. Every once in a while a war comes along that allows us to play that role: The Allied Forces in the Second World War in general had that role to play. The United States in particular, victim of a sneak attack at Pearl Harbor that seriously damaged our Navy, played that role throughout the war. With World War II in our immediate past, within the living memory of many of us, the frustrations of the United States military engagements since that time rankle with special bitterness. Korea, where we were not allowed to proceed into Chinese territory to clean out the sanctuaries used by the North Koreans; Vietnam, where we were not even supposed to *think* of winning, and our allies seemed considerably more corrupt and cowardly than our enemies seemed evil; Lebanon, where 250 Marines were killed by no identifiable entity at all, and where the "innocent, noncombatant" civilians robbed the American bodies and sniped at the rescuers. Is Central America next?

The theorist would point out that we have lost the thread of the good soldier if we dwell on this point. The soldier's duty does not change just because the policy he is carrying out changes. Policy may be made for good or ill, more or less wisely; if only it is the real policy of the authentic policy-makers, it is legitimate and binding on the nation. It may or may not involve deploying troops. If it does involve deploying troops, it is probably crucial to the policy that the troops do exactly what they are told. But then the police action or politically motivated engagement becomes one more case of the "diversionary tactic." In the longer light of the whole policy of the nation, the military action may be essential, possibly the key to the success of the policy, and the soldier who loves his country must fight on with the same will as he would fight under direct attack.

In summary: We have seen that the loyalty of the soldier in combat differs from loyalty generally in two ways:

1. As the part differs from the whole. For Royce, "loyalty" includes the whole of the duty to be moral: to accept the responsibility to choose our commitments, to make moral obligations our own, to discover and create the means of carrying them out, to stand firm against all efforts to sway us from those commitments by fear or temptation, and to sacrifice, if necessary, pleasure, property, even life itself, in their service. For the military, the choice of commitment, obligation, and manner of carrying them out are given; only the last two are the business of the armed services. Military loyalty is loyalty to your own country, whatever that may be; to the honor of your unit, to which you are assigned; and to your duty, as it is presented to you.

2. In its life-and-death implications. Rarely in other than military service does loyalty require your life. You have seen the problems of loyalty agonizingly focused—as duty seems to require that you take human life, and equally that you spare it; that you bend all to accomplish the mission,

and equally that you keep some part of yourself prepared to question your orders; and simultaneously, that you do whatever has to be done to protect your unit, to serve your country, and to serve your own ideals.

There is no easy resolution to these conflicts. Human life is sacred, and yet, in the situations dramatized here, we as a nation require frightened youngsters to sacrifice their own lives and the lives of others for some higher value. What value could be higher?, we are sometimes forced to ask. At the least, we must reflect on this question, and keep in mind the real situations of military combat, with all the human agony they involve, before we casually decide that we are "hawks" or "doves" on foreign policy. Our instructions to our elected representatives, on how they should vote the next time someone proposes to send our troops somewhere in the world to enforce our policies, must incorporate our personal conclusions on the value of military action, our knowledge of the situations to which we are subjecting our sons, and our recognition of the tragic life and death choices that will be made in the course of any military engagement.

QUESTIONS FOR YOUR REFLECTION

1. The Greek poet Homer (c. 800 B.C.) once claimed that "War is the business of men"; much of the rest of our inherited culture contains an undercurrent of admiration for military action and adventure. You have seen some of the best members of the armed services describing and discussing the kind of situation that men under fire will encounter. What is your reaction?

- To work for peace at all costs?
- To agree with Homer and the others that this enterprise brings out the best in men, and should be encouraged as part of every young man's life?
- Somewhere in between? Where?

2. What do you think of the participants in the discussion (especially Frederick Downs, who agreed to defend the most controversial positions)? Are they monsters? Heroes? Decent people in extraordinary situations?

3. What does loyalty mean in your life? To what extent does it encompass every virtue? To what extent is it narrower, because, like the military officers you have seen on the program, you have accepted some of the objects of loyalty as "given?" At some point in your life, should you reexamine these original commitments?

Which ones take priority? Can you list your loyalties in order of priority? In what order would you put, for instance, the items on the following list:

- Family
- Friends (social group)
- Colleagues (the people you work with)
- Calling (your life's work)
- Employer
- Town or region
- Country
- Church or religious group

Which of these loyalties limit others? Which of them reinforce others? Say how, in both cases.

4. What is your evaluation of the Platonic/Stoic ideal of life—living without passions, or at least with passions sufficiently under control that you can act without letting them rule you? Is it possible? Is it desirable?

5. How does Royce's notion of loyalty complement Plato and Epictetus in describing an ideal for military life?

SUGGESTIONS FOR FURTHER READING

Special Supplementary Text:
MICHAEL WALZER. *Just and Unjust Wars: A Moral Argument with Historical Illustrations.* New York: Basic Books, 1977.

ARON, RAYMOND. *Peace and War.* New York: Praeger, 1967.

BEER, FRANCIS A. *Peace Against War: The Ecology of International Violence.* San Francisco: WH Freeman & Co., 1981.

BOULDING, KENNETH. *Stable Peace.* Austin, TX: University of Texas Press, 1978.

BROWN, HARRISON. *The Human Future Revisited.* New York: Norton, 1978.

CLAUSEWITZ, KARL VON. *On War.* trans. Michael Howard and Peter Paret. Princeton: Princeton University Press, 1976.

EISENHOWER, DWIGHT D. *Crusade in Europe,* New York: Doubleday, 1948.

GRAVES, ROBERT. *Goodbye to All That.* (rev. ed. New York: Doubleday, 1957).

GRAY, J. GLENN. *The Warriors: Reflections on Men in Battle.* New York: Harper and Row, 1967.

KISSINGER, HENRY A. *Nuclear Weapons and Foreign Policy.* New York: Doubleday Books, 1958.

PAULING, LINUS. *No More War.* New York: Dodd Mead, 1975.

RAMSEY, PAUL. *The Just War: Force and Political Responsibility.* New York: University Press of America, 1968.

SCHELL, JONATHAN. *The Fate of the Earth.* New York: Alfred Knopf, 1982.

YOUNG, DESMOND. *Rommel: The Desert Fox.* New York: Harper & Row, 1958.

chapter 9 _____

CONFIDENTIALITY:

Under Orders, Under Fire (Part 2)

QUESTIONS TO KEEP IN MIND AS YOU READ THE CHAPTER

1. How important is it to keep a secret—especially if it is wrongdoing that is being concealed? Why does someone place you under an obligation by merely telling you that something is "confidential"?

2. We are studying military life—one of the most mercilessly open lives there could be. How does "confidentiality" play a role in the soldier's life?

3. Should national policy be made on these matters? Should military chaplains be forbidden to keep the soldiers' secrets if they are of importance to the military? Is secrecy or openness the best policy for the development of military policy (for instance, on nuclear weapons)?

THE CONCEPT OF CONFIDENTIALITY

Confidentiality holds a curious place in our value structure. We have no doubt that it *is* a value: that the ability to trust another implicitly, and the certainty that what we confide to another will not be published abroad, are essential to our lives and our sanity. Yet secrecy and confidentiality appear primarily as limitations to other moral imperatives; they often act as a counterbalance, in opposition to the moral demands legitimately made by the society.

Consider the first exercises of secrecy: Adam and Eve, having eaten the apple and known guilt and shame, hide when they see God coming; Cain, having killed his brother, denies any knowledge of Abel's whereabouts under God's questioning (*Bible*, **Source Reader** pp. 67, 68). These two first hidings in the Bible perfectly capture the child's earliest experience of concealment—hiding from the returning parent who will discover the mess, hiding the evidence of wrongdoing, hiding things stolen, or hiding cookies so they need not be shared. The concealments of the young child are almost always guilty concealment, hiding something from parents or other authorities. It is worth noting, even at this rudimentary stage, that the ones from whom the secret is being hidden have a legitimate right to know every detail of the young child's life; the child and the society ultimately benefit when parents know enough about what their children are doing to keep them under control.

A new dimension is added to concealment when the child gets old enough to have friends, who become sharers in the extensively controlled life of childhood. As sharers, they are eligible to be confidants—to hear and keep the secrets and to know about the concealments. Sharing guilty secrets, of course, only makes the guilty one freer to commit the sins concealed, by giving them a certain legitimacy. Revealing the secrets to the relevant authorities—parents or teachers, as the case may be—would facilitate justice and, for the child's own good, allow those authorities to make sure that the wrongdoing did not occur again.

Yet even parents and teachers detest "tattlers." Why?

Following confidentiality into adult life, we are struck by the recurrence of the paradoxical childhood patterns: confidentiality is antisocial at the core, and usually invoked against a clear and immediate public interest; yet the public, and usually the law, defend it, and will not allow its abolition even in defense of legitimate public aims. Confidentiality in the practice of medicine, for instance, has been held to require a physician to conceal a patient's previous back problems from a jury about to award damages for back injury; a patient's active syphilis from his fiancee; a patient's heart problems from his employer (the airline for which he works as a pilot); and a patient's AIDS from just about everyone, especially insurance companies. Public law has supervened in some of these cases; but always, where the law requires breach of confidence for the public safety, the breach required is for a very carefully defined and narrow band of cases, and leaves the institution of confidentiality untouched elsewhere.

Similarly, confidentiality in the practice of law requires that a lawyer conceal from the court, of which he is an officer, that an uncalled witness has sure evidence of his client's guilt; that evidence material to the case has been destroyed (but not by him); and that his client, all through her testimony under oath on the witness stand, was lying through her teeth. Confidentiality in the practice of psychiatry, or in the Church, means that the confidant may not even admit in public that the confider came to see him, let alone that the confidence included a tale of rape and mass murder. Yet we protect by law, by custom, and by popular outcry the institution of confidentiality. Even in borderline cases, we tend to sympathize with the keeper of the guilty secrets. We support the reporter's attempts to keep confidential the (often criminal) sources of his stories; we support the teacher's insistence on keeping the confidences of her students, even though the teacher is an employee and not an independent professional. Why?

Why do we value confidentiality, when its major function seems to be to thwart the public interest, by withholding from the public information that is needed to protect the welfare of the greatest number of citizens? The answer seems to be that confidentiality lies at the intersection of three essential social values—the weakening of which would render society impossible or hopelessly immoral—and that a serious threat to confidentiality would damage any one of them, or all three. The three values are privacy, trust, and promise-keeping.

Privacy is the condition essential to the development, nurture, and fulfillment of the individual *qua* individual. Without privacy, there can be no self—and therefore no self-consciousness, self-law (autonomy), self-respect, moral agency, and individual responsibility. Privacy has its own chapter in this volume, and you are referred to the essay in that chapter for further elaboration. Suffice it to say at this point that protecting the inner process of the self is essential for the development of the habit of reflection on one's own deeds, and even for the knowledge that one's deeds are one's own. As we value moral agency, we must protect privacy.

Trust, or fidelity, is the condition of friendship at its outset, according to Aristotle (Book VIII of the *Nicomachean Ethics*). Its root meaning is mutual good will: the recognition, on the part of both parties, that the other person means you well for your own sake, and will do you no harm. Fidelity, or faithfulness, is simply the extension of trust over time, as you recognize that this mutual good will and harmlessness will continue on your own part and may safely be expected of the other. Where firm trust exists, the barriers between the individuals have broken down to the point that they need not maintain their privacy vis-à-vis each other any more. The boundaries between them become fluid, sometimes disappearing altogether; at these times they can think and work as one person. In that ability we see the value of trust for the society at large. We are many, and we are social animals. We have to live and work together. Some of the things we work on are enormously complex. For these things to flourish, many people have to work as one, relying on the others to do their jobs, not guarding themselves against possible treachery from their coworkers, but concentrating on the common task. Without trust, the corporation perishes, commerce dies, education ceases, civil government becomes impossible—"and the life of man, solitary, mean, poor, nasty, brutish, and short" (Hobbes, **Source Reader** p. 105). If we cannot trust each other, we die, and whatever protects trust, protects us.

Promise-keeping means doing what you said you would do. Promises bind human beings over time—in fact, they are the *only* way human beings can be bound over time. Time is a succession of instants, each one the end of all the time that ever was. The future does not exist. There is no structure out there in front of us in time that we can attach our scaffolding to, to make sure that the step we planned lands where we aimed it. When it comes to simple physical things, like the position of the sidewalk, we can count on the regularity of physical nature to make our predictions about walking come true. (When it comes to complex physical things, like the car's battery on cold days, predictions are not so sure.) But there is nothing to assure that the human will, like the sidewalk, is going to remain firm from day to day, or even from minute to minute. Because the will is free, it can be anchored only by the free commitment of its owner, by a resolution that a decision made today for tomorrow will be carried out tomorrow, even though we know today that tomorrow may bring very different attractions and inclinations.

If I have the strength to carry out such resolutions, *my* future will be predictable to *me*. But recall that we are many, and must work together on very complex projects. If I am supposed to be working with you, *your* future is as interesting to me as my own; for instance, will you come to work tomorrow? If there is work that you now intend to have finished by that time, will it be done? Only your free action will get it done; only your commitment to getting it done will set the action in motion; and only your statement of that commitment to me—your promise—assures *me* that it will be done and allows me to plan my own life accordingly. It is your promise, and mine, that bind our relationship over time, and permit trust to mature into fidelity.

The notion that human society is an enormous contract occurs and recurs in the history of philosophy, from the Biblical covenant to the materialist Hobbes to the great contract rights theorists of the seventeenth and eighteenth centuries (*Bible*, **Source Reader** p. 69; Hobbes, **Source Reader** p. 106; Locke, **Source Reader** p. 119). Promise is the origin of contract; it is one person's side of contractual obligation. Each of our social institutions—the professions of law and medicine, the corporation, the schools—can be seen as an incredibly complex web of promises. Society as a whole is simply all these institutions promising each other to keep their place and fulfill their role in the entire polity for the good of all. That huge collective promise is the "social contract" that frees us from the whims and demands of the moment, binds time, and makes long-range planning possible in society.

Again, without these values, we die, at least as humans. First, the protection of *privacy* allows us to be aware of ourselves, our acts, and our responsibilities; we can recognize our obligations, make free and knowledgeable promises to fulfill them, and carry them out. We dare not crush that small and fragile self, so we place heavy limits on the society's means of getting to the heart of it and finding out what it is really thinking, or even doing (for instance, in the Constitutional provision that forbids a court to force us to testify against ourselves). Second, the protection of *trust* makes it possible for individuals to work together as one, at work or in the family, and we need that. We dare not terrorize people out of trusting each other; as we limit society's right to penetrate the self, so we limit society's right to intervene in private relationships, or to turn people against those who trust them (for instance, in the custom of the law that forbids spouses to testify against each other in court). Some nations have tried abolishing trust by terrorism (one recalls the Soviet Union under the rule of Joseph Stalin), in the name of public objectives; the results they have obtained provide salutary warnings to the rest of us as to the consequences of such attempts. And third, the protection of *promise-keeping* supports contracts, social and private. We dare not endanger the contract, so we teach people to keep promises, regardless of the content of the promises, with only a very few exceptions (for instance, a contract to perform an illegal act is not enforceable at law).

Confidentiality nestles safely among these essential values. It provides an interesting example of society consciously limiting its Utilitarian pursuit of the greatest happiness for the greatest number at the moment, in favor of long-range goals having to do with the protection of certain professional pursuits and a certain way of being human.

We are familiar with the protected pursuits: the physician must protect confidences because all medical information is potentially embarrassing; if there were the least question about the confidentiality of your conversations with your physician, you would have no such conversations, and your health, and by extension the health of all the people, would be endangered. The lawyer must keep client confidences for the same reasons. Those who have committed crimes, especially, need assurances that all communication will be kept secret so that they can openly discuss their situations with their attorneys, thereby ensuring the best protection for their rights, and by extension the rights of all the people. The Church and the psychiatrist could not carry on their separate ministries to the souls of the people if confidences were not sacred. To ensure the long-term functioning of essential professional services, then, society protects the confidentiality of professional communications, even against the public interest in disclosure.

But our protectiveness with regard to confidentiality goes beyond mere consequentialist reasoning, which justifies confidentiality by appeal to the greatest happiness of the greatest number in the long run. There is something sacred, something inviolable, about the private self, and something inviolable about that self keeping faith, to its own vows, to the friends it trusts, and to the causes that it has chosen as its own (see the chapter on Loyalty for more on this aspect of the topic). When we protect the keeping of secrets, and internalize strict limits on what we may do to others to ferret out secrets, we are really protecting the uniquely human in the unique individual human being. In social terms, we are protecting those conditions, psychological and social, that make it possible for people to work, trust, grow, love, and dream of the future. In short, we are protecting the conditions that make it possible for people to be the sorts of beings about whose greatest happiness we might appropriately care. In the end, the public interest is only the interests of all human beings. By protecting the intimate dimension of human existence, we create the condition for those beings to thrive.

THE TELEVISION PRESENTATION: SELECTED QUESTIONS ON THE MILITARY EXPERIENCE

This section considers the television presentation or videotape. The recapitulation of the dialogue that follows is not meant to be a word-for-word transcript of the tape, but a summary of the major themes, issues, and opinions that emerged in the conversation. It is for review, and for use as a resource if you include this topic in your term project.

TITLE: "UNDER ORDERS, UNDER FIRE" (PART 2)

Moderator: Professor Charles Ogletree, Jr.

Participants: from left to right on your screen

NEWT GINGRICH
U. S. Representative from Georgia

EVELYN P. FOOTE
Brigadier General, AUS

LOUIS STOKES
U. S. Representative from Ohio

BRIAN JENKINS
Chair, Political Science,
RAND Corporation;
Captain, U. S. Army Special Forces
(1965–68)

TIMOTHY TATUM
Chaplain, (Colonel)
U. S. Army War College

EDWARD C. MEYER
General, AUS (Ret.);
Chief of Staff, (1979-1983)

PETER JENNINGS
Anchor, Sr. Editor, ABC News

FREDERICK DOWNS, JR.
Director, Prosthetic/Sensory Aids,
Veterans Administration;
Lieutenant, U. S. Army (1966-1969)

DAVID C. JONES
General, USAF (Ret.);
Chairman, Joint Chiefs of Staff
(1978–82)

WILLIAM C. WESTMORELAND
General, AUS (Ret.)

GEORGE M. CONNELL
Colonel, USMC

MIKE WALLACE
Correspondent, CBS News

BRENT SCOWCROFT
Lt. General, USAF (Ret.)

J. BRYAN HEHIR
Department of Social Development and
World Peace,
U. S. Catholic Conference

ROBERT C. STUART
Major, USMC

JAMES E. SERVICE
Vice Admiral, USN (Ret.)

THE COURSE OF THE DIALOGUE

Ask yourself as you review the dialogue:

1. How much can a soldier be expected to "keep secret" about his military experience? Why?
2. Are all these officers, including the chaplains, acting appropriately? How would you defend their actions to one of your teachers? Or to a pacifist?

The scene opens where the "Loyalty" program left off. Our unit has been pursuing guerrillas into a hostile village, a mission that is not only dangerous, and terrifying for the untried troops, but also very frustrating for those trying scrupulously to distinguish between "civilians" or "noncombatants" (the villagers) and "guerrillas" or "combatants," who dress and act like the villagers but will kill you if they get a chance.

Means and Ends

Phase one of the hypothetical: six American soldiers have been seized by the guerrillas and are being held somewhere in the area. Our unit seizes several Kosanese reliably identified as guerrilla fighters of the same group. They probably know where the prisoners are. What do we do now? Do we torture them to make them tell us where the prisoners are being kept?

Frederick Downs says yes, we do. "This is not a pretty situation you've put me in, but this is a situation in which I've been ordered to get results, and the results to me are of the highest value, which is to save my fellow soldiers, and I'm going to do it. If I have to kill you to prove a point to the other five guerrillas, I may go that far."

Principles and Laws
Brian Jenkins disagrees. "There will be no torture...I can't guarantee that people wouldn't be shoved around, made to feel fear. But to...apply torture in order to get information, no. And it has nothing to do with the lives of my fellow soldiers. It has to do with principles and laws, and if some soldiers are going to die, even my own comrades, because I'm going to make a decision to obey those laws, and to uphold those principles, then so be it."

Asked to comment, Fr. Bryan Hehir agrees that sometimes torture does happen, but denies that it ought to happen, if only because the effects are as terrible on our own soldiers as they are on the tortured enemy. First, "When you torture somebody, it isn't just the other person that is affected; you do something to the human being that does it....Expand that order....up the chain of command, and you get not just torture, but in the nineteenth and...twentieth century, you get a kind of warfare where there are just no limits at all, because there are all kinds of orders that can be given....Secondly, our men are taken prisoners. We want some restraint on the other side about what they can do to our men. Once it becomes clear that anybody who's got an order can do whatever they want to do,...what are you going to lodge against the other side, when your own men are held prisoner?"

Downs is undaunted. Those are my men in enemy hands. They are not going to be left behind just because one man doesn't have the intestinal fortitude to bend the rules. This is my decision to make, if I'm the one on the spot. I will have to live with it. I will make it, and I think that I have the moral strength to live with myself afterward if I succeed in releasing the prisoners of war. Admiral Service is sympathetic. This is an imperfect world. If I *knew* that I could get that information, and that that was the *only* way I could get that information, I might go ahead and do it. I am working, after all, for an ethical entity, my country, and I have to believe that my orders are ethical. General Westmoreland is *not* sympathetic, not with any suggestion that our troops, including their officers, might violate the Geneva Conventions, to which we as a nation are signatories. We do not do things like this, and it is repugnant to him that Downs should suggest the contrary. General Jones is less certain about what he would in fact do, faced with this very difficult situation: the enemy "soldiers," after all, are irregulars, not in uniform, not covered by the Conventions, and if he thought he could save six of his men, he would face a terrible moral dilemma.

Atrocity

Phase two of the hypothetical opens with another attempt to get information from people suspected of killing Americans. No techniques of torture are in use here; a lieutenant, in company with an enlisted man, has simply captured several villagers, or guerrillas, and is shooting them, one after another, until they agree to tell him what he wants to know. Should another lieutenant happen on the scene, what should *he* do? Major Stuart, what do you do about it? Major Stuart's answer: stop him immediately. Talk him out of it, threaten him out of it, if necessary shoot him, but stop him. No perception of "Americans" vs. "Enemy" is relevant here: the lieutenant is committing cold-blooded murder; he must be stopped.

Suppose instead that no one happened along to stop the carnage. Suppose all the victims are shot, so there are no sure witnesses, at least not in the immediate area. Lieutenant and private return to camp. The private (GI Joe), terrified at the events in which he has played a part, seeks out the chaplain, and asks to go to confession. He tells the whole story to Chaplain

Confidentiality
vs. Truthtelling
Tatum. Will the Lord forgive him? Certainly, Tatum assures him, but you must go at once to the military authorities and turn yourself in and tell them the story, for this is a serious violation of the Rules of Land Warfare. Joe finds those instructions much too difficult to follow, and fades back into the camp. Now what is Tatum's responsibility? Would he go to the authorities? No, he would not.

General Scowcroft finds himself in charge of the base and worried about the rumors of a nasty incident, in which innocent civilians were shot. He has reason to believe that Chaplain Tatum knows something about the incident. Would he approach Tatum and ask for information? Yes, he would. And he would remind Tatum that part of penance is the obligation to set the situation right, and that he shouldn't tell a penitent that God will forgive him if he *won't* set it right. In fact, "I hope you would at least indicate that he may go straight to hell if he doesn't try to set that situation right," by going to the appropriate authorities.

Tatum will not break the confidence, on grounds that it is important that a soldier should have someone he can talk to totally without fear. Therefore confidentiality should be kept in these cases.

Fr. Hehir finds that rationale a bit anemic. He believes that the seal of the confessional is absolute. In his case, he could not even acknowledge that someone had come to him as a penitent. He will answer hypothetical questions—how do you handle this type of confession—but he will allow no discussion of individuals. Suppose by chance one of the chaplains should say something that might incriminate the lieutenant. Would General Scowcroft use it at the court-martial? He certainly would. *He's* under no obligation of confidentiality.

**The Case for
Confidentiality**
Hehir continues: "There's another question. Can the institution live with what he did? And it's the institution of the confessional that's always at stake when you have an individual case. No matter how urgent and overwhelming the reasons are in the individual case, if you crack the confidence in the institution of the confessional, you're finished. If you crack the confidence in the institution of the military, that they tell people to torture, or that they look benignly on people torturing, then you endanger the institution. It is not enough for the individual to ask, can I live with something? The institution has to ask, can *we* live with it?" Can the institution survive, and command the allegiance of the next generation?

There seems to be agreement, as Generals Jones and Foote conclude, that the military as a whole may be no party to covering up the ugly incident—that the affair should proceed to a court-martial, which will find attenuated guilt for the private acting under direct orders, guilt for the lieutenant, and no guilt for any officer who stopped the incident, even at the cost of killing the lieutenant.

Journalists in the Enemy Camp

**Protecting
Sources**
Phase three of the hypothetical brings the journalists into the war. Now Peter Jennings is on the spot: suppose you are an American journalist on the battlefield, and you get a chance to go behind the enemy lines as a guest and observer, to film the North Kosanese in action. Do you take the

offer? Answer: Yes! Very well then: now suppose that the North Kosanese unit you are attached to, and filming, sets up an ambush. They are going to kill as many as possible of a unit of South Kosanese coming up the road now. Do you try to warn the South Kosanese? Answer: No. As a reporter, in this situation, you make a commitment going in that you will be an observer only. You film the ambush as it happens. You made that decision at the beginning.

Very well: now suppose that the unit approaching is American. Do you warn them? This is not an easy question. Jennings' answer, after deliberation: yes, he would warn them. But his answer is based on his feelings and not on what he thinks he ought to do.

Mike Wallace immediately takes the other side. He *wouldn't* warn them. This is a good story. As a matter of fact, he finds it difficult to believe, as a reporter, that Peter Jennings would act as he says he would act. But the lives of Americans will be lost? Answer: "You're a reporter. Granted you're an American, but you're a reporter covering combat between North Kosan and South Kosan...and I'm at a loss to understand why...you would not have covered that story....You're a reporter, your job is to cover what is going on in that war. People know that Americans are going to be killed in that war."

Country vs. Profession

Jennings wavers; intellectually, he agrees with Wallace. Generals Scowcroft and Wallace disagree where the American journalist's obligations might lie: with his country or profession. General Westmoreland comments that he finds it repugnant that the American networks should be, or seem to be, in league with the enemy. Wallace begins to answer full tilt, fades in the stretch: "General, the same question is raised in the cities of this country:...if you knew that a murder was going to take place, ahead of time, would you cover that story, or would you let the object of that murder know, or would you let the police know? I think, and I've answered this question before, I think...that I would surely not let the man, or the woman, be murdered. I would...I would let the authorities know. And then you say, all right, under those circumstances, now move it over in to war. And I...I'm going back and forth as I sit here. I understand all of the stresses and strains that are going on....It's a hell of a dilemma to be in. I think...I don't know what the hell I think."

Granted that an American journalist will find it very hard to say what he would in fact do, what, Fr. Hehir, *should* he do? Hehir points out that this case is different from those that have come before, where we dealt with actions that are absolutely prohibited—torture and killing of the innocent. We can say that violating such prohibitions is absolutely wrong. But here we have two conflicting affirmative obligations: to report the news, and to warn Americans in danger. It isn't that clear which duty takes precedence, especially when warning the Americans will result in the instant death of the reporter.

What do the military men think of the reporters' duty to protect the news—even when it involves an ambush of American soldiers? Major Stuart acknowledges his distaste for the situation, but points out that reporters are not expected to be heroic, and put their own lives in danger. Colonel Connell expresses, with uncharacteristic vehemence, his "utter contempt" for the journalists. Two days later, they'll be ambushed, and lying wounded, and expect him to send marines to rescue them. "They're just journalists, they're not Americans....But I'll do it, and that's what makes me most contemptuous of them. And marines will die going to get a couple of journalists."

Newt Gingrich points out that this curious case, of the reporter whose loyalties are divided simply by location, is typical of the chaotic environment we live in, with its small wars and high-tech worldwide communications. Recall, for instance, the American reporters in Libya during a real bombing raid, who held telephones outside on the balcony so their home offices could hear the American bombs exploding before the raid was officially acknowledged. These agonizing conflicts of loyalty mean that we are not yet very good, as a people, at deciding who we are. Meanwhile, the military has done a vastly better job of systematically thinking through the ethics of behavior in a violent environment than have the journalists.

Nuclear Bullet

Phase four of the hypothetical opens with a major North Kosanese base under construction. It has immense potential for visiting damage upon American troops. The charismatic (if slightly crazy) North Kosanese leader, Major Madness, cult figure for the guerrilla fighters, likes to stay on this base—he's there most afternoons. Admiral Service, shall we bomb the base? Answer: Yes. Shall we bomb it when Major Madness is there? Answer: Definitely. He's as much a military target as the base itself, and more valuable to disable. What if we think his family might be there? Answer: They are not the targets, but we bomb anyway.

No disagreement yet. Let us continue. The bombing raid has failed. The base is very dangerous to us. In fact, we are losing the war. I am President, and I say we must destroy the base to cut our losses. We have the perfect weapon for that: a "nuclear bullet" that one man can carry in a backpack. When he gets into the area, he can fire it off, and it will just destroy the base—there will be no wider damage. General Jones, I'm going to order you to shoot off that weapon.

General Jones will not do it. It will not be as decisive as you think, Mr. President. Such escalation is not warranted. Let's talk to the Secretary of Defense about it.

The Value of Public Disclosure

As President, I order you to obey or resign. But General Jones has no intention of doing either. We need full discussion on the decision to go nuclear, and we will get it. We must include the Secretary of Defense, and carefully consider this in the National Security Council. This is a step that needs to be pondered very carefully in this country. Very well, then, says the President, I will fire you and order the next in command to use this nuclear device. General Meyer, I order you....No, General Meyer would refuse also, and retire or resign. General Scowcroft, will *you*....No, he will not, and will resign publicly to make sure this idea gets the national attention it deserves. There are global implications to going nuclear, and it would be a move of monumental stupidity to do it without full consideration of the consequences. Newt Gingrich concurs; the concept of nuclear destruction sets the use of these weapons apart, as a peculiarly serious type of escalation of warfare.

Let us finish the hypothetical. Suppose the use of the nuclear bullet *has* been approved by the proper chain of command. Fred Downs is ordered to carry out the mission to fire the bullet. Would he do it? Yes, he would, but to the moderator's suggestion that he would probably *enjoy* the job, and the general laughter following, he asks to add a final word:

"Let's put this all in context, from an infantryman's point of view...I think a lieutenant who has to make these kinds of stressful decisions—highly stressful for the purpose of this conference—you have to understand one thing. This is one man, by himself. He must make these crucial life and death decisions. He has to have a higher ethic, a higher morality, than people who do not make these decisions, and then he has to live with them afterwards." We have here an infantryman, whose major goal is to return home to his family, who has to make decisions, split-second and combat-oriented, in the heat of battle —and what makes him less moral than the person who drops a bomb and kills hundreds of innocent civilians? "Without ethics, without morals, without control, you become a mob, your army disintegrates and you lose your honor and dignity as a nation."

A REVIEW OF SELECTIONS FROM THE SOURCE READER

Before going on to discuss the philosophical background and the television presentation, this might be a good time to review certain of the readings in the history of ethics that pertain especially to this topic.

Confidentiality is rarely mentioned in the classical literature, save disapprovingly. Yet, as the opening essay for this chapter explains, in a world that is increasingly alienated and lacking in privacy, the preservation of individual dignity depends on trust in another, necessary for confidentiality. Therefore the selections we have chosen for this chapter echo the classic theme of the dignity and freedom of the individual, and the trustworthiness of the individual who has been trusted.

Selections for this chapter:

> Epictetus, *The Moral Discourses of Epictetus*, **Source Reader** p. 93
> Immanuel Kant, *Foundations of the Metaphysics of Morals*, **Source Reader** p. 136

Epictetus gives us the first solid portrait of the good man in the hostile world, whose responsibility it is to do his duty to the extent that it is within his power. Keeping secrets is one of the few specific tasks that is clearly within his power. Kant speaks more generally of the worth and dignity of the human being, and the inclination to do one's duty, not for the good results it will achieve, but for the sake of obedience to law.

SYNTHESIS AND DISCUSSION

Let us attempt to unify the dialogue in the presentation with the opening essay. The dialogue reinforces, in part, the claim that confidentiality is very important to us; that we will protect it from invasion even for very powerful public purposes. But it also points out the limitations on that duty: where an act is clearly morally wrong, from the point of view of our profession or our principles, we will tolerate no secrecy concerning it.

1. Note, first, the way the protection of "confidentiality," or secrecy, works against the public interest every time it gets a chance, just as it does in the several peacetime contexts of confidentiality mentioned in the Meditation.

　　a. We object to torturing prisoners to ferret out information, even though that information might save American lives; although the end is desirable, the means, and the consequences of using those means, are unacceptable, so the end is regretfully abandoned, at least for the moment. For the majority of the military men, there can be no question about the status of the order to get information by torture if necessary. That part of the order is illegal and is not binding. It's a matter of ends justifying means; when the means are clearly immoral, you can't use them.

　　b. We know that the chaplain has information about a dirty incident that we're going to have to deal with sometime, but we are deeply divided even about the justifiability of reminding him that we'd like to know it, and that we'd like him to tell us. As for the chaplain, he is clearly protected in his unwillingness to discuss the issue at all.

　　c. Can we really tolerate the reporter's protection of the group of enemy soldiers, who are carrying out an ambush on our own soldiers? How can we justify participation in an incident in which Americans are killed?

2. Note, further, the *power* of the value of confidentiality, at least in these contexts.

a. Why is torture clearly morally wrong? One major reason, of course, is that torture entails the deliberate infliction of extreme pain on another human being. And we would object to sadism, or infliction of pain on the prisoners simply for the fun of it, simply because we don't want to see prisoners brutalized, for obvious reasons, including the ones mentioned by Fr. Hehir. But torture to obtain secret information is worse: the objective is not just to make the other person feel pain, which is bad enough in itself, but so to weaken the psychological constitution and moral fiber of the person that he becomes unable to do what every human being can do from childhood—keep his thoughts inside him, elect his speech, choose what shall be concealed and what shall be revealed. Such torture is an assault on the peculiarly human, while torture just for the fun of inflicting pain is an assault only on the animal part of us.

b. Again, the sanctity of the confessional is not challenged. In a very sticky military situation, where a leak from an unsuspected source to one of those omnipresent journalists could unleash a scandal in the stateside press, the military authorities are hobbled in their investigation by a clergyman. He apparently knows what happened in detail, but impudently starts chatting about the World Series when asked just *what* he knows! Do the generals press for information? The clergyman, after all, has *not* been through basic training, and may very well yield to pressure. But no ranking military officer even considers invading that secrecy.

c. The reporters, again, claim it as their right to conceal information that might save American lives, in the name of a promise given, to an enemy, not to reveal his position. The promise is justified in the name of finding out the truth from a source who demands that promise as the price of access. Keeping the promise requires participation in the ambush. In this case at least one military man was willing to say that the goal, the promise, and the journalists, were all worthy of total contempt. Across the country, they command a bit more respect than that.

3. But note, especially, the limitations on this power. Where the moral imperatives are clear, the question of confidentiality does not seem to arise. Consider the two cases where the dilemma of whether or not to keep a secret was raised in the presentation, but where the decision went the other way.

d. Does anyone remember My Lai? It was a village in Vietnam where a platoon of Americans, frustrated by recent defeats and the loss of men, summarily shot a few dozen noncombatant men, women, children, grandparents, and babies. The officers conspired to keep the incident quiet until one of the enlisted men blew the whistle. A similar incident is portrayed in the television presentation, and a brother officer, happening along, is invited to choose sides. Will he choose to support the offending officer's crimes and conceal them from the authorities? Not on your life.

Major Stuart, the only military officer asked to comment on the incident, replies immediately that he would shoot his brother officer if necessary to stop the killing of innocent civilians. We do not condone illegal acts. A glance around the stony-faced generals yields no sympathy for the offender in this case. This is one of those areas where, as Newt Gingrich puts it, the military has done a very good job of thinking through the ethics of behavior in conditions of violence.

e. The President has ordered the use of a nuclear device to blow up a base. You, as General, think the decision is wrongheaded, but it *is* an order from your Commander-in-Chief. Do you just carry it out, without mentioning it to anyone? After all, leaking the story to anyone could ensure that it reached the enemy, and that in turn could provoke the enemy to use nuclear weapons preemptively. If this mission is to be carried out, secrecy is essential for national security. Do you tell just a few? Who? Or do you go public and blow the whistle, because the decision to go nuclear is so serious? This whole scenario posed no dilemma at all for the people who were asked to respond. The first general to be asked this question announced that he had no intention of carrying out the order without much wider discussion with the appropriate bodies, including the National Security Council. The second, on the assumption that the first had resigned or been fired, would also resign, but discreetly. The third would resign too, but very publicly, and the moderator abandoned the question just as that third general was about to call a news conference. When this sort of issue is at stake, national secrecy simply doesn't have a chance. Again, the generals seem to have thought the issue through before this telecourse asked them to talk about it.

4. In summation: with the military scenarios before us as samples, we may say that confidentiality remains valuable even under the most extreme conditions. Even the soldier must have someone he can talk to without fear, and we provide chaplains precisely so that he can reinforce in himself that privacy, that inner space that is all his own, without fear of it being opened to inspection by those authorities who exercise absolute power over all the rest of his life. We have decided that even in combat secrecy is permissible, because even in combat it is necessary to remain a human being, and stripped of his secrets, a being is not human. That is the real subject of Downs' last speech: Without ethics, without morals, we become a mob, or a herd of animals. Without protection of basic values, we lose the right to fight to protect anything, even ourselves.

QUESTIONS FOR YOUR REFLECTION

1. Epictetus asserts (Epictetus, **Source Reader** p. 93) that the keeping of a secret is the most obvious exercise of free choice, since the choice

of whether or not to reveal it is clearly within your power. They can chain your leg, of course, if you will not tell, and even cut off your head; but they cannot make you reveal the secret. What do you think are the limits of human freedom? What would make it *impossible* for a person to keep a secret? (You may consider historical examples in your answer to this question.)

2. Sometimes, as the generals made clear, secrets ought not to be kept, because some higher principle makes the act so seriously immoral that confidentiality becomes nothing but accessory to crime. Review the moral principles in Chapter 1, and ask yourself in which of the following cases confidentiality should prevail, and in which it should be overridden. When it should be overridden, be prepared to say *why*, and who should be told. Assume that all the following are told to you in confidence:

- A 14-year-old friend tells you that he's been sniffing cocaine for a year.
- The building contractor working on the house next door tells you on his lunch break that he can't stand having blacks (not his word) working for him; as a matter of fact he has managed to get three of them fired from a federal project he's contractor for.
- Drunk one night at a block party, a neighbor tells you that he's cheating on his wife.
- Another neighbor's wife tells you that her husband sometimes beats the children very badly, and sometimes terrorizes her.
- A friend in his early sixties confides that he's found a sure way to use his computer to siphon off small amounts of his employer's money into his own bank account, and plans to use the transferred money to bolster his upcoming retirement.
- A building contractor (maybe the one above) tells you that federal specifications are unrealistically high for multistory buildings, and that it is common practice to save money on building projects by using a much lower grade of concrete for the floors than is specified; in fact, he tells you that in one of his buildings, he's doing just that.

SUGGESTIONS FOR FURTHER READING

Special Supplementary Text:
SISSELA BOK. *Secrets: On the Ethics on Concealment and Revelation* New York: Pantheon Books, 1982

BRANDT, ELIZABETH A. "On Secrecy and the Control of Knowledge: Taos Pueblo" in *Secrecy: A Cross-Cultural Perspective*, ed. S. K. Tefft. New York: Human Sciences Press, 1980; pp. 123-144.

COX, ARTHUR MACY. *The Myths of National Security: The Perils of Secret Government*. Boston: Beacon Press, 1975.

DERLEGA, VALERIAN J. AND ALAN L. CHAIKIN. "Privacy and Self-Disclosure in Social Relationships," *Journal of Social Issues*. 33(1977):102-115.

FRENCH, PETER, ED. *Individual and Collective Responsibility: The Massacre at My Lai*. Cambridge, MA: Schenkman Publishing Company, 1972.

GOFFMAN, ERVING. *Asylums: Essays on the Social Situation of Mental Patients and Other Inmates.* Chicago: Aldine Publishing Co., 1961.

HALPERIN, MORTON H. AND DANIEL N. HOFFMAN, *Top Secret: National Security and the Right to Know.* Washington, DC: New Republic Books, 1977.

ORWELL, GEORGE. *Nineteen Eighty-four* (1949). New York: New American Library, 1961.

ROBERTSON, KENNETH G. *Public Secrets: A Study of the Development of Government Secrecy.* New York: St. Martin's Press, 1982.

SIMMEL, GEORG. *The Sociology of Georg Simmel*, ed. Kurt H. Wolff. New York: Free Press, 1950.

TEFFT, STANTON K. "Secrecy as a Social and Political Process," in *Secrecy: A Cross-Cultural Perspective,* ed. S. K. Tefft. New York: Human Sciences Press, 1980, pp. 319-41.

chapter 10 _____

TRUTHTELLING:
Truth on Trial

QUESTIONS TO KEEP IN MIND AS YOU READ THE CHAPTER

1. Why does our society teach the value of telling the truth? Can you imagine what life would be like if people in general told lies in all their dealings? (Try.) What does telling a lie do for you? What does being lied to do *to* you?

2. What is the function of the civil law in the nation, and of the lawyer in that system? Why do we do things this way? Other nations don't, at least not all of them. What values do we protect by doing things this way?

3. Is it all right to conceal the truth when you are protecting someone you have promised to protect? What is required of the lawyer in a civil case in weighing truth, justice, and the public good against the duty of zeal on behalf of the client? If you had to make new policy in this field, how would you make it?

THE CONCEPT OF TRUTHFULNESS

We begin by distinguishing "telling the truth" from "Truth." "Truth" is some final Good, some value so exalted that it can justify any means to attain it and spread it to all nations—including, I suppose, lying. Does service to the highest justify engagement with the lowest? Possibly, but that is not our problem. Truthtelling, truthfulness, is a much humbler value. It is simply the total worth of people trying not to deceive each other, or at least not trying *to* deceive each other.

Truthtelling is one of the easiest social values to establish; it is derivable in one move from each of the three primary ethical principles with which we began this inquiry: respect for persons, concern for welfare, and justice. It may be unique in this respect. It is certainly unique in its time of acquisition. It is the earliest value taught the child, inculcated from the time that the child acquires the power of speech, and it is the only virtue that can be entirely actualized by the child. For the young, wisdom is impossible, courage only an imitation, and self-control only present potentially. But a truthful child is as truthful as an adult, and as praiseworthy for that virtue, for the choice to tell the truth or tell a lie is entirely the child's own.

Why is truthfulness valuable? If only for purposes of review, it is worth going through the derivation of truthfulness from the primary ethical concepts.

Truthfulness is valuable, first, because we are moral agents; we must make choices, for which we are, and will be, held responsible. Our dignity as humans comes from this characteristic, and if our attempts to exercise moral agency are systematically frustrated, we are deprived of that dignity. To be effective, our choices must be rational—reasonable under the circumstances and appropriately fashioned as means to our ends. For the choice to be rational, we must possess correct information about the situation in which the choice is made, the conditions in which it will be carried out, and the likely consequences of the actions chosen. When we are wrong about any of these, our choice is less rational than it might be. When we are dependent upon others for the information on which we must act, deception on their part will render the choice irrational, the power of choice useless, and the moral agency null and void (since we cannot be held accountable for actions performed when we were deceived). Put another way, if I lie to you on a matter of importance to you, a matter on which you must act, I turn you into a dupe and a fool, your choice into an exercise in futility, and your action against you, rendering it useless and counterproductive. Minimal respect for the human dignity of another requires at least that we tell that person the truth.

That is the first and most important derivation of the value of truthtelling. Second, and possibly most obvious, truthtelling is important for the welfare of the whole society. Try to count, some average day, the number of transactions you complete in which you are, at some crucial point, utterly dependent upon the word of another. You may separate these dependencies into categories, if you like. Sometimes you are dependent upon oral information from another ("Sally? The meeting's been changed. It'll be at two, at my place...."), or from a machine (!) ("The number is: 9-4-3-2-6-..."), or on the air ("The offer has been extended an extra week...."). You can be dependent upon written information through the mail ("Property taxes are due and payable on the 15th of the first month...."), on a sign ("Exit 28: Pembroke Street..."), on a poster ("Mendelssohn's *Elijah* is to be performed March 5, 8:00 PM..."), flashing from a dashboard ("CHECK OIL CHECK OIL CHECK...."), dangling from a new appliance ("To avoid severe electric shock, replace this plate *before* plugging in...."). But the list could go on indefinitely. Note that all of the examples contain information on which you might be expected to act to achieve some end—to attend the meeting, to call or visit a friend, to get your taxes in on time, enjoy a concert, avoid electric shock. If the information on any one of them is wrong, the result will be disappointment, wasted time, possible loss of money, or injury. If they are all wrong, and you try to act on all of them, you will not be functioning very well by the end of the month. If all such information were as likely to be wrong as right, in business and commercial transactions as well as the home-oriented matters chosen for these examples, the society as a whole would cease functioning even sooner. (A point to ponder: could the dashboard have been "lying"?)

The value of truthfulness can as easily be derived from the principle of justice, for when I decide that I will lie to you, I choose to make myself an exception to a universal rule, and gain an unfair advantage from that exception. For my lie will do me no good unless it is told against a background of general social honesty. Your expectation that I will tell the truth makes my lie effective. It means that I can rely on everyone else's word, and indeed I do take their accounts to be true in framing my lie to do me the most good. My lie, in this climate of expectation, is a clear violation of a rule that I apply to everyone else, a violation calculated to give me an advantage, and is therefore unjust.

The principle of truthfulness, or veracity, then, is easy to validate, but its range is not as easy to establish. Granted that truthfulness is valuable in general, is it absolute? Must we *never* lie? We could hold, as a limiting case of the principle, that one should never lie. But this position is too open to immediate refutation. Where innocent lives are at stake, and only a lie can deflect harm from these people, it is right to lie. (There is the traditional schoolchildren's case: If a murderer, weapon in hand, pursues a victim, who hides near you and begs you not to tell where, and the murderer comes up to you and asks, "Where did she go?" must you tell him? The answer is no, you need not. You can think of other instances, possibly from incidents of war, where the only moral imperative that makes sense requires a lie.)

If we must preserve truthfulness in general, but may not make it absolute, what rules are appropriate for determining when we may make an exception? Some rules are clearly unacceptable. We may not, for example, adopt a purely utilitarian rule: that whenever it will maximize happiness in the long run for the greatest number it is all right to lie. Numerous arguments speak against this. We may argue, for example, that justice should prevail against utility in clear cases. (You may not hand over the innocent man to the lynch mob to be killed in order to prevent a race riot that will kill hundreds.) Or that respect for moral agency should prevail against the sum of happiness (in which case you must tell a dying man the truth about his condition, no matter how much it distresses him and his relatives, so that he may set his affairs in order according to his desires). Or that the awful command of the Lord requires that the sinner be told his sin for the sake of his soul (which is why Samuel had to tell Eli that his family would be deprived of priesthood, I *Samuel* 3).

But the strongest argument against the utilitarian rule is utilitarian. In the nature of the situation, the only person who is in a position to decide, in advance of the lie, whether *this* lie will serve the greatest happiness of the greatest number in the long run, is the liar; and the liar's perspective is totally skewed by self-interest, fear, and desire, the most benevolent interpretation of his own motives, and the rosiest view of the future to be achieved by the lie. The liar, then, is hardly objective. At the least, he is in no position to judge the effect of the lie on his own character, which is one of the more serious consequences of his action.

Then what tests will tell us which lies are justified? Some tentative, and probably satisfactory, rules emerge from the debate. First, as above, any lie is justified that saves human life, or saves a human being from serious injury, in the absence of other ways to bring about the same result. Second, any lie that has the approval of the dupes (those who are to be lied to) is probably all right. You might protest, what person would be *willing* to be lied to, and would agree publicly that lying to him is acceptable? But this is what we do all the time, when we authorize our police to travel in unmarked cars, set up speed traps in the bushes, and conduct nonconsensual surveillance in pursuit of illegal drugs. Of course we don't think that *we're* going to be the ones under surveillance, or caught in the trap. But we agree to the practice, nonetheless.

Beyond that limiting case, many not-quite-consensual deceptive practices are accepted in this society. The two parties to any negotiation (labor negotiations, for example), will commonly begin by telling lies about what they and their membership consider a minimally adequate settlement. Advertisers lie, but not very much. Poker players lie with their body language; that's part of good playing. Door-to-door salesmen probably lie, on the pretense that "everyone understands the rules of the game, so no one gets hurt." We play lots of these games. Should we play *quite* so many? It's a good question.

The rules of the game of trial at law are in question in the hypothetical that follows. Is it all right to lie, or hide the truth, or mislead, or make one who lies appear to tell the truth and one who tells the truth appear to lie, on the justification that these are the rules of the game? How much lying, or untruth, is needed to destroy the law entirely?

The answer to that may be, quite a bit. The legal system does not owe its origin or justification to any dedication to the truth. Its foundation is in the need for survival, and derived from that need, the "natural law," as Hobbes called it, to seek peace, and failing that, to prepare for war (Hobbes, **Source Reader** p. 107). The laws of crime and punishment (examined elsewhere in this volume) preserve peace by simultaneously satisfying and moderating the natural desire and social need for revenge for criminal injury. The civil law preserves peace by settling all disputes that do not involve crime; that is, all injury, real or alleged, that the society has not declared to be so obviously violative of order that it must be dealt with using the whole force of the state.

When a citizen (or noncitizen under some circumstances) perceives that some right has been violated, or injury suffered, and that another is to blame for the injury, he may, if he likes, bring suit against that person to recover the amount by which he has been damaged. Should the alleged offender agree that she is at least partly to blame for the damage, the suit may be settled—with an appropriate amount of damages agreed upon and paid by the defendant to the plaintiff. (Sometimes a judge monitors the settlement process, but usually plaintiff and defendant are free to settle any way they like.) In the absence of quick settlement, an elaborate process is set in motion, leading to trial and decision, usually by jury, on the proper allotment of rights and damages. The legal process ordinarily entails a series of steps that appears to be directed to finding out what the facts of the matter are, and the appropriate degree of responsibility to be ascribed to the defendant. Indeed, the whole language of "discovery," "examination," "cross-examination," not to mention the oath taken by everyone who speaks, to tell "The Truth, the Whole Truth, and Nothing But the Truth (so Help Me God)" suggests that the purpose of the process is to find out that truth, so we may all know who is *really* responsible for the damage, and the outcome will be just. But the suggestion is an illusion.

Consider the law this way: If A injures B, and B is too witless to know that she is injured, or too phlegmatic to take offense, or too intimidated to press the matter, then the matter will go no further. There will be no truth, and there will surely be no justice, but there will be peace, so the law is satisfied. As long as the injury is not of criminal dimensions, the law is not interested in finding out about it. But then the law must equally be satisfied if the parties agree to go home and remain at peace with each other after settling the case out of court, even without looking to see if the settlement is "just." And it must, within limitations, be satisfied if the parties are content (more or less) with the verdict handed down by the court, even if the testimony consisted of lies, good lies, and nothing but consistent lies, and the verdict was flatly unjust. (The limitations involve appearance more than anything else. The court must have rules that forbid fraud—for instance, the example given in the program, forbidding a favorable settlement based on misinformation—if only to retain the credibility it needs to function as peacemaker.)

Then the object of the expedition, as far as the civil law is concerned, is only civil peace, and it adopts only those means to find out the truth and to do justice which are necessary to bring about peace in the present case and preserve its ability to do so in the future. If we use perfect truth, or even perfect justice, as our standard, we must find the system sadly wanting. About the only thing that can be said in its defense is that, as a general proposition, it beats civil war.

THE TELEVISION PRESENTATION: SELECTED QUESTIONS ON THE CONDUCT OF CIVIL LAW

This section considers the television presentation or videotape. The recapitulation of the dialogue that follows is not meant to be a word-for-word transcript of the tape, but a summary of the major themes, issues, and opinions that emerged in the conversation. It is for review, and for use as a resource if you include this topic in your term project.

TITLE: "TRUTH ON TRIAL"

Moderator: Professor Charles R. Nesson

Participants: from left to right on your screen

JOHN SMITH
Clark Professor of Philosophy, Yale
University

JAMES NEAL
Partner,
Neal and Harwell

ROBERT MAYNARD
Editor and President,
The Tribune

FLOYD ABRAMS
Partner,
Cahill, Gordon and Reindel

THEODORE COOPER, M.D.
Chairman and CEO, The Upjohn
Company

SHEILA BIRNBAUM
Partner, Skadden, Arps, Slate, Meagher
& Flom

ROBERT BANKS
Vice President, General Counsel, Xerox
Corporation

ANTONIN SCALIA
Justice, Supreme Court of the United
States

STANLEY CHESLEY
Partner, Waite, Schneider, Bayless &
Chesley

JOSEPH COTCHETT
Partner, Cotchett & Illston

ROBERT MERHIGE, JR.
U. S. District Judge, Eastern District
Virginia

MARILYN HALL PATEL
U. S. District Judge, Northern District
California

STEPHEN GILLERS
Professor, School of Law, New York
University

As you read through the dialogue, ask yourself:

1. Where are the lawyers' interests in each stage of the case?
2. Where are the clients' interests? Do they always coincide with the lawyers'
    interests?
3. In whose interest is it for the truth to be revealed (if anyone's)? Are the
    restrictions on lying that we just talked about being taken very lightly here?
4. Do you approve of this competitive situation, this adversary system, that
    systematically obscures the truth?

THE COURSE OF THE DIALOGUE

First Signs of a Problem

Let me introduce myself, the moderator begins. I'm Hyram Powers,
CEO of Hot Products. One of our big products is the Hot Boy, a space heater

at the low end of the market. Big seller. Mr. Abrams, "you and I are having lunch and you're the counsel to this company. Can I talk to you in confidence?" "Sure, sure," says Abrams. "Well, there's something I wanted to run past you." I got this memo from Nellie Barnes yesterday—safety engineer, been with the company from the beginning, I call her "Nervous Nellie"—seems she's worried about the Hot Boy. Worried that under some circumstances it might tip over, the shut-off wouldn't trip, and there'd be a fire. Well, space heaters always cause fires. But I sat down and costed out a new emergency shut-off, and it would price our product right out of the range we're in. We'd have to go after a whole new market. It really isn't clear that we've got a problem, so I decided to forget the whole thing. That's my decision. Any problems?

Floyd Abrams thinks there could be. Better check up on the product. Anybody gets hurt, the company's liable, augmented by the fact that now you're on notice that there may be something wrong with it. Powers protests that Nellie brought in the only copy of that memo by hand; they can just destroy it. Abrams wouldn't count on that; there are Xerox machines, you know, and if anything ever happened, she'd have to testify. So would you.

What does James Neal think of the situation? Neal has all of Abrams' worries, and points out, further, that there may be a zealous prosecutor out there who'd want to prosecute Powers as a criminal, for reckless conduct. He would stop right now and determine whether that space heater is dangerous. He might even want to consider a recall. Hy Powers does not look happy. I just lost my position, didn't I? comments Neal. Out on the street with me.

Powers wants to know if Neal really thinks it is the lawyer's place to tell the CEO how to make his business decisions. Neal's answer is instructive: "Yes, I think it's my place to tell you that that's bad judgment and you've also put me on the spot because I don't know what my ethical responsibilities are now....I think my primary responsibility is to the Board of Directors....now that I think about the danger to the company in continuation of the marketing of this Hot Boy heater, I think I've got to go to the Board of Directors and tell the real bosses of the corporation just exactly where we are."

Abrams thinks that Neal shouldn't be this worried this soon (he wants to keep *his* job). There's only one memo, at this point.

The Smoking Gun

Cost/Benefit Ethics

Let's get Sheila Birnbaum in on the consultation. The way I make these decisions, Powers continues, is to make two lists for myself, all the pros on one side and the cons on the other. I used to do it longhand, but now I use my little computer. "And I show you a memorandum that I did, my notes, just me to me. And there it's all laid out. Nellie's description of the difficulties, my estimate of how many fires this might cause, maybe forty fires a year, if what she says is true, which may not be true at all. Some people might get killed, maybe six. An estimate of how much it would cost to settle those lawsuits, maybe $200,000 apiece, a judgment about how much it would cost to reposition the product or recall the product: out of sight. And my conclusion: better to study this problem further, keep producing and, after all, I say at the bottom of the memo, the kind of people that use these Hot Boys, cheap space heaters, they're not really into lawsuits that much. They're much more interested in tacos and watermelons." Birnbaum immediately identifies that set of notes as a smoking gun document: if that's discovered, you're in for punitive damages as well as compensatory damages in suits that will follow "if you don't do the right things from that point forward."

Oh, in that case, I should destroy it, Powers figures. Get rid of it, right?

Wait a minute, says Birnbaum. Remember, "the documents that get destroyed or lost are...even worse than documents that are found, because of the inferences that juries make, and probably accurately, that if the document has been destroyed it says terrible things."

Abrams concludes that this document can fairly be viewed as "notes to yourself." So this is a much closer call. But please, don't *do* memos like that. Just don't write them.

Mr. Gillers, is there a problem in destroying that document? Steven Gillers doesn't think there is, not in any jurisdiction he knows of. And if it's tactically wise to destroy it, go ahead. The lawyers may have to deal with that later. "But it's not their job to help your future adversary down the line...Floyd and Sheila and Jim are perfectly within their rights to say, 'Get rid of it Charlie.' We'll deal with the fact that it doesn't exist if they discover that it ever did exist later. Right now you are legally permitted to get rid of it. We are ethically permitted to allow you to get rid of it. Get rid of it. They'll never think to ask the question about tacos and watermelon."

Stanley Chesley protests that that is incredible and wrong. Others agree. In this controversy, the moderator turns to Justice Scalia. Justice Scalia, is it all right for him to destroy that document? Over the same objections, Scalia shrugs: Sounds all right to me. Of course, Gillers adds, if legal action has begun, or you have reason to believe that one will begin soon, then you may not destroy any documents.

The Lawsuit

Let's go back in your career a few years, Mr. Chesley. You're in your office and fire engines roar by. Do you go after them? This ploy is a bit obvious for Chesley, and he refuses to play: No. Never chased fire engines, or ambulances. Will Mr. Cotchett chase them? No. "I might go out of interest, of course. Get to the bottom line. Would I chase a client down the street looking for the..." The moderator protests that he likes to get to bottom lines slowly. Anyway, you go. While at the fire, you see an ambulance preparing to take away the burned body of a girl killed in the fire. Her father is grieving beside the ambulance. You overhear conversation to the effect that the fire was caused by a space heater. Would you say anything to the father? Yes, I would. "I'd go right up to that father and I'd say, 'Sir, you better investigate what caused that fire. And you better make sure you get someone who's good and competent and understands the problem.' Absolutely, without a question." Would you give him your card? No. "But I'd certainly make him aware." How, the moderator wants to know, is this tenement dweller going to pay for your services? Cotchett will take the case on a contingency basis, and proceeds to characterize this way of practicing law as "opening the courthouse door" to the poor person in society.

Games

Legal action has begun. And in the discovery process, Hy Powers is being asked questions by the plaintiff's attorney. How do I prepare for this deposition? he asks Sheila Birnbaum. Birnbaum gives the standard reply. "I would tell you to tell the truth, to not volunteer and expand on answers, but answer the question directly that's being given to you. And to only answer if you're sure that you know the answer. That you shouldn't guess at things if you don't know something. You can tell somebody you don't remember or you don't know something." "You would never tell me to lie, would you?" "Absolutely not."

What about "I don't remember"? Neal is called back into consultation, only to point out that if you *do* remember, "I don't remember" is just as much of a lie as anything else, and if you say it when it isn't true, you perjure yourself. And if I know you plan to perjure yourself, then I'm going to have to withdraw (second job I've lost today). "If I'm an honest, ethical counsel, I would have to withdraw."

Maybe Abrams will be more helpful. Mr. Abrams, do I have to spill my guts to them? No, says Abrams, but you have to tell the truth, and answer the questions. As narrowly as possible, right? Yes, generally narrowly. "Suppose they ask me, 'Mr. Powers, were any memos written in response to the Nellie memorandum?' I don't want to tell them....I don't really consider it a memorandum....It was like personal notes." The lawyers agree with Birnbaum that denying you wrote a "memo" on grounds that the document was really "notes" is a fine cut. Well, says Powers, those were notes to myself, not really a memo. So, Mr. Abrams, can I just say, There was no memo? Abrams doesn't think so, and would urge him not to do it. Well, what if we get him to clarify that question—say, that memo means some communication to someone else? Sure, says Abrams, "if I could get him to say in some fashion on the record that he wants something which we don't have, then the answer is 'we don't have it.' And if I could get him to clarify his request in a way which cuts out notes to myself or doodles on a piece of paper or things I said to people other than Nellie, for example. It depends on what the question is and how the question can be fairly understood."

Truth or Gamesmanship

But isn't this all gamesmanship? Mr. Cotchett, suppose you're representing the defendant in a suit over an automobile accident. Your client tells you, 'you know, I'm supposed to wear prescription glasses when I drive, and I wasn't wearing them. I was wearing my sunglasses.' Now the question comes down: "Were you wearing your glasses at the time of the accident?" Can your client say yes? Yes, he can, but then there will be a follow-up question. No, there's no follow-up. Then it's all right? Well, says Abrams, if it was a material fact in that accident, I might have a tough time with that.

Judge Merhige, what do you think of this? Is this the real world we're talking about? Merhige answers, "I'm afraid we are. I'm not very proud of it. It seems to me that we're forgetting the oath that you take in the first place, and that is 'to tell the truth, the *whole* truth.' If he asked you for glasses, you knew what he meant. Prescription glasses, glasses you usually wear. You ought to tell him."

Stephen Gillers points out that this is the way the process works—both sides carefully weigh their words. Everybody becomes a literary critic, and if it's notes and not a memo it doesn't count, if it's reaction and not response, it doesn't count. "And if the other side did not frame the question more particularly, we play blame the victim. That's what we do. We've done it for generations and we do it today." Justice Scalia points out that's why we hire lawyers for this sort of thing. Yes, Chesley responds, and that's why lawyers learn to talk about *all* kinds of writing—"memo, note, letter, or any other kind of document in reaction, response, reply, or in any other way caused by" that Nellie memo. And that's why cases are not likely to stand or fall on these words. Gillers comments that not all lawyers are smart enough to do that, and the ones who don't are taken advantage of.

Blaming the Victim

Professor Smith has had enough of this. This is *supposed* to be conversation on *ethics* and the law. I know you talk inside the house, as lawyers, in strict utilitarian terms, using cost-benefit analysis. "Now that's not the only ethical tradition that we have. And if you're telling me that, in effect, what you call ethics of the law is simply utilitarianism or cost-benefit analysis, how do you plug someone's death into cost-benefit?...You said before, when we were talking about people dying from this damn heater, that you were willing to pay the price. How're you going to pay the price of death?..." Gillers concludes that Immanuel Kant would have made a lousy lawyer but a fine judge.

Your Witness

So we go to law. In discovery, Hyram Powers turns out not to recall whether or not there was any writing at all about the Hot Boy. But towards the end of the trial, Tess Trueheart shows up in Chesley's office. Seems she used to be secretary to Hyram Powers, and she found this memo on a disk in her files. It turns out to be the cost-benefit analysis of changing the switch on the Hot Boy. She doesn't have a copy, but she remembers it word for word and she recites it, down to the tacos and the watermelons. Mr. Chesley, can you use her evidence? He certainly can, and goes to court immediately to have her name added to the list of witnesses he intends to call.

Mr. Neal, you're representing Hot Products. What are you going to do about this testimony? Are you interested in Tess's background? He certainly is. This testimony is devastating, and I must destroy Tess's credibility or my client is destroyed. Would you hire a private investigator? Sure. OK, here's what he finds out: Tess Trueheart has not always been her name. She changed it about five years ago, after a history that included drugs, mental illness, and a very messy divorce. Are you going to use this information? Neal hopes that he really doesn't know she's truthful. No such luck. "So I know she's telling the absolute truth; I know it's in my power to make her appear to be a liar....It's the most difficult decision, I think, that a trial lawyer faces. I think I would come down, God forgive me...Make her look like a liar." Cross-examine, then.

"Your name is Tess Trueheart?...How long's it been Tess Trueheart, Tess? Were you ever known as anything else, Tess?" Will the judges make her answer that? Judge Merhige will. Judge Patel is having none of this. Counsel will not call the witness "Tess" in her courtroom, and once past that, we will have a session *in camera* to find out what he's doing with this line of questioning and whether or not he will be permitted to proceed with it. Suppose he gets a straight answer—changed my name five years ago—he will proceed to bring out the history of mental illness. "Miss Trueheart, you said you saw this mythical document you've been talking about up here on the stand. Have you ever had any occasions in the past to have auditory hallucinations or to see things that didn't exist?" And when the history of institutionalization and hallucinations comes out, Neal says "Aha!" and sits down.

But (setting aside the fate of the witness for the moment) look at your use of the word "mythical." How can you call that document "mythical" when you know it existed? Well, the judge might get after me for that one, Neal says. But if I can get away with it, I'll call it that. "An adversary society puts us in all these ethical dilemmas at all times, because the whole concept is that that man is going to do his job, I'm going to do my job, and out of the clash of these jobs will come the truth and justice....I would have to destroy Tess. I would have to do it even though I knew [she told the truth about the document]. Because I'm using the truth. The truth is that she's changed her name. The truth is that she's been institutionalized, having auditory hallucinations and seeing things that didn't exist. I'm putting out the truth....Now my goal, I guess you'd say, is to deceive the jury, but I think that's permitted in our system."

John Smith disagrees. "If what you're telling us you have to do is necessitated by the system, we have to take another look at the system." Truth does not come out through conflict. The best you can expect from conflict is a better definition of the issues.

Judge Patel reminds us that she would not let him get away with any of this. Some power to protect the truth resides in the judge: "I have the power to correct what I may believe is an effort on both sides to deceive the jury...". As to the mental history, it depends on how proximate it is to the event. If there's a lengthy history of no problem, then we must omit it. Judge Merhige agrees that it depends on the relevance of the testimony.

Merhige goes on to point out that the adversary system has worked for a long time. Lawyers are not always looking for the truth. But if they stay within the rules, the system works all right. We have a jury there, and the jury can pass on the credibility of the witness. Justice Scalia agrees. He can understand why Smith might want to scrap the adversary system, but look at the alternatives. "The adversary system has been described...as based on the premise that if you take two photographs, one focused too far and the other focused too close, you can superimpose the two to get a sharp image." Patel respectfully dissents. All too often the only effect is to obfuscate the truth.

Stephen Gillers tries to put the whole thing in perspective: "Judge Patel's problem is that she doesn't know if the witness is telling the truth, and Mr. Neal is not going to tell her, and she can't ask him because he knows that as the result of a privileged communication." Can't you at least ask him not to deliberately lead the system to an untruth? "Listen, for better or worse, and it may be worse and we could all vote to change it tomorrow, but Mr. Neal has the opposite ethical obligation. As Justice Scalia correctly says, his obligation is to introduce that truth that helps him, and to encourage the jury to disbelieve what he knows to be the truth if it helps the other side. And the other side is going to do the same thing and the truth that we finally get, the so-called courtroom truth, may be false but it's true for the purposes of our justice system. Sounds odd? It *is* odd. But that's the system we've been living with for hundreds of years."

The Courtroom Truth

Terms of Settlement

Well, the trial is drawing to a close, Mr. Neal. The last statements are made, it's Friday afternoon, and you're sitting enjoying a Jack Daniels. Monday the case goes to the jury. Then a young associate of yours comes in, ashen-faced. Seems he's found a disk in the files, put it on the screen, called up an index entry "Nellie," and there's that note, down to the tacos and the watermelons. Now what do we do?

I have to produce that, says Neal. I go to the limits of what the Code of Professional Responsibility will allow me, and at this point the Code says that I must produce that document.

What should he do, Mr. Cooper? Settle on the spot. Chesley wants a million; give it to him. Nope, says Neal; I'd have to tell Chesley that document exists before we settle. Scalia agrees; a settlement offer cannot be based on misinformation.

A Confidentiality Agreement

So you reveal the document and the offer goes up, to three million. You'd settle for three million but you want the documents back. Sheila Birnbaum agrees that this sort of confidentiality is often requested. You can get all the documents back that were subpoenaed. Plaintiff and defendant often agree on that point, and there may already have been a protective order in the case requiring that.

Chesley would prefer not to return the documents, or at least he would like a guarantee that they will not be destroyed so that he can sue again. But he has an obligation to maximize recovery for *this* client. And if he turns down the settlement terms—so many million in return for the right to destroy the documents—and the case goes to trial and his client loses, his client has a valid complaint against him. But he still doesn't want to give them the right to destroy the document. That's unethical. It means that no one could ever sue Hot Boy again. Scalia suggests he could quench his unhappiness with more money—ask for six million. That's not the point, retorts Chesley; he wants a guarantee that the documents will not be destroyed so that they will be available for use by future claimants. And if Hy Powers won't make that deal, maybe he has an obligation to go to court. Scalia points out that that course of action means making his present clients pay so that future clients can recover.

Robert Maynard is the most likely representative of the public interest here. What does he think of these terms? He doesn't like them. "The public interest in knowing how these matters are resolved is frequently compromised by settlements in which part of the understanding of both parties is that all of the documents that have been identified as confidential in litigation will be destroyed upon the settlement. And history, as well as news, suffers as a result of that practice. We have, here in California, companies that exist solely for the purpose of making certain that confidential documents at the conclusion of litigation are not just burned, but burned and then boiled in sulfuric acid....And I think it's a troublesome aspect of our system...I

Public Obligations

heard Judge Merhige use the term, well, it's private litigation. Well, I'm not so sure that after the taxpayers of the nation have paid what they pay for the cost of litigation that, indeed, it is fair to construe the product of that event as being private." In the case of this company, and this document, there may be an overriding public obligation to keep those documents and not let them, as they do in all too many cases, disappear.

Mr. Cooper, you're chairman of the board of Hot Products. You just had to pay six million dollars to get the documents back. Now what do you do? First, I fire Powers and I give Mr. Neal a raise. We should have pushed this issue at the beginning; fixed the product and avoided all this.

Robert Banks is not convinced. I still don't see the product as bad, and I certainly don't see the issue as public. In any case, the corporation has got to fix its own product.

Judge Patel will not sign the order. The parties may stipulate or agree to anything they want, but it's not her job to supervise secret agreements. Furthermore, secrecy is virtually impossible at this point; by now half the plaintiff's bar may know about it. The parties will be back if I sign it, looking for enforcement, but any court order of this type is essentially unenforceable. If they insist on a court imprimatur, they can let the issue go to trial; that's what the system is all about.

Keeping Secrets

Maynard comments that nothing will remain secret. If the reporter he puts on the case does not have the terms of settlement in 24 hours, he'll put someone else on the beat. He'll find out from all the blabbermouths in the legal community, second only to journalism in its inability to keep a secret. Sometimes those lawyers like publicity, and they'll leak it themselves. Or go talk to the court reporter. Don't try finding out from the judge.

Disturbed by all this, the moderator puts one last question: Justice Scalia, we have been through a lawyer's story here in an exercise that was meant to explore truth and ethics. We haven't heard a whole lot of truth and we haven't heard a whole lot of ethics. Now let me ask you. Does this system simply put lawyers into roles that other people couldn't stand, that would be immoral for a regular citizen?

Scalia replies, "Of course they're put into roles. That's a very good word for what the common law adversary trial is, that is, a play....We do it all as a drama and the lawyers from both sides do play roles. That's the system we have. It's the system we've had for hundreds of years, and I think by and large it works well. What we've been talking about today are largely questions at the margin....consider the alternatives. What do you do? Do you put the witness on the stand and let the lawyer ask as broad and unskilled questions as 'tell me everything relevant about this case....' The only alternative is to go to the inquisitorial system and have an investigating judge. And then you're going to win or lose depending on how good a judge you happen to have gotten. At least when you pick your lawyer you know that if he's bad it's your fault."

Truth or Justice

Neal gets in a final sortie: "I don't want to be put in a position that I ever said that I'm out for the truth. The adversary system is not a system calculated to produce the truth....It is calculated to produce, instead, justice in the criminal system; and justice is totally different from truth."

A REVIEW OF SELECTIONS FROM THE SOURCE READER

Before going on to synthesize the philosophical background and the television presentation, this would be a good time to review certain of the readings in the history of ethics that pertain especially to this topic.

The tension felt throughout the discussion comes from one very basic tradition in philosophical ethics: truth is good, and therefore the whole business of civil law—suits, claims and counterclaims, verdicts reached heaven knows how—is wrong. We have always known that under the stress of verbal combat, verbal virtue would give way to verbal sin, and lying. While we prefer verbal combat to combat with guns and grenades (that's why we invented the court system, after all), we recognize the warping effect it has on human candor. And we do not like it.

Selections for this chapter:

> Immanuel Kant, *Foundations of the Metaphysics of Morals,* **Source Reader** p. 127
> The *Bible*, Sermon on the Mount, **Source Reader** p. 81

For Kant, the only society worth having was totally honest: the Kingdom of Ends, an ideal of a rational community, where each, having the knowledge available to all and desiring only to honor the law, decides on courses of thought and conduct ruled by reason, honor, duty, and concern for others. Since there are no opposed interests, there is no temptation to engage in untruthfulness to protect them. The suits avoided by Kant are foreseen by Jesus of Nazareth, who urges his followers to make peace with their adversaries on the steps of the court rather than going through with the trial—the better to avoid the distractions, the anger, and the deception that destroy the soul. What can the lawyer offer in defense of her profession? Does the moral ideal of the ethical lawyer depend essentially on an imperfect world and the self-interested and short-sighted people who live in it?

SYNTHESIS AND DISCUSSION

Truth and the lawyer coexist very uneasily in the American practice of law. As we have seen in the television presentation, the lawyers' duty to serve the client's interest first and only (within the bounds of their Code) puts enormous pressure on truthfulness. As representative of the distortions introduced, consider some of the decisions taken in the course of the dialogue:

- the decision not to reveal the defects of the product (the Hot Boy space heater);
- the decision to conceal from the court the reasoning, especially the record of the reasoning, that went into the first decision;
- the decision to make Tess Trueheart look like a liar;
- the decision to make the right to destroy the crucial documents a condition of settlement of the case.

First of all, what is the truth about the product? That it is an inexpensive way to keep your rooms warm, especially in areas where landlords are notoriously lax about keeping the furnace going? Or that it is unsafe, a threat to your family, likely under some (unusual) conditions to tip over and fail to shut off, starting a fire that could be fatal? Both are true, as it happens. But which is the important truth?

The American business system does not prosper by publishing all the truth about its products. It chooses to publish, in its advertising, only that part of the truth that serves its interests. (It used to tell outright lies in its advertising, but the federal laws that regulate such communications put a stop to that.) The situation here is a bit different: we are not asking how to advertise the Hot Boy, but how to react to the news that there may be a safety problem with it. But the businessman's reaction, as here portrayed, echoes the public relations attitude of the advertiser: only the truth that is known to the public counts as real truth, and only the truth that serves our interests should be released to the public. Dissent is expressed by the other panelists; interestingly, the lawyer Neal, who adopts a very different role later in the dialogue, is one of those to express it. Should the businessman have told the truth at this juncture? We will let this question hang in the air, for the moment.

At the point of the second decision, the safety of the product is a matter for litigation, and the plaintiff's side wants to know if there is any record of the decision to market this dangerous product. For if there is evidence that those responsible knew that the product was dangerous, they are much more culpable than if they did not (see *Exodus*, **Source Reader** p. 73). There is such evidence, a note that any plaintiff's attorney would pay any price for—it is written by the CEO, who had full power to recall the product, so it is no academic exercise. It contains a callous cost/benefit analysis in which the CEO puts a monetary value on a human life ($200,000), which is guaranteed to send any jury through the roof; and to put the icing on the cake, it finishes with a racial slur aimed at the largest minority populations of our largest cities. (Incidentally, it is highly unlikely that the CEO in this situation would actually be aware of the product's defects. "Plausible deniability" was invented in the business world, not in government. But let us continue with the hypothetical.) Let the note be read to the jury, and judgments in the millions are ensured.

The attorneys agree that the pretrial "discovery" process is going to be very important for this case. For the purpose of this discovery process is to bring all documents material to the case into the court for all parties to examine. The note is clearly material to the case at hand. The CEO knows of the existence of the note, as does his attorney. The rules governing discovery make it *very* inadvisable to lie, as all the attorneys agree. The CEO is the one being questioned, and his lawyer is scripting his answers. The person asking the questions is the one who has the most to gain from finding this document or anything like it. Then how can the document possibly be kept concealed from the court? By scripting responses so that the CEO is not-quite-telling-the-truth while not-quite-lying. Your job, as CEO, is to hope that the questioner does not quite describe the document correctly, to construe the question in the narrowest possible way, and then to deny, altogether innocently, that the document *asked for* exists. Judge Merhige testily points out that that, too, is a lie, relative to the witness's duty to tell the *whole* truth, but the attorneys agree that such a response is entirely proper.

As a point of interest, this is one of the few places in the dialogue where the inherent conflict of direction between judge and attorney comes to the surface. A judge trying to reach a decision that will not be reversed is at a tremendous disadvantage when the "smoking gun" turns up only after the decision is reached; the judges really are interested in getting the "whole truth." Thus when John Smith, the philosopher, objects that this whole quibbling enterprise is nothing but unethical, citing Immanuel Kant as his source, Stephen Gillers quips that Kant would have made a lousy lawyer but a great judge. Not considered in the hypothetical is the possibility that Kant may not have the whole ethical truth. We do not permit our legal system to force individuals to incriminate themselves, on grounds that protection of individual rights is more important than protecting the nearest possible access to the truth. Possibly the protections surrounding the discovery process in such cases constitute a rule forbidding self-incrimination for corporations: corporate officers may not be forced to testify truthfully on corporate misdeeds.

But whatever face we put on it, the obvious purpose of the exercise is to conceal the truth from those who seek it. What are we to make of this mendacious exercise? Can we live with the situation that Gillers refers to as "blaming the victim"—blaming the interrogating lawyer if he phrases his questions in such a way that the witness can give him false answers without landing in jail for perjury? We want truth in our courtrooms, and the judges need it. Our lawyers are advocates for their clients, but they are also officers of the court, with a duty of candor to the court on all matters relevant to the case at hand. What evidence is there of that duty in the behavior here? Why do we tolerate this?

The third decision, James Neal's decision to destroy Tess Trueheart's character in order to render her true testimony unbelievable, is clearly wrong. Further, Neal knows it is wrong, and piously asks God's forgiveness for doing it as he launches into it. But he thinks his client's case requires it, and that's all that matters, he seems to think. But is it all that matters? Doesn't this decision take us past the limits of the tolerable?

Elsewhere in this volume there is a chapter on the criminal law, in which a superficially similar question is put: does the lawyer have the right to impugn the character of the murder victim in order to make his client, charged with her murder, look less guilty? Possibly, in that case, the lawyer has that right: the woman is dead; the presumed killer's life is at stake; and there is some reason to believe that the character and behavior of the victim may have contributed to the crime. But this case is different: We are talking about attacking the character of a living woman making a difficult recovery from illness; the only thing at stake is the client's money; and the attorney knows that there is no connection between anything he will bring to light and the testimony that she gave. He knows the testimony was true.

Yet the only hope that he can hold out to us, that the witness may be rescued from destruction and the testimony allowed to stand, is the slight hope that the judge will figure out what he's up to and put a stop to his shenanigans. "Stop me before I kill again" is usually the cry of the desperate psychopath, not the plea of one of the most respected practitioners of an ancient and honorable profession. Yet Neal is helpless to stop his own depredations as long as they serve his client. What form of coercion is this?

And finally, there is the willful destruction of the evidence, connived in by both parties. The note having been found, Hot Products wants nothing more than its destruction. The plaintiffs want nothing more than lots of money. The public interest would best be served by publication of all documents relating to the safety of the Hot Boy in *Consumers' Report*, or better yet, in the most widely read newspaper in the parts of town where tacos and watermelons are most in favor. That word should get out to all who have suffered (how many fires have actually been caused by that product?), so that they may seek legal relief themselves. It should certainly get out to all who own Hot Boys, so that they may take measures to protect themselves. And the word is now available to the court, a public organ if ever there was one, since it is figuring in the rapid settlement of a court case on the point of going to the jury. Yet here are the parties to the dispute, agreeing to bury the truth and destroy the documentation of the truth, in return for a rich settlement. As public policy, does this make any sense at all?

In all of this, how does the lawyer define his own task and ethic? The panel strongly suggests that there may no longer be a single ethic for lawyers. "Loyalty to the client" claims pride of place among their values, but that leaves the definition of the value dangling from the identity of the client. Chesley has made his fortune representing injured plaintiffs against corporations with deep pockets. Therefore he identifies his motive as "concern for the underdog" and his task to preserve any and all evidence that will permit suits and more suits. Abrams casts himself here as the defendant's lawyer; his motive is protection of privacy, and he therefore counsels maximum concealment of any damaging communications. More to the point, he counsels nonproduction of such communications and periodic destruction (the shredders and the sulfuric acid) of any and all records that might ever be used against the company. Neal, consulted in confidence by the CEO of a company, does not immediately know who his client is, and finally goes to the Board of Directors (his "real bosses") to tell them what the CEO said. The company lawyer is lawyer for the entity, and it is never quite clear just what may be said to him, by whom, in confidence. In practice, the corporation lawyer often must remind corporate officers that his confidentiality is limited by his responsibility to the corporation—a sort of "Miranda Warning" for civil proceedings.

Recall, the criminal law justifications for absolute loyalty do not apply to lawyers in civil cases. The lives at stake are those of the future sufferers from the product; truth will save their lives. At stake for the defense lawyer's client is only money, the tender devotion to which got him into this jam to begin with. In these cases, it would seem appropriate that the interests of truth and public policy should triumph over the protection of the client. As all the lawyers point out, these interests cannot triumph under the Code which currently governs the legal profession.

Meanwhile, even as the habit of concealment and ruthless defense of the client has turned half the bar into connivers at falsehood, it has turned the other half of the bar into ambulance chasers on a grand scale. The reason why the plaintiff's bar, the trial lawyers, have such a field day in the courts is that any persistent investigation of any corporate malfunction inevitably turns up a trail of lies, cover-ups, and the unmistakable smell of sulfuric acid from the last batch of memos destroyed; and that is all you need for generous, indeed unreasonably large, awards from the jury. So plaintiffs' attorneys prosper, to the horror of the insurance companies, Boards of Directors, and all whose financial fate in any way rests with the companies they sue.

Why is this? Why are juries so generous? The answer brings us full circle. The truth of the matter, the real truth (since that is our subject), is that as a people we value the truth, and honesty, and the telling of the truth especially by those in a position to conceal the truth. And if that value seems to have no place in the Boardroom and the courtroom, very well then, we will champion it from the lonely outpost of the jury box, at whatever expense to our Hy Powered corporations, until the CEOs and the judges and the lawyers get the message.

QUESTIONS FOR YOUR REFLECTION

1. Can the lawyer's role in society be portrayed as an ethical role, based solely on the materials presented in this chapter? (Do not take into account the role of the criminal lawyer.) How? Pick one of the lawyers' presentations and evaluate it. Is that lawyer's approach likely to advance justice?

2. Whom does the corporate lawyer represent? He is supposed to be loyal to "the corporation." In the case presented, the lawyer immediately decided that the CEO was too dangerous to keep around, and went to the Board of Directors and revealed what had been told him in confidence. Is this right? Who could trust the company lawyer, then?

3. Can you draft a rule that would preserve the lawyer's ability to cast doubt on doubtful testimony in cross-examination, but would prevent the kind of defamation of character recommended by Neal for Tess Trueheart?

4. Stephen Gillers points out a few times that we could change the system tomorrow. The others agree, but are dubious about the alternatives available. What are the alternatives? See what you can find out about the judicial inquisitorial method and other types of court systems in other countries. Do they provide genuinely different ways of doing things? What are their disadvantages?

5. The Biblical injunction against lawsuit follows from a recognition that involvement in suit is normally distracting, hostile, and dangerous. Is it possible to have a court system that embodies the law of love? How?

6. Find out what you can about Alternative Dispute Resolution in your area. It wasn't mentioned in the program, but it shows promise for settling some large civil suits under some conditions. What are its advantages and disadvantages?

SUGGESTIONS FOR FURTHER READING

Special Supplementary Text:
SISSELA BOK. *Lying: Moral Choice in Public and Private Life*. New York: Random House, 1977.

ARONSON, ROBERT. *Problems in Professional Responsibility*. St Paul, MN: West, 1978.

FEINBERG, JOEL, AND HYMAN GROSS, EDS. *Philosophy of Law*, 3rd edition. Belmont, CA: Wadsworth Publishing Co., 1986.

FREEDMAN, MONROE. *Lawyers' Ethics in an Adversary System*. Indianapolis, IN: Bobbs-Merrill, 1975.

FRIED, CHARLES. "The Lawyer as Friend: The Moral Foundations of the Lawyer-Client Relationship," *Yale Law Journal* 85 (1976):1060.

GOROVITZ, SAMUEL, AND BRUCE MILLER. Professional Responsibility in the Law: A Curriculum Report. Council for Philosophical Studies, 1977.

HAZARD, GEOFFREY C., JR. *Ethics in the Practice of Law*. New Haven, CT: Yale University Press, 1978.

KAUFMAN, ANDREW. *Problems in Professional Responsibility*. Boston: Little, Brown, 1976.

KELLY, MICHAEL. *Legal Ethics and Legal Education*. Hastings-on-Hudson, NY: Institute of Society, Ethics and the Life Sciences, 1980.

LUBAN, DAVID, ED. *The Good Lawyer: Lawyers' Roles and Lawyers' Ethics*. Totowa, NJ: Rowman and Allanheld, 1983.

MORGAN, THOMAS, AND RONALD ROTUNDA. *Problems and Materials on Professional Responsibility*. Mineola, NY: Foundation, 1976.

PATTERSON, L. RAY. *Legal Ethics: The Law of Professional Responsibility*. New York: Matthew Bender, 1982.

POSNER, RICHARD A. *Economic Analysis of Law*, 2nd edition. Boston: Little, Brown, 1977.

REDLICH, NORMAN. *Professional Responsibility: A Problem Approach*. Boston: Little, Brown, 1976.

SCHRADER, DAVID E., ED. *Ethics and the Practice of Law*. Englewood Cliffs, NJ: Prentice Hall, 1988.

SCHWARTZ, MURRAY L. "The Zeal of the Civil Advocate." *American Bar Foundation Journal*, 1983 (1983):543.

STEWART, JAMES B. *The Partners: Inside America's Most Powerful Law Firms*. New York: Simon and Schuster, 1983.

chapter 11 _____

HELP AND HARM:

The Human Experiment

QUESTIONS TO KEEP IN MIND AS YOU READ THE CHAPTER

1. Utilitarianism tells us to "maximize human welfare," or to produce as much happiness as possible for as many people as possible, minimizing pain for everyone. Do you sometimes have to cause pain, or harm, in order to do good? (Think of examples.) Do you think it is right to adopt policies which are clearly beneficent (that is, they produce good on balance), but involve harming a few people along the way?

2. I've been told that many medical advances simply would not be possible without the opportunity to test drugs and procedures on human subjects. Do you think the fact that future generations will benefit justifies using human beings as guinea pigs—or laboratory mice?

3. Research with human subjects is an area of moral dilemmas where, in response to a particular popular outcry, Congress established a commission specifically to investigate the ethical problems of the practice. Do you think this approach would work in other settings for other problems?

4. Do the financial pressures in testing new drugs make all such testing suspect? Is there inevitable distortion of results and choices?

THE CONCEPT OF BENEFICENCE

On the face of it, the moral imperatives "to do no harm" (nonmaleficence) and "to help others where possible" (beneficence), seem simple enough. They are easily understood, we might think, and always applicable. To disabuse us of *that* impression, Plato has Socrates show us their complications in the second major interchange in the *Republic*, the dialogue with Polemarchus. Polemarchus foolishly claims to know that "justice," or the moral life, is identical with "helping friends and harming enemies," as you will recall (if you do not, reread Plato, **Source Reader** p. 19). By the time Socrates finishes asking those infernal questions of his, Polemarchus can no longer tell friend from enemy nor help from harm (having been forced to admit that a "friend" is anyone who "helps" you, and that "help" is anything that makes you better, stronger, healthier, or more virtuous). Where moral attributes like "virtue" are fed into the help and harm equation, the implications of those imperatives turn out to be very difficult to discern. After all, if one result of my action is to make people more loving, while another result is to decrease their felt happiness, who can say which result is more important?

But the modern world is in no mood for complications of that sort. For a variety of historical reasons—the rise of individualism in the Renaissance, entailing more trust in the perceptions and desires of the individual; the rise of science, entailing more trust in the plain evidence of the senses— the modern mind, unlike the ancient, is perfectly willing to let each human define her own happiness, and to base that definition on her own experience of pleasure and pain. It is on this foundation—the universal experience of pleasure and pain—that Jeremy Bentham erects the system of Utilitarianism.

Utilitarianism is a compact theory, adequately and succinctly stated in the writings of its two major exponents, Jeremy Bentham and John Stuart Mill. There is no need to clarify, summarize, or interpret the theory; Bentham and Mill write with a clarity, elegance, and command of the English language that writers since their time have struggled in vain to imitate. The purpose of this essay is to explore some of the implications of the theory, especially as they appear in our considerations of the permissibility of research with human subjects.

The first of the implications is that the prescriptions (commands) and proscriptions (prohibitions) derived from this or any consequentialist theory are not absolute, but require balancing by their very nature. Harm, pain, discomfort, or at least blank spaces in the pleasure, are inescapable, and we seek only that life, or course of action or treatment, which will minimize the pain and maximize the pleasure. This implication is in bright contrast with the conclusions of deontological or nonconsequentialist theories like that of Immanuel Kant or Thomas Aquinas, not to mention Amos. For any deontological theory, injustice is not to be "balanced" with justice; it is to be avoided, condemned, and punished. Truth is not to be doled out in appropriate measure, "balanced" with untruth; it is to be told, and respected, and followed. Utilitarianism denies all absolutes; it recognizes no devils, no terrible moral pitfalls, no evil save the ordinary suffering in body and mind to which our mortality is subject.

When we turn to clinical research—the attempt to discover generalizable truth about matters of health and medicine, where human beings take the place of the test tubes and white mice used in other scientific laboratories—utilitarian calculations are put to a severe test. What is the appropriate formula for balancing the pain, discomfort, and inconvenience of the tests, examinations, doses of medicine, or whatever procedures the research subject is to endure, against the long-term gains for medical science of the knowledge that will be acquired? Before tackling this question, a few distinctions will help us keep the field in order.

We may begin with the distinction between "research" and "practice," with a side comment on "experimentation." (These and all distinctions, definitions, and citations in the remainder of the essay are derived from the first two chapters of your supplemental text, *Ethics and Regulation of Clinical Research* by Robert Levine.) "Research" refers to a class of activities designed to develop or contribute to generalizable knowledge—theories, principles, or relationships that can be corroborated by ordinary scientific observation. "Practice" of medicine refers to a class of activities designed solely to enhance the well-being of an individual patient or client. The purpose of practice is to diagnose and treat; the standard for practice is a reasonable expectation of success for this patient. Success is not certain, and sometimes treatments do not work as they are expected to work. At this point a practicing physician may try a drug in a new application, or a combination of drugs that he has not used before—in short, he may "experiment" with treatments to see what, if anything, will help this patient. To experiment means to try; to depart from the usual schedule of practice to find something brand new and just right for this individual. Experimentation is specifically forbidden in research. If the protocol (the design of the research) calls for two milligrams of the drug being tested to be administered to each subject each day, that is what must be done, and the trials will be useless if the investigators depart from their schedule.

We should also understand the phases of new drugs research. The Food and Drug Administration (FDA), which must approve every drug sold in America, requires different types of tests for each proposed new drug. Drugs must first be tested on animals (hence the strains of white mice whose sole function is to develop tumors to be treated with new drugs). If the animal trials offer some indication that the drug may be useful to humans, the company recruits normal, healthy volunteers to receive measured doses of the drug to determine, over a period of time, whether the drug has dangerous or undesirable side effects. These tests on normal volunteers are called "Phase I Clinical Pharmacology," and are designed to determine levels of toxicity—whether, in short, the drug is safe.

With some types of drugs, research begins directly on sick patients, people who might be expected to benefit from the treatment. "Phase II Clinical Investigation" consists of controlled clinical trials designed to demonstrate effectiveness and relative safety. A "controlled" trial is one in which only some (usually half) of the patients in a group of equally sick people get the drug. The other half, known as "controls," don't get the drug that is being tested. Then if the half getting the drug gets better, and the other half doesn't, the investigators know the drug is effective. On the other hand, if the half getting the drug starts suffering intense abdominal pain, while the other half does not, we know that the problem is the drug and not just the hospital food. (Incidentally, J. S. Mill, whose *Utilitarianism*, p. 166 in your **Source Reader**, is one major text for this chapter, also wrote a book called *Logic*, in which he sets forth the "Methods of Similarity and Difference," used in those last two sentences.)

Controlled trials are more complicated than just described because we are dealing with human psychology, and humans are impressionable beings. Whether or not we heal from injury or illness often depends on our state of mind, especially on our confidence in the quality of our care. So we can't just give the control group *nothing*; their depression at being left out of the drug trial would worsen their condition all by itself. So we give them a "placebo," an injection or a pill (whatever the real drug looks like) of some inert substance, so they'll think they're getting the drug. For the same reason, we can't tell them that they're the control group; that is why these trials are called "blind."

But the problem of getting solid, objective results in these trials lies as much with the psychology of the investigator as with that of the subject. Built into the structure of the scientific profession in this country is the fact that the investigators desperately want the drug to succeed. They may have helped to develop the drug, and have at least an emotional investment in its success; increasingly, they may also have a financial investment in it, and be interested in seeing it get to market. If they are to choose, from the initial group of subjects, which are to receive the drug and which the placebo, they will, even unconsciously, choose those that seem to have the best chance for recovery anyway. So we don't let them choose. We assign subjects to groups by rolling the dice, or, if dice are unavailable, by some other random procedure. That is why these are called "randomized" clinical trials; the investigators have no role in choosing which "arm" of the research protocol each subject goes to, but have only to report the results. They may not do *that* objectively if they know which patients have been put on which arm, since they'll see improvement in patients on the drug before they see it in the controls. So the assignment is done by a computer, the doses are labeled by patient number only, and only at the end, when the protocol is opened, do the physician investigators find out which of their patients have been receiving the drug (by that time all the reports are filed). That is why these randomized trials are called "double blind": neither patient nor investigators know whether or not any given patient is receiving the drug.

So the investigator-subject relationship bears no relation at all to the doctor-patient relationship, even when the same doctor who is treating me for my disease is also testing a new drug for that disease on me. In her role as my doctor, she knows all about me, as a person as well as a "case," and individualizes every aspect of my care for my good. As investigator, she doesn't know if I'm getting this new experimental wonder drug or if I'm getting pink aspirin, and she can't find out. Are these two roles compatible? It doesn't help the matter that Phase I trials are conducted on sick people rather than healthy volunteers only when the disease is so deadly that no possible remedy should be withheld from its victims (AIDS and cancer come to mind). So the patients who are used to test the efficacy of drugs *before* they've been tested for toxicity, or potential for harm, are precisely those most vulnerable patients with the least ability to evaluate what the doctor says. We will come back to this question later.

At the end of the Phase II trials, if effectiveness is basically established, we continue with Phase III Clinical Trials, controlled and uncontrolled. These will give us additional evidence on the effectiveness of the drug under different conditions, and more data on adverse side effects.

Incidentally, we need not always use a parallel group of patients as controls. Especially in the case of really deadly diseases, like AIDS, where everyone dies of the disease, it seems pointless to give half the group of patients aspirin "to see what happens"; what happens to AIDS patients who take aspirin is that they die. With that record, we can give the drug to everyone eligible, and any improvement at all that they enjoy has to be due to the drug; this procedure uses what are called "historical controls." The only reason for a controlled trial in a deadly disease protocol is to test the safety of the new drug—it might, after all, turn out to hasten death or make it more horrible. And the time frame of a randomized clinical trial is not set in iron: as soon as it becomes clear that some patients are doing much better or worse than others, the investigators can, in fact must, break the computer code, open the protocol and establish the actual effect of the drug being tested.

The ethical principles governing the use of human beings in scientific research are straightforward enough, and by now familiar. We must respect human dignity, autonomy, and the right to make choices. Human dignity, as Immanuel Kant points out, is not served when a person is used as a means to someone else's end rather than as an end in himself; the subject of research is certainly being used as a means. Then why not forbid such research on the grounds that it offends the dignity of the person? Because sometimes people want to be used as such means; if I am dying of a fatal disease, and know it, and know that nothing else can help me, I can still derive satisfaction from participating in a protocol that might, someday, help someone else. For that matter, as a healthy volunteer or general patient, I might not mind taking part in such research, if it isn't too inconvenient and might eventually be useful, just as I don't mind giving a pint of blood occasionally. All I ask is that I be told the purpose of the research, told what to expect in the way of inconvenience and side effects, told, if I am a patient and my disease is being studied, what alternative treatments are available to me—in short, that I go into this protocol fully informed about what is being done and why. This requirement is called "informed consent," and it is usually enforced, from the hospital's point of view, by having the subjects sign a "consent form," stating that they know the implications of the study and are willing to participate in it. Justice is also a requirement; we must guard against the tendency to do our research always on the disadvantaged or the institutionalized, simply because they are more available to the research community.

From the utilitarian point of view, the most important aspect of any acceptable research protocol is the risk/benefit ratio. The projected benefits of the study, multiplied by the probability of their occurring, must exceed the possible harms multiplied by their probability—by a good deal. This requirement throws us into all the difficulties of measuring benefits and harms inherent in Utilitarianism, and adds the difficulties of calculating probabilities, spread over an indefinitely large population. Most of the ethical restraints and procedures in the research process derive from the imperative to maximize the possibility that benefit will be realized and to minimize the risks to the subjects. Thus good research design is an ethical, not just a technical, imperative; the competence of the investigators, the importance of the knowledge to be gained, the necessity of the study in order to acquire that knowledge, and the efforts to keep the number of subjects to the minimum required for valid results, and to obtain results as soon as possible, are all part of the ethical framework of the study.

The field of research with human subjects enjoys (figuratively speaking) a distinction among professional fields: it is the only one whose conduct was discovered to be so abhorrent to human morals that a special federally sponsored commission, the National Commission for the Protection of Human Subjects of Biomedical and Behavioral Research, was established by Congress to make it more ethical. Highlights of that peculiarly lurid background are worthy of note.

Scientific research itself is not very old, so its abuses are recent history. For a long while we thought they began with the Nazis. The Nazis slaughtered upwards of six million Jews, plus other "undesirables," in their death camps. When the evidence of the slaughter of these millions at the hands of the Third Reich was presented at the War Crimes

Trials at Nuremberg after the war, attention was drawn not only to the brutal, but simple, killings by guards and executioners, but also to the very complex killings of prisoners by the doctors of the Third Reich in the course of what they called "research." "Research" was done, for instance, on how long it takes a woman to freeze to death in ice water, and how long men live when air is evacuated from their airtight cell. Surgeons did research on "bone grafts," for instance, and on the usefulness of electric shock to sterilize women. Their "experiments," done totally without controls, usually without documentation, often without hypotheses, were variations on torturing people to death, not variations on science. Nevertheless they were condemned as "scientific research" that had been conducted without the "informed consent" of the subjects. The Nuremberg Code that emerged from the trials laid down ten sensible rules limiting human subjects research, specifying protections for those subjects from harm and from coercion of any sort (see Appendix).

A more established history of abuse, this time on American soil, began to emerge in the early 1970s. It came out, for example, that since 1932 400 black men with syphilis had, quite without their knowledge, been subjects of research to determine the natural history of their disease if left untreated. In 1932 the research itself made sense (although the choice of subjects had more to do with the social position of blacks than it had to do with the nature of the disease, which knows no racial boundaries), since no one knew if the available cures might be worse than the disease. Late in the 1940s, when penicillin was readily available and 100 percent effective against the disease, it made no sense at all; but the men were not told, and the study continued until 1972 when it was called to an overdue halt.

The Tuskegee Syphilis Study was not alone. At about the same time it was revealed that retarded children had been infected with hepatitis at Willowbrook State School in New York to study therapies for the disease; that elderly patients at the Jewish Chronic Disease Hospital had been injected with cancer cells, quite without their knowledge, to see how fast their bodies would reject their cells; and that, in fact, in hospitals all over the country, physicians were carrying on their favorite research on patients forcibly recruited into protocols without any clue that they could or should protest. The icing on the political cake came with rumors of research on aborted fetuses, immediately after the 1973 Supreme Court decision legalizing abortion; protest marches in front of the National Institutes of Health were led by the twelve-year-old niece of Senator Edward Kennedy, and Congress immediately realized that it had to act.

In July 1974, Congress passed the National Research Act, which established the National Commission named above. Among the charges to the Commission were: "The Commission shall (i) conduct a comprehensive investigation and study *to identify the basic ethical principles which should underlie the conduct of biomedical and behavioral research involving human subjects,* (ii) develop guidelines which should be followed in such research *to assure that it is conducted in accordance with such principles...*" and recommend to the Secretary of Health, Education and Welfare (Health and Human Services) how those guidelines should be enforced (emphasis added). To the best of my knowledge this was the first time that Congress undertook to establish a Commission to look after the ethics of any enterprise save its own.

Part of their work was to recommend much more extensive review of research protocols, and to bolster the position of the Institutional Review Boards (IRBs). IRBs are committees established, in any institution in which research is carried on, to pass on the ethical merits of all proposals for federally funded research that will be conducted on patients or clients of the institution; they are charged, in brief, with deciding for each protocol whether the benefits foreseen outweigh the harms, whether the right of the subject to informed consent is adequately respected, and whether there is no injustice in the selection of the subjects. (In practice, all research, no matter how funded, passes before the IRBs.)

The Commission's work was, in the event, well done, although here as elsewhere the bureaucrats who followed the physicians and philosophers have been challenged by the job of translating excellent precept into sensible enforcement practice. But the idea remains promising. Should we try this elsewhere? Represented in this course are nine different areas of professional practice in this nation. How many of them could profit from the attention of a panel of intelligent public officials and professionals, staffed by philosophers, working to enunciate the ethical guidelines of the field?

Ultimately, to return to the first phase of this essay, we must decide who is at risk and who benefits from research with human subjects. And we must decide if the balance of good and painful consequences in each case justifies the research. Possibly the situation portrayed in the television presentation will throw some light on the subject.

THE TELEVISION PRESENTATION: SELECTED QUESTIONS ON RESEARCH WITH HUMAN SUBJECTS

This section considers the television presentation or videotape. The recapitulation of the dialogue that follows is not meant to be a word-for-word transcript of the tape, but a summary of the major themes, issues, and opinions that emerged in the conversation. It is for review, and for use as a resource if you include this topic in your term project.

TITLE: "THE HUMAN EXPERIMENT"

Moderator: Professor Lewis B. Kaden

Participants: from left to right on your screen

CHASE N. PETERSON, M.D.
President, University of Utah

THOMAS CHALMERS, M.D.
Boston Veterans Administration
Medical Center; Lecturer,
Harvard School of Public Health

ELLEN GOODMAN
Columnist, *The Boston Globe*

ARNOLD RELMAN, M.D.
Editor, *New England Journal of
Medicine*

ROBERT OLDHAM, M.D.
Chairman and Scientific Director,
Biotherapeutics, Inc.

JOSEPH CALIFANO, JR.
Secretary of HEW, 1977–79;
Senior Partner,
Dewey, Ballantine, Bushby,
Palmer and Wood

ANTONIN SCALIA
Justice, Supreme Court
of the United States

C. EVERETT KOOP, M.D.
Surgeon General, U. S. Public Health
Service, Department of Health and
Human Services

FRANK YOUNG, M.D.
Commissioner, U. S. Food and Drug
Administration

THEODORE COOPER, M.D.
Chairman of the Board and CEO,
The Upjohn Company

VINCENT T. DEVITA, M.D.
Director, National Cancer Institute

ALEXANDER CAPRON
Professor of Law, Medicine and Public
Policy, University of Southern California

PAUL MARKS, M.D.
President and CEO, Memorial
Sloan-Kettering Cancer Center

J. BRYAN HEHIR
Senior Research Scholar,
Kennedy Institute of Ethics,
Georgetown University

As you read through the dialogue, ask yourself:

1. Can a person who is very sick, probably dying, make objective decisions about his own case?
2. Should a doctor be allowed to double as an investigator on a protocol for experimental drugs?
3. Does the profit motive distort the process of developing drugs and treatments?
4. Is Bill Parker's anxiety reasonable? Do you think that you, in his position, would be calmer and more accepting of your situation?

5.   Would you spend all your money to prolong your life for a little while? (Have you ever thought about that before?)

THE COURSE OF THE DIALOGUE

Getting on the Protocol

I'm Bill Parker, the moderator begins, and I'm your patient, Dr. Koop. I came to you with a suspicious red spot; sure enough, it's Kaposi's Sarcoma, and I test positive for AIDS—a type of AIDS, in fact, that is resistant to AZT. Am I going to die?

Koop replies that as far as he knows Bill's going to die, sooner than some: "We don't have a thing to do for you except to treat you symptomatically."

But I know, continues Parker, that Dr. DeVita at the National Disease Institute has just started a test of a new drug called H.O.P.E. Will you try to get me into that experiment? He will. DeVita will see him. All DeVita wants to know is, does he fit the conditions for the protocol? And does he understand the risks and benefits? "Do you really understand that we really don't know the effect of this drug?" If he does, then DeVita will gladly accept him.

A Question
of Fairness

Suppose "Paul Duncan," a former messenger for Califano, shows up with AIDS and wants to get on the protocol. Will Califano help him get on the protocol? Sure. Sort of thing he does all the time. The moderator pushes: Will DeVita take me even if the protocol is full, if Califano calls? Well, with these protocols, unless we have another drug we want to test now ("son of H.O.P.E."), there really isn't any clear end point. Sure, we'll fit him in. Yes, but does it matter that *Califano* called? Yes. Influence does make a difference.

Would Justice Scalia make such a telephone call for a nephew of his? Yes. No question. Would Ellen Goodman? Yes. But she wouldn't feel very good about it. But the sick nephew takes precedence even if I feel uncomfortable. If it were a reader who asked me, I wouldn't do it; but I might assign a reporter to do a story on the distress of this member of the community.

If it were Dr. Oldham doing the test, would it matter who calls? Of course it matters. "I don't think there's any question that...political influence plays a role in entering patients on protocol. What's the frequency? I don't know. What are the number of calls? When I was there they were frequent. They're real. They have influence. And they're part of the political system of research in this country."

Justice Scalia adds a qualification: I will call only if there are no cases before my court that involve the NDI. There must be no appearance of a *quid pro quo*. "I figure I can get through to the director simply because he may have heard of my name or heard of the Supreme Court, with no implication that 'you do this for me and I'll do something for you.'" Suppose you're the head of the Appropriations Committee, controlling the funds for the NDI. Would you make the call? Yes, definitely, answers Scalia. "Politics is...the trading off of favors. Justice isn't." It's part of politics that when the chairman calls, you take care of him.

What does Father Hehir say? That "the commitment of the legal system and the procedural system to fairness ought to be the presumption." He would make a call for a relative. It's the leverage you use *after* the call—that protocol had *better* be open—that makes the use of influence wrong.

The Placebo Possibility

Bill Parker is back at the interview with DeVita. Will DeVita try to make him better, to cure him? Well, yes. But wait a minute. According to your description of this protocol, there are 200 of us; 100 will receive H.O.P.E. and the other 100 will get a placebo. Suppose I get the placebo—how will that help me? In any randomized clinical trial, DeVita points out, half must receive the placebo in order to tell if the drug really does any good. Right now we don't know if the drug does more good than harm. Actually, I have doubts about the use of such a trial in this case.

The Ethics of Placebos

Chalmers says that "it has to be made clear to the patient that there's a large number of drugs introduced every year for a serious disease like this and very few of them survive. And the reason they don't survive is they make the patients worse or they're ineffective. So I would say that the patient getting the placebo is much more likely to be the lucky one." DeVita objects that patients are *not* generally harmed, and personally, he would prefer *not* to randomize to a brand new drug. Frank Young comments that Chalmers hit the nail on the head: 73 percent of investigatory drugs fail, over one third because they are not safe. But Bill, while you're on this protocol, we'll give you the best medical care available. We'll watch you, we'll treat you, and as soon as we *know* that this drug is any good, we'll open the protocol and give everyone the drug.

Scalia is puzzled by the mathematics. What percent of the placebos "fail," after all? If the choice is between 100 percent failure and 75 percent failure, you're better off with the 75. Yes, says Young, but remember that over one third were safety problems—drugs that resulted in accelerated death. "And tomorrow there might be Son of H.O.P.E. [a drug that is really effective against the disease], and that acceleration of death could really be a major problem."

Alex Capron comments that he is "happy to see the physicians trying to insist to Bill that there is a reason for doing the placebo that's to his benefit, but I haven't heard anybody really acknowledge the conflict of roles that does exist here. It isn't just to be better for Bill that we're using the placebo. It's to gain knowledge. And the researcher is wearing both of those hats."

Arnold Relman comments that a randomized trial for a deadly disease is not ethically justified. If everyone dies of the disease, then you can use past experience as your control. "If before 95 percent or 100 percent died in a month or two months, and now without placebo 20 percent died or 40 percent died, it would be very clear. And I don't think it would be ethical [to run a randomized clinical trial] if they felt they could find the answer to their question without a placebo."

Autonomy in the Face of Death

Bill Parker is still in DeVita's office. This protocol is his only hope; where does he sign? DeVita hands him the consent form.

Alexander Capron is distressed at the speed of this choice. You need not only freedom to choose, to sign or not to sign, but information to base the choice on and time to think about it. You may be making a decision you don't want to make. Autonomy requires that you wait, think, absorb the information, ask questions.

Informed Consent under Pressure

Does Justice Scalia think that somebody in Bill's state can make a consent that reasonable people would view as informed? "I think so. If you're dying and this is your last chance, it is inevitable that you'll take that last chance. I don't know why that makes it an uninformed choice. If all you're saying is that because you're dying and because it seems to you that there are no other options, you're bound, of course, to sign the form, that just means it's a good choice...the mere fact that the individual is under a lot of pressure to make the choice one way or another, by the circumstances, doesn't seem to me to establish that the choice is coerced, unfair or uninformed."

Califano rejoins that there is desperation in this choice, made without viable alternatives. He would like to see the primary care physician be a large part of any such decision.

Scalia wonders if the physicians are just as reassuring to the patients who are receiving the placebo. DeVita points out that they wouldn't know which patients are on the drug and which on placebo—that's part of the nature of a double-blind protocol. "Parker" is very unhappy with this development. "My problem is, Dr. Young, I keep looking for somebody to have my interest at heart, to be my champion. And now I'm told that everybody's blind. Nobody knows what I'm getting or how I'm doing. I want somebody who can see." Young tells him we need the double blind structure, so the investigator won't see improvement where there isn't any. It's to keep him objective.

Then who protects Bill Parker's interest? Capron finishes the section with the suggestion that the type of research being done on this protocol just doesn't protect the interest of the individual patient. The point is to develop the knowledge that will be useful for the future. Part of Bill's role is "to give something to the society."

Research for Profit

Well, the tests at DeVita's establishment haven't been very successful, and Bill Parker is getting even more desperate. He comes to the clinic you have started, Dr. Oldham, BioClinics, Inc. Tells you he's been in DeVita's study and he isn't getting any better; will you take him as a patient?

Yes, but there are conditions. First, he has to drop out of DeVita's study, and treatment cannot start for two weeks after he does; the drugs might not mix well. (DeVita releases him, a bit sorry he's leaving before the protocol is finished.) Second, he must realize that we are not government-funded. We're in the private sector. We take no public funds. So the patient and his insurance company must arrange to pay the cost of the treatment. The kind of treatment he has in mind for Parker, for starters, costs about $4,000. Another treatment modality that he might find himself using costs $30,000 to $35,000.

Bill goes back to his family doctor for advice. Bill, says Koop, "you have to realize eventually that things may not work out the way you'd like. You can't keep jumping from protocol to protocol."

Chase Peterson continues: "Bill, you've got a disease that will almost certainly kill you in the next months. There's no medicine now known to experimental science or to any investigative company that's likely to save your life...." It's not a bad idea to join the protocol. But "do it in the context of saying, 'I'm dying and I'm dying in the immediate future. Now if it's useful for me to make a contribution to medical science by joining a protocol at NDI or going with a private company in their protocol, I should do that and derive some satisfaction from that.' But not very much hope....But I wouldn't take all your money out of the bank. I wouldn't ask all your brothers and sisters in California to raise money. I wouldn't call on the governor to have a fundraising drive to get you money for this. Because the chances of this helping you in the near future, in your lifetime, are very small."

"Look," Parker wails, "if I don't try it, I'm dead."

"And you want to live your death," continues Peterson, "with as much dignity as you want to live your life. And for that reason you should not bankrupt your family and do a whole lot of strange things for a small point." Still, he knows the company, and thinks they're doing exciting work. If Parker has no wife and children, and he does not, then go for it.

Oldham agrees that Bill should listen to what all those other people have said. He must remember that just like DeVita's protocol at the NDI "this is unproven treatment." He should talk it over with any physician. And then he should make his choice. He has a right to be concerned.

Dr. Relman is certainly concerned about this for-profit research. But the integrity of the research itself interests him even more. Is Dr. Oldham following a protocol that will eventuate in real results, ultimately for publication? "As far as I know, I read the medical literature very carefully, Bill, and I haven't seen any reports anywhere indicating that what Dr. Oldham says he's going to do for you helps anybody. We're talking about the ethics of responsible research. When you use a new drug or a new treatment, the safety of which, as well as the effectiveness, is not known, the ethical justification for doing it is that it will be administered in a way that will tell you...as quickly and as safely as possible whether it's any good....So I would like to know from Dr. Oldham whether he is going to follow the same rigorous, controlled, appropriately controlled protocol which will be open to public scrutiny, as [would] any other protocol...followed at the NDI."

The Ethics of Responsible Research

Oldham retorts that we do, too, publish our results, when we get them. This particular set of treatments is not on a randomized protocol. But we will keep very careful track of our results. Oh? "How many patients so far?" Relman asks. "How many reports on this have you published in the medical literature so I can tell whether it looks promising or not?" I wish I could help you, Doctor, Oldham replies, but this patient happens to be the first and I just developed the treatment last week. Stalemate.

Ellen Goodman questions the distinction between privately and publicly funded research.

Relman asserts that it is a terribly important distinction. But let's stick with the previous point. "Dr. Oldham now tells us that the 'treatment' or the experimental treatment that he proposes to give to my patient and charge $30,000 for, he's never given to anybody else before. He doesn't know whether it's going to work or not. I would have very serious doubts in my mind whether I could in good conscience tell my patient to take this treatment when there's no evidence by Dr. Oldham's statement that it's going to work. Then add to that the fact that I know that Dr. Oldham is the officer of an investor-owned company...their financial interests and their financial future depends on their persuading patients like my Bill Parker to take this unproven treatment of unknown safety and unknown value at a time when they're scared to death, they're desperately seeking for something. And it awakens memories in my mind of snake oil salesmen who used to go around doing this sort of thing with unproven, untested remedies saying, 'Trust me. It'll work. I know it'll work. Just give me your money.' And poor, desperate, sick people would extend themselves to pay for it. Now I'm not impugning Dr. Oldham's integrity. I'm just saying the situation that he puts me in is very uncomfortable."

Financial Interests and the Patient's Best Interest

Oldham points out that Bill Parker, dying of AIDS, has every right to choose: to go to the NDI and go on a randomized clinical trial or come to him or someone else and try a treatment they might have.

DeVita, having looked into BioClinics at Parker's request, thinks that Oldham has nothing to offer that hasn't been developed elsewhere; would Bill like him to see if he can get the same stuff that Oldham is peddling somewhere else—cheaper?

Who Looks
after the
Patient?

Young does not think that the critical distinction is between for-profit and not-for-profit establishments. The critical thing is the patient's estimate of whether or not he'll benefit. But all the people I talk to, Parker complains, say they don't know. And that, says Young, is where the state of the art is today. We wish we had cures and guarantees but we don't. Why don't you go back to Dr. Koop? "He's your family friend. He's taken care of you all these years. Ask him for his unbiased judgment because he's the one that has no vested interest in the trial. He's only concerned with you."

Koop says that his only interest is in sparing Bill Parker any further disappointment. "And I can understand the desperation of people in your situation, with a fatal diagnosis, no cure on the horizon that anybody has any faith in. And you get this desperate feeling that you've got to do something....But...I don't think there's enough credibility in what's going on in Dr. Oldham's laboratory to give you the satisfaction that you're going to do something that might work. I think it's one more disappointment. You can't take many more."

Califano doesn't think that the profit is the problem. "Pharmaceutical companies every day are operating at a profit in testing drugs and have brought upon us a tremendous number of miracles....And universities, in their own ways,...bring in people; they want them to be superstars, they want to get lots of research bucks. That's profit for the university."

Treatment vs. Research

Justice Scalia raises a new question: Is there that clear a distinction between "treatment" and "experimentation?" In both cases the physician makes a guess at what will help. If I come to a doctor with a vague pain in my side and we don't know what it is, he'll have to make that kind of guess. Isn't the difference between that guess and the investigator's guess just a matter of degree?

Relman replies that this is a bad analogy. To be sure there is "a good deal of uncertainty in the practice of medicine....But what the physician does in the face of uncertainty is pretty well established and pretty well agreed on to be the best thing to do under the circumstances. It's clearly advancing the patient's welfare as best you know how and clearly calculated not to do harm. In this circumstance, what Dr. Oldham is proposing to do has never been done before, whereas...if you come to me with a pain in your side of uncertain etiology, I've dealt with that a lot of times before, Justice Scalia. I may not know in a particular case what the pain is due to, but I know how to find out."

Alexander Capron points out that the variation in medical response to uncertainty, and the inevitable differences in medical judgment, do not justify accusations of "snake oil." Further, medical research at the NDI isn't paid for by patients not because the doctors there are altruistic but because it's paid for by government grants. Or by the drug companies, Relman adds. The question is, Capron continues, is this going to be good science or not? And there is no reason to believe that the profit motive leads to more bad science than any of the other motives that drive people.

Profit vs. Non-Profit Science

Oldham tends to agree, that the work his people do is little different from that at the non-profit or government establishments. There is a different mechanism for funding, that is all. If no one joins on his protocols, his company will fail. If no one joins the protocols I would be writing if I were still at the NDI, I'd lose my promotion.

Marks adds that quality control is the most important thing. We need mechanisms to assure quality. The profit motive might make a difference. Quality control is in the best long-range interests of the company.

Whether or not the long-range interests of the company, or the society, are served by such research, what will serve Bill's interests? The bottom line for Bill is, Scalia points out, is this procedure going to help him?

Publish and Perish

The moderator moves to a new phase of the research. We have an important breakthrough—a killed-virus vaccine for AIDS. This may be the cure we've been looking for! Now you get a call, Dr. DeVita, from a colleague at Rival University. He's been working on the same thing; he doesn't seem to be as far along as you are. He wonders if you might get together on the research to help each other out. Will you share your information? Sure, DeVita says; if there's anything to gain by collaborating, we'll collaborate. Capron agrees that sharing would be the best course.

Keeping Company Secrets

As for Dr. Theodore Cooper, CEO of Upjohn, he would have a real problem with any of the scientists on his payroll sharing information. He would have to know that there will be a clear benefit to his company before he'd permit it.

Chalmers is annoyed by this attitude. "This session is about ethics, isn't it? Bad science is unethical." And the one thing we know is that "good science requires communication. Free, frequent, complete, detailed communication. So to the extent that we are forced by economic circumstances to cut back on that free communication, we cut back on the quality of the science, and, therefore, on the ethics of the effort we're all making."

The tests continue. The killed virus vaccine is really working. De-Vita writes it up for publication in a peer-reviewed professional journal. Now that colleague from Rival University calls Ellen Goodman to tell her all about it. He eventually tells her that DeVita did most of the work. So Goodman goes off to talk with DeVita. Will he talk with her? Of course, but he will give her no details. The public will misinterpret details. "Are you suggesting that I would miswrite this?" Goodman asks. "No," replies DeVita, "but I think the public is not in a position to really understand all the nuances nor will your editor probably give you enough space to cover the material sufficiently nor will any scientist peer review your article."

The Ethics of Prior Publication

She writes the story anyway, in her column, three weeks before publication in *The New England Journal of Medicine*, which has accepted the article under expedited review. Dr. Relman, do you publish the article anyway if DeVita talked to the reporter? Maybe not. He made an agreement when we accepted the article that he would not release the results to the press; he's broken the agreement. We make exceptions in cases where the publication of findings a few days earlier will make a real difference to public health. But this isn't one of them. If she got the story without his help, we run the article; he lived up to his part of the bargain. But if he helped her—bad judgment. We pull the article.

Why? "Because Dr. DeVita violated an agreement that he made with me voluntarily which, presumably, he made because he agrees with me and the vast majority of his colleagues that that is not the best way, in the public interest and in the interests of science, to disseminate new scientific information. And he may have violated that." Goodman figures that he's just calling it "unethical" because she beat him to a story. Relman denies that they are doing the same job. Medical scientists and physicians need this rule. They cannot base their recommendations to patients on the *Boston Globe*.

Frank Young comments further on what happens when the press breaks a story before the medical journals have had time to get the word to the physicians—the phone rings off the hook with people asking for answers and advice, and we have none to give them. On the other hand, he does not agree with Relman that the article should be yanked from *The New England Journal of Medicine* just because it has appeared in the popular press; that's when the physicians need it most, and pulling it would be unethical.

The Most Good in the Long Run

What would Justice Scalia say? "You make your judgments on the basis of what produces the most good in the long run. Now it may well be that in this particular case it would be less harmful and do more good to publish it in the *Journal* despite the fact that it's been leaked. But if the consequence of that is to induce leaks in innumerable cases in the future, if that's the only feasible sanction, which is I think what has been said, then in the long-range good, which is what you always have to consult, the thing to do is to force people to abide by their contracts by refusing to publish this."

A REVIEW OF SELECTIONS FROM THE SOURCE READER

Before going on to synthesize the philosophical background and the television presentation, this would be a good time to review certain of the readings in the history of ethics that pertain especially to this topic.

For the concept of "beneficence," the general duty to do good to other persons, up to and including the community of all humankind, there can be no better sources than the ones mentioned in the opening essay for this chapter, Jeremy Bentham and John Stuart Mill.

Selections for this Chapter:

> Jeremy Bentham, *Principles of Morals and Legislation*, **Source Reader** p. 158
> John Stuart Mill, *Utilitarianism*, **Source Reader** p. 166

In rereading the selection from Bentham, pay special attention to the "felicific calculus." In medical research, we are balancing the interests of research subjects now with the interests of patients in the distant future. How do we weigh the known interests of a finite set of living people against the presumed interests of an indefinite set of unborn people? Can we measure interests in this way? (Try: measuring along Bentham's suggested dimensions, decide whether it is more to your interest to finish your ethics homework, prepare for lunch with the boss tomorrow, take your child to the movies, go to a party, or go to bed and get a good night's sleep.)

John Stuart Mill's formulation is the classic exposition of this approach to ethics and cannot be improved upon. Review of this work is absolutely essential to understand the moral basis on which most of our institutions stand.

SYNTHESIS AND DISCUSSION

What points in that interchange struck you as worth remembering? We are talking primarily about help and harm, about benefit and risk of suffering. The question that comes up over and over again in that presentation is, benefit for whom?

Benefit for whom? Utilitarianism in its strict form (Bentham's) requires us to specify the group that is to be counted before doing any counting. (In its later form, Mill's exposition, the whole universe counts every time.) Who counts here? Bill Parker keeps asking: who's looking out for me? who will benefit me? and he keeps getting evasive answers, because that seems to be the wrong question.

The point here is that no course of action will benefit Bill Parker, at least not in any way that he is thinking about. He wants his life saved and his disease cured, and that can't happen. Occasional discussants suggest that the greatest benefit they can give him now is the opportunity to help others in the future by participating in research, but Bill doesn't seem interested in that. Then the constant advice of the "family physicians" that are assigned to him—come home, come to terms with your disease, at least let us keep you comfortable while you die—is the only sensible counsel for him, on his terms. Should those be his only terms? Are we all obliged to help the community in whatever way we can? Is Bill Parker being selfish? In the course of an hour presentation, we may think about the situation as the first hour after hearing that we have AIDS—all the thoughts are selfish. But Bill, in the hypothetical, has had months to get used to the idea, months to realize that he is going to die, soon, and to decide how he wants to die.

Clearly future sufferers from AIDS will benefit from this research, eventually. A darker note is sounded by several of the participants in the discussion, with reference to the other parties who stand to benefit. Every activity in this society is carried on by someone, for money. The someone in this case is the scientist, living in a world of grants and promotions and publications that accompany a very interesting and comfortable career path. These accompaniments lead into each other: if I have a good publication record, I will have a much easier time getting funds for the research that I want to do. Those funds allow me to work on the problems that interest me, rather than those that interest my boss, and the stipends attached to them provide me with a nice income besides. They also make me much more desirable as a member of a university faculty, since some part of those grants is paid as overhead to the university at which I work, so I will have my choice of positions. The quality of the grants and publications determines my ability to dictate salary and working conditions (how many classes I have to teach, for instance) at that university. All in all, a pleasant life awaits the successful investigator; but first, I have to get those publications, and that means I have to conduct my research quickly and I must get results. On occasion, that pressure leads to scientific fraud. If my research demands the use of human subjects, it can also lead to all manner of coercion to recruit the subjects I need to get the study done. That is why we require signed consent forms for all funded research, and why we have the Institutional Review Boards, in the hospitals and other places where such research is done, to review those forms, and to make sure that the research will be conducted in accordance with ethical guidelines. Without such controls, I might very well be tempted to understate the risks and inconveniences entailed by participation in my study, and possibly do a little arm-twisting to get my patients to sign on for it.

Another party that will clearly benefit from the research is the drug company that plans to produce and market the drug. The shareholders' interest in quick results, and the right kind of results, is perfectly obvious, and therefore several layers of controls are interposed between the officers of the company and the determination of the results of the research. In general, the outside pressure put on the scientist by the drug companies is less dangerous to the integrity of the enterprise than the pressure that comes from the inside, from the scientist's own normal greed and career aspirations.

Yet another beneficiary of the research is a new type of enterprise, the research-and-medicine-for-profit corporation ("BioClinics" in the video presentation; Oldham's own company, Biotherapeutics, is the model). This type of corporation bypasses many of the inefficiencies of the usual system, where grants from the federal government fund research at universities, often on drugs produced by private companies. At private companies like Biotherapeutics, the scientists proceed directly to the research, paid by the patients or by private insurance companies, and profit directly from the results. The danger often feared in this way of operating is that there are fewer controls between the profit motive and the recruited patient; the temptation to promise a desperately sick patient a little too much in order to finish the research might be overwhelming. But then, as Oldham points out, that temptation might be overwhelming to an academic scientist as well.

And when the system works the way it is supposed to work, society at large benefits as well. It could be argued that the American system of medical and pharmaceutical development is one of the lasting triumphs of capitalism. We have the best medicine in the world, and we get it by channeling the private greed of manufacturers, physicians, universities, research scientists, hospitals, insurance companies, and patients into a structure that motivates the companies to develop the drugs, hospitals to allow them to be tested, physicians and scientists to perform the research, and all concerned to worry about the quality of the treatment that eventuates and the truthfulness of the results. Altruism would never produce the same excellence in the field. It should be pointed out that the FDA and other government agencies are partners in this enterprise, funding the research and monitoring the results.

The burden of keeping the system moral falls, ultimately, on the individual investigator; the benefits to be derived by all concerned depend, to a very large degree, on his integrity. The welfare of the patient, the institution, the drug company, the patients of the future, and the system at large depends on the truthfulness of that one person, and the willingness to take pains to ensure that the results are accurately reported. All the pressures of the system converge on that one person. The controls in place may keep some of the pressures at a distance; except in these new medicine-for-profit institutions, the pressure from investors to realize a return on their investment will not be felt immediately by the persons doing the actual work and recording the results. The double blinding reduces the subjectivity of the findings in all cases. But ultimately, in no matter what kind of institution they work, and no matter how closely they are monitored, the scientists can simply lie about the nature of the work they are doing, and they can lie about the results they got, and there will always be cases when it will be to their advantage to lie. Here as elsewhere, the ethics of the system depends on the ethics of the individual within it. Fortunately for us, the level of integrity in this enterprise is high, as high in the for-profit sector as in the not-for-profit; but it is up to us as citizens to find some way to reward the vigilance of the profession in guarding against its own corruption.

QUESTIONS FOR YOUR REFLECTION

1. As the television presentation made clear, the research subject may be at risk of harm, if the drug or treatment being tested turns out to have nasty side effects. How should the subject weigh that harm against possible benefit? How should we, as makers of policy?

2. The physician's obligation is to care for the patient. That is a fiduciary obligation, like the professional obligation that a lawyer has to the client. Is that compatible with a role as investigator for an experimental drug? Can the same person wear both hats? Would you trust a physician who you knew was doing research on you? Would your tendency to trust that physician change if you knew he stood to make a terrific profit on his stock in the company that produced the experimental drug, if the experiments seemed to be successful?

3. Utilitarianism requires that we count every person as one and no person as more than one. How do we count children? Shall each of them be accorded one count? What about unborn children? still in the womb? not yet conceived? when do we stop counting? How do we weigh the indefinite interests of unborn generations against the very clear interests of the people here and now? Try your hand at that one.

4. Can Jeremy Bentham's Felicific Calculus actually be used to decide real cases? See if you can demonstrate that it can, by using it to choose between two common options (do the housework or do volunteer work at the hospital, for instance; write part of a term paper or go cheer for the basketball team). If it doesn't work, why doesn't it work?

5. Do some kinds of felt happiness or felt unhappiness count for more than other kinds? How would you weigh the following kinds of felt pain:

- The pain of a sprained ankle
- The pain of the death of a friend
- The pain of living near a smelly dump
- The pain of losing quite a bit of money on a stock transfer
- The pain of knowing that undesirable "minorities" are moving into the neighborhood
- The pain of childbirth
- The pain of losing the game
- The pain of having to write a paper on ethics

What criteria control the weights you put on these pains?

SUGGESTIONS FOR FURTHER READING

Special Supplementary Text:
ROBERT J. LEVINE. *Ethics and Regulation of Clinical Research*, Baltimore: Urban and Schwarzenberg, 2nd edition 1986.

CANADIAN MEDICAL RESEARCH COUNCIL. *Ethics in Human Experimentation*. Report Number 6, Ottawa, Canada, 1978.

FREUND, PAUL A. *Experimentation with Human Subjects*. New York: George Braziller, 1970.

FRIED, CHARLES. *Medical Experimentation: Personal Integrity and Social Policy*. New York: American Elsevier Company, 1974.

GAYLIN, WILLARD, AND RUTH MACKLIN, EDS. *Who Speaks for the Child? The Problems of Proxy Consent*. New York: Plenum Press, 1982.

KATZ, JAY. *Experimentation with Human Beings*. New York: Russell Sage Foundation, 1972.

LEBACQZ, KAREN. *Professional Ethics: Power and Paradox*. Nashville, TN: Abingdon Press, 1985.

LEBACQZ, KAREN, AND ROBERT J. LEVINE. "Informed Consent in Human Research: Ethical and Legal Aspects," in *Encyclopedia of Bioethics*, ed. Warren T. Reich, pp. 754-762. New York: The Free Press, 1978.

MITFORD, JESSICA. *Kind and Usual Punishment: The Prison Business*. New York: Vintage Press, 1974.

By all means look up other relevant articles in the *Encyclopedia of Bioethics*. Two Congressionally authorized Commissions took up the subject of the ethics of research with human subjects, and issued reports on it.

From The National Commission for the Protection of Human Subjects of Biomedical and Behavioral Research:

Research on the Fetus (1975)

Research Involving Prisoners (1976)

Research Involving Children (1977)

The Belmont Report: Ethical Principles and Guidelines for the Protection of Human Subjects of Research (1978)

Behavioral Research; Institutional Review Boards (1978)

Research Involving Those Institutionalized as Mentally Infirm (1978)

From The President's Commission for the Study of Ethical Problems in Medicine and Biomedical and Behavioral Research:

> Protecting Human Subjects: The Adequacy and Uniformity of Federal Rules and their Implementation
>
> Compensating for Research Injuries: The Ethical and Legal Implications of Programs to Redress Injured Subjects
>
> Making Health Care Decisions: The Ethical and Legal Implications of Informed Consent in the Patient-Practitioner Relationship
>
> Splicing Life: The Social and Ethical Issues of Genetic Engineering with Human Beings

These publications are available from the Government Printing Office.

chapter 12 _____

PRIVACY:
Politics, Privacy, and the Press

1. How valuable is your privacy to you? Do you become angry when you think people have been watching you, or trying to find out about you—not from malice, but just from curiosity? How easily do you share information about yourself?

2. How do you react to media exposure of the private lives of public figures— movie stars, politicians, and the like? Do you enjoy it? think they deserve it? feel embarrassed and resent it? Why?

3. How would *you* reconcile the fundamental American freedoms: the freedom to be left alone to live your own life as you see fit, and the freedom of the press fearlessly to report all the facts that come to its notice? Which of those freedoms is more important in a democracy? Or is that the wrong way to put the choice?

THE CONCEPT OF PRIVACY

The impulse to protect our own privacy is fundamentally an impulse of self-defense. Human beings are very vulnerable animals in their natural state, a fact that tends to get lost in the present justifiable concern to protect from extinction the animals that used to make regular lunches of us. The desire to get away from possibly dangerous stimuli, to be alone and therefore protected against invasion, has been ingrained in our genes since we came down from the trees. At the beginning, I want to protect myself, my skin, the space around me, for simple reasons of physical survival.

But the function of privacy in the individual human life goes well beyond the primitive need for physical protection. We have not only a physical skin to protect, but a complex mental and spiritual life to defend against invasion. This life is present only in embryo in the child, develops rapidly in adolescence and continues to grow, develop, and refine throughout adulthood. It is at least as vulnerable as the physical life that supports it.

We are social animals: we exist primarily as members of a group, and our individuality is a hard-won achievement of self and group together. For me to be myself, to be *my* self, I must have your agreement that that is what I am. I am truly an individual only when the group addresses me by my name, recognizes my individuality and respects it. For a short time, if I am normally strong, I can maintain my identity against group denial, but ultimately I will be what the group expects me to be; to be, as an individual, is to be perceived as such.

Even as reasonably strong adults, we are full of conflicting impulses and desires, some of them quite unworthy of ourselves and the kind of person we would hope to be. What the group sees us to be, that we will be; it is essential that we be able to keep to ourselves aspects of ourselves that are incompatible with the person we want the group to confirm. This is not just the simple matter of protecting our reputation, maintaining an image that we want the group to accept. What we are seen to be, that we will become in fact; the way I establish my character is by projecting an image of that character into my society and growing into it, much as shellfish grow into the new shells they have constructed for themselves.

So the protection of privacy is essential for the individual to develop character, personality, singularity, and strength as an individual. Paradoxically, privacy is also essential for intimacy, for a life closely shared with intimate friends. Relationships with others vary on a scale from the aloof to the intimate, and intimacy is prized. The intimacy of a relationship is established and confirmed by the sharing of personal secrets; secrets enhance intimacy to the extent that they are hidden from the public at large, as jewels gain value from rarity independent of other characteristics. Privacy, the protection of the ability to keep personal information from the public, preserves the secrets that are shared in intimate relationships.

Privacy, then, is not permanent or accidental "hiddenness." Rather, it is control: the control of personal space, so that others may not come in without permission; the control of all mental and spiritual life, so that access to it shall be only at the discretion of its possessor; and above all the control of information about any aspect of the self, past, present, or future, which may be withheld or released only at the desire of the self.

If that is privacy, what is invasion of privacy? At one level it is any unsolicited or undesired penetration of personal space—any taping, photographing, watching, taking notes, any observation that causes an unconsenting person to live under the gaze of another. At a second level, it is any noising abroad of what has been observed—loose chatter, gossip, or published revelations of any sort. At a third level, it is any of the above that materially injures the person who is observed and about whom the revelations are made.

Any injury, by definition, violates the interests of the person injured. Clearly unwanted revelations can be injurious in several ways. Suppose in my youth I was a thief and confidence man, in a distant place, crimes for which I have long since repented and been punished. Now I am attempting to set up an adult life for myself, and am doing rather well at it, successfully pursuing a career, raising a family, contributing to my community. Now suppose that some local newspaper reporter uncovers my juvenile record and publishes it. How am I injured? First, there is the sheer fact of violation, producing fear all by itself, the instant reaction of every householder who discovers a burglary. The consciousness of having been observed, or found out, is painful all by itself. After that, the revelation of that secret information, obtained by violation, is an assault whether or not any further harm is done. In this instance, of course, there is the obvious harm, the damage done to my reputation and credit in the community. The bank is hesitant about advancing credit for my business, my suppliers think twice about waiting for their payment, my customers wonder about the quality of the goods I sell, the Rotary wonders if I should continue to be a member and the Boy Scouts rethink their decision to appoint me as regional delegate. A hundred areas of personal enjoyment and fulfillment are affected, as the country club holds up my application and my wife hesitates to hold our annual Christmas Open House. For purposes of this essay, we will take those invasions in reverse order.

Material injuries. Where material injuries occur, the law provides remedies for the person whose privacy is invaded. The retention of control over the details of our personal lives has traditionally been recognized as essential to our welfare, and the law protects us in the privacy of our secrets as in the privacy of our houses. But it does not protect all of us equally. There is no reason why I should have a right to know that my innocuous neighbor was a thief in his youth, and no justification for the damaging publication of the record. But I do have a right to know if the people who are governing me have incidents in their pasts that would embarrass them, if only to rule out the possibility that their actions in my regard may be distorted by blackmail or fear of exposure. Beyond that, if I am to trust them with custody of my public life, and pay their salaries for exercising that custodianship, I have a right to know about their past and their character, as I have such a right when I hire a personal servant. As a citizen, I have the right to know anything that would influence my decision to hire them.

Because of this conflict between the right of privacy and the public's right to full disclosure from their officials, the law draws a line between the "private person," who has a right to keep secret anything about which no public record is mandated (for instance, private financial affairs); and a "public figure," who is legitimately the subject of curiosity and about whom anything may be published, even falsehoods, as long as it shows no "actual malice" or "reckless disregard for the truth." The result of this distinction is that journalists or other publicists are in trouble if they publish anything damaging about a private person, unless the damaging information is contained in the public records (juvenile criminal records are not public); but if the person damaged is a public figure of any sort, he will have the very devil of a time getting a court to do anything about the injury, for "actual malice" and "recklessness" are very difficult to prove.

The problems of public figures, the press, and the law form a recurring theme in the television presentation accompanying this chapter, and we will return to this theme in the synthesis below. For the present, in order to ground the right disputed in that presentation, it will be worthwhile to follow out the case begun above, tracing the problems I face as a private person because of unwanted revelation. We have seen that I am injured in every facet of my life in which my enjoyment of my community depends upon my neighbors' perceptions of me. But the damage does not stop at the observable and legally actionable.

Public revelations. Here we have perhaps the most important injury, the interruption of inner process and growth: I was in the process of becoming, not just an honest person, but the sort of person who would be *incapable* of thievery and deceit. Now it is clear that I will never be that. From now on my group sees me as one who clearly is capable of the kind of fraud I detest. However they may approve the sort of person who repents of crime and becomes better, they will never see *me* as the type of person *I* wanted to be. From that it follows that my relationships with others are badly threatened. Those who did not share my secret now regard me as a hypocrite and liar; those who did share it are themselves exposed as hypocrites for concealing it all this time. All in all, a great deal of damage has been done.

Penetration of personal space. Because of that damage, we try to protect the privacy of the private individual, to protect personal welfare. But at the initial level of invasion mentioned above, welfare does not seem to be involved. What if I am *just* watched, *just* found out about, without my consent? What if the person who watches me takes notes, if at all, only for his own benefit or for some work to be published only after I die and have no interests left to protect? (The law protects my estate, but only for financial purposes. *I* have no interests beyond the grave.) Would there be anything wrong with that? Or rather, since we know full well that there *is* something wrong with sneaking, eavesdropping, peeping from behind the curtains, or just *watching* someone who does not want to be watched, *why* is it wrong? Here we tend to appeal to another fundamental value: the dignity of the individual, the requirement of respect for persons.

It is simply disrespectful to spy on others, even if you mean to use what you find out for the benefit of the one spied upon. There may be situations when that disrespect is tolerated for the sake of that benefit—for example, when psychiatric observation is done for medical purposes. But it is disrespectful all the same, when carried on without the person's consent. When the purpose is not to benefit the observed, but simply to satisfy the curiosity of the observer, the observation is without excuse. The very fact that we are social animals makes the presence or absence of others, and their consciousness of us, a factor in our existence. Like it or not, an act observed is different from an act unobserved, all other things being equal. If it is my act, respect for my autonomy dictates that I should have the right to choose whether the act is done observed or unobserved. The uninvited gaze of the stranger estranges my action from me, making it partly his action; the integrity of my self, at several levels, requires that I have a way to escape from that gaze.

THE TELEVISION PRESENTATION: SELECTED QUESTIONS ON THE DILEMMAS OF JOURNALISM

This section considers the television presentation or videotape. The recapitulation of the dialogue that follows is not meant to be a word-for-word transcript of the tape, but a summary of the major themes, issues, and opinions that emerged in the conversation. It is for review, and for use as a resource if you include this topic in your term project.

TITLE: "POLITICS, PRIVACY, AND THE PRESS"

Moderator: Professor Charles R. Nesson

Participants: from left to right on your screen

SUZANNE GARMENT
Resident Scholar,
American Enterprise Institute

R. W. APPLE, JR.
Chief Washington Correspondent,
The New York Times

TOM FIEDLER
Political Editor, *The Miami Herald*

KATHERINE FANNING
Editor, *The Christian Science Monitor*

PAUL TAYLOR
Reporter, *The Washington Post*

GERALDINE FERRARO
U. S. Representative, 9th District NY
(1979–84)

PETER JENNINGS
Anchor, Senior Editor, ABC News

JEANE KIRKPATRICK
U. S. Permanent Representative to the
United Nations (1981–85)

KATHARINE GRAHAM
Chairman of the Board, CEO,
The Washington Post Company

LIZ SMITH
Syndicated Columnist,
New York Daily News

MIKE WALLACE
Correspondent, CBS News

ALAN SIMPSON
U. S. Senator, State of Wyoming

LYLE DENNISTON
Washington Correspondent,
The Baltimore Sun

WILLIAM C. WESTMORELAND
General, AUS (Ret.)

JEFF GREENFIELD
Media and Political Analyst, ABC News

BARNEY FRANK
U. S. Representative, 4th District MA

THE COURSE OF THE DIALOGUE

The original tape of the seminar on privacy and the profession of journalism was of such broad interest that in cutting it down for the purposes of this course, two one-hour tapes were produced instead of the one
that had been anticipated. You may have seen the first part of the seminar when it was broadcast during the year prior to the first offering of
this telecourse. If the tape of it is available to you, you are encouraged
to see it, just from interest. It is not part of the required materials of
this course. For background, however, "highlights" of that first tape will
be shown prior to the airing of the second tape; a brief summary of those
highlights is included here.

Highlights of the First Presentation on Privacy and the Profession of Journalism:

Should Journalists Socialize with Newsmakers?

In response to the moderator's questions, Katharine Graham denies that entertaining politicians at her home will get them any different, let alone improved, treatment in her newspaper. Lyle Denniston tells us that, from the perspective of the journalist, it seems unethical to "rub elbows" with the "unwashed masses" who are likely "to become part of my news coverage." Editor Fanning respects the position, but wonders if refusal to be "part of the human race" might make it more difficult for a reporter to know what's going on. "It's a question of proportion." Peter Jennings insists that it is possible to go to a party *just* as a guest, to be Off Duty. Ah, but if some news comes wafting by? Well, you sometimes go *on* duty again. Congressman Frank protests that this is very much a one-way street: the journalists can go off duty, but whenever they want to be, they're *on* duty, and we're always fair game.

Ferreting Out the Candidate's Secrets

Senator Simpson asserts that there is no such thing as keeping secrets from the public, not any more. Ambassador Kirkpatrick protests that the American public does not expect as a precondition of candidacy full confessions of its candidates, extending, like St. Augustine's, to earliest youth. Geraldine Ferraro, speaking from a wealth of experience, points out that people love gossip, and to have their curiosity satisfied; but the duty of the press is only to give them the information they need to vote intelligently. Columnist Smith points out that we don't just elect a candidate, we elect a whole family, and make the wives and children suffer as human beings have not suffered before (at least in this context). Katharine Graham protests that the press is being maligned; we cover elections much better than we used to. We do describe everyone's stands on the issues, much more than is read. This is not just titillation that we're talking about here.

The Right
to Know

THE COURSE OF THE SECOND PRESENTATION

Ask yourself, as you review the dialogue:

1. Why do journalists try so hard to get these stories? Try sorting out their motives: money? fame? some primitive sense of triumph in uncovering what another wanted kept secret? duty to the public?

2.   Were you Senator Valentine, would you be resentful, angry, at the media attention? Would you feel yourself unjustly treated? Would you have been much more careful?

We continue from where the first presentation left off. Joe Valentine, an attractive young Senator running for the Presidency, is seated next to a lovely movie starlet at a benefit dinner. A picture is taken. Miss Smith, what do you do with the picture? Answer: Print it without comment. No implications will be made at all. Well...if she's *very* well known, I might bend my ethics just a *little* bit and make something of it. On the other hand, no, not if he's married. Married people have enough problems.

Midnight at the Motel

The next phase of the hypothetical opens with a problem for Tom Fiedler. You get a telephone tip from an anonymous young woman that Joe Valentine is having an affair all right, and that he'll be found tonight (under cover of a conference of fundraisers) in one of the Cozy Condos at Lake Ardor in company with Debbie Spice. Are you going up there to find out what's going on? Answer: Well, I have to know more than that. This might be a purely professional relationship. She might be just a terrific pollster. And I need to know more about the caller, and her motivation. Of course, if there have been previous indications of this, I might be interested. Would the interest be different if it were not Debbie Spice, but Eleanor Truelove, a distinguished professional woman whose relationship with Valentine has been going on for some time? Well, if this is a candidate for President we're talking about, and there are rumors out already, this might be important.

Peter Jennings loses patience with this equivocation: look, in the case of a call like this, a reporter *will be sent*. That's what *any* newspaper will do. And further, I think you want a camera up there. Ms. Fanning, do you agree? "I think I'd agonize a lot." But this is not an issue yet. Valentine has made no point of his fidelity or his family, and has not challenged reporters to follow him. At this point, this affair is not an issue in the campaign. Johnny (R. W.) Apple differs: I agree completely with you, but only if the Gary Hart affair had not occurred. Hart changed the landscape? Yes. The issue is not just recklessness, but from our side, simple fairness. We can't go after Gary Hart and not after the others.

Jeff Greenfield comments, "I find it amusing—almost hilarious...that if the candidate didn't say 'Follow me,' that's ok...the judgment about his behavior is not conditioned on whether he says 'Put a tail on me.'" Just because he tells us to go away and leave him alone after 10 o'clock at night doesn't mean we shouldn't follow him. "There's more to it than that. Any candidate who would go up to a conference of fund raisers at this Cozy

**Fairness in
Campaign
Coverage**

Condo cottages with a woman to whom he is not married, with whom he is planning to spend a nonworking night, is the biggest idiot that ever walked the face of the earth, and for that alone is unqualified to be President of the United States. You don't have to get to the morality issue. You don't have to get to the character issue. This is the guy who wants to be in charge of covert operations for the United States of America? Forget it. And I say you'll send that photographer up there, send a camera crew, because you are dealing with the biggest moron in the United States Senate."

The hypothetical advances. Mr. Denniston, you are the reporter assigned to cover this rendezvous. What do you do? Ask at the front desk if Senator Valentine and friend are registered? No. That's nine steps too far forward. First, I get in the bushes. In the bushes? Denniston calmly continues as the other journalists cringe. Yes, in the bushes. See who comes and goes for awhile. Then I look for open windows, especially open windows with the shades down. What about checking the garbage? Oh, that comes later, Denniston continues. Then, having found the open windows, I start listening at the windows. If I hear a baby crying, that's probably not it. If I hear passionate groans, I figure I'm on the way.

Senator Simpson can take no more of this. How would you like it if someone did that to you? Let me ask you that. "If we all got back to the point in this city of Washington where it simply comes down to how would I feel if that happened to me, as a human being, we'll make some progress."

Fiedler agrees, that's an excellent rule, and he'd be very unhappy if any of *his* reporters did anything like that. Jennings isn't so sure. It's a good thing the journalists are "being so gingerly" with this. We don't like to think of ourselves as people in bushes. But this is the way it is. He feels guilty about it; he was part of the effort that brought about Mrs. Ferraro's demise— *political* demise, that is. But that's the way the game is played at this point, and as Apple pointed out, we don't have any choice in the matter.

The ball passed to her, Geraldine Ferraro changes the hypothetical slightly. What if this is a longstanding extra-marital relationship, and the man decides to run for President? Do you report it? The question goes to Paul Taylor. Yes, ultimately, he would. But look what you've done, Ferraro persists. The candidate retires from the race to save his family. Then the voters have one less choice, and it may have been an important choice. Greenfield demurs: the voters can always decide, as they did with Grover Cleveland, that they don't care about private playing around. Ferraro: yes, but since television they won't. So in reality, you have unilaterally narrowed the field of candidates.

Back to Denniston, plying his trade at the Cozy Condos. Suppose you find a waiter taking drinks to the senator. Do you offer to help? Climb a tree to peek through the window? Certainly, if there's an appropriately placed tree. Listen at air vents? Yes. Sneak around the back....Mike Wallace enters the conversation. There is *nothing wrong* with sneaking

The Ethics of Spying

and skulking to get a story. I'm with Denniston all the way. I'd have a camera going, I'd knock at the door, and whoever opens that door, I'd get a picture.

What do you advise Joe Valentine to do now? He calls his campaign manager (Jeff Greenfield) at 3:30 in the morning: I think I've got a batch of reporters outside. What do I do? Well, are you alone? Silence. Senator? Ah, there's this pollster with me, Debbie Spice...the conversation continues, but the conclusion is clear: For the woman's sake, get her back into her own room now. Come see me in the morning and we will prepare a graceful withdrawal statement from the campaign. It's too bad, Senator, but you're too dumb to be President.

Simpson, still enraged by these tactics, comes up with a novel idea: By now, the reporter who got Valentine is a public figure in his own right, is he not? Because of all the press coverage on Valentine's problems. Now can I send my staff after him, try to catch him doing something embarrassing? General Westmoreland is also turned off by the "Gestapo" tactics. When it became clear that Valentine did not have the right moral character for the Presidency, he should have been quietly told to get out. Suzanne Garment points out that the problem is not just the press. Watergate changed our notion of public morality, and the women's movement changed our attitudes "towards what was cute and what wasn't when it came to fooling around." The press just reflects those changes in its pursuit of people. Asked for her advice on whether to get out, Ferraro points out that he had a very good group of advisors already, and should have gotten their advice *before* running off to the motel.

Does This Game Have Any Rules?

Katharine Graham points out that the rules *have* changed, for the better as far as the voter is concerned. The press now has the function that used to be exercised by the smoke-filled room of politicians—to find out what has to be known and to screen the candidates accordingly.

It is the next morning, and you, as journalist, confront Valentine. What are you going to say to him?

Denniston: I'll say, "Senator, it's 9:00 in the morning. I've got a 1:00 deadline. I've got a story and I'm going to say that you spent the night with Debbie Spice. And I'm going to go with that story unless you tell me right now that you didn't and you show me that you didn't and you get Miss Spice out here and you have her attest in her own way that she didn't spend the night with you. But if you don't say anything, I'm going with that story." Probably I'm lying, because I haven't checked with my editor, but that's what I'll say. Simpson hits the ceiling. "Ethics is good for us but not for them, is the way it works." Denniston shrugs. "There isn't anything that I know of

The Ethics of Publishing the News

that constitutes a commonly accepted uniform code of ethics when one is engaging in the haphazard enterprise of communicating information."

Simpson hopes that Denniston has the tables turned on him some day. Denniston thinks that if he ever did, he would feel badly, but just a little of him would congratulate the guy that got him. "Journalism isn't child's play. And journalism, when you're dealing with public affairs and people who are maneuvering in power entities and power relationships, and they stand in the position to make one whole hell of a lot more difference than Lyle Denniston with his pathetic little pad and his pencil...." You think Joe Valentine will secretly congratulate you for getting him? "No, because Joe Valentine is not a journalist and Joe Valentine has not spent 39 years of his life trying to figure out what it is to have this incredible, incredible opportunity to be the first kid running down the street to say what I heard."

The Ethics of Doing Harm

Fiedler comments that you as journalist are sensitive to the human pain and anguish that you cause by this sort of thing. Fanning finds that justification insufficient. You have to ask, when you publish a piece that will hurt someone, what is the public interest? What is the relevance, what purpose is served?

Ferraro is not interested in Denniston's feelings about being first with the story. If the object is information, then OK. If a Pulitzer, no. If you're just trying to sell papers, she thinks it's unethical. She is not sure of the relevance of private lives. She agrees that the sexual indiscretion in this particular case is a matter of intelligence and judgment and so the public should know.

Smith denies that journalists are after stories that sell papers. That's not their concern.

Jeane Kirkpatrick reflects on the whole account of journalism presented by Lyle Denniston. He starts by saying he will not socialize with the people he covers, and ends with a great feeling of triumph at having exposed them. In between, we have the bushes, the transoms, and the keyholes. Journalism is too important for this.

Buying the News

The next phase of the hypothetical opens with Michael Marsh, a photographer for the Audubon Society, arriving at your desk with some pictures. Seems he was out by Lake Ardor, behind the Cozy Condos, taking pictures of the mating displays of birds, when he heard some splashing, looked over at the lake, and saw what seemed to be Candidate Valentine swimming with someone, possibly a woman. The light wasn't too good, but he got some pictures. Would your newspaper be interested in buying the pictures (you're the editor)?

Fanning's newspaper would not. This is beyond the ethical line, and not in the public interest. Denniston would not buy them. We may have noticed that his ethical perceptions tend to differ from Ms. Fanning's, but here he agrees with her. Wallace has no objection to buying good information, but these pictures aren't worth buying.

Why is it unethical to buy these pictures, Ms. Fanning? First because they are bought; second because they don't prove anything.

Garment wonders if there should be some agreed upon ethical standards for the press, possibly a self-governing body to supervise the profession. But no: "I don't see any possibility of developing a code of standards definite enough so that you can entrust the governance of the trade to any single body."

Graham worries about the tone of the presentations. We do care about the pain we cause, we do supervise the reporters, we do worry. It bothers her that people hate the press. We try to confine ourselves to those private issues that influence public affairs.

The Right to be Left Alone

Ferraro maintains that while she does not hate the press, the press often reaches over "that very fine line which you have described; and takes their rights that they have and forgets their responsibility to the public and, I think, to the public officials that they're covering; and when they cross that line and don't exert responsibility, they start moving in and affecting the private lives and the privacy rights of the individual." As a public official, you should *not* have to give up those rights. Along with the freedom of the press, there has to be some responsibility.

Simpson points out that different standards were used when Judge Bork was being covered prior to the hearings for an appointment to the Supreme Court. What did the press do about him? First, it kept a record of the videotapes he rented from a video store. How would you like it if some one did that to you? And it decided that he "didn't have enough compassion"; evaluating the quality of his feelings. For an ethical standard on these things, how about what Griffin Bell said it was, respect for "the right to be left alone"? Simpson concludes: "By God, and you'd like that, every one of you."

A REVIEW OF SELECTIONS FROM THE SOURCE READER

Before going on to discuss the philosophical background and the television presentation, this would be a good time to review certain of the readings in the history of ethics that pertain especially to this topic.

The concept of "privacy" has no history in the literature of philosophical ethics. As a single concept, it owes its origin to the law, which decided only recently to offer it Constitutional protection; as a value, it is much older, as a welcome refuge from an unpleasant world. For its philosophical foundations, we look to the literature of human dignity and the literature of private property: odd as the term may seem, one's property in one's own dignity may be the best cognate of privacy.

Selections for this chapter:

> John Locke, *Treatise of Government*, II, **Source Reader** p. 114
> Immanuel Kant, *Foundations of the Metaphysics of Morals*, **Source Reader** p. 136

Locke sets the bounds of all our senses of "property." We have property in ourselves, our own minds and bodies. He gives no philosophical derivation of this assertion, for he means it to be the head of a train of implications, not the conclusion. If we had to provide one, we might be forced back to the Greek/Judaeo-Christian concept of the individual who is individually answerable to God; if I must give an account of my actions to God, then I must have the right to act, or at least to control the conduct of my own body. From property in my body I derive property in my labor; from that I derive property in those things with which I have mixed my labor; and all else follows from that. Meanwhile, my body, myself, is my own.

Kant asserts the dignity of that self. As a mental exercise, see if you can reconcile the passages here with Jeremy Bentham's "Felicific Calculus" (Bentham, **Source Reader** p. 165). Does Bentham's "Calculus" make as much sense for all higher mammals as it does for humans?

SYNTHESIS AND DISCUSSION

The television presentation raises three sets of ethical tensions in our understandings of privacy and the press, which we may relate back to the introductory essay on the concept of privacy: the tension between the portrait of the professional journalist and the notion of a decent human being; the tension between the public's right to know and the public figure's right to privacy; and the tension between the need to limit the increasingly ingenious media invasions of privacy and the need to preserve the Constitutional protections of the free press. We will take them in that order.

1. There is a professional ideal of the journalist, just as there is of the doctor, the lawyer, or the soldier. At best, or purest, the journalist embodies the impersonal gaze of observation unmixed with emotion. As

Denniston articulates the ideal, reporters care nothing for the doings or feelings of their subjects, save as events take a turn that yields a better story. Their only passion is to get the story and to get it first; their only joy is in success in that quest, their only sorrow to find the story has slipped away or been missed.

This orientation turns all humankind into "material." Under the reporter's gaze, you are dehumanized, and any human relationship between you and the reporter is impossible. Denniston cheerfully concedes the point, and simply avoids humankind. To fulfill his chosen professional mission, he adopts an ascetic regime in which he is not prey to compromising human attachments. The other journalists, more or less uncomfortably, disagree with Denniston. You should, they insist, be able to have friends other than journalists, to go to parties, to relax, to be human. But then, what if juicy bits of news come drifting through the delectable scents of French cooking and fine brandy? Do you have the right to stop being human and start being a reporter again, or does your acceptance of the invitation forbid you to turn that impersonal, judgmental gaze on the host and the guests? Or is journalism one of those callings that requires you to act as a professional at all times? Do you have an absolute *duty* to go back to work when news presents itself?

Journalism is not like the profession of medicine. If someone suddenly takes ill in the middle of a party, we will call for an ambulance, but we will also ask if there is "a doctor in the house," and expect any physician to respond. Physicians are never "off duty" because we might unexpectedly need their help. Journalists, on the other hand, are not very helpful, at least not to the people who claim their attention in the middle of a party. On the contrary, they are very likely to do a fair amount of damage. Is there no safety from their invasions? If I am in the company of a reporter, am I liable at any moment, as Barney Frank complains he is, to find my life under that impenetrable gaze, swiftly to be turned into print and exposed to all the world? Can this be right? The television presentation shows us beyond doubt that the matter has not been resolved in the journalistic profession itself.

2. How much of a public figure's private life is not private? Here the journalists seem to have reached at least a theoretical consensus: to the extent that the private life bears on the public activity, the public that is affected by that activity should know about it. Determining on a case by case basis what aspects of that private life have such effects is, of course, another matter. When homosexuality was clearly beyond the pale of acceptable lifestyles, evidence of homosexuality was relevant to public life, because the homosexual was subject to blackmail. Now that the homosexual can tell would-be blackmailers to go ahead and publish their discoveries, is the condition less likely to affect public life?

Some public figures have, in fact, announced their homosexual preferences. In such public "confession," three ethical questions are raised. First, to what extent may we simply acquiesce to popular perceptions of the right and the good, and to what extent should we stand against them or insist on a more reasoned perception? Granted that the popular perception of homosexuality is much more tolerant now than it was in the 1950s, is it not still incumbent upon us, as moral citizens, to reach our own conclusions on the moral weight, if any, of sexual preference? If a history of fraud in business dealings becomes widely acceptable (say, as a result of the large number of people convicted for insider trading), should we acquiesce to a generation of public figures with a proven propensity for fraud? Or is it still our duty, as rational moral agents, to form our own opinions on matters of morals? Or is that duty overridden for these purposes by the presumption of democracy—that what the people are willing to accept just *is* moral enough for the people's representative?

Second, what aspects of the internal life of the person shall count as likely to affect the public interest? How much, and what, do we *need* to know? The journalists do not seem to reach a consensus on this one. Marijuana use? But then why not alcohol consumption? At a certain level of consumption, of course, alcohol does become an issue. But what level is that? Sexual liaisons in the past? How many? And how far in the past? The more recent they are, the more serious; but at a certain number, they become significant no matter when they occurred. What number is that? Cheating, lying and, in general, fraud, seem much more serious, as deeply reflective of the character and courage of the person. But here also the signals are not clear. We have seen (in this country, not in the hypothetical) one political candidate virtually destroyed by revelation of cheating in school, while another went on to the Senate. Meanwhile, the members of a person's family have more effect on his actions than any other group or influence. Should the activities of the candidate's family become public knowledge? At what distance of consanguinity? Brothers, sisters, parents, distant cousins—where shall we stop?

And third, whatever the real moral quality of the private acts or propensities in question, whatever their influence or lack of it on the conduct of public office, to what extent can the right of privacy be asserted—the simple right, in Simpson's words, to be left alone—to counter efforts to find out about those private acts or propensities? This is the primary issue for this presentation, although the other two cannot be completely excluded from the discussion.

3. If the issue is one of privacy—the right of individual privacy asserted against the public's right to know and the journalist's consequent duty to make known—how shall we determine the appropriate limitations on reportorial activity? The end of that activity is given: to provide the people

with the knowledge they need in order to govern themselves rationally. If our collective decisions are to be rational, we need to know the truth about the world for which those decisions are to be made, about the condition of our nation's institutions, and about the public officials who are making the decisions in our name. Jefferson once said that newspapers were more important than government to the life of the people; in the First Amendment to the Constitution he protected their right to publish. No doubt an important social value is at stake here, and the press has an important task to accomplish. But given the potential for injury to human beings, is it not appropriate to limit the means that may be employed to accomplish that task? What about all this sneaking, skulking, spying, listening at windows and transoms and vents? Gathering information in this way violates the dignity of the reporter, the subject of his report, and the profession of journalism. Surely we can agree that these means, at least, are ethically unacceptable?

It is not clear that we can. The use of covert means to gather information for purposes of law enforcement is well established and accepted. As a people, we have authorized wiretaps, police decoys, stakeouts, and all manner of police following and spying to gather evidence against serious lawbreakers. More interesting, we have even authorized radar traps and in-store cameras, more likely to catch us or our neighbors at petty lawbreaking. As long as the behavior targeted clearly violates the law, we have no real objection to using secret means to detect it. The criminal, we would probably be willing to say, has no right of privacy where criminal behavior is concerned.

But that principle has unsettling extensions. One such extension, beyond the scope of this essay, is that suspicion of any actions temporarily declared to be "criminal" automatically abrogates the right of privacy, with no notification required. Thus during the 1950s "Red Scare" anyone remotely suspected of "Communist" activity could be subjected to criminal investigation; much the same phenomenon occurred in the 1920s and, to a much lesser degree, during the protests against the war in Vietnam.

Another such extension is that with public figures, the public's "right to know" may authorize the same sort of surveillance for activities not contrary to law, but probably contrary to the public interest. That, of course, is the case that interests us here. Were the police hiding in those bushes at the Cozy Condos in hopes of trapping the leaders of the Mafia in some ungodly scheme of murder and grand theft, we would applaud. But the attempt to catch out an indiscreet married man, keeping company with a young lady in compromising circumstances, hardly seems worthy of the means necessary to succeed. It is marginally illegal for a married man to have an affair with an unmarried young woman; laws against adultery are still on the books of most states, but they are never enforced for their own sake. But the illegality is not the source of our interest in this act, and it is doubtful whether our interest in such doings should be satisfied. As General West-moreland suggested, once the immorality was discovered, the candidate should quietly have been told to withdraw, quite without the national peep show the press is promising us. But absent the kind of zeal displayed by the *Miami Herald* reporters in the coverage of Gary Hart during the 1988 Presidential campaign, and articulated by Lyle Denniston, how will we ever find out about these things?

All of this raises a peculiar possibility: that we as a people may not be able to live without the press and its revelations, while we as a people may not be able to tolerate the systematic invasions of privacy that the press seems determined to commit. Resolutions to this dilemma may be difficult to find. Several plausible candidates for resolution were advanced in the TV presentation:

1. Senator Simpson's appeal to the Golden Rule—or as Philosophy would recognize it, the Principle of Universality that lies at the foundation of Kant's Categorical Imperative (Kant, **Source Reader** p. 131). How would you like it if someone did that to you? If you, Mr. Denniston, would not like someone hiding in the bushes outside *your* home watching *you*, listening at *your* windows, going through *your* garbage, then don't do it to us.

Simpson's appeal has the virtue of simplicity, not to mention wide applicability elsewhere in the moral life of the individual and the nation. But while we may want the members of the press to be sensitive to the feelings of those they cover, we do not really want them to limit their reportorial zeal, at least not when important public issues are at stake. After all, while we want our police to be sensitive to the human feelings of those with whom they deal, we do not want them restrained from making arrests by the thought of the anguish that will be felt by the criminal and his family if he should be caught. The press has a job to do in the life of the nation, and we want it done regardless of feelings. So this elegant solution will not do us much good.

2. Ms. Garment's suggestion that a professional association of jour-nalists might be the appropriate body to set the standards and limits for journalistic coverage also has a certain logic to it; after all, we as "laymen" vis-à-vis these professionals cannot foresee all the ethical dilemmas that will confront the professional in his or her career. Because of the technical na-ture of many occupations, we have come to trust internal organizations (like the American Medical Association for the profession of medicine, or the American Bar Association for law) to set and enforce the ethical rules for their practitioners. This is the way we have always expected our professions to govern themselves.

But professional self-governance raises as many problems as it was designed to solve. Newspapers, unlike physicians, are in head-to-head competition, and their survival depends upon their ability to outmaneuver their rivals. The temptation to use any such standard-setting board as an instrument for your own profit—by setting rules that would work against the competition more than against your own paper—would have to be irresistible to any participating publisher. Further, any attempt to enforce standards, for instance by forbidding the publication of stories that were obtained in violation of an accepted code of procedure, would violate the First Amendment guarantee of freedom of the press. And any standards adopted by such a body, whether or not enforceable, would be binding only on its own membership; membership could not be coerced without further First Amendment violations. There is always the further objection that any professional organization must be self-serving, since it is dedicated to protecting its members from complaints and regulation in the name of the public; certainly the AMA and the ABA have been criticized on that score. The self-governing professional association will have to be given more thought before we adopt it as our solution.

3. Another possible solution lies just below the surface in some of Jeff Greenfield's remarks: that we draw a bright moral line, parallel to the bright line the law tries to draw in these cases, between the private person, who desires only to be left alone and whose right to be left so should be scrupulously respected, and the public figure. The public figure has sought publicity for some purpose of his own, and has therefore entered into a "Faustian bargain," or pact with the devil, to trade privacy for the power, fame, and glory that come in the wake of public recognition. Public figures implicitly ask for and deserve constant attention from the press, and rapidly become very good at manipulating the press to serve their own image and publicity purposes. Where Presidential candidates are concerned, as Ms. Graham suggested, this constant press attention fulfills the function of the Old Pols of the back rooms, finding out all that is significant in the candidate's background.

Crucial information may not lie ready to hand. Who would have suspected that the delightful Senator Eagleton, late of George McGovern's campaign for the presidency, had a history of mental illness? Nor would any of us have suspected the apparently dubious side of the business transactions carried on by the husband of the scrupulously honest Geraldine Ferraro. But old friends, old pols, would have known about these things, and thought to bring them up before the campaign began. (Had that happened, perhaps both sets of problems would have been resolved through appropriate disclosure and public discussion, and two excellent candidates would have run more successful races.) Now we must rely on the press to uncover events from the past, or from the family, and air them for discussion.

Then perhaps all this press tracking, trailing, peeping, and spying is, after all, when applied to Presidential candidates, good for the nation in the long run. Again, one of Jeff Greenfield's remarks, made when the hypothetical candidate had been found compromised at the Condos, sticks in the mind: "This man wants to be in charge of all of the covert operations in the United States? Forget it!" As leader of the Free World, the President will have to keep its secrets, and if he cannot keep even his own, how can we trust him with ours? As Commander-in-Chief of its armed forces, he will have to control his temper and watch his tongue. A careless remark made in anger during the campaign can bring him unwanted headlines, but such a remark made as President can bring us unwanted war. And so forth. The press is often praised as the nation's teacher. It has also become the educator of Presidents. All this attention will, at the least, school the future President in caution. That may be the greatest help the press can provide in the preparation of our statesmen.

QUESTIONS FOR YOUR REFLECTION

1. Privacy is one of those moral principles that has different values to different people (unlike, say, honesty, which is vitally important to everyone). How would you rank privacy among your own values: very important, moderately important, not very important at all? Can you say why?

2. What is the value of the free press? Can you imagine living in a country with no newspapers, radio, TV, or newsmagazines? Or a country where the press was firmly controlled by the government? Suppose you had to defend our protection of the freedom of the press to someone from that country. How would you go about doing it?

3. What did you think of the participants in the discussion (especially Lyle Denniston, who took all the hard positions)? With whom did you find yourself in sympathy? Denniston? Ferraro? Simpson? Why?

4. What, if anything, defines the appropriate barrier of "the private" in the life of even a public figure? How shall we determine when that barrier is breached? Who (what body or person or procedure) should make that determination?

5. What legal invasions of privacy would you be willing to justify in the name of public policy? Would you be able to defend regular surveillance for the purposes of:

- Making sure that people stay within the law;
- Making sure that people are behaving themselves morally;
- Making sure that people are healthy;
- Making sure that people are happy.

Try. Some defenses are easier than others.

6. Given Hobbes' notion of the "natural rights" of human beings, would invasion of privacy be a violation of those rights? What about on Locke's notion of rights, or Jefferson's? Cite evidence from your **Source Reader**.

SUGGESTIONS FOR FURTHER READING

Special Supplementary Text:
KEITH S. COLLINS, ED. *Responsibility and Freedom in the Press: Are They in Conflict?* Washington, DC: Citizen's Choice, Inc., 1985.

ALLEY, ROBERT S. *Television: Ethics for Hire.* Nashville, TN: Abingdon, 1977.

CHRISTIANS, CLIFFORD G. AND CATHERINE L. COVERT. *Teaching Ethics in Journalism Education.* Hastings-on-Hudson, New York: Institute of Society, Ethics and the Life Sciences (Hastings Center), 1980.

DENNIS, EVERETTE E. AND JOHN C. MERRILL. *Basic Issues in Mass Communication: A Debate.* New York: Macmillan Publishing Company, 1984.

HODGES, LOUIS. "The Journalist and Privacy," in *Social Responsibility: Journalism, Law, Medicine,* Vol. IX, ed. Louis Hodges. Lexington, VA: Washington and Lee University, 1983.

McCULLOCH, FRANK, ED. *Drawing the Line: How 31 Editors Solved Their Toughest Ethical Dilemmas.* Washington, DC: American Society of Newspaper Editors Foundation, 1984.

MERRILL, JOHN C. AND RALPH BARNEY, EDS. *Ethics and the Press.* New York: Hastings House, 1975.

OLEN, JEFFREY. *Ethics in Journalism.* Englewood Cliffs, NJ: Prentice Hall, 1988.

PENNOCK, ROLAND AND JOHN CHAPMAN, EDS. *Privacy* (*NOMOS* vol. XII) New York: Atherton, 1970.

POWELL, JODY. *The Other Side of the Story.* New York: Morrow, 1984.

PURVIS, HOYT H., ED. *The Press: Free and Responsible?* Austin, TX: The University of Texas Press, 1982.

ROWAN, FORD. *Broadcast Fairness: Doctrine, Practice, Prospects.* New York: Longman, 1984.

RUBIN, BERNARD, ED. *Questioning Media Ethics.* New York: Praeger Special Studies, 1978.

SCHMUL, ROBERT, ED. *The Responsibilities of Journalism.* South Bend, IN: Notre Dame Press, 1984.

SHAW, DAVID. *Press Watch: A Provocative Look At How Newspapers Report the News.* New York: Macmillan, 1984.

SWAIN, BRUCE M. *Reporters' Ethics.* Ames, IA: Iowa State University Press, 1978.

THAYER, LEE, ED. *Communication: Ethical and Moral Issues.* New York: Gordon and Breach, 1973.

chapter 13 _____

THE LAST WORD

Writing a final chapter is always difficult. It should sum up the course, present (or re-present) it on a platter, neat and laid out. It should be clear and certain about what has been said, and done, and learned, in the course of the semester. But ethics simply does not lend itself to such neat summaries.

We will follow a more tentative course. We will summarize briefly what we can know for certain (the area is very small), indicate what cannot be certainly known (the territory is vast), then try to indicate what sort of journey should be undertaken, and what sort of explorer should undertake it, in order to bring more of the territory of ethics within reach of the understanding.

WHAT WE CAN SAY FOR CERTAIN

Ethics has some permanent elements, changeless over time since the first discussions of the topic began. For starters, we might review the implications of the first statements in the first chapter of this book.

1. Ethics is intelligible, and we must resist the recurring temptation to cynicism—the strong desire to believe, with Thrasymachus, that

there *is* no right or wrong, but only the desires of human beings and the strength they have to satisfy them. ("Might makes right," we may call it, Plato, **Source Reader**, p. 8.) We do not find this view articulated on our video programs, because those who hold such positions do not tend to take days out of their profitable schedules to engage, for no compensation, in public debates on ethics. But we know this temptation exists in our own lives, and we have seen it at work among our coworkers and classmates. There is an overwhelming tendency, in pluralist America, to assume that "you have a right to think anything you want" means that "anything you want to think is right," that ethics, like taste in ice cream, is just a matter of personal policy, and that therefore no real study of ethics is possible. But that is a great fallacy, and one that we ought to be prepared to contest whenever it arises. Trying to do the right thing all the time is burdensome, and it would be pleasant to abandon the effort. The belief that there *is* no right, except as you or I happen to feel at the moment, permits us to abandon the effort for good. Hence the temptation to cynicism, which we must learn to resist.

2. Ethics is serious, and very difficult. If we are not to think that there are no right answers at all, our next temptation is to find one simple answer that takes care of all problems once and for all. In this error we may include the relatively simple fallacies of egoism ("whatever helps me in the long run counts, and nothing else counts") and cultural relativism ("whatever my group thinks is right to do, right now, *is* right to do, for me, right now"). Both stop short of including human beings beyond the immediate group, and so fail as ethical theories.

In this category of ethical failing we include the recurring tendency to fanaticism. The phenomenon of fanaticism has as many definitions as it has manifestations, but we may take the simplest definition: Fanaticism is the zealous dedication to a system of beliefs that excludes all doubts about their truth, all respect for those who believe otherwise, and all qualms about any action that must be taken to advance the cause. Fanaticism also is absent from the programs we have watched; fanatics are very difficult to have on a panel that discusses ethics, because they do not believe in reasoning— at least, not the kind of reasoning that might challenge their axioms.

In one sense, fanaticism is the opposite pole from cynicism: fanaticism is an excess of moral belief, and cynicism is a lack of the same. In another sense, fanaticism is exactly like cynicism: both abolish the need to reason, to think, to deliberate and debate, to agonize, to suffer remorse when your difficult choice turns out to be wrong. Both vices of moral belief are ways out of the necessary pain of moral reflection; as such, they are equally attractive and equally wrong.

3. And third, ethics is about human beings. If we are looking for constants in the human pursuit of right and wrong, we must include the

recurring and sincere desire of human beings to live as they ought to live, to adhere to a standard of right conduct or virtue—to avoid the extremes of cynicism and fanaticism and to be good. This determination to do the right thing has three different expressions.

First: the attempt to help others, to protect them from harm, to heal their illness and, on occasion, to save their lives. This attempt often showed up on the television programs as dedicated professionalism, i.e., the determination of a professional to do his or her job, to protect the patient or client (or readers or constituents) no matter what conflicts complicate the job. Thus we have Mortimer Rosen trying to save the life of a baby, Sally Quinn and Ellen Goodman trying to get the story for their readers, Willard Gaylin trying to get help for a disturbed street person, and James Neal trying by all means, fair or foul, to make his client seem innocent. On occasion, concern for welfare extends to the entire nation, or world, in the long run, even at the cost of some present unhappiness. So, at least, argued Sir James Goldsmith about the effects of his business dealings, so the journalists explained their right to expose the private lives of public people, so the military men justified the loss of lives in the "diversionary tactic," and so ran the justification for research with human subjects.

But the dedication to help often seemed to have limits that the professionals did not notice. The desire to help the street person sometimes runs afoul of the civil rights of that person, including the right to resist incarceration. The desire to save the baby can conflict with the mother's right to refuse invasion of her body. And the pursuit of the story, the deal, the client's benefit, maximal efficiency of the market, and the ultimate drug for AIDS can violate privacy, justice, truth, workers' rights, and the right of the patient to die with dignity (in that order). These failings are not due to lack of moral fiber on the part of the members of the panels. As above, in these programs we are unlikely to find amoralists, arguing that the strong can do what they want and the weak simply have to suffer. We find instead practitioners who pursue the limited objectives of their profession with a single-mindedness that rules out a wide range of ethical considerations. We may not assume that the people who presented such views actually believe them and act on them in their own lives. They may have been presenting their views only as hypothetical positions in response to the hypothetical problem. But there is a consistency in their presentations that belies that speculation.

Second: the pursuit of justice. Another note that sounds through the conversations of the seminars is justice, or fairness. It is the central subject of the dialogue on business practices (how can it be fair for those few to be that rich—for that little work?) and criminal law (where Will Gaylin forcefully defended the proposition that some crimes simply demand certain penalties, regardless of benefit). It also runs through the product liability case, where Chesley and Cotchett try to obtain justice for the poor against the rich corporations; through the conversations on journalism and government service, where fairness in the treatment of public servants is discussed; and even through the family ethics case, where Justice Scalia must decide (in his role as Father) whether to turn in his own son for cheating on a test.

Third: sensitivity to individual freedom and dignity. In the cases of the pregnant cancer patient and the homeless street person, we find the panelists agonizing between the obligation to help a person who is suffering and the obligation to honor that person's firm choice. Individual dignity pervades the Law cases; we allow lawyers to obfuscate the truth, destroy witnesses' characters, and pull a thousand technical tricks in order to provide protection for one individual against the society that (probably with justification) wants to change or destroy him. The same value fuels the demand for privacy (against the depredations of the journalists), confidentiality (against the legitimate demands for information posed by military authorities), and liberty (to carry on business as profitably as possible, regardless of justice or the pain of those who are hurt).

These values—beneficence, justice, and respect for persons—are the three to which we have referred in the course of this *Study Guide*. We know that we can explain most correct moral judgment in terms of these values. We do not know how to decide which takes priority over which. That problem lies at the heart of all real ethical conflict. Once we've got past our attempts to find an easy way out of thinking at all, and confronted real ethical problems on their own terms, this is the source of all indecision, as it was for our panelists, week after week. Here is where the choosing person enters at the level of ethical theory (as opposed to the level of moral conduct): each of us must choose which pattern of values will inform our lives, our day-to-day choices, and our careers, and, for purposes of those choices, must subordinate all others to that. But in this, too, there are dangers.

It is the highest virtue of the human race, Royce argued (**Source Reader** p. 139), to make a value your own, the object of your loyalty, and devote yourself thenceforth to that. Yet we must also step back from professional or otherwise limited goals and evaluate them in terms of the larger commitments. It is our duty to be loyal and obedient; it is also our duty to be critical and to question authority; it is our duty, further, to accept the conflict between those two duties, and set a course for ourselves that incorporates both of them.

So far our list of certainties is not very long. We are sure to find cynicism in every age, in every type of society. We are sure to find fanaticism, with its passion that destroys all reason, all doubt, and all opponents in its quest for total domination. And we are sure to find good people, torn between the loyalty that borders on fanaticism and the criticism that borders on cynicism. We acknowledge certain basic values (welfare, justice, and respect for persons), we know those values cannot be proved or placed in clear priority, so we acknowledge further that we must live with the resulting conflicts and uncertainty, and must find some personally acceptable, and publicly defensible, way to chart our course among them.

TRAGEDY AND VISION; ACCEPTANCE AND COURAGE

Conflict, then, and divergent perspectives, are essential to the notion of ethics. We may not be doing ethics in good faith, of course; the cynic and the fanatic, no matter how well behaved they are in polite company, are not working in good faith. They listen to "reasoning" only until they find the weak points to insert their single-minded blades, and treat debates as means only to secure converts. But ethics in good faith provides no certainty except that we will find ways to disagree, if somewhat more painfully than the cynic and fanatic.

We need a sense of the tragic, a sense that over a very large area of our choices, there will be no right one. Some choices are easy, some are difficult, but we know when we have made the right one. But over that large area, there will only be more or less unacceptable alternatives, more or less wrong decisions. Nor will that fact exempt us from responsibility for the inevitable consequences of those choices. Conflict and divergence of perspective are inevitable; responsibility is also inevitable.

Beyond a sense of the tragic, we need a vision of the possible. What understanding of the good life will help us chart the way through conflicts? It might be helpful to review Chapter 2 at this point, and remind ourselves of the four visions of the moral life emerging from the history of ethics. Of those four, which did you prefer?

A rational life of virtue, as the Greeks? Was Plato's proof in the *Republic* valid after all (Plato, **Source Reader** pp. 25, 43)?

A life of love of God and neighbor, as set forth in Moses' last sermon (Bible, **Source Reader** p. 75), and the Gospel according to John (Bible, **Source Reader** p. 87)?

A stern life of adherence to the moral law, expressed most eloquently by Epictetus the Roman slave (Epictetus, **Source Reader** p. 93)? A life according to the law, maintaining respect for the dignity of the human as an end in itself (Kant, **Source Reader** p. 127)?

A moderately happy life of gratifying our desires, well within limits, along lines suggested by Epicurus (**Source Reader** p. 157; codified by Jeremy Bentham, **Source Reader** p. 158; best articulated by John Stuart Mill, **Source Reader** p. 166)?

Ask yourself which of these lives appeals to you. Or are there other visions that you find more attractive? When you try to sort out your own life for yourself, and try to say what kind of person you should be, and what kind of life you should live in order to be happy, which of these visions of human life is closest to your description?

GOING ON FROM HERE

If you decide to join the generations of travelers, a few in each generation, who have gone in search of the moral life, you must be prepared for a difficult journey, with no sure rewards along the way and no sure notification when its end is reached. We have tried, in these pages, to provide the compass for that journey. But you are the one who must decide how it is to be used. All a compass can do is tell you what directions are open; it will not tell you which one you must follow at any given point.

For this type of journey, the qualities of the explorers are more important than the excellence of the instruments at their disposal. Consider the following, as a brief and partial list of the personal equipment you should take with you:

1. You will need sensitivity, especially to human suffering; you will need the moral imagination to see the world as another sees it, especially as that "other" is bound by personal moral imperatives.

2. You will need self-discipline, or courage; the willingness to do something that is right even if it is unpleasant. Moreover, you will need the willingness to persevere in that right even if the world proceeds to make it somewhat more unpleasant. In the end, the name of the quality is integrity: the way of being one person, not whatever person the powers around you have created.

3. You will need a sense of humor, or a sense of tragedy (they come to the same thing); a recognition that not everything (and that nothing, eventually, in this very imperfect world) is going to come out right, and that we must therefore be satisfied in doing the best that we can. Despair is the punishment for ignorance of this point. Cheerfulness is the reward, and the condition, for its acceptance.

4. And as you set out, you will need that moral compass: a personal orientation to the recognized values of ethics, freely and knowledgeably adopted, that will provide firm directions for personal behavior in situations where extended reflection is impossible.

We have not left you with a simple moral agenda. But we can state it simply enough: our job is first, to respect, and have faith in, each other; second, to employ, and have faith in, reason; and third, to continue the conversation on ethics ourselves and to teach it to our children. The last word in ethics will be written by you, in your own lives.

AUDIOCASSETTE 3

The audiotape that accompanies this final chapter features a dialogue led by Professor Fred W. Friendly and Professor Thomas Pogge. A group of students from Columbia University weigh some tough ethical questions posed by Professor Friendly. These are questions that you could easily face tomorrow, or next week.

As you listen to the students on the tape, ask yourself whether you agree with their reasoning. In light of what you have learned in this course, what decisions would you make? Are your decisions different from or similar to the decisions made by these students? Can you explain in ethical terms why your decisions are different? You might stop the tape after each of the case studies to give yourself time to think about your answers to these questions.

APPENDIX

THE NUREMBERG CODE[1]

The Proof as to War Crimes and Crimes against Humanity

Permissible Medical Experiments

The Proof as to War Crimes
and Crimes against Humanity

Judged by any standard of proof the record clearly shows the commission of war crimes and crimes against humanity substantially as alleged in counts two and three of the indictment. Beginning with the outbreak of World War II criminal medical experiments on non-German nationals, both prisoners of war and civilians, including Jews and "asocial" persons, were carried out on a large scale in Germany and the occupied countries. These experiments were not the isolated and casual acts of individual doctors and scientists working solely on their own responsibility, but were the product of coordinated policy-making and planning at high governmental, military, and Nazi Party levels, conducted as an integral part of the total war effort. They were ordered, sanctioned, permitted, or approved by persons in positions of authority who under all principles of law were under the duty to know about things and to take steps to terminate or prevent them.

[1]Reprinted from *Trials of War Criminals before the Nuremberg Tribunals under Control Council Law No. 10*, Vol. 2 (Washington, D.C.: U.S. Government Printing Office, 1949), pp. 181-182.

Permissible Medical Experiments

The great weight of evidence before us is to the effect that certain types of medical experiments on human beings, when kept within reasonable well-defined bounds, conform to the ethics of the medical profession generally. The protagonists of the practice of human experimentation justify their views on the basis that such experiments yield results for the good of society that are unprocurable by other methods or means of study. All agree, however, that certain basic principles must be observed in order to satisfy moral, ethical and legal concepts:

1. The voluntary consent of the human subject is absolutely essential.

This means that the person involved should have legal capacity to give consent; should be so situated as to be able to exercise free power of choice, without the intervention of any element of force, fraud, deceit, duress, overreaching, or other ulterior form of constraint or coercion; and should have sufficient knowledge and comprehension of the elements of the subject matter involved as to enable him to make an understanding and enlightened decision. This latter element requires that before the acceptance of an affirmative decision by the experimental subject there should be made known to him the nature, duration, and purpose of the experiment; the method and means by which it is to be conducted; all inconveniences and hazards reasonably to be expected; and the effects upon his health or person which may possibly come from his participation in the experiment.

The duty and responsibility for ascertaining the quality of the consent rests upon each individual who initiates, directs or engages in the experiment. It is a personal duty and responsibility which may not be delegated to another with impunity.

2. The experiment should be such as to yield fruitful results for the good of society, unprocurable by other methods or means of study, and not random and unnecessary in nature.

3. The experiment should be designed and based on the results of animal experimentation and a knowledge of the natural history of the disease or other problem under study that the anticipated results will justify the performance of the experiment.

4. The experiment should be so conducted as to avoid all unnecessary physical and mental suffering and injury.

5. No experiment should be conducted where there is *a priori* reason to believe that death or disabling injury will occur except, perhaps, in those experiments where the experimental physicians also serve as subjects.

6. The degree of risk to be taken should never exceed that determined by the humanitarian importance of the problem to be solved by the experiment.

7. Proper preparations should be made and adequate facilities provided to protect the experimental subject against even remote possibilities of injury, disability, or death.

8. The experiment should be conducted only by scientifically qualified persons. The highest degree of skill and care should be required through all stages of the experiment of those who conduct or engage in the experiment.

9. During the course of the experiment the human subject should be at liberty to bring the experiment to an end if he has reached the physical or mental state where continuation of the experiment seems to him to be impossible.

10. During the course of the experiment the scientist in charge must be prepared to terminate the experiment at any stage, if he has probable cause to believe, in the exercise of the good faith, superior skill and careful judgment required of him that a continuation of the experiment is likely to result in injury, disability, or death to the experimental subject....

THEORY	GOOD TO BE REACHED AS A CONSEQUENCE	VERIFICATION PROCEDURE: HOW TO KNOW WHAT TO DO AND WHEN IT'S DONE
	Consequentialist Theories	
Utilitarianism **1. Hedonism** **(Bentham)**	Maximum pleasure for the greatest number.	The ability to discern what is pleasurable is innate. The criterion for maximized pleasure is the number of moments of pleasurable consciousness felt by those affected, and only asking them will determine what result has been achieved.
2. Utilitarianism **(J.S. Mill)**	Maximum utility (pleasure or any other good—virtue, education, achievement) for the greatest number.	Utility, which includes judgments of quality of pleasure and long-term enlightenment, is much more difficult to quantify.
3. Rule utilitarianism	Formation of, and obedience to, rules of conduct of general obedience that will produce the greatest good for the greatest number.	Rule utilitarianism requires two-step verification; the good act is one in obedience to rule; and the rule must be utilitarian.
Intuitionism **(G.E. Moore)**	Goodness, a non-natural universal quality intuitively recognizable.	Each person is intuitively able to recognize goodness and distinguish it from all natural properties.
Self-realizationism or Virtue (Aristotle, Maslow)	Achievement of full development of human nature.	Very difficult to say. Attainment is usually associated with culturally approved characteristics: virtue, happiness, and success.

Note: "Egoism," a purported form of consequentialism in which the good sought is the happiness of the actor alone, contradicts itself at the first level of any analysis and is not therefore treated here as a valid theory.

BACKGROUND: ETHICAL ORIENTATIONS

THEORY	SOURCE OF OBLIGATION	VERIFICATION PROCEDURE: HOW TO KNOW WHAT TO DO AND WHEN IT'S DONE
Non-consequentialist Theories		
Law-based theories: Natural Law Theory (Aquinas)	Eternal Law of God.	That portion of God's law which is necessary for the moral life is immediately known to reason, engraved on the heart.
Formalism (Kant)	Nature of morality itself; moral law.	Act so that the reason for your act is generalizable to all moral agents (first formulation of the Categorical Imperative).
Rights-based theories: (Hobbes, Locke; Nozick)	The inalienable rights that persons have by nature, that others must respect.	Each person deserves at least to be regarded as a person, entailing at least the right to be free (to be left alone) and to be regarded as equal to other persons. Other rights (like property) are derived from liberty or equality, or established by contract (see below).
Contract-based theories: (Hobbes, Locke; Rousseau, Rawls)	Agreements made by the agent (explicitly or tacitly).	Obviously, all contracts (or promises) explicitly undertaken create moral obligations. Beyond that, the conventions that make society possible are "tacitly" agreed to by all who accept the benefits of those conventions.
Principle-based theories: (Ross, Fletcher, Royce, et al)	A variety of moral principles (gratitude, honesty, compassion, etc.), which are *prima facie* binding on all agents.	These principles are intuitively known and need no external warrant. They occasionally conflict, which is why they do not bind absolutely. Reflection must determine which principle takes precedence in a given situation.

ISSUES OF LAW & SOCIETY

ISSUE	CONSEQUENTIALIST CONSIDERATIONS	NON-CONSEQUENTIALIST CONSIDERATIONS
Issues of Justice and Public Responsibility		
Defense of the clearly guilty	Preserves legal system vs releases criminals into the street.	Rights of each person to a vigorous defense in court vs demands of retributive justice.
Plea bargaining	Needed for legal system's viability vs encourages criminals to repeat crimes.	Right to accept any offered deal vs society's right to appropriate punishment of crime.
Media candor: pre-trial publicity	Prevents coverups, informs public vs creates bias among potential jurors.	Public's right to know vs accused's right to a fair trial.
Media candor: TV in the courtroom	Educates and informs the public vs turns trials into circuses, rewards spectacle and gimmicks.	Public's right to know vs accused's right to a reasonable trial.
Capital punishment	Ultimate deterrence for worst crimes and criminals vs possible death of innocent, brutalization of society.	Right of society to full retribution for worst crimes vs duty not to take any human life.
***Pro Bono* Work: Donating Community Service**	Provides legal help for those who couldn't get it otherwise vs brings matters to court that otherwise would not be in litigation.	Right to representation by attorney; also duty of lawyers to use talents for benefit of the poor.
Alternative dispute resolution	Tremendous saving of money, time, nerves and energy. No evil consequences.	Timely justice vs right to full trial, including jury of peers.

DUTY	CONSEQUENTIALIST CONSIDERATIONS	NON-CONSEQUENTIALIST CONSIDERATIONS
	Issues of Truth and the Client	
Full knowledge of the case: the lawyer's duty to find out all the facts	Without full knowledge, the lawyer will not be able to plan a rational strategy to serve the client. The lawyer must know where to look for evidence, what witnesses to question, and what lines of inquiry to avoid, and only with full knowledge can that be done.	*Trust:* the lawyer-client relationship is one of trust, and it must start with a willingness to reveal even embarrassing information. *Integrity:* like any professional, the lawyer will not proceed without knowledge. *Contract:* attempt to get full information implicit in contract with client.
Confidentiality: the lawyer's duty not to reveal anything the client discloses if it would embarrass the client	Guarantee of confidentiality is the only way to ensure that the client will feel able to reveal the most troubling facts, or seek out a lawyer to begin with. Only this way will fearful clients be able to exercise their rights and avoid being victimized by bolder participants in the legal system.	*Trust:* confidentiality justifies the client's trust in the lawyer, is part of any trusting relationship. *Integrity:* revealing confidence is beneath professional dignity. *Contract:* confidentiality is the major provision (besides competent representation) in the contract with the client.
Candor with the court: the lawyer's duty to reveal to the court at least any planned or ongoing wrongdoing	Ultimately, the system of public order will not survive if a privileged class of consultants will not reveal planned harms. The contemplated victims have rights, too, and nothing is more demoralizing than seeing wealthy men protect wrongdoers in their crimes.	*Trust:* his relationship with society, as with client, depends on it. *Integrity:* the lawyer is, first and foremost, an officer of the court, sworn to uphold the legal system. The lawyer above all cannot countenance lawbreaking. *Contract:* his professional license depends on it.

ISSUES OF MEDICAL ETHICS

ISSUE	CONSEQUENTIALIST CONSIDERATIONS	NON-CONSEQUENTIALIST CONSIDERATIONS
Issues of Professional Responsibility		
Shaping the provider-patient relationship	Need to get patient well, keep patient calm and compliant with treatment.	Respect for patient's autonomy, provider's integrity.
Avoiding malpractice suits	Need to practice good medicine and document everything done; avoid costly "defensive" medicine (excess tests, etc.).	Patient's right to compensation for injury, right to use of courts; good medicine is good law.
Research with human subjects	Need to develop generalizable knowledge for the progress of medicine and welfare of all.	Respect for rights of subject; informed consent, voluntary participation.
Harvesting the organs from the dead	Need to have organs available for transplants to vastly improve chances of survival and quality of life for very sick patients.	Respect for feelings of family, religious objections.
Developing allografts, xenografts, and artificial organs	Need to supplement living donations. Watch for large research costs, diversion of resources into these new, exciting fields.	Respect for patient's and family's privacy and dignity; right to withdraw from experiment.
Developing rationing schemes to cut costs of health care	Need to cut costs before health care consumes disproportionate amount of our budget. Need to limit escalating technology.	Right of every patient to care available; duty of physician to concentrate on care for this individual patient.
Advising on lifestyle legislation	Tremendous health gains from losing weight, stopping smoking, eliminating alcohol from diet, etc.	Respect for liberty and privacy.

ISSUES OF MEDICAL ETHICS

ISSUE	CONSEQUENTIALIST CONSIDERATIONS	NON-CONSEQUENTIALIST CONSIDERATIONS
Issues of Life and Death		
Artificially assisted reproduction	Desire of couple to have a child vs possibility of exploitative commercialization.	Value of life, right of contract vs separation of marriage and reproduction.
Surrogate motherhood	Above; plus advantage to surrogate vs possibility of fostering callousness in contracting parents.	Above; plus possible injustice, unnatural use of reproductive capacity.
Abortion	Prevents birth of unwanted or defective children vs fosters callousness toward life.	Right of woman to control own body vs right of fetus not to be subject to lethal attack.
Refusal of vigorous treatment for imperiled newborns	Ends suffering of infant and parents, avoids low-quality life of suffering and burdensome treatments vs ends lives, misses opportunity to develop and test medical technology.	Right of family to refuse treatment on behalf of the infant when interests so indicate vs right of all infants to whatever level of care they need.
Allowing competent patient to die on request	Minimizes suffering and expense for patient and family vs may lead to death under pressure, shortens possibly good life.	Right of any conscious, competent patient to refuse unwanted treatment vs requirements of law and medical ethics to preserve life.
Deciding to terminate life support for irreversibly comatose	Minimizes expense, suffering of family, futile use of scarce resources vs if hastily done, may kill recovering patient; may usher in euthanasia.	Right of next of kin or guardian to exercise substituted judgment for incompetent vs duty to sustain life.

FUNDAMENTAL DUTIES

	BENEFICENCE: PROMOTING HUMAN WELFARE	JUSTICE: ACKNOWLEDGING HUMAN EQUALITY	RESPECT FOR PERSONS: HONORING INDIVIDUAL FREEDOM
BASIC FACT ABOUT HUMAN NATURE THAT GROUNDS THE DUTY	Humans are animals, with vulnerable bodies and urgent physical needs, capable of suffering.	Humans are social animals, who must live in communities and therefore must adopt social structures to maintain communities.	Humans are rational, free, able to make their own choices, to foresee the consequences, and to take responsibility.
VALUE REALIZED IN PERFORMANCE OF DUTY	Human welfare, happiness	Human equality	Human dignity, autonomy
WORKING OUT THE DUTY IN ETHICAL THEORY	Best modern example is Utilitarianism, from Jeremy Bentham and John Stuart Mill, who saw morality as that which produced the greatest happiness for the greatest number. Reasoning is consequential, aimed at results.	Best modern example is John Rawls' theory of justice as "fairness," maintaining equality unless inequality helps everyone. Reasoning is deontological: morality derives from duty, not consequences.	Best modern example is Immanuel Kant's formalism, where morality is seen as working out the Categorical Imperative. Reasoning is deontological.
SAMPLES OF IMPLEMENTATION IN BUSINESS	Protecting safety of employees; maintaining pleasant working conditions; contributing funds to the local community.	Obedience to law; enforcing fair rules; non-discrimination; no favoritism; giving credit where credit is due.	Respecting employee rights; treating employees as persons, not just as tools; respecting differences of opinion.

THE DUTIES OF CORPORATIONS

DUTY	EXAMPLES OF IMPLEMENTATION	GROUNDS: LEGAL, MORAL, AND PRACTICAL

Duties to the Community: The External Constituencies

A. Customers

1. Product Safety — Maintain highest standards of quality control in design and manufacture. — *Legal:* Strict liability; negligence; implied warranty. Consumer protection laws.

2. Truth in selling — Choose marketing media and messages carefully. — *Moral:* Avoid harm (customer welfare); avoid deception (customer autonomy).

Practical: Shoddiness and dishonesty generally backfire on sales.

B. Local Community

1. Economic stability — Do not close plant on which community depends. — *Legal:* Tax and zoning laws, local regulation.

2. Philanthropy — Support non-profit enterprise. — *Moral:* Duty to help neighbors.

Practical: Keep workers and their families happy.

C. Natural Environment

1. Non-pollution — State of the art scrubbing devices; monitoring beyond legal requirements. — *Legal:* DEP (direct regulation); superfund; user fees and taxes.

2. Safe disposal of wastes — Continue research into recycling and neutralizing of harmful waste substances. — *Moral:* Obligation to protect health, to preserve nature for future generations.

Practical: Good PR; easier to work in pleasant surroundings.

D. Third World

1. Questionable payments — Avoid all payments that distort market or deflect officials from their jobs. — *Legal:* Foreign Corrupt Practices Act; treaties; restrictions such as tariffs, quotas or embargoes.

2. Marketing harmful substances — Follow same safety standards abroad as at home, even where law is more permissive. — *Moral:* Obligation to other nations to help them develop on their own, independent and unexploited.

3. Support of racist, corrupt, or oppressive regimes — At minimum: Abide by Sullivan Principles, U.S. law, and supply no instruments of oppression. — *Practical:* Violent change in regime can wipe out trading partners and investments.

THE DUTIES OF MANAGERS

DUTY	EXAMPLES OF IMPLEMENTATION	GROUNDS: LEGAL, MORAL AND PRACTICAL

Duties to Employees: The Internal Constituencies

A. Respect for Rights

1. Nondiscrimination in hiring

Affirmative action program at all levels.

Legal: Broadly, the Constitution. Then: civil rights legislation and court decisions, labor laws, Equal Employment Opportunity Commission, use of federal contract requirement.

2. Reward for performance

Scrupulous adherence to contract, fair and thorough personnel records, incentives.

3. Privacy

Personnel inquiries strictly job-related; no polygraphs.

Moral: Respect for autonomy of persons, equality, individual dignity.

4. Participation in community, exercise of rights of citizen

Noninterference in non-company related political activity.

Practical: Attitude of respect is essential to foster integrity, initiative, and moral behavior in the employees.

B. Concern for welfare

1. Safety

Constant concern for safety: education, regulations, enforcement.

Legal: Labor laws, OSHA, workmen's compensation, income security and maintenance programs.

2. Health

Maintenance of medical, exercise facilities.

Moral: Love of neighbor; especially responsibility for those in your care.

3. Economic security

Job stability, generous retirement benefits.

Practical: Genuine concern, regularly manifested, is associated with increased productivity, lower absenteeism and fewer errors in work.

4. Personal and professional growth

Reimbursement for education, in-service training.

5. Community participation and recreation

Contribution to recreational and other community activities in which employees participate.

GLOSSARY

As you may have discovered by now, philosophers spend most of their time pondering the meanings of words—their core meanings, their associations, and their logical connections with other words. Given this perennial activity, there can be no "true" or final definitions for the key ethical terms we have used in this work. But with the help of a few dictionaries, common usage, and common sense, we can usually come up with a definition adequate to start us thinking. With this in mind, the editors at WNET offer the following brief definitions of some of the key words, as generally used in this text. We hope you will find them useful.

a priori: statements that we can know to be true prior to any examination of the facts of the world.

a posteriori: statements that can be determined as true only after investigation of the world.

accountability: the quality or state of being answerable, liable, or responsible.

altruism: unselfish consideration of, or devotion to, the well-being of others.

analytic: logically true or necessary, or reducible by definition to logical truth.

applied ethics: ethics put to practical use: concerned with concrete dilemmas rather than with fundamental principles. Also professional ethics, as in business ethics, medical ethics, legal ethics, military ethics, government ethics, journalistic ethics, and the ethics of scientific research.

arete: Greek term for excellence, valor, and virtue, which together comprise character.

autonomy: the power to make moral choices and be self-governing; an ethical principle based on the union of rationality and freedom.

axiom: a proposition, principle, rule or maxim that is generally regarded as true on the basis of its intrinsic merit or an appeal to self-evidence.

beneficence: an ethical principle of helping others wherever possible; active goodness, kindness, or charity.

categorical imperative: a moral obligation or command that is unconditionally and universally binding. "Act so that you can simultaneously will that the maxim of your action should become universal law."—- Immanuel Kant.

causation: the agencies or the processes that bring about an effect.

civil society: an association organized under law composed of or shared by individuals living and participating in a community.

collective: by, characteristic of, or relating to, a group of individuals, especially a public group such as social class or a whole society.

collectivism: a theory or system in which the group or the state takes responsibility for the social and economic welfare of its members; a social theory or doctrine that stresses the importance of the collective rather than the individual.

community: any organization that exercises limited political authority over a small region, such as a town or village; in ethics, a pattern of life where collective demands and interpersonal relations are as important as individual goals and choices.

consequentialist reasoning: in which the rightness of an act is linked with the goodness of the state of affairs that it brings about.

deontological reasoning: a type of reasoning which focuses not on the consequences of an action but on the theory or study of duty or moral obligation.

descriptive ethics: a theory which holds that only descriptive or empirical statements are meaningful; a branch of ethics that discusses the moral and ethical beliefs and customs of the peoples of the world.

distributive justice: the ethical principle that is concerned with the fair allocation of privileges, duties, and goods within a society in accordance with merit, need, work, or other agreed upon criteria.

duty: behavior required by moral obligation, whether or not it will make anyone happier, or make us better people.

empirical statements: factual assertions about the world and our physical environment, verifiable by controlled observation, experiment, or direct sense experience: usually opposed to theoretical statements.

epicureanism: the philosophy of Epicurus and his followers, who considered emotional calm the highest good and valued intellectual pleasures above all others.

epistemology: the field of philosophy concerned with the theory of knowledge.

ethical egoism: the belief that the only principle you should use to guide your life is the principle of advantage to yourself.

ethics: the study and evaluation of human conduct in the light of moral principles.

felicific calculus: Jeremy Bentham's method for measuring value in terms of happiness.

fiduciary: involving confidence or trust; a fiduciary obligation is one arising out of trust.

good samaritan: one who gives people in need as much help as possible, and gives it to them immediately.

heteronomy: lack of moral freedom or self-determination; control by others.

hypothetical: involving supposition; logical but not necessarily so.

ideal: a standard of perfection or excellence; a goal which we strive to realize.

imperative: an act that must be carried out; a duty.

informed consent: a term used in medical ethics to indicate the patient's approval of a procedure or treatment, based on possession and understanding of all relevant information.

institution: a significant and established element within a society that reflects that society's needs, activities, or values; it may be an organization such as the family, schools, or courts; or a practice, such as marriage or slavery.

justice: fair dealing or right action: the principle that demands that we subject our actions to rule and that the rule be the same for all.

law: an authoritative system for governing human conduct by rules.

lex talionis: the law of retaliation, which says that no vengeance shall exceed the original hurt: an eye for an eye, a tooth for a tooth.— *Bible*

libertarian: a theory which gives priority to the principles of individual liberty and freedom of thought and of action, no matter how unwise the choice may seem to others.

logic: the field of philosophy concerned with the validity of argument.

logical statements: formal statements. Statements derivable from definitions, which can be verified by a formal procedure drawn from the definitions that govern the field in question; includes the entirety of mathematical discourse. True formal statements are analytic.

loyalty: in ethics, the principle of fidelity or allegiance to an overarching concept, such as a government, belief, person, country, or other principle.

mass society: a mechanistic or bureaucratic organization of people and resources characterized by a lack of communal relationships and a sense of anonymity.

maxim: a general truth, basic principle, or rule of conduct, often expressed as a proverb or saying.

mean: moderate actions or attitudes appropriately chosen between two extremes; identified with virtue.

mens rea: "guilty mind" or intent to injure; the assignment of lesser penalties for lesser degrees of guilt.

metaethics: theoretical ethics. A discipline which considers the foundation of ethics, specifically the meaning of ethical terms and the forms of ethical argument.

metaphysics: the branch of philosophy concerned with questions about reality and the nature of existence.

moira: Greek word for order of the universe.

moral: pertaining to principles or considerations of right and wrong behavior or good and bad character.

moral agency: the ability to make ethical choices, and to take responsibility for those choices.

moral law: a rule or group of rules of right living conceived as universal and unchanging.

morality: a doctrine or system of ideas concerned with imperatives, duties, or right conduct.

natural law: a body of law arising out of nature, which governs human society; may function independently or in addition to societal law.

non-maleficence: avoiding harm or evil.

normative ethics: a discipline dealing with the nature of ethical principles that have been accepted as norms of right behavior.

objective: considered by rational minds to be real, true, or valid; observable or verifiable; based on interpersonal truth; opposed to "subjective."

paradox: an argument or statement that seems to contradict itself, yet may be true.

paternalism: in ethics, the principle of caring for and controlling the behavior of subordinates (workers, patients, citizens) in a fatherly fashion, for their own good.

philosophy: critical reflection about fundamental beliefs and questions about life and death. Includes metaphysics, epistemology, logic, ethics, and aesthetics.

polis: a Greek city-state: ideally, a community that embodies the organization and fulfillment of social relations.

privacy: the ability of the individual to keep large portions of his or her life away from the observation of others; the control of personal space.

rationality: the capacity to consider abstract concepts, use language, think in terms of categories, classes, and rules; the ability to evaluate situations accurately and to choose appropriate means to cope with them.

relativism: characterized by the notion that no point of view is more correct than any other; in matters of policy and ethics, the belief that there is only subjective (personal) opinion, and no objective (interpersonal) truth.

relativization: using our own intuitions of adequate freedom and reason as the measure of the case before us.

retributive justice: in ethics, the principle of justice that is concerned with punishing an individual for his or her actions.

retributivists or retributionists: those who emphasize the requirement under justice to punish crime simply because it is crime.

social contract: an agreement which brings a society into being and regulates the relations between the members of the society with each other and with their government.

social technology: the success of the forces of individual and mass society through technology.

socratic method: the method of questioning that Socrates used to get at the truth, which is assumed to be implicitly known to all rational beings.

sophists: literally "wise ones," they were professional teachers of rhetoric in ancient Greece, who taught that the selfish life was the best life.

stoicism: a philosophical system of the Stoics, which held that our duty is to conform to natural law and accept our destiny and that wise human beings should remain unswerved by joy or grief.

subjective: based on personal opinion, rather than universal or certifiable conditions; opposed to "objective."

syllogism: deductive logical scheme of a formal argument; consisting of a major premise, a minor premise, and a conclusion.

synthetic: statements that put together in a new combination two ideas that do not initially include or entail each other. Empirical statements are synthetic.

utilitarianism: the most common form of consequentialism, based on the pursuit of the greatest happiness of the greatest number in the long run.

value judgment: a judgment that assigns good or evil to an action or entity.

BIOGRAPHICAL SKETCHES
OF TELEVISION PANELISTS

FLOYD ABRAMS is a lawyer specializing in media and the First Amendment, and has argued many cases on behalf of newspapers, broadcasters, and journalists at the Supreme Court level. He was co-counsel for the *New York Times* in the Pentagon papers case and argued before the Supreme Court in *Nebraska Press Association vs. Stuart*. He has taught at Yale Law School and Columbia Graduate School of Journalism.

MARCIA ANGELL, M.D. is Senior Deputy Editor of the *New England Journal of Medicine*. Her recent writings include "The Baby Doe Rules" (*New England Journal of Medicine*) and "Medicine: The Endangered Patient-Centered Ethic" (*Hastings Center Report*). She is a frequent lecturer on medical ethics.

R. W. APPLE, JR. is Senior Correspondent and Deputy Washington Editor in the *New York Times* Washington bureau. He joined the *Times* in 1963. In a newspaper career spanning more than a quarter century, he has covered the civil rights movement in the American South, the wars in Vietnam and in Biafra, the Iranian revolution, five American Presidential elections, the White House, the Kremlin, and Watergate.

ROBERT S. BANKS joined Xerox Corporation in 1967 and has been Vice President and General Counsel since 1976. He is a member of the American Bar Association, and the Standing Committee of the Second Circuit Court of Appeals on the Improvement of Civil Litigation.

ROBERT BECKEL runs National Strategies, a political consulting organization. He was Walter Mondale's campaign manager in the 1984 Presidential election.

JAMES F. BERÉ is the Chairman and Chief Executive Officer of Borg-Warner Corporation and successfully fended off an attempted takeover of the company. Beré's directorships include Abbott Laboratories, American Information Technologies Corp., Baker/Hughes Company,

K Mart Corp., Temple-Inland, Inc., Time, Inc., Tribune Co., and York International Corp.

SHEILA L. BIRNBAUM heads the products liability department for Skadden, Arps, Slate, Meagher & Flom, a New York law firm. She is lead defense counsel for Jewel Stores and American Stores, Inc. in litigation stemming from salmonella contamination of milk in the midwest, and has defended a diversified chemical manufacturing company in DDT exposure cases. She also represents a major insurance company in cases involving DES, Agent Orange, and hazardous wastes.

STANLEY M. BRAND is a former General Counsel to the clerk, the chief legal officer to the U.S. House of Representatives (1976 - 83). In this role he represented the House and its committees and Members in cases involving subpoena of records, contempt proceedings, legislative vetoes, and many aspects of Constitutional and common law. From 1971 to 1974, he was a legislative aide to Thomas P. O'Neill, Jr., then Majority Leader of the House. Brand is a partner in the law firm of Brand & Lowell.

WARREN E. BUFFET is Chairman of the Board and Chief Executive Officer of Berkshire Hathaway Inc., a conglomerate whose activities include insurance underwriting, newspaper publishing, and retail sales.

CALVIN O. BUTTS, III is the Executive Minister of the Abyssinian Baptist Church of the City of New York. He is President of Africare, an independent organization dedicated to the improvement of the quality of life in rural Africa, Chairman of the Board of Managers of the Harlem Branch YMCA, and Adjunct Professor in the African Studies Department, City College, New York. Dr. Butts is the President of the Organization of African American Clergy, who led the fight against police brutality in New York City.

JOSEPH A. CALIFANO, JR. was Special Assistant to President Lyndon B. Johnson from 1965 to 1969. From 1977 to 1979 Mr. Califano served as Secretary of Health, Education and Welfare, mounting major preventive health programs, including childhood immunization and an anti-smoking campaign. From 1982 to 1983 he served as Special Counsel to the House Committee on Standards of Official Conduct. Califano is a senior partner in the firm of Dewey, Ballantine, Bushby, Palmer and Wood based in Washington, D.C.

ALEXANDER MORGAN CAPRON is Topping Professor of Law, Medicine and Public Policy at the University of Southern California, where he teaches in both the law and medical schools. From December 1979 to March 1983 he served as Executive Director of the President's Commission for the Study of Ethical Problems in Medicine and Biomedical and Behavioral Research. In 1987, he was appointed to the Biomedical Ethics Advisory Committee of the U.S. Congress.

THOMAS C. CHALMERS, M.D. is a professor and lecturer of medicine at Harvard, Tufts, George Washington, and Boston Universities, and Mount Sinai School of Medicine of the City University of New York. In addition, he has managed an active clinical career, winning the New York Academy of Medicine's Research Medal in 1987.

STANLEY M. CHESLEY has been involved as a plaintiff's attorney in major mass disaster and product liability cases including the Union Carbide disaster in Bhopal and the litigation over Agent Orange. He is a partner in the law firm of Waite, Schneider, Bayless & Chesley Co. in Cincinnati, Ohio.

GEORGE MURDOCK CONNELL is a Colonel in the U.S. Marine Corps. While serving in Vietnam he was wounded and decorated three times for bravery. Currently an intelligence officer, Colonel Connell has served as a Soviet specialist for the past eight years. He has advanced degrees in international relations and Russian studies.

THEODORE COOPER, M.D. is Chairman of the Board and Chief Executive Officer of the Upjohn Company. Among the positions he has held are: Director, Center for Cardiovascular Research, St. Louis University; Assistant Secretary for Health, Department of Health, Education and Welfare; and Dean, Cornell University Medical College.

JOSEPH W. COTCHETT serves on the California Commission on Judicial Performance, a constitutional body of judge and lawyer members that oversees discipline and disability for all California judges, and on the Board of Directors of Hastings College of Law. He is a member of the Board of Directors of Trial Lawyers for Public Justice.

LLOYD N. CUTLER is a member of the law firm of Wilmer, Cutler & Pickering in Washington, D.C. Among the positions he has held are: Co-Chairman, Lawyer's Committee for Civil Rights Under Law (1971-73); Chairman, District of Columbia Committee on the Administration of Justice Under Emergency Conditions (during the April 1968 riots in that city); and Chairman, Section of Individual Rights and Responsibilities, American Bar Association (1969). He served as Counsel to the President from 1979 to 1980, as Special Counsel to the President on Ratification of Salt II Treaty from 1979 to 1980, and as Senior Consultant to the President's Commission on Strategic Forces from 1983 to 1984.

MIDGE DECTER is an author and editor in the area of social and political policy criticism. Her articles have appeared in *Commentary*,

Harper's, Atlantic, Esquire, and *Saturday Review.* She was one of the founders of the Coalition for Democratic Majority, of which she is a past National Chairman, a co-chairman of the Advisory Committee on European Democracy and Security, a member of the board of the Committee on the Present Danger, the Council on Foreign Relations, the National News Council, and the Ethics and Public Policy Center. She also serves on the board of the Heritage Foundation.

LYLE WILLIAM DENNISTON is a reporter for the *Baltimore Sun* (Washington Bureau). Assigned primarily to the U.S. Supreme Court, he also covers legal affairs and legislation. He is the author of *The Reporter & The Law: Techniques of Covering the Courts,* and writes a column on media law for the *Washington Journalism Review.*

VINCENT T. DEVITA, JR., M.D. has been Director of the National Cancer Institute since his Presidential appointment in 1980. He has been frequently cited for his accomplishments in the development of curative chemotherapy. Dr. DeVita is a member of the editorial boards of numerous scientific journals. He has received many awards, including the Albert and Mary Lasker Medical Research Award, and is a member of the Institute of Medicine of the National Academy of Sciences.

FREDERICK DOWNS, JR. was a Lieutenant in the U.S. Army in Vietnam from 1966 to 1969. Downs now works for the Veteran's Administration as Director of Prosthetic and Sensory Aides Services. He lectures frequently at military institutions and has written two books on his Vietnam experiences: *The Killing Zone* and *Aftermath.*

RODERIC DUNCAN is a Judge of the Superior Court assigned to Family Law in Alameda County, California. He has served as a faculty member at over 50 educational programs for judges on the subjects of media relations, landlord-tenant law, consumer law, and small claims. From 1978 to 1979 he was a member of the Chief Justice's Special Committee on Courts and the Media, which opened California courtrooms to cameras.

LINDA ELLERBEE joined ABC News in 1986 as host and writer of the prime-time TV series "Our World." She is currently working on a similar series for PBS/WNET. For eleven years at NBC News, she held a variety of positions including contributing correspondent for "NBC Nightly News." From July 1982 until December 1983, she was a co-anchor and general editor of the late-night news program, "NBC News Overnight." Her book, *And So It Goes,* recounts her experiences in the broadcast field.

EDWARD JAY EPSTEIN is the author of eleven books. His most recent is *Soviet Deception.* He is a contributing editor for *Manhattan, Inc..* His writings have been published in *New Yorker, Commentary,* the *New York Times,* the *Wall Street Journal,* and *Atlantic.*

KATHERINE FANNING is Editor of the *Christian Science Monitor.* Before that she was editor and publisher of the *Anchorage Daily News.* She is the first woman president of the American Society of Newspaper Editors.

GERALDINE A. FERRARO was the first woman vice presidential candidate on a national party ticket (1984) and has since written and lectured extensively on the media, politics, and privacy. She served three terms (1978-84) in the United States House of Representatives. She is a board member of the National Democratic Institute of International Affairs and a member of the Council on Foreign Relations.

TOM FIEDLER has been Political Editor of the *Miami Herald* since 1984. His paper broke the Gary Hart-Donna Rice story in 1987. Fiedler has been involved in public affairs reporting on the national, state, and local levels since becoming a newspaperman in 1971.

JOSEPH H. FLOM is one of the foremost lawyers involved in corporate mergers and acquisitions. He is credited with developing some of the best-known offensive and defensive strategies. He is a partner in the New York City law firm of Skadden, Arps, Slate, Meagher & Flom, a firm with a broad commercial law practice.

EVELYN P. FOOTE is a Brigadier General in the U.S. Army serving as Deputy, the Inspector General. Prior to that, she was Special Assistant to the Commanding General, 32nd Army Air Defense Command, United States Army, Europe. She served with the Information Office at Headquarters, U.S. Army Vietnam in 1967. Her awards and decorations include the Meritorious Service Medal.

BARNEY FRANK, Democrat from Massachusetts, is serving his third term in the United States House of Representatives. He chairs the Subcommittee on Employment and Housing of the Government Operations Committee and is a member of the Judiciary, Banking, and Aging Committees. He is National Chairman of Americans for Democratic Action and the brother of panelist Ann Lewis.

LEONARD GARMENT is a Washington attorney. Among the many public officials he has represented are Richard Nixon during Watergate, Judge Robert Bork during the hearings on his nomination to the Supreme Court, and Robert McFarlane during the Iran-Contra investigations. He is the husband of Suzanne Garment, another participant in these programs.

SUZANNE GARMENT is writing a book on the politics of scandal from Watergate to the present. As Associate Editor of the editorial page of the *Wall Street Journal,* she wrote the weekly column, "Capitol Chronicle." From 1975 to 1976, she was special assistant to the U.S. Permanent Representative to the United Nations, Ambassador Daniel P. Moynihan, and wrote with Ambassador Moynihan the account of his U.N. years, *A Dangerous Place.* She is the author of *Decision to Prosecute,* a study of decision making in the Justice Department's Antitrust Division, and the wife of panelist Leonard Garment.

WILLARD GAYLIN, M.D. is President and co-founder of the Hastings Center, an institution engaged in research on ethical issues in the life sciences. He is Clinical Professor of Psychiatry at Columbia College of Physicians and Surgeons and maintains a private practice. Dr. Gaylin serves on the boards of directors of The Field Foundation, Helsinki Watch, Columbia Psychoanalytic Center, and Workplace Health Fund. He is the author of *The Killing of Bonnie Garland.*

STEPHEN GILLERS is a professor of law at New York University, where he teaches Regulation of Lawyers and Professional Responsibility, Evidence, and Federal Courts. His books include *Regulation of Lawyers: Problems in Law and Ethics.* From 1987 to 1988 he was Counsel to the Blue Ribbon Commission to Review Legislative Practices in Relation to Political Campaign Activities of Legislative Employees.

NEWT GINGRICH, Republican from Georgia, is serving his fourth term in the U.S. House of Representatives. He serves as Ranking Minority Member of the House Subcommittee on Investigations and Oversight of the Public Works and Transportation Committee, as well as on the House Administration Committee. Gingrich taught History and Environmental Studies at West Georgia College for seven years before winning election to Congress in 1978.

RUDOLPH W. GIULIANI became the United States Attorney for the Southern District of New York in 1983, representing the U.S. in all criminal and civil court proceedings in that district. From 1981 to 1983, Giuliani was Associate Attorney General of the United States, the third-ranking official in the U.S. Department of Justice. During his early years as a prosecutor he pursued many cases involving corruption in the New York City Police Department.

HARRISON GOLDIN is the Comptroller of the City of New York. Among his duties is management of all the investment portfolios for the city.

JAMES M. GOLDSMITH is the founder and Chief Executive of a number of industrial, commercial, and financial enterprises. A specialist in mergers and acquisitions, he launched an attempted takeover of the Goodyear Tire and Rubber Company while Robert Mercer (also a participant in these seminars) was Chairman. He is Chairman of the Editorial Committee for *Express News Magazine* in Paris.

ELLEN GOODMAN has been with the *Boston Globe* since 1967. In 1976, The Washington Post Writers Group began syndicating her column, which in 1980 won the Pulitzer Prize for distinguished commentary and now appears in 325 newspapers. Three collections of her columns have been published.

KATHARINE GRAHAM has been Chairman and Chief Executive Officer of The Washington Post Company since 1973. Before that she was publisher of the *Washington Post* and President of the Washington Post Company. Graham is a trustee of the Urban Institute and a member of the Council on Foreign Relations. She is a past Chair and President of the American Newspaper Publishers Association and a former board member of the Associated Press.

JEFF GREENFIELD is a journalist who has also worked for such political figures as Robert Kennedy and David Garth. He joined ABC News in 1983 and is a regular correspondent for ABC News and "Nightline." He has reported on a wide variety of issues including the media's coverage of Presidential campaigns, political campaign videos, and the emergence of political figures as commercial spokespersons. Mr. Greenfield's syndicated column on politics appears in some 80 newspapers across the U.S.

JOHN H. GUTFREUND is Chairman, President, and Chief Executive Officer for Salomon Brothers, Inc. In the past, he has served as Vice Chairman of the New York Stock Exchange, President of the Bond Club of New York, Chairman of the Syndicate Committee of the Investment Bankers Association, and on the Board of Directors of the Securities Industry Association.

LESLIE YALE GUTTERMAN is past President of the Rhode Island Board of Rabbis and former Chairman of the Rhode Island Committee for the Humanities, an affiliate of the National Endowment for the Humanities. He is Honorary President of the Jewish Family Service and has been a member of the Governor's Committee on Ethics in Government.

SCOTT HARSHBARGER is serving a second term as District Attorney of Middlesex County, Massachusetts. Prior to that, he was the General Counsel to the State Ethics Commission, established in 1978. From 1975 to 1978, he was Chief of the Public Protection Bureau of the Department of the

Attorney General. The Bureau implemented the concept of a governmental public interest law practice dedicated solely to aggressive affirmative legal action on behalf of citizens whose rights and interests had never before been protected or asserted.

DIANE H. HEGENER, M.D. is Medical Director of the Cancer Treatment Center at Central Maine Medical Center in Lewiston, and Assistant Clinical Professor in Radiology at Boston University School of Medicine. She has been a Professional Advisor to Can Help, a cancer hotline, and a member of the Board of Directors of Hospice of Western Maine.

J. BRYAN HEHIR is Secretary of the Department of Social Development and World Peace of the U.S. Catholic Conference. At Georgetown University in Washington, D.C., he is a Senior Research Scholar for the Kennedy Institute of Ethics and Research Professor of Ethics and International Politics at the School of Foreign Service. Fr. Hehir is a member of the Board of Directors of Bread for the World and the International Human Rights Law Group, the Catholic Theological Society of America, and The American Society for Christian Ethics. He writes and lectures widely on moral and political topics.

BRIAN JENKINS is an authority on international terrorism. One of the first analysts to conduct research on the topic, he currently directs The Rand Corporation's research program on subnational conflict and political violence. A former captain of the elite Green Berets, Jenkins served in the Dominican Republic during the American intervention and later in Vietnam, where he was on several occasions decorated for valor in combat. He is the author of many reports, chapters, and books on terrorism and is Editor-in-Chief of *TVI Report,* a journal dealing with political violence.

PETER JENNINGS has been a journalist for more than 25 years and has reported for many years from the wartorn Middle East. In 1983 he became Anchor and Senior Editor of ABC's "World News Tonight." Previously, he was Chief Foreign Correspondent for ABC News and "World News Tonight's" Foreign Desk Anchor based in London.

DAVID C. JONES, now retired, was Chief of Staff, United States Air Force, from 1974 to 1978, and Chairman of the Joint Chiefs of Staff from 1978 to 1982, serving four different Presidents and four different Secretaries of Defense. Since his military retirement he has lectured and written on national security matters.

FREDERICK H. JOSEPH is Chief Executive Officer and Vice Chairman of the Board of Drexel Burnham Lambert. From 1983 to 1984, Joseph served as Chairman of the Corporate Finance Committee of the Securities

Industry Association. He has testified before Congress on issues relating to the capital markets. He is a member of the Board of Directors of the Legal Aid Society.

JEANE J. KIRKPATRICK was the first woman to serve as chief United States Representative to the United Nations (1981 to 1985). Since then, she has resumed her position as Leavey Professor at Georgetown University and as Senior Fellow at the American Enterprise Institute. Kirkpatrick is the author of five books on American political issues and foreign policy. She is a syndicated columnist for the *Times-Mirror.*

C. EVERETT KOOP, M.D., SC.D. is Surgeon General and Deputy Assistant Secretary for Health, U.S. Public Health Service. Before joining PHS, Dr. Koop, a pediatric orthopedic surgeon with an international reputation, was Surgeon-in-Chief of Children's Hospital of Philadelphia and Professor of Pediatric Surgery and Pediatrics at the University of Pennsylvania. As Surgeon General, Dr. Koop advises the public on health matters such as smoking, diet and nutrition, environmental health hazards, the importance of immunization, and AIDS prevention.

ROBERT M. LEVY is Staff Attorney for the New York Civil Liberties Union. One of his clients is Joyce Brown (sometimes known as Billy Boggs), the homeless woman who was institutionalized by the City of New York. Previously he was Director of the Mental Patients' Rights Project of the New York Civil Liberties Union; Staff Counsel to the Mental Patients' Rights Project; and Staff Attorney to the Legal Aid Society of New York City, Juvenile Rights Division.

ANN F. LEWIS was Political Director of the Democratic National Committee, and was an advisor to Jesse Jackson's Presidential campaign. From 1985 to 1987 she served as National Director of Americans for Democratic Action. Prior to that she was the Political Director of the Democratic National Committee (1981- 1984). An active feminist, Lewis was one of the founders and co- leaders of the Massachusetts Women's Political Caucus and subsequently held national office in the National Women's Political Caucus. She is the sister of panelist Barney Frank.

ARTHUR L. LIMAN was Chief Counsel for the Senate Select Committee on Investigation of Military Sales to Iran/Contra (1987). He is a partner in the law firm of Paul, Weiss, Rifkind, Wharton & Garrison. In 1985, he was Chairman of New York City's Department of Investigation, Medical Examiner's Office. Liman has served the Governor of New York on both the New York State Executive Advisory Committee on Sentencing and the Executive Advisory Committee on Administration of Justice. He is Chairman of the Legal Action Center.

JACK LITMAN is a criminal defense attorney in New York City. His clients have included Richard Herrin, in the Bonnie Garland murder case, and Robert Chambers, who pleaded guilty in connection with the death of Jennifer Levin in New York's Central Park.

PAUL A. MARKS, M.D. is President of Memorial Sloan-Kettering Cancer Center in New York City and Professor at Cornell University Graduate School of Medical Sciences. From 1978-82 he was Editor-in-Chief of the journal *Blood*, and is currently on the editorial board of *Cancer Treatment Reviews*.

C. VERNON MASON, civil rights advocate and community activist, maintains a private law practice in Manhattan. Since 1972, he has provided legal assistance to those without access to private representation. Mason has provided *pro bono* legal services in cooperation with organizations such as the NAACP Legal Defense and Education Fund, The Center for Constitutional Rights, and the National Conference of Black Lawyers.

ROBERT C. MAYNARD is Editor and President of *The Tribune,* an Oakland, California newspaper, and a nationally syndicated columnist. His many affiliations include a position on the Board of Directors of the Associated Press, and membership on the Pulitzer Prize Board and the Board of Trustees of the Foundation for American Communications.

ROBERT E. MERCER is Chairman and Chief Executive Officer of The Goodyear Tire & Rubber Company. He held this position at the time Sir James Goldsmith (another participant in these seminars) attempted a hostile takeover.

ROBERT R. MERHIGE, JR. is United States District Judge for the Eastern District of Virginia. He presided over the Dalkon Shield product liability trial. He is the John A. Ewald Distinguished Visiting Professor of Law at the University of Virginia.

EDWARD C. MEYER was Chief of Staff of the United States Army for four years until his retirement in July 1983. He has served in various command and staff assignments with the U.S. Army including tours in Korea, Europe, and Vietnam. He is a Director, Executive Vice President and General Manager of Parks-Jaggers Aerospace Company and has served on the President's Strategic Defense Initiative Panel, the Defense Science Board, and other governmental advisory boards and panels.

JAMES F. NEAL has served as a plaintiff's lawyer in many mass disaster and product liability cases, including the Ford Pinto suit and "The Twilight Zone" movie accident trial. He also served as a Watergate prosecutor. He was Chief Counsel to the Senate Select Committee to Study Undercover Operations of the Department of Justice. He is presently a partner in the law firm of Neal & Hartwell in Nashville, Tennessee.

ROBERT K. OLDHAM, M.D. is the founder and Director of the Biological Therapy Institute, and the founder and Chairman of Biotherapeutics, Inc., both for-profit health care organizations. He is also founder and Editor of the *Journal of Biological Response Modifiers.* He is active in cancer research and was involved in the development of many innovative treatments and therapies.

MARILYN HALL PATEL is a Judge of the U.S. District Court, Northern District of California. She has written numerous articles and reviews on tax and corporate law and the legal rights of women. She is a faculty member at Hastings College of Law in San Francisco.

CHASE N. PETERSON, M.D. is President of the University of Utah. He has been widely acknowledged for his innovative leadership in university administration, as well as his achievements in medicine. A graduate of Harvard Medical School, he has both taught and practiced medicine.

T. BOONE PICKENS, JR. is a geologist by training. In 1964 he founded Mesa Petroleum, which has grown to become America's largest independent producer. He has been actively involved in major corporate mergers and acquisitions. In August 1986, Mr. Pickens founded the United Shareholders Association. The Washington-based organization champions the rights of America's 47 million shareholders.

ANNA QUINDLEN writes a weekly column for the *New York Times* called "Life in the 30s." She was a reporter and editor at the *Times* from 1977 until 1985, first as a general assignment and City Hall reporter, then as the author of the "About New York" column, and finally as the Deputy Metropolitan Editor.

JANE BRYANT QUINN is a leading commentator on personal finance. In addition to a personal finance column in *Newsweek,* her twice-weekly column is syndicated by *The Washington Post* to more than 200 newspapers. Her business news reports have been seen on CBS Evening News, CBS Morning News, and other nationwide programs. She is the author of *Everyone's Money Book,* a complete guide to personal finance.

ARNOLD S. RELMAN, M.D. edits the *New England Journal of Medicine,* teaches medicine at Harvard Medical School, and practices medicine at Brigham and Women's Hospital. He is a member of the Council of the Association of American Physicians and was its president from 1983 to 1984.

MORTIMER GILBERT ROSEN, M.D. is Chairman and Rappleye Professor of the Department of Obstetrics & Gynecology at Columbia University's College of Physicians & Surgeons. He is the Director of Obstetrical & Gynecological Service at The Presbyterian Hospital in the City of New York.

ANTONIN SCALIA took the oath of office as U.S. Supreme Court Justice on September 26, 1986. Before that he spent four years as Judge for the U.S. Court of Appeals for the District of Columbia Circuit. Justice Scalia has taught at the University of Virginia and the University of Chicago. He spent a year as a Scholar in Residence at the American Enterprise Institute.

BRENT SCOWCROFT served as Military Assistant to the President in 1972 and 1973, then as Deputy Assistant and Assistant to the President for National Security Affairs until January 1977. He was retired from military service in 1975 with the rank of Lieutenant General. General Scowcroft served on the Tower Commission appointed by President Reagan to investigate the Iran- Contra affair. He is a member of the Advisory Council of the Georgetown University Center for Strategic and International Studies and of the Johns Hopkins University School of Advanced International Studies.

JAMES E. SERVICE, Vice Admiral in the United States Navy (now retired), was appointed President of Naval War College in 1982. A carrier aviator, he has served numerous tours in fighter, attack, and reconnaissance squadrons since joining the Navy as a Naval Aviation Cadet in 1952. His last tour of duty was as Commander of the Naval Air Force in the Pacific. In 1977 he served in Washington, D.C. as Executive Assistant to the Vice Chief of Naval Operations.

DONALD W. SHRIVER, JR. has been President of Union Theological Seminary in New York City since 1975. Before that he was Professor of Ethics at Emory University and Professor of Religion at North Carolina State University. He is an ordained Presbyterian minister and has spent most of his career in university and church settings in the South. As a teacher, writer, and administrator, he spent many years organizing dialogues and study around ethical issues in the professions of science, engineering, business, politics, and medicine.

ALAN K. SIMPSON is a Republican Senator from Wyoming. His committee assignments include Chairman of the Committee on Veterans' Affairs, Chairman of the Subcommittee on Immigration and Refugee Policy of the Judiciary Committee, and Chairman of the Subcommittee on Nuclear Regulation of the Environment and Public Works Committee.

LEAH A. SIMMS is Assistant U.S. Attorney for the Southern District of Florida. Prior to that she served as Judge for the County Court for the 11th Judicial Circuit, Dade County, Florida (1981-1987); and Special Attorney for the Department of Justice, Organized Crime Strike Force, in Detroit, Michigan (1977-1980). Her career has centered on criminal prosecution.

JOHN E. SMITH is the Clark Professor of Philosophy at Yale University. He writes and lectures extensively and is on the editorial board of many philosophy journals. He is the husband of panelist Marilyn Smith.

LIZ SMITH writes a "gossip" column published in the *New York Daily News* and some 65 other newspapers serviced by the Chicago Tribune Syndicate. In addition to her work in print journalism, she does a twice-weekly spot on "Live at Five," NBC's local news telecast in New York City.

MARILYN S. SMITH is an Associate Professor of Philosophy at the College of Basic Studies, University of Hartford. She is the coauthor of three editions of *Living Issues in Philosophy*, and the wife of panelist John Smith.

MILDRED STAHLMAN, M.D. is Professor of Pediatrics and Pathology and Director of the Division of Neonatology at Vanderbilt University School of Medicine in Nashville. A pioneer in the field of neonatology, she is a member of the National Institute of Child Health and Human Development, for which she serves on the Special Review Committee for Physician Manpower Applications.

LOUIS STOKES was elected Congressman of the 21st Congressional District of Ohio on his first try for public office in 1968. By virtue of his election, he became the first black member of Congress from the State of Ohio. He is currently serving his tenth term in Congress. Rep. Stokes served on the House Select Committee to Investigate Covert Arms Transactions with Iran.

ROBERT C. STUART has been promoted from Major to Lieutenant Colonel, U.S. Marine Corps, since the television filming. He is Deputy Staff Advocate for the Western Recruiting Region. From May to September 1972 he was naval gunfire liaison officer to the Vietnamese Marine Corps, Republic of Vietnam. He received his J.D. in May 1976.

TIMOTHY C. TATUM is a Colonel and the Director of Ethical Studies, U.S. Army War College. He has served as an army chaplain for many years, including a tour in Vietnam.

PAUL TAYLOR is a political reporter for the *Washington Post*. At a press conference, he once asked Gary Hart whether he had ever committed adultery.

LESTER THUROW is Dean of the Sloan School of Management at the Massachusetts Institute of Technology. His widely published writings on economics won him the Gerald Loeb Award for Economic Writing in 1982 and the 1983 Champion Media Award for Economic Understanding.

MIKE WALLACE, a CBS News correspondent, has been co-editor of "60 Minutes" since its premiere. His experience as a newsman dates back to the 1940s, when he was a radio news writer and broadcaster for the *Chicago Sun*. His timely interviews include: Yasir Arafat, Ayatollah Khomeini, Ronald and Nancy Reagan, Mikhail Baryshnikov, Jeane Kirkpatrick, Johnny Carson, and Kurt Waldheim.

FAYE WATTLETON, as President of Planned Parenthood Federation of America since 1978, has been on the cutting edge of shaping national policy. She is the first woman and the youngest person to head the nation's oldest voluntary family planning organization.

WILLIAM C. WESTMORELAND, a General in the U.S. Army (now retired), served in 17 battle campaigns in three wars, received four Distinguished Service Medals, and was decorated in 16 foreign countries. He commanded U.S. troops in Vietnam and advised the South Vietnam military for over four years. The General sued CBS News and Mike Wallace (also a panelist) for libel arising from a "60 Minutes" report "Vietnam: The Uncounted Enemy." He served as Chief of Staff for the U.S. Army for four years.

TIMOTHY E. WIRTH, a Democrat, was elected in 1986 as the 28th United States Senator from Colorado, after representing Colorado's Second Congressional District for 12 years. He has been appointed to four Senate committees: Armed Services; Budget; Energy and Natural Resources; and Banking, Housing and Urban Affairs.

ELLEN C. YAROSHEFSKY recently left the Center for Constitutional Rights, where she handled litigation in state and federal courts on trial and appellate levels. She is now an adjunct faculty member at Cardozo Law School in New York City and is in private practice.

FRANK E. YOUNG, M.D., PHD. is Commissioner of the Food and Drug Administration. From 1979 to 1984 he was Dean of the School of Medicine and Dentistry and Director of the Medical Center of the University of Rochester. Concurrently he served as Chairman of the Executive Hospital Committee of Strong Memorial Hospital. His area of research is biotechnology, including the fundamental genetics of pathogenic and nonpathogenic bacteria.